Navigating Collective Intelligence for Sustainable Futures

Tania Elena González Alvarado
University of Guadalajara, Mexico

Pablo Cabanelas Lorenzo
University of Vigo, Spain

IGI Global
Scientific Publishing
Publishing Tomorrow's Research Today

Vice President of Editorial — Melissa Wagner
Managing Editor of Acquisitions — Mikaela Felty
Managing Editor of Book Development — Jocelynn Hessler
Production Manager — Mike Brehm
Cover Design — Phillip Shickler

Published in the United States of America by
IGI Global Scientific Publishing
701 East Chocolate Avenue
Hershey, PA, 17033, USA
Tel: 717-533-8845
Fax: 717-533-8661
Website: https://www.igi-global.com E-mail: cust@igi-global.com

Library of Congress Cataloging-in-Publication Data

Names: González Alvarado, Tania Elena, editor.
Title: Navigating collective intelligence for sustainable futures / edited by Tania González Alvarado, Pablo Cabanelas.
Description: Hershey, PA : IGI Global Scientific Publishing, [2025] | Includes bibliographical references and index. | Summary: "This book analyzes the role of collective intelligence in adapting businesses to external shocks and its contribution to resilient organizations"-- Provided by publisher.
Identifiers: LCCN 2024053065 (print) | LCCN 2024053066 (ebook) | ISBN 9798369372722 (hardcover) | ISBN 9798369372739 (paperback) | ISBN 9798369372746 (ebook)
Subjects: LCSH: Organizational resilience.
Classification: LCC HD58.9 .N39 2025 (print) | LCC HD58.9 (ebook) | DDC 658.4/06--dc23/eng/20250203
LC record available at https://lccn.loc.gov/2024053065
LC ebook record available at https://lccn.loc.gov/2024053066

British Cataloguing in Publication Data
A Cataloguing in Publication record for this book is available from the British Library.

Table of Contents

Detailed Table of Contents

Changes in the environment and the speed with which many companies adapt to them lead to exploring the adaptation process. In other words, the authors question the development of dynamic capabilities and how it is linked to resilience and organizational ambidexterity. Companies that effectively address these challenges will be better positioned to thrive in the environment. This chapter attempts a detailed analysis of the interactions between dynamic capabilities, resilience, and ambidexterity.

The chapter explores the transformative impact of collaborative business ecosystems on organizational success and innovation. Collaborative business ecosystems, comprising interconnected organizations, suppliers, customers, and stakeholders, are reshaping traditional business models by fostering cooperation, co-creation, and shared value. This chapter delves into the key dynamics of these ecosystems, including trust-building, shared governance, resource integration, and digital connectivity, highlighting their role in enhancing competitiveness and resilience. It examines how businesses can leverage these ecosystems to drive innovation, reduce costs, and adapt to rapidly changing market conditions. The chapter addresses the challenges associated with managing collaborative ecosystems, such as balancing competition with collaboration and navigating complex stakeholder relationships.

This chapter explores the convergence of sustainability, intelligent methods, and smart grids as a solution to the escalating energy demands and environmental concerns of the 21st century. It investigates how smart grids, empowered by machine learning, artificial intelligence, and other advanced techniques, can create a more efficient and environmentally friendly energy ecosystem. Key applications in load forecasting, demand management, renewable integration, and grid optimization are examined. The chapter acknowledges challenges like resource intensity and data privacy, advocating for robust regulations and responsible development to ensure equitable access to smart grid benefits. Ultimately, it presents a comprehensive analysis of this synergy, aiming to equip readers with the knowledge to navigate the complexities of the energy landscape and build a sustainable energy future.

This chapter examines how collective intelligence is transforming the mobility industry into the era of "new mobility." Collective intelligence—the collaborative problem-solving and knowledge-sharing of groups—is reshaping traditional paradigms, business models, and global value chains (GVCs). Furthermore, this explores new business models emerging from digitalization and collective intelligence, such as mobility as a service (MaaS) and car-sharing platforms. The shift from traditional mobility to new mobility that emphasizes alternative energy sources, sustainability, connectivity, and user-centric services, is driven by advancements in electric vehicles (EVs), connected and autonomous vehicles (CAVs), digital platforms, big data, and artificial intelligence. Collective intelligence is redefining relationships within the mobility value chain, moving from OEM-dominated hierarchies to collaborative networks involving diverse stakeholders like tech companies and public entities. This necessitates shared knowledge, data exchange, and cooperative innovation.

This chapter focuses on a relevant topic, an element of India's freedom struggle called Khadi or the homespun cloth made of cotton on spinning wheels as an example of product stewardship in terms of ethics and environmental impact. Product stewardship is identified as businesses with commitments to a healthy, safe, and environmentally friendly society. This closely aligns with the philosophy of a circular economy that adheres to lean production principles of manufacturing and business processes that are eco-friendly and sustainable. Textile industries around the world are integrating manufacturing towards a circular economy and green practices due to an increasing need to reduce the environmental impact. Social entrepreneurship as an alternative has been in focus as a sustainable business model and the popularity of Khadi, arts, crafts, and cottage industries in India is growing in today's internet economy. This study has explored how social entrepreneurship is providing numerous opportunities for growth and sustainability and a solution to social problems.

Sustainability is a catchword of the present generation. The evolution of sustainability through the sustainable development model of Brundtland report and Sustainable Development Goals (SDGs) affirms that the present generation is not only focused on its developmental needs but also concerned about the survival needs of the future generations. This constructive and progressive vision emerged from the positive mentality of many people affirming that the existence of collective intelligence (CI) is advantageous to society. CI insists that open dialogue, mutual sharing, and collaborative efforts can make wonders in human existence. Human coexistence becomes more meaningful with CI. It has also shaped the idea of corporate social responsibility (CSR), which stands for the firms' responsibility towards society. CSR also tries to share a portion of the economic benefits to the marginalized sections of society. From this perspective, the chapter analyzes the role of CI-guided CSR for establishing a sustainable society.

Preface

In an increasingly interconnected world, the challenges faced by businesses are more complex and unpredictable than ever before. As editors of *Navigating Collective Intelligence for Sustainable Futures*, we are acutely aware of the critical need for organizations to cultivate resilience—not merely as a reactive strategy but as a proactive foundation for sustainable growth and innovation.

Resilience, we argue, is not just a trait found in individual leaders or isolated teams; it is a collective phenomenon. It emerges from the shared knowledge, diverse perspectives, and collaborative efforts of all stakeholders within an organization. In this volume, we explore the intricate interplay between collective intelligence and resilience, particularly in the context of adapting to external shocks and fostering long-term sustainability.

Drawing insights from business experts, entrepreneurs, government agencies, and educators, we delve into the various dimensions of resilience—organizational, entrepreneurial, and collective. Each chapter serves as a testament to the power of collaboration and shared intelligence in navigating the complexities of today's economic landscape. The contributions herein emphasize that resilience is integral to competitive advantage, shaping decision-making processes and strategic directions.

As we confront the multifaceted challenges of our time, from economic fluctuations to environmental crises, the role of collective intelligence becomes paramount. It is through collaborative ecosystems that organizations can harness their collective capabilities, turning challenges into opportunities for growth. We examine how artificial intelligence and technological advancements can further enhance these collaborative efforts, offering tools to analyze data, foster innovation, and drive sustainable practices.

We invite readers to engage with the rich tapestry of ideas presented in this book. Our hope is that it serves as a valuable resource for business leaders, policymakers, researchers, and educators alike, inspiring a deeper understanding of resilience as a collective endeavor. Together, we can build a more sustainable future, one that thrives on the synergy of our collective intelligence.

In Navigating Collective Intelligence for Sustainable Futures, each chapter contributes uniquely to our understanding of how collective intelligence underpins resilience and sustainable practices across various domains.

Chapter 1: Orchestrating Collective Intelligence: Conceptual Pathway to a Sustainability-Oriented Future lays the foundation for our exploration by systematically examining the components of collective intelligence—collectives, systems, and infrastructures. This chapter offers a practical framework aimed at enhancing innovation and decision-making among organizations and policymakers. In an era of increasing globalization and environmental challenges, it emphasizes that true resilience stems from the interconnectedness of all system elements, urging us to leverage collective intelligence to foster solidarity and sustainability.

Chapter 2: Managing AI in the Workplace to Enhance Collective Intelligence and Resilience shifts our focus to the integration of Artificial Intelligence within organizational settings. It investigates the relationship between AI, collective intelligence, and collective resilience, highlighting the importance of aligning technology with human values. This chapter provides a conceptual framework for managers, offering strategies to navigate the complexities of AI integration while enhancing collaboration and trust among team members.

Chapter 3: Dynamic Capabilities through Resilience and Ambidexterity delves into how organizations develop dynamic capabilities in response to environmental changes. It explores the interconnections between resilience, ambidexterity, and adaptability, illustrating that companies with a robust understanding of these concepts are better equipped to thrive amid uncertainty.

Chapter 4: Synergizing Success: The Dynamics of Collaborative Business Ecosystems examines the transformative potential of collaborative ecosystems in driving innovation and organizational success. It highlights the essential dynamics of these ecosystems, such as trust-building and resource integration, and discusses the delicate balance between competition and collaboration necessary for fostering resilience in rapidly evolving markets.

Chapter 5: The Synergy of Sustainability, Intelligent Methods, and Smart Grid Applications focuses on the convergence of sustainability and advanced technologies, particularly smart grids. It investigates how machine learning and AI can optimize energy systems while addressing environmental concerns, advocating for responsible development practices to ensure equitable access to these innovations.

Chapter 6: Collective Intelligence Approach for New Mobility analyzes the mobility sector's evolution through collective intelligence. It highlights emerging business models, such as Mobility as a Service, that prioritize sustainability and user-centric services, facilitated by advancements in technology. This chapter emphasizes the importance of collaboration among diverse stakeholders in reshaping the mobility value chain.

Chapter 7: Adaptive Capacity in the Tourism System: Resilience and Collective Intelligence explores the interplay between resilience and collective intelligence within the tourism industry. It argues for a systemic approach to understanding how businesses adapt to changes, emphasizing that collective intelligence is crucial for fostering creative problem-solving and survival in unpredictable environments.

Chapter 8: Building Resilient Companies through Internal Marketing discusses the role of internal marketing in fostering company resilience. Through a case study of a transnational corporation, this chapter reveals how talent attraction, internal communication, and empowerment can significantly enhance organizational resilience, drawing on empirical data to support its conclusions.

Chapter 9: Khadi, Arts, and Handicrafts as India's Symbol of Freedom and Fashion in Today's Internet and Circular Economy presents a unique perspective on product stewardship through the lens of Khadi, emphasizing its ethical and environmental significance. This chapter connects social entrepreneurship to sustainability, demonstrating how traditional practices can thrive in the modern digital economy while addressing social issues.

Chapter 10: Collective Intelligence for Sustainable Society: A Study through the Lens of Corporate Social Responsibility highlights the evolution of sustainability and corporate social responsibility (CSR). It underscores the positive impact of collective intelligence on societal well-being, arguing that collaborative efforts can drive meaningful change and ensure that economic benefits are shared with marginalized communities.

Chapter 11: Organizing in Democratic Organizational Forms and Constitution of Collective Intelligence concludes the volume by investigating how democratic organizational structures foster collective intelligence. By promoting participation and diversity, these structures enhance problem-solving capabilities within groups. The chapter calls for further research to optimize these organizational forms, illustrating their potential to cultivate innovative and resilient environments.

Together, these chapters weave a comprehensive narrative on the vital role of collective intelligence in shaping resilient, sustainable futures. We invite you to engage with these insights and consider their implications for your own work and practice.

Tania Elena González Alvarado
University of Guadalajara, Mexico

Pablo Cabanelas Lorenzo
University of Vigo, Spain

Chapter 1 Orchestrating Collective Intelligence: Conceptual Pathway to a Sustainability-Oriented Future

Renata Kubus
https://orcid.org/0000-0002-7133-8290
Complutense University of Madrid, Spain

Ignacio López Domínguez
https://orcid.org/0000-0001-5929-9308
Complutense University of Madrid, Spain

Inés Martín de Santos
https://orcid.org/0000-0003-1674-2415
Complutense University of Madrid, Spain

ABSTRACT

This chapter explores in a structured way different aspects of collective intelligence, such as collectives, systems, and infrastructures, as well as their orchestration. It aims to contribute to the existing body of knowledge and provide a practical and actionable conceptual framework. The benefits of this study extend beyond academia to organizations and policymakers with the potential to drive innovation, improve decision-making, and address complex challenges in various domains. Globalization and technological change, increasing interdependencies, and optimizing some variables, such as resource extraction or consumption, have diminished the resilience of the global (eco)system. In the long run, the system is only as strong as its weakest element. Thanks to collective intelligence, these shocks could allow us to resize the global vision of solidarity and boost true resilience and sustainability.

DOI: 10.4018/979-8-3693-7272-2.ch001

INTRODUCTION

The phenomenon of collective intelligence is a multifaceted and intricate concept that cannot be easily simplified or reduced to a singular explanation or definition. It necessitates a systematic approach to its introduction and exploration, which must be executed carefully considering its various components and implications. Attention must be directed toward the diverse aspects inherent in the study of collective intelligence, including but not limited to collectives, systems, and infrastructures, as well as the orchestration of these elements in tandem. Consequently, the objective of this chapter is to make a significant contribution to the expansive existing corpus of knowledge on this subject, while simultaneously providing a practical and actionable conceptual framework that can serve as a guide for future inquiries and applications. The implications and advantages of this scholarly endeavour are not confined solely to the academic realm, as they also extend to organizations and policymakers who stand to benefit immensely from insights that have the potential to catalyse innovation, enhance decision-making processes, and tackle complex challenges that arise across a multitude of domains.

The structure of this chapter unfolds in a systematic manner: Initially, a succinct review of the need and evolution of the collective intelligence concept will be conducted, aimed at delving into both the historical and contemporary understanding of collective intelligence, exploring its origins, and tracing its development over time. Following this, the concept of nature as a source of inspiration for collective intelligence will be introduced, examining not only human interactions but also considering other living organisms within the biosphere and the invaluable insights and principles that can be gleaned from them in terms of designing and enhancing collective intelligence while simultaneously enriching the understanding of its dynamics and resultant outcomes. Subsequently, the discussion will shift to the perspective of machines, systems, and infrastructures, with a concentrated focus on the technological and material dimensions that facilitate and support collective behaviour, thereby illuminating the importance of knowledge infrastructure and processes, along with their normative dimensions, which are both shaped by and shape the values, norms, and regulations that govern the collectives and the broader society.

In the next section, the chapter will address collectives' intelligence, primarily focusing on the c-factor, which pertains to the measurement and orchestration of collective intelligence as a dynamic process, thereby differentiating between the organizing principles of collective intelligence and the balance that must be maintained among them. Furthermore, the concepts of sustainability and resilience will be examined, albeit briefly, as they represent essential characteristics of collective intelligence that relate directly to its capacity to sustain and enhance the well-being of the biosphere in the face of environmental changes and uncertainties. The importance of sustainability and resilience cannot be overstated, as they are critical for ensuring the long-term viability, success, and meaningful contributions of collective intelligence to the pressing global challenges we currently face. Finally, the concluding section of this chapter will present a reframed concept of collective intelligence, which is articulated as a comprehensive and integrative framework that synthesizes the findings and insights derived from the preceding sections, thus providing both a conceptual and practical tool that can be utilized for the purposes of understanding, designing, and evaluating the multifaceted nature of collective intelligence.

Why Collective Intelligence?

In order to effectively elucidate the intricate concept of Collective Intelligence, it is both appropriate and beneficial to initiate the discourse by examining the fundamental necessity underpinning this phenomenon, as it plays a crucial role in comprehending its significance within various contexts. This necessity serves not only as a foundational element but also as a poignant problem statement that encapsulates its challenges and opportunities. In this sense, some examples of myxobacteria and others, such as Acrasis rosea (Brown et al., 2012), explain the relationship between collective intelligence and resilience for sustainable future. In this simple biological analogy, if the environmental conditions (humidity, temperature) are good, each bacterium and other organisms live independently. To bring it to human reality, they function under the individualistic premise of the market. Each of the bacteria, fighting for its good, achieves the good of the collective itself. However, when the conditions are no longer favourable, these bacteria unite and function as one organism. Their behaviour evolves from the individualistic to the collective one. Functioning under the collective premise allows individuals to survive, be resilient, and be sustainable in the long run. In human terms, this could be compared to the significant challenges of our time that no one can solve individually, such as the environmental crisis or air pollution.

In this sense, interregnum is a period of discontinuity or interval in a government, organization, or social order. Archetypically, this was known as the period between the reign of a monarch and the assumption of his successor (from the Latin inter-, "between" and regnum "sovereignty, reign") (Interregnum | Search Online Etymology Dictionary, n.d.). Historically, the longer an interregnum has been, the longer it has been accompanied by disorder, civil wars, and wars of succession, as well as power vacuums filled by the invasion of a foreign power or the emergence of a new internal power. The current era is often called a time of interregnum due to the need for a paradigm shift (Sanahuja & Rodríguez Díaz, 2023; Kuhn, 2017). As presented in Figure 1, the last industrial revolution started with sustainability (Demir & Cicibaş, 2019), and the collective intelligence approach is taking the lead.

Another essential concept is a complex or wicked problem, a challenge in which no straight-forward solution exists. There are different approaches, but no single solution unambiguously solves the problem. An example would be the health issue; one is healthy, not so much by the sum of healthy body elements, such as the finger, hand, and liver. It is something more than a mere sum. There are elements, but the interrelation between them is very relevant. It is the main difference with complicated problems.

Figure 1. Industrial revolutions as paradigm shifts

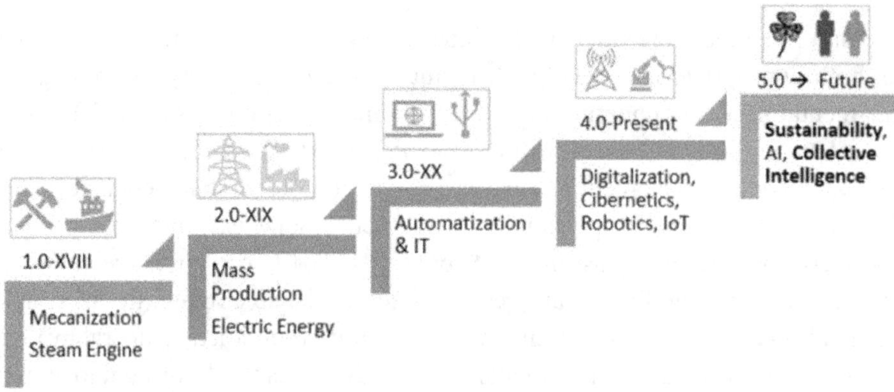

Source: Own elaboration.

Wicked problems are also related to the dimensionality of choice, as presented in Figure 2. It is the difficulty of making decisions or managing oneself in an environment. It can be divided into three dimensions (Mulgan, 2018b):

- Cognitive: the way of thinking, models, and disciplines, such as those used to understand and analyse the situation. The more transversal the subject, the more complex it will be.
- Social: the way people and entities influence thinking and the conflict of interests and power plays that may be in place among stakeholders. The more diverse and interdependent the agents, the more challenging it will be to coordinate and cooperate.
- Temporal and spatial: a decision has short-, medium- and long-term results. Sometimes, it takes years to see the result. For instance, in the case of environmental sustainability, ocean plastic pollution was not an issue noted at the very beginning, mainly because there was no conscience and knowledge regarding its scale and nature, i.e., the dissolution in microplastics. Now, track-

ing the fundamental responsibility of the plastic pollution issue is complex. Thus, it is a question with short-term benefits but with negative results in the long term. With time, it is more difficult to distinguish the influence of the factor because many other factors will be added. The longer the period, the more uncertain and unpredictable the outcomes. It is analogical with the spatial distribution (Alañón & Arauzo, 2011).

Figure 2. Dimensionality of choice

Source: Own elaboration.

A global example of a complicated problem that is not complex can be chess. The rules are complex, but only in the logical field do they not entail emotions. There is no need to use physics. There are only two opponents, and it is known that each of them wants to win. There are 3-4 outcomes: win, lose, draw, or cancel. So, as complex as it may seem, chess, from the point of view of dimensionality of choice, is not complex, and hence, it can be done well by machines within narrow and not global intelligence. All things considered, collective intelligence has gained significant attention in recent years due to its potential to address complex challenges and drive innovation in various domains, leading to resilience and sustainability (Puerta et al., 2023).

COLLECTIVE INTELLIGENCE EVOLUTION

The word collective comes from the Latin *collectivus*, meaning “pertaining to a collection or assemblage,” which is derived from the verb *colligere*, meaning “to gather together” or further on 'plurality of individuals) (Collective I Search Online Etymology Dictionary, n.d.). Moreover, the word intelligence comes from the Latin *intelligentia,* meaning “understanding, knowledge, power of discerning”, which is derived from the verb *intelligere*, meaning “to understand, comprehend, come to know" (Intelligence | Etymology, Origin and Meaning of Intelligence by Etymonline, n.d.).

At least partially, the concept of collective intelligence is probably as old as the intelligence and collectives themselves. It can be traced back to ancient civilizations, where communities relied on group decision-making for survival and progress. In ancient Greece, the Athenian democracy exemplified collective intelligence through its system of governance, where citizens participated in public debates and decision-making processes (Uña, 2023). Similarly, indigenous societies across the globe, such as Native American, Australian and African tribes, practiced collective decision-making and problem-solving through consensus-building and communal knowledge sharing, emphasizing the group's wisdom over individual expertise. They relied on shared knowledge and collaboration to survive and thrive (Spencer & Gillen, 1899; Landemore & Elster, 2012).

The Enlightenment era of the 17th and 18th centuries witnessed the emergence of influential thinkers (Locke et al., 1960) who laid the groundwork for the modern understanding of collective intelligence. John Locke, Hume, and Voltaire advocated for the power of reason, individual liberty, and, once again, the importance of collective decision-making. Jean-Jacques Rousseau's concept of the "general will" emphasized its importance for the common good. These thinkers' ideas set the stage for the development of democratic systems, where collective intelligence became a central pillar for governance and social progress of democratic systems, where citizens collectively shape policies and laws. In the 19th and early 20th centuries, we witnessed the rise of social sciences, which further explored collective intelligence dynamics. Émile Durkheim, a prominent sociologist, studied the collective consciousness of societies and highlighted the role of shared beliefs and values. Durkheim's work (Durkheim, 1995) laid the foundation for understanding the social factors that influence group intelligence and behaviour. The scientific method, pioneered by Francis Bacon and others, also further on (Franck, 2012), emphasized the importance of collaboration, peer review, and collective knowledge accumulation.

The advent of the internet and advancements in communication technologies in the late 20th century revolutionized collective intelligence. The internet provided a platform for global connectivity, enabling individuals to share information, collaborate, and collectively solve problems on an unprecedented scale. The emergence of online platforms, such as wikis and social media, and open-source software projects enabled large-scale collaboration and information sharing in distributed networks of contributors. Howard Rheingold (2002) explored how mobile technologies and social networks empowered collective action and decision-making, predicting the transformative potential of collective intelligence in the digital age. Surowiecki (2004) popularized the "wisdom of crowds" concept. He argued that diverse groups, when aggregated, often make more accurate decisions than individuals or experts.

He highlighted examples from various fields, including finance and prediction markets, to demonstrate the effectiveness of collective intelligence.

The rise of different types of crowdsourcing platforms (Flórez et al., 2020) in the 21st century further propelled collective intelligence. The success of platforms like Wikipedia and open-source software projects showcased the potential of collective intelligence in producing high-quality, crowdsourced knowledge and action. It can be seen in the scientific research areas where 'collective intelligence' is one of the keywords. Computer sciences stand for more than one-third of the topic-related research. The other third part of the research areas is constituted by Engineering (13.1%) and Mathematics (11.3%), followed closely by Social Sciences (9.9%). The last third part is much more divided; it includes, among others, Business, Management (4.7%), Decision Sciences (3.8%), Arts and Humanities (3.7%), and Psychology (2.0%). (Figure 3)

Figure 3. Collective Intelligence research by scientific area.

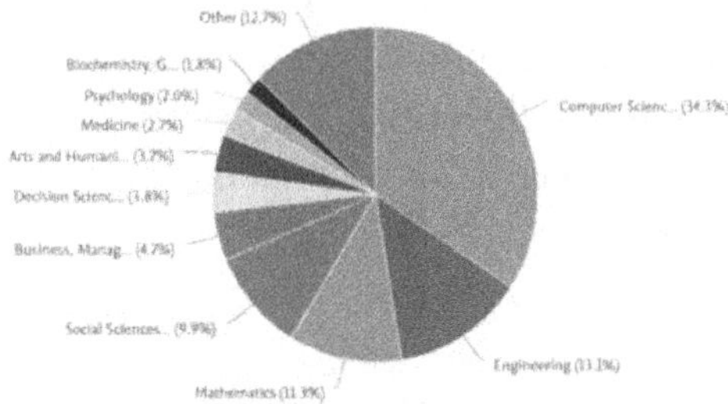

Source: Scopus Data Base, November 2023.

Today, collective intelligence continues to evolve with the integration of artificial intelligence and machine learning algorithms (Mulgan, 2018a). These technologies enable the analysis of vast amounts of data generated by online communities, facilitating more accurate predictions and decision-making. Additionally, the field of collective intelligence is expanding into diverse domains, highlighting its relevance and potential impact on societal and environmental challenges. Summarizing, collective intelligence is an ancient concept that has gained renewed attention in the digital era. It has a rich historical background. As we move forward, further exploration and understanding of collective intelligence will undoubtedly shape our ability to tackle complex challenges and harness the potential of diverse communities in their eco(system).

Nature-Inspiration in Collective Intelligence

On the one hand, human, animal, and plant collectives represent life on planet Earth. They are in the same boat regarding sustainability and resilience in the face of environmental challenges. Plants and animals can help directly in collective intelligence projects (Mulgan, 2018b). As for animals, vultures in Peru are used to detect illegal dumps and pigeons in London to measure air pollution levels. As for plants and forests, when trees pass food to each other to help the sick, this can be thought of as an example. Another one can be using strawberry plants to measure the pollution in the 'Vigilantes del aire,' a citizen science project by Ibercivis.

On the other hand, living nature represents a source of inspiration for human technologies and infrastructure development, e.g., swarm intelligence (Pham et al., 2021). Engineers can draw from nature's principles and patterns to design and implement practical solutions for human and environmental challenges. Moreover, there are nature-based solutions when tackling socio-environmental issues (EC et al., 2023; Voskamp et al., 2021). Nature-based solutions refer to a set of actions or policies that harness the power of nature to address some of the most pressing societal challenges, such as the threat to water availability, the increasing risk of natural disasters, or climate change. These solutions involve protecting, restoring, and sustainably managing ecosystems to increase their resilience and capacity to address these societal threats while safeguarding biodiversity and enhancing human well-being.

Stigmergy is another fitting concept that relates to collective intelligence and nature. It is a self-organization first observed in the animal kingdom by Grassé (1959) that produces complex, seemingly intelligent structures without any observable central planning, control, or even direct communication between the agents. It is a mechanism of indirect coordination, through the environment and context, between agents or actions, where the trace left in the environment by an individual action stimulates the performance of a succeeding action by the same or different agent. It creates feedback that leads to the emergence of collective patterns, structures, and systems. Stigmergy is often observed in social insects, such as ants, bees, termites, and wasps, to coordinate their actions and achieve global objectives, such as foraging, sorting, building, and exploration. For example, ants exchange information and collectively develop a network of trails to get the best way to food sources by laying down pheromones on their way back to the nest. The network of trails functions as a shared external memory for the ant colony. Stigmergy can explain how collective intelligence emerges from the interactions of individuals, organizations, communities, markets, and networks using signs, symbols, artifacts, and technologies. It is critical in a collective intelligence branch, i.e., swarm intelligence (Beni & Wang, 1989; Pham et al., 2021) that can be used to design, implement, and coordinate systems that can adapt, learn, and optimize their performance in complex and dynamic environments, such as swarm robotics, artificial neural networks, and genetic algorithms (Heylighen, 2016).

An associated term can be collaborative intelligence, which tries to mirror natural ecosystems. Each organism's unique signature is derived from its genetics, circumstances, behaviour, and position in the ecosystem (Brooks, 1991). Furthermore, some collective intelligence theories lead to a vision like Acrasis rosea, presented at the beginning, and they see the groups of organisms working together in a synergetic, self-organized way as one superorganism to achieve a higher-level intelligence, functions, and behaviour. In this sense, superorganisms are more specific to biological systems, depending on genetic and evolutionary factors. At the same time, collective intelligence includes systems and infrastructures and can be influenced by sociocultural factors. There were visions of Gaia (Lovelock, 1979), or the Earth as a single superorganism (like Pandora's views in the Steven Spielberg movie 'Avatar'), or the biosphere as one (Vernadsky, 1998). There is also an organismic view of society incorporating concepts from cybernetics, evolutionary theory, and complex adaptive systems (Heylighen, 2002).

MACHINES, SYSTEMS, INFRASTRUCTURES

The emergence of collective intelligence from machines and human interactions is studied under the umbrella of symbiotic intelligence. Not only do these two sides of collective intelligence complement each other, but they also create new forms of proceeding. Symbiotic intelligence extends human-computer symbiosis (Licklider, 1960), leading to distributed intelligence (Johnson et al., 1998).

Machines, systems, and infrastructure are essential for Collective Intelligence. It is not easy to distinguish between them. Moreover, in some cases, the same thing considers all these concepts simultaneously. For instance, a computer can be seen as a machine that processes data, a system consisting of hardware and software components, or, more broadly, as an infrastructure enabling communication and information access. The distinction between these three notions can be associated with complexity and integration or, in a sense, abstraction. A machine is generally considered a single device that performs a specific function. Meanwhile, a system is a collection of devices or elements that interact together to allow the performance of a more complex function. An infrastructure, in turn, can be considered a network of systems that can provide essential services and support for a larger collective, sometimes an entity such as a country or a city. Another discernment leading to the same hierarchy of conceptions will be provided according to purpose and scope. As previously explained, a machine will be used to perform a specific task or problem.

The system is usually thought for a broader range, i.e., domain or field of tasks. Infrastructure, in turn, will have a much more general purpose and a broader scope, facilitating different collective life areas, such as social welfare or national security.

Machines can extend or augment human intelligence. They are 'knowledge storage,' and they can perform difficult or tedious tasks, such as data processing, pattern recognition, optimization, and prediction. Machines, especially AI (Mulgan, 2018a), can also assist humans in decision-making, creativity, and learning by providing feedback, suggestions, and insights. Systems are complex, adaptive, and dynamic (Gross, 2008). They can organize and manage the interactions and contributions of multiple human and machine agents to achieve a common goal. Systems can also facilitate the sharing and integration of diverse perspectives, knowledge, and skills and the evaluation and improvement of collective outcomes. For example, online platforms can enable crowdsourcing, crowdfunding, peer production, and collective deliberation for various purposes, such as innovation, democracy, and social good (Flórez et al., 2020; Uña, 2023).

Infrastructure can support and sustain the development and deployment of machines and systems. It can provide the necessary resources, implying standards, protocols, and policies. Infrastructure can also ensure quality, security, and reliability by addressing the technical, ethical, and social risks. Thus, it is considered the set of services, facilities, and systems that support the functioning of a collective, an organization, or a society. An illustrative example that underscores the critical importance of considering all dimensions of collective intelligence can be observed in the context of automobile traffic management. In the early days of motor vehicles, the typical speed limit for cars was a modest 30 kilometres per hour, and at that juncture, there was a limited reliance on horse-drawn carriage pathways for transportation purposes. It is quite surprising and noteworthy that, during that era, the incidence of accidents on the roads was alarmingly high despite the relatively lower speeds and fewer vehicles on the road. Nevertheless, as time progressed, an increasingly intricate and multifaceted system of roads emerged, accompanied by essential artifacts such as traffic lights and designated crosswalks, which were systematically implemented to enhance safety and efficiency. Furthermore, the establishment of comprehensive traffic regulations, codes of conduct that align with various traffic signs, and the delineation of specific roles for different participants in the traffic ecosystem—including but not limited to traffic agents, drivers, co-drivers, and pedestrians—has significantly contributed to improved safety and efficiency outcomes. This case indicates that, despite the exponential increase in traffic volume over the years, there has been a notable decline in the frequency of road accidents. In contemporary times, we are witnessing further advancements in this domain, exemplified by the emergence of innovative technologies such as Cooperative Vehicle-Infrastructure Systems (CVIS) (Verweij et al., 2010).

There are different types of infrastructure, depending on the classification's perspective and purpose. The first distinction will be between physical and logical. The first refers to the tangible assets that enable the movement of people, goods, information, and energy, like bridges, power plants, telecommunication, and buildings. The logical infrastructure, in turn, refers to the abstract or virtual elements that enable the processing, storage, transmission, and analysis of data and information. Examples of logical infrastructure are digital networks, platforms, databases, software applications, cloud computing, and cybersecurity. Digital platforms and technologies are especially relevant as they facilitate communication, collaboration, and information sharing. Online platforms, such as social media, crowdsourcing, and collaborative tools, have significantly enabled collective intelligence. These platforms allow individuals to connect, share knowledge and insights, and collectively work towards a common goal. Additionally, as previously mentioned, advancements in artificial intelligence and machine learning have further enhanced collective intelligence by enabling automated analysis of large datasets, pattern recognition, and decision support (Mulgan, 2018a).

Other relevant infrastructure types will be socio-economic and environmental ones, i.e. (eco) systems where humans are considered part of a natural world. Hereupon, there is a concept of infranomics (Gheorghe et al., 2014), a term that combines infrastructure and economics and refers to the study of the economic and social impacts of infrastructure systems, such as transportation, energy, water, and communication. Infranomics also explores infrastructure systems' optimal design, planning, management, and governance, considering the uncertainties, risks, and resilience. Agents are understood as individuals and collectives, environmental and information resources, and systems become the elements of infrastructure when they are essential for the functioning and performance of the infrastructure system.

Knowledge Infrastructure

Another type of infrastructure pertinent to collective intelligence is knowledge, as it is currently the knowledge or information society turns (Drucker, 2017; Webster, 2006). Information presents a quality evolution with data-information-knowledge-wisdom processes, and information society is seen as an evolution of hunting, agriculture, and manufacturing. Knowledge infrastructure is the set of resources, tools, and systems that enable the creation, capture, storage, sharing, and use of knowledge within collectives or their network. It can include human, information, technology, and organizational resources. These last ones refer to the policies, procedures, norms, and culture that support the governance, coordination, and evaluation of knowledge activities, such as strategies, plans, rules, incentives, and values, and are related to another type of infrastructure, which embraces legal and normative dimensions. They articulate two aspects of the regulatory framework that governs the provision and use of infrastructure facilities and services. Legal infrastructure also establishes the mechanisms for dispute resolution, enforcement, and compliance, while the normative one sets universal access, affordability, and social inclusion criteria. It resonates with the division of knowledge into conceptual and procedural (Scheffler, 1967).

Figure 4. The interplay of knowledge and reality

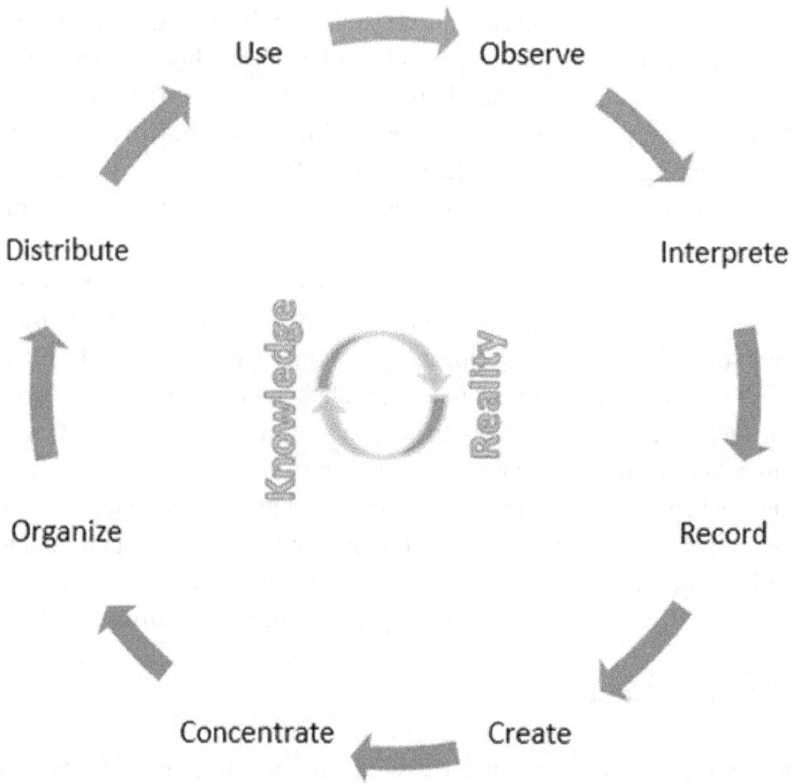

Source: Own elaboration.

As exposed in Figure 4, the interplay of knowledge and reality is an entrenched process. First, reality and its different aspects must be observed/perceived and interpreted. After that, it is stored in the form of memory. Information aggregation techniques, such as voting, rating, and reputation systems, help filter and prioritize the contributions. Knowledge synthesis involves the integration of diverse perspectives and expertise. Consequently, insights and solutions can be generated thanks to actionable elements and issues. Judgment allows for the right choice for action and reflection. Decision-making mechanisms, such as consensus-building processes or deliberative democracy, ensure that collective decisions are made fairly and inclusively. That, in turn, provides the knowledge and sometimes wisdom (when context is considered) in what refers to reality. The knowledge to be manageable needs to be concentrated and, afterward, distributed and used for the change. Lastly, learning mechanisms enable the collective to adapt and improve based on feedback and experiences. And the spiralling process restarts.

There are several challenges and risks on the way. Being too much wrapped in the memory, the collective intelligence can be trapped by the past. It leads to a time lag between the present and future. It can be observed in AI issues, which cause ethical controversies, for instance, by not representing properly different minority views. Knowledge is entirely concentrated on rationality; intuition and emotion have a restricted representation. It can negatively impact the human quality of collective intelligence and creativity. From the human perspective, too much focus on observation and data and their diversity can lead to paranoia, so the organizing principles of focus and granularity are essential here. The constant struggle, communication, and responsiveness prevent the creation of the necessary distance to acquire a more holistic vision. Human consciousness and mental activity can be considered part of the knowledge field. They influence the biosphere and evolution through symbiotic intelligence, leading to the noosphere (Levit, 2000) and the world brain (Wells, 1938).

Currently, knowledge management is related to the 'open' movement, which includes open intelligence, open innovation, and open science (Wilkinson et al., 2016). The distinction is based on the phase of the knowledge creation and application processes they cover. The idea is to make data FAIR (Findable, Accessible, Interoperable, and Reusable), which is a relevant part of the methodology of the European Union (EC, 2016). They are crucial to allow for a level playing field in knowledge, its development, and thus collective intelligence processes. They face challenges and risks, especially when facing Intellectual Property rights and dynamics (Liu & Yu, 2022). Participatory movements are another social phenomenon associated with collective intelligence. They implicate an active citizens' involvement in various aspects of public life, especially science and democracy. Even with its ethical and epistemic issues, citizen science can contribute to 'a commons' (Pelacho et al., 2021). Participatory democracy or governance is the participation of citizens in political processes through voting, deliberation, consultation, and co-creation (Fischer, 2012), as seen in initiatives like e-democracy and crowdsourced legislation. Participatory movements can enhance legitimacy and accountability and increase participants' consciousness and literacy, citizens' engagement, responsiveness, and trust between the participating institutions or entities and citizens. Thus, it boosts citizens' empowerment, inclusion, and diversity. They can be seen as an expression of collective intelligence.

Collective Intelligence Measurement

A general attempt is made to find a factor called 'c' to measure collective intelligence, similar to the 'g' factor of general intelligence in psychological terms of an individual, and that could determine cognitive performance in various tasks. The picture would be much more complex for the collective intelligence, as shown in Figure 5.

Figure 5. Collective Intelligence measurement

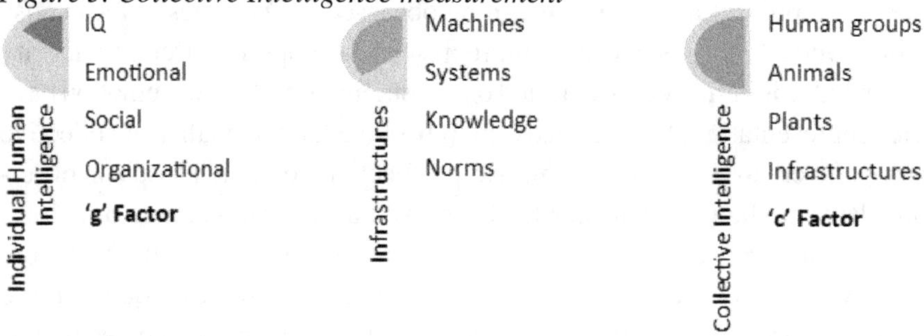

Source: Own elaboration.

The current studies on the c-factor are concentrated only on the human group's intelligence, a kind of group IQ test, as an indicator to predict its performance (Williams et al., 2010). This c-factor does not need to correlate strongly with the group members' intelligence, average, or maximum intelligence. It can be analysed in terms of functional elements (observation, prediction, creativity, judgment), feedback learning loops, and forms of organization. As it is centred on human groups, their diversity, social sensitivity, and turn-taking of the members are considered relevant conditions. It does not need to correlate strongly with the group members' individual intelligence, average, or maximum intelligence. It is an emergent property. However, it is challenging to conclude even its existence due to the complexity of the question and the difficulty of considering the infrastructure part. Another approach is to consider that all intelligence is collective intelligence, with some relevant dimensions of difference such as 'spatiotemporal scale, interdependence of elements, rate of information transfer, task diversity, network structure, transient diversity (i.e., the degree to which elements of a system resist consensus), and mechanisms of interaction (e.g., collaboration vs. competition)' (Falandays et al., 2023).

Collective Intelligence Orchestration

There are two different streams of the collective intelligence term understanding; one is an emergent property of a crowd when the quality of several contributions provides superior value when compared to the individual one so that the process is more on the level of information aggregator (Engert, 2020) or crowd wisdom (Surowiecki, 2004). Another understanding (Mulgan, 2018b) shared because of this is that collective intelligence in order to be achieved requires careful orchestration. Thus, this last conceptualization implies that different dimensions of collective intelligence require planning, monitoring, and revisions. At this moment, the action of arranging collective intelligence is defined as orchestration. The term organization seems more suitable; however, it is applied more to human groups, their order, structures, and even systems. Organization entails coordination of planning, management of collective action, and collaboration of collective members. It shapes how people work together.

An organization is more focused on defining roles and where they belong in the structure. Orchestration, in turn, is more concerned with how things work together. Furthermore, organizations are generally more static and prescriptive. Orchestration is a term quite used within machines and systems (as an orchestra that generally plays musical instruments) working together with human teams. Orchestration works at a higher level and is expected to make decisions based on changing conditions and requirements; it is more dynamic and adaptative. Another relevant term is governance, especially as this concept forms part of ESG or Environmental, Social, and Governance aspects of sustainability. Governance is the framework and process that defines the orchestration's authority, accountability, and legitimacy. Its mechanisms also provide rules for participation and conflict resolution, and they help ensure fairness, transparency, and trust. Governance can include the normative and legislative infrastructure: rules, norms, and values that guide the orchestrators' and participants' decision-making and display. The degree of directness and hardness is higher in governance than in orchestration.

Orchestration can be seen as a specific, soft, and indirect type of governance, overcoming some of the limitations or challenges of other modes of governance (hierarchy, collaboration, or delegation), such as lack of capacity, legitimacy, or consensus. The idea is that the actor that seeks to govern or orchestrate does not apply coercive or binding instruments (e.g., responsibilities, laws, contracts, incentives, or sanctions) to influence other actors. He or she applies persuasion or consultancy to implicate others in the process, perhaps turning them into orchestrators themselves, thus guiding the collective intelligence functioning and action. In this sense, orchestration helps leverage different actors' advantages or opportunities, such as expertise, networks, or reputation within the systems and infrastructure domains.

Infrastructure governance is conformed by the rules and mechanisms that shape the decision-making and behaviour of the actors involved in developing, operating, and using an infrastructure system. Orchestration can be used in various contexts and fields, such as global governance, informal international organizations, or digital platform ecosystems.

ORGANISING PRINCIPLES OF COLLECTIVE INTELLIGENCE

Different authors provide different guidelines or criteria that help to achieve collective intelligence; however, they are mainly addressed to human collectives (Mulgan, 2018b; Woolley et al., 2015). When applied, these organizing principles of collective intelligence have advantages and disadvantages, as seen in Figure 6. Thus, they should be seen from a prudent perspective, and the main challenges should be observed and addressed. Moreover, they are only sometimes easy to implement and may require appropriate tools, methods, and cultures to support them (Mulgan, 2018b).

Figure 6. Collective Intelligence organising principles and their challenges

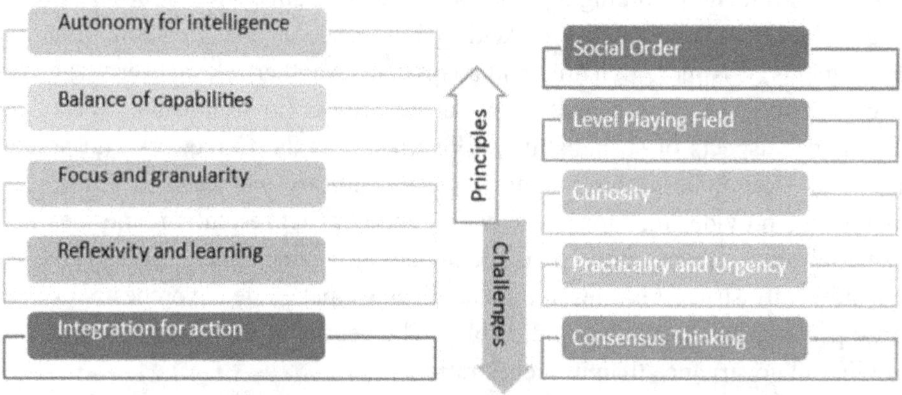

Source: Own elaboration (Mulgan, 2018b).

Autonomy for intelligence implies that the collective should respect the independence and freedom of its members, who should be able to express their opinions and ideas without being influenced by external factors, such as authority, hierarchy, or conformity. Autonomy also implies that the members can self-organize and self-regulate and identify and correct errors and opportunities for improvement. They are to avoid the comfort zone and the false deception that can lead the organization to the precipice, as is often the case with charismatic leaders, which leave no space for dissension. This autonomy strongly depends on the availability of resources and a level playing field for the stakeholders. They can be affected by the availability of infrastructural resources in their different dimensions. Furthermore, it should be kept in mind that having a certain social order, with roles and responsibilities, is necessary so that a collective does not become chaotic.

The collective should have diverse members with different capabilities, backgrounds, skills, and perspectives. It should bring complementarity rather than uniformity. It allows the collective to avoid biases and groupthink and to generate more creative and innovative solutions to complex problems. Diversity also fosters inclusion and representation of different stakeholders in the collective process. Nonetheless, there is a need to balance the capabilities well and to have a good level playing field because the bearers of those diverse capabilities will have their distinctive status and influence in the group decisions and acting, by the capabilities which are valued in the society and thus in the group. The collective should have a focus on a clear and shared goal. It should concentrate its attention and resources on the most relevant and essential aspects of the problem. Focus also implies that the collective should avoid distractions, conflicts, and irrelevant information that could hinder its performance. Thus, focus and granularity help the collective achieve higher efficiency, quality, and creativity in solving complex problems. They also enable the collective to leverage its members' diversity and autonomy and integrate their contributions into a coherent and meaningful whole. Conversely, too much focus can hinder curiosity and, thus, learning.

Collective is to adjust the level of detail and complexity of the problem according to the context and the needs of the situation, bringing the situations or issues to their corresponding level without trying to make a decision taken in a particular case applicable to all types of cases, placing excessive weight on its resolution. It is often an overseen issue leading to paralysation or inaction, used throughout history in sabotage (CIA, 1944). There is only collective intelligence with the capacity for reflection and interest in learning. The collective should constantly monitor, evaluate, and improve collective intelligence processes and outcomes and adapt to changing circumstances and challenges. Learning also requires that the collective is open to new information and knowledge and can learn from its own and others' successes and failures. Moreover, learning implies that the collective can unlearn obsolete or irrelevant practices and beliefs. Nonetheless, it must be considered that sometimes there are urgent issues, and practicality wins over. The collective should apply what it has learned in action and in this way, transform its collective reality according to its expectations and aspirations. Integration for action also means that the collective can align its actions with its values and principles and measure and communicate its impact and achievements. Integration for action is the key, but in the end, it requires choosing only options for action that, without other elements such as reflexivity, can lead to the consensus or single dominant thinking.

Collective Intelligence for Sustainability and Resilience

Most of the intelligence recognized and functioning today, especially at the systems and infrastructure level, is aimed not at preventing problems but at fixing or correcting them. As shown in Figure 7 below, this kind of intelligence has been developed for fields like military, finance, or marketing (García et al., 2024). It is also used in elections or voting when it tries to answer questions like how many people will vote or have voted for a candidate. It is more concerned with solving existing problems than with avoiding them. For instance, in the health sector, the prevalent approach is to treat diseases rather than to predict and prevent them. Nonetheless, in the face of the Anthropocene era and climate crisis, there is a need to act before things get worse, not after. For global challenges like the UN's sustainable development goals (SDGs), focusing more on preventing and forecasting potential scenarios and finding better ways to act is intelligent.

Figure 7. Current vs required intelligence

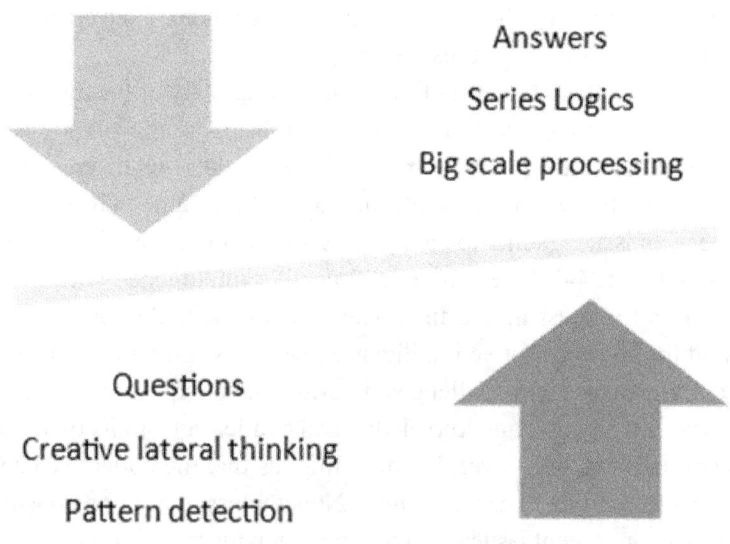

Source: Own elaboration (Mulgan, 2018b).

Collective intelligence should play a relevant role in dealing with problems like health, pandemics, the environment, community, or prosperity, which affect the whole planet. It helps to ask the right questions, to use comprehensive, creative lateral, out-of-the-box thinking beyond the usual logic (de Bono, 1995; Almond & Iszoro, 2023), and to identify divergent patterns.

The term sustainability can be drawn back to the Triple Bottom Line or Triple Balance concept (Elkington, 1998). Nowadays, it encompasses ESG or Environmental, Social, and Governance dimensions in the first place related to sustainable finance (Who Cares Wins. Connecting Financial Markets to a Changing World, 2004) but also to Corporate Social Responsibility. Sustainability has a strong temporal and spatial dimension, as it can be defined as the capacity to provide the needs of the present time without compromising future generations (Wood et al., 2021). In this sense, the Doughnut Economy (Raworth, 2018) can contribute an interesting framing for sustainability. It is a theory that states that economic activity should take place in the space between a social base and an ecological ceiling. In practice, everyone should have access to basic goods - food, housing, and health - but within the means and resources available on the planet.

In the neoliberal context, as in the European Union, when government intervention is only to be applied in case of market failure, a relevant theoretical framing is provided by the 'externalities' and the Coase Theorem (Deryugina et al., 2021; Schoenmaker & Schramade, 2019). These are the impacts generated by an economic actor but afterward suffered or benefited by others. However, the market with its 'free hand' does not return these impacts correspondingly on the originating actor. It can be drawn back to the dimensionality of choice. While facing climate change, there is an obligation to prepare for extreme, environmental, and social events (Firlej et al., 2023). Resilience is the ability of the (eco)system to withstand shock while maintaining its integrity and purpose (Holling, 1973; Zolli & Healy, 2012). The systems and infrastructures, as well as how the collectives are conceived and operate, need to be designed and redesigned to absorb disruption, operate under different critical circumstances, or transit more smoothly between one circumstance and another. To sustain integrity and purpose can also imply change, especially if the shock is disruptive. The alternatives are to increase the capacity to resist adverse conditions or to end up with less resilience and degrade or even disintegrate. Fine-tuned feedback, dynamic reorganization, built-in response mechanisms, decoupling, diversity, modularity, simplicity, readiness for readjustment, withdrawal, deployment, and clustering form the characteristics of systemic resilience, as shown in Figure 8 below.

Figure 8. Systemic resilience characteristics

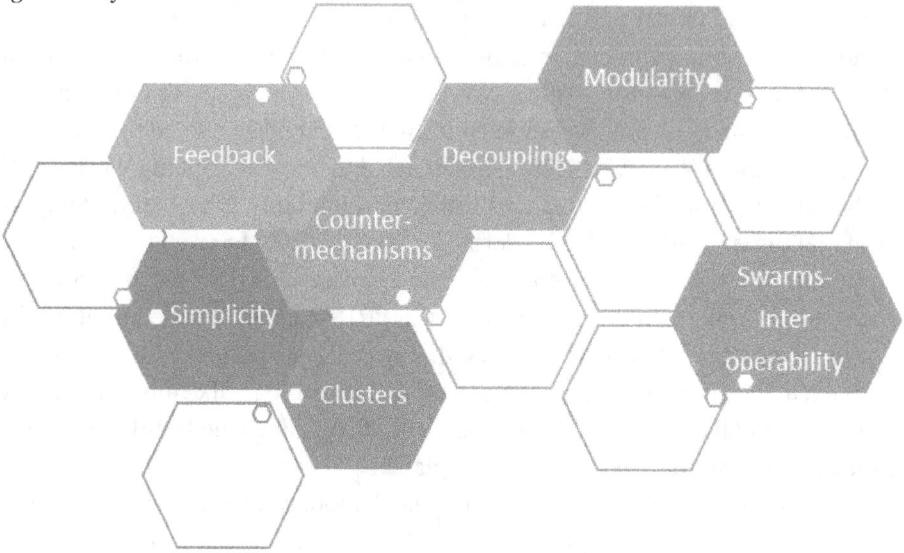

Source: Own elaboration (Zolli & Healy, 2012).

As in the case of collective intelligence, feedback mechanisms are relevant when it comes to detecting the approach of the critical threshold and the subsequent management of the situation. Industry 4.0 can be especially relevant in this context, enabling the collection, screening, combination, and interpretation of operational and performance data in real-time, monitoring the performance of the system and extending its resilience, allowing a faster and more focused response to the focus of the problem, i.e., dynamic reorganization with the sensor or IoT usage it implies. Another relevant aspect is decoupling the system from its underlying requirements regarding the material resources it needs for its operation, ensuring sufficient available reserves, and diversifying inputs to minimize dependence on any of them. Thanks to the increased autonomy of the constituent parts, under special conditions, some systems can separate themselves from their wider environment, reducing their overall localization and dependencies.

The modularity of the structure of an (eco)system grants the reduction of its operation to critical elements, disconnecting or leaving aside other non-critical ones. It also allows for on-the-fly retraction and reconfiguration in case of disruptive shocks, avoiding the cascade effect on the whole system and changing the scale according to the situation. Firewalls are foreseen to prevent disruption in one part from affecting the rest. Hence, many resilient (eco)systems can be diversified and complicated at their edges but are simple in their hardcore and basic infrastructure requirements. Modularity, simplicity, and interoperability allow system components and, thus, infrastructure to deploy and retract as needed.

In this sense, resilience is also enhanced by appropriate, niche-style clustering, which enables resources to be brought together in proximity environments, with the intensified density and diversity of talent, resources, tools, models, and ideas to realize the innovations necessary for resilient reconfiguration and growth (Cánovas, 2014; Encinas, 2021; Vu et al., 2020). However, resilience is not always good. Some resilient (eco)systems have pejorative implications per se, e.g., criminal or terrorist networks and organizations, from which much can be learned in this regard.

Figure 9. Resilience advantages and challenges

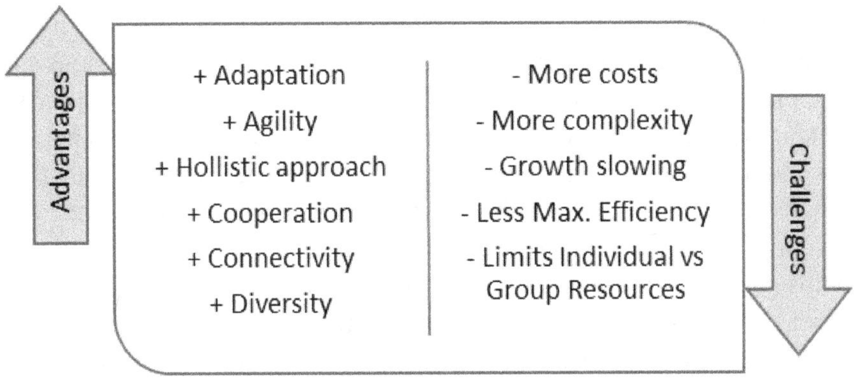

Source: Own elaboration (Mulgan, 2018b).

(Eco)systems operate in conditions of constant dynamic disequilibrium, which does not imply an unconditional naturalism but a balancing of the advantages and challenges, as exposed in Figure 9. Living with applicable, rarely employed, yet critical mechanisms in shock situations implies costs for the (eco)system. Furthermore, it increases complexity, compromising and slowing down its growth capacities or decreasing peak performance. Favouring a holistic approach limits the resources to feed an individual component when it is to be done at the expense of the whole system. What is suitable for the system is only sometimes good for every element of the system or at any given time. Putting resilience mechanisms in place is a challenging decision, especially at the political level. Nevertheless, when considering the cyclical nature of everything, including the economy, the requirement is to get rid of the short-term vision of maximizing the immediate gains of one element at the expense of the survival of the whole.

CONCLUSION

Collective intelligence has emerged as an exceedingly influential concept within the contemporary landscape of academic discourse and practical application, particularly in this era characterized by rapid technological advancements and complex social dynamics. Nevertheless, it is critical to note that this concept is frequently focused on domains or sectors, limiting its broader applicability and understanding. The research proposal that is being put forth in this context endeavours to build upon and expand the existing body of studies by synthesizing their various findings and insights, ultimately aiming to provide a comprehensive vision that will facilitate the effective harnessing of collective intelligence to achieve both resilience and sustainability in various (eco) systems. Living collectives encompass a diverse array of entities, including but not limited to the natural environment, various animal species, plant life, and human beings, all of which interact in complex ways that warrant further examination. Conversely, within the proposed collective intelligence framework, machines, systems, and infrastructural elements are conceptualized as serving the collective interests of these living entities, thereby forming an intricate ecosystem in which each component plays a vital role.

In this regard, infrastructures possess logical representations, such as networks and other abstract forms, and a tangible physical dimension that is sometimes inadequately addressed or considered in relevant academic research. Throughout this intricate process, knowledge is generated and subsequently managed in a manner that is closely intertwined with normative frameworks that guide societal interactions and expectations. The existing 'hard' infrastructures, which are characterized by considerable inertia at higher levels, necessitate a thorough reconsideration to adapt to the evolving demands of collective intelligence. Such a re-evaluation requires adept orchestration that harmonizes the existing power dynamics and relationships that shape the current landscape. It is imperative to establish a metaphorical level playing field that ensures the emergence of collective intelligence is both equitable and effective across different domains. The notion of the intelligence of intelligence, or what can be termed meta-intelligence, necessitates the establishment of a proper balance among diverse factors and stakeholders. These conceptual frameworks and ideas are capable of providing a practical guide that can be utilized to leverage collective intelligence effectively while simultaneously illuminating critical areas that warrant further research and development efforts.

This comprehensive and holistic conceptual framework, which is visually represented in Figure 10 and has been thoroughly introduced and discussed in this chapter, makes a substantive contribution to the existing corpus of knowledge surrounding the phenomenon of collective intelligence. In doing so, it lays a robust foundation for future studies and investigations within this multifaceted domain, serving as a guiding resource for organizations, policymakers, and researchers who are keen to harness the full potential of collective intelligence in their respective fields. Furthermore, it is essential to recognize that collective intelligence is undergoing rapid evolution, necessitating ongoing research that delves into the potential challenges, ethical considerations, and best practices that accompany the effective harnessing of collective intelligence in diverse contexts.

Figure 10. Collective intelligence conceptualization

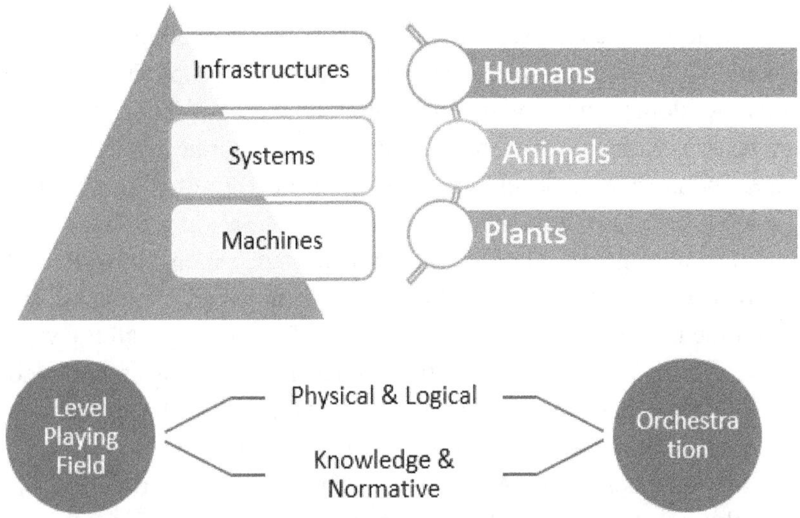

Source: Own elaboration.

The approach towards collective intelligence necessitates a thorough and all-encompassing framework, as any attempt to implement it in a fragmented or incomplete manner has the potential to result in catastrophic and far-reaching consequences, which are subsequently addressed and analysed in greater detail throughout the remainder of the conclusions section. The rules implied in the system, and infrastructure govern societies towards what can be considered collective intelligence and wisdom or towards collective stupidity and madness. Science distribution across fields and their specialization makes it difficult to find a creative and innovative global perspective. Even how the scientists are rewarded or evaluated for their activities impacts it. For instance, finance and economics, critical fields in managing society and its relations with the natural environment, favour almost exclusively relatively short scientific articles centred on econometric models, studying details rather than the whole (Garayalde et al., 2019). Thus, the main proposals of holistic views come from fields like journalism, philosophy or art (Castro, 2019; Fisher, 2009; Morozov, 2013).

Furthermore, the STEM (Science, technology, Engineering, and Mathematics) areas are now strongly promoted by different governments (Kubus, 2020), as their results can relatively quickly turn translational in the sense of turning them into innovations, while social sciences are losing their weight (Figure 3), so that we have the innovations implementations without their proper negotiation and unforeseen negative impacts on the society, stressing their pharmakon (Stiegler, 2010) dimensions as a cure and a poison at the same time.

The terms defining collective intelligence have many overlapping areas. Thus, it takes work to have a clear-cut concept of it. A good example is the comparison of collective wisdom with a more spiritual vibe (Landemore & Elster, 2012). All in all, the collectives without sufficient resources, both economically and in a physical, knowledge, and normative or relational sense, will be prone to display much less collective intelligence in their actions. Even if, in principle, they have the same other properties regarding group intelligence. They are much more likely to suffer the negative processes and enter vicious instead of virtuous cycles. In a sense, this is the same for the individuals and collectives; even if displaying high IQ, vulnerable collectives have different life perspectives when level playing is not adequately balanced. The same goes for developing countries; the liberalization and deregulation in the sense of normative setbacks in a level playing field lead to inequality, exclusion, and peripherisation. As for what regards the free market, there is more wishful thinking in the case of de facto monopolies or oligarchies. In resilience terms, one more privileged actor or a limited group like financial investors when not concerned with sustainability can be growing and maximizing their performance at the expense of the whole, i.e., the sustainability and resilience of the planet Earth.

Infrastructure is challenging to develop and scale and is associated with high inertia; a significant part of it is already embedded. For instance, how the cities or their quarters are built can influence how the society is configured and its ability for collective intelligence. This is the case, if they are developed in a way that promotes individualization with reduced public space and require the use of cars (Dioni, 2021), leading to gentrification and 'touristification' of city centres. The concept of 'infrastructure apartheid' has been introduced by the Liberatory Infrastructures Labs, and this term serves to effectively interrogate and challenge existing theoretical frameworks as well as engineering methodologies that have traditionally dominated discourse in this field (Carrasquillo, 2023). This notion encapsulates a collective intelligence conundrum, wherein the systemic processes of de/humanization, which are manifested through both material and social entities, must be critically examined and understood in relation to how these processes are experienced and enacted across various dimensions of racial, economic, and geographic spatialization. Concurrently, the phenomenon of information overload, coupled with the pervasive presence of misinformation, emerges as yet another formidable obstacle that complicates our understanding of these intricate dynamics. A parallel situation can be observed within the realm of artificial intelligence, which heavily relies on data or information infrastructures that are often reflective of historical perspectives that, in contemporary contexts, can no longer be regarded as ethical—such as those encompassing elements of racism and other forms of discrimination—or may exhibit inherent biases that undermine their validity. Therefore, it becomes imperative to engage in a thorough and nuanced exploration of these challenges to fully comprehend their implications on societal structures and individual experiences. In doing so, we can aspire to create more equitable and just frameworks that address the multifaceted nature of these issues and promote a deeper understanding of the interconnectedness between technology, society, and ethical considerations.

In some cases, however, what grows and is mythicized as collective intelligence is just the financialization of cooperation and collaboration. Platform capitalism, associated with terms such as collaborative economy or sharing economy, can lead to what is called a digital divide (Gainsworth, 2021). Globalization and technological change, increasing interdependencies, and optimizing some variables, such as resource extraction or consumption, have diminished the resilience of the global (eco)system (Vlados & Chatzinikolaou, 2024). However, the climate crisis and associated social issues affect everyone. The system is only as strong as its weakest element in the long run. Thanks to collective intelligence, let us hope that these shocks will allow us to resize the global vision of solidarity and boost true resilience and sustainability. As we navigate the complexities of the modern world, harnessing the potential of collective intelligence will continue to be crucial.

REFERENCES

Alañón, A. & Arauzo, J. (2011). On the Geographical Scope of Location Decisions: Empirical Evidence from Spanish Municipalities. *The Empirical Economics Letters*, 10(2).

Almond, K., & Iszoro, E. (2023). Virtual Reality as a New Means of Communication: A Case Study Analysis of Fashion Brand, Accidental Cutting. *Fashion, Style & Popular Culture*, 10(3).

Beni, G., & Wang, J. (1989). Swarm Intelligence in Cellular Robotic Systems. *NATO Advanced Workshop on Robots and Biological Systems*, 703–712.

Brooks, R. (1991). Intelligence without representation. *Artificial Intelligence*, 47(1-3), 139–159. DOI: 10.1016/0004-3702(91)90053-M

Brown, M., Silberman, J., & Spiegel, F. (2012). A contemporary evaluation of the acrasids (Acrasidae, Heterolobosea, Excavata). *European Journal of Protistology*, 48(2), 103–123. DOI: 10.1016/j.ejop.2011.10.001 PMID: 22154141

Cánovas, P. (2014). Innovación tecnológica y crecimiento en la Unión Europea. *Revista Universitaria Europea,* 20.

Carrasquillo, M. (2023, November 15). Infrastructure Apartheid to Liberatory Infrastructures. *Shareable.*

Castro, F. (2019). *Filosofía tuitera y estética columnista.* Micromegas.

CIA. (1944). Simple Sabotage Field Manual. In *Strategic Services* (p. 20). Office of Strategic Services.

Collective | Search Online Etymology Dictionary. (n.d.). Retrieved November 12, 2023, from Link https://www.etymonline.com/search?q=collective

de Bono, E. (1995). *De Bono's Thinking Course.* BBC Books.

Demir, K., & Cicibaş, H. (2019). The Next Industrial Revolution: Industry 5.0 and Discussions on Industry 4.0. *4th International Management Information Systems Conference "Industry 4.0,"* February, 247–260.

Deryugina, T., Moore, F., & Tol, R. (2021). Environmental Applications of the Coase Theorem. *Environmental Science & Policy*, 120, 81–88. DOI: 10.1016/j.envsci.2021.03.001

Dioni, J. (2021). *La España de las piscinas.* Arpa.

Drucker, P. (2017). *The Age of Discontinuity. Guidelines to our Changing Society.* Heinemann. DOI: 10.4324/9781315130873

Durkheim, É. (1995). *The Elementary Forms of Religious Life.*

EC. (2016). *Open Innovation, Open Science, Open to the World - a Vision for Europe.* European Commission.

EC: Directorate-General for Research and Innovation. (2023). *Harnessing the power of collaboration for nature-based solutions – New ideas and insights for local decision-makers*, Publications Office of the European Union.

Elkington, J. (1998). *Cannibals With Forks. The Triple Bottom Line of 21st Century Business.* Capstone Publishing Limited. DOI: 10.1002/tqem.3310080106

Encinas, M. (2022). *La innovación disruptiva como recurso para la transformación de modelos de negocios en medios de comunicación.* Complutense University of Madrid.

Engert, A. (2020). *Collective intelligence: Crowd Wisdom versus Herding Collective Intelligence* (44).

Falandays, J., Kaaronen, R., Moser, C., Rorot, W., Tan, J., Varma, V., Williams, T., & Youngblood, M. (2023). All intelligence is collective intelligence. *Journal of Multiscale Neuroscience.* https://doi.org/DOI: 10.56280/1564736810

Firlej, K., Firlej, C., & Luty, L. (2023). Economic growth and decent work as a goal of sustainable development in the European Union in the pre-pandemic and pandemic period. *International Entrepreneurship Review*, 9(1), 61–76. DOI: 10.15678/IER.2023.0901.05

Fischer, F. (2012). Participatory Governance: From Theory to Practice. In *The Oxford Handbook of Governance.* Oxford University Press.

Fisher, M. (2009). *Capitalist Realism: Is There no Alternative?* Zero Books.

Flórez, J., Rubio, G., & Rapallo, C. (2020). Corporate social responsibility and crowdfunding: The experience of the colectual platform in empowering economic and sustainable projects. *Sustainability (Basel)*, 12(13), 5251. Advance online publication. DOI: 10.3390/su12135251

Franck, G. (2012). Modern Science: A Case of Collective Intelligence? On the Role of Thought Economy and Gratifying Attention in Knowledge Production. *Angewandte Chemie International Edition*, 51(29), 7088–7092. Advance online publication. DOI: 10.1002/anie.201201013 PMID: 22707208

Gainsworth, S. (2021). *Airbnb Ciudad Mercancía. Historias de resistencia a la gentrificación digital.* Marmol Izquierdo Editores.

Garayalde, M., González, S., & Mascareñas, J. (2019). *"Project Finance" y desarrollo económico. Estudio de un caso.* REVESCO. DOI: 10.5209/reve.64302

García, J., Fernández, J., & Mascareñas, J. (2024). Cómo financiar un futuro sostenible: un estudio descriptivo del mercado de bonos verdes europeo. *Revista Universitaria Europea,* 41.

Gheorghe, A., Masera, M., & Katina, P. (2014). *Infranomics. Sustainability, Engineering Design and Governance.* Springer. DOI: 10.1007/978-3-319-02493-6

Grassé, P. (1959). La reconstruction du nid et les coordinations interindividuelles chez Bellicositermes natalensis et Cubitermes sp. La théorie de la stigmergie: Essai d'interprétation du comportement des termites constructeurs. *Insectes Sociaux,* 6(1), 41–83. DOI: 10.1007/BF02223791

Gross, C. (2008). *Complex and Adaptive Dynamical Systems: A Primer.* Springer-Verlag. DOI: 10.1007/978-3-540-71874-1

Heylighen, F. (2002). The Global Superorganism: An Evolutionary-cybernetic Model of the Emerging Network Society. *Journal of Social and Evolutionary Systems,* 1–37.

Heylighen, F. (2016). Stigmergy as a universal coordination mechanism I: Definition and components. *Cognitive Systems Research,* 38, 4–13. DOI: 10.1016/j.cogsys.2015.12.002

Holling, C. (1973). Resilience and Stability of Ecological Systems. *Annual Review of Ecology and Systematics,* 4(1), 1–23. DOI: 10.1146/annurev.es.04.110173.000245

Intelligence | Etymology, origin and meaning of intelligence by etymonline. (n.d.). Retrieved November 12, 2023, from https://www.etymonline.com/word/intelligence

Interregnum | Search Online Etymology Dictionary. (n.d.). Retrieved September 28, 2024, from https://www.etymonline.com/search?q=interregnum

Johnson, N. L., Rasmussen, S., Joslyn, C., Rocha, L., & Smith, S. (1998). Symbiotic Intelligence: Self-Organizing Knowledge on Distributed Networks Driven by Human Interaction (1998-05–039).

Kubus, R. (2020). *Innovation Ecosystems in the European Union.* UNED.

Kuhn, T. (2017). *The structure of scientific revolutions.* The University of Chicago Press.

Landemore, H., & Elster, J. (Eds.). (2012). *Collective Wisdom: Principles and Mechanisms*. Cambridge University Press. DOI: 10.1017/CBO9780511846427

Levit, G. (2000). The Biosphere and Noosphere theories of V. I. Vernadsky and P. Teilhard de Chardin: A Methodological Essay. *Archives Internationales d'Histoire des Sciences*, 50(144), 160–176.

Licklider, J. (1960). *Man-Computer Symbiosis. IRE Transactions on Human Factors in Electronics*, 4–11.

Liu, T., & Yu, Z. (2022). The Relationship between Open Technological Innovation, Intellectual Property Rights Capabilities, Network Strategy, and AI Technology under the Internet of Things. *Operations Management Research : Advancing Practice Through Research*, 15(3–4), 793–808. DOI: 10.1007/s12063-021-00242-8

Locke, J., Hume, D., & Rousseau, J. (1960). *Social Contract, Essays by Locke, Hume and Rousseau*. Oxford University Press.

Lovelock, J. (1979). *Gaia: A New look at Life on Earth*. Oxford University Press.

Morozov, E. (2013). *To Save Everything, Click Here. The Folly of Technological Solutionism*. PublicAffairs.

Mulgan, G. (2018a). Artificial intelligence and collective intelligence: The emergence of a new field. *AI & Society*, 33(4), 631–632. DOI: 10.1007/s00146-018-0861-5

Mulgan, G. (2018b). *Big Mind. How Collective Intelligence Can Change Our World*. Princeton University Press. DOI: 10.1515/9781400888511

Pelacho, M., Rodríguez, H., Broncano, F., Kubus, R., García, F., Gavete, B., & Lafuente, A. (2021). Science as a commons: Improving the governance of knowledge through citizen science. In *The Science of Citizen Science* (pp. 57–78). Springer International Publishing. DOI: 10.1007/978-3-030-58278-4_4

Pham, Q., Nguyen, D., Mirjalili, S., Hoang, D., Nguyen, D., Pathirana, P., & Hwang, W. (2021). Swarm intelligence for next-generation networks: Recent advances and applications. *Journal of Network and Computer Applications*, 191, 103141. DOI: 10.1016/j.jnca.2021.103141

Puerta, M. E., Pindado, J., González, T. (2023). The resilience of corporate tourism: bleisure, digitalization, and sustainability. *Mercados y Negocios*, (48).

Raworth, K. (2018). *Doughnut Economics: Seven Ways to Think Like a 21st-Century Economist*. Random House International.

Rheingold, H. (2002). *Smart Mobs: The Next Social Revolution*. Perseus Books.

Sanahuja, J., & Rodríguez Díaz, J. (2023). The European Union and Latin America in the Interregnum: Limits and Challenges of a Needed Partnership. *Development Corporation Review*, 6(3).

Scheffler, I. (1967). *Science and Subjectivity*. The Bobbs-Merrill Company.

Schoenmaker, D., & Schramade, W. (2019). *Principles of Sustainable Finance*. Oxford University Press.

Spencer, B., & Guillen, F. (1899). *The Native Tribes of Central Australia*. The Macmillan. DOI: 10.2307/2842887

Stiegler, B. (2010). *What Makes Life Worth Living: On Pharmacology*. Polity Press.

Surowiecki, J. (2004). *The wisdom of crowds*. Anchor Books.

Uña, R. (2023). *La humanidad como ente político soberano: Una aproximación al cosmopolitismo jurídico-político*. Dykinson.

Vernadsky, V. (1998). *The Biosphere*. Springer Science+Business Media.

Verweij, F., Hoose, N., Kuiken, M., Pommer, J., & Savenije, W. (2010). *Cooperative Vehicle- Infrastructure Systems. Deployment Roadmap*. Report D.DEPN.8.1. ERTICO – ITS Europe.

Vlados, C., & Chatzinikolaou, D. (2024). The emergence of the new globalization: The approach of the evolutionary structural triptych. *Journal of Global Responsibility*. Advance online publication. DOI: 10.1108/JGR-04-2023-0063

Voskamp, de Luca, C., Polo, M., Hulsman, H., & Brolsma, R. (2021). Nature-based solutions tools for planning urban climate adaptation: State of the art. *Sustainability*, 13(11).

Vu, K., Hanafizadeh, P., & Bohlin, E. (2020). ICT as a driver of economic growth: A survey of the literature and directions for future research. *Telecommunication Policy*, 44(2).

Webster, F. (2006). *Theories of the Information Society*. Routledge. Taylor & Francis.

Wells, H. (1938). *World Brain*. Double Day, Doran & Co.

Who Cares Wins. (2004). *Connecting Financial Markets to a Changing World*. UN Global Compact.

Wilkinson, M., Dumontier, M., Aalbersberg, J., Appleton, G., Axton, M., Baak, A., Blomberg, N., Boiten, J.-W., da Silva Santos, L. B., Bourne, P. E., Bouwman, J., Brookes, A. J., Clark, T., Crosas, M., Dillo, I., Dumon, O., Edmunds, S., Evelo, C. T., Finkers, R., & Mons, B. (2016). Comment: The FAIR Guiding Principles for Scientific Data Management and Stewardship. *Scientific Data*, 3(1), 1–9. DOI: 10.1038/sdata.2016.18 PMID: 26978244

Williams, W., Chabris, C., Pentland, A., Hashimi, N., & Malone, T. (2010). Evidence for a Collective Intelligence Factor in the Performance of Human Groups. *Science*, 330(6004), 683–686. PMID: 21030660

Wood, S., Luers, A., Garard, J., Gambhir, A., Chaudhari, K., Ivanova, M., & Cronin, C. (2021). Collective foresight and intelligence for sustainability. *Global Sustainability*, 4.

Woolley, A., Aggarwal, I., & Malone, T. (2015). Collective Intelligence and Group Performance. *Current Directions in Psychological Science*, 24(6), 420–424. DOI: 10.1177/0963721415599543

Zolli, A., & Healy, A. (2012). *Resilience: Why Things Bounce Back*. Headline Publishing Group.

Chapter 2
Managing AI in the Workplace to Enhance Collective Intelligence and Resilience

Michael Steggemann
https://orcid.org/0009-0008-2693-4289
La Salle University, Mexico

ABSTRACT

This chapter examines the integration of artificial intelligence (AI) in the workplace and its impact on collective intelligence (CI), collective resilience (CR), and experienced integrity (EI)—the alignment of individual and organizational values. Building on CI and CR concepts, it explores how AI shapes collaboration, trust, and meaning-making for individuals and teams. While AI boosts efficiency and innovation, its integration requires balancing technology with human values, focusing on ethical considerations, transparency, and maintaining integrity. The chapter presents a conceptual framework, enriched by the author's experiences, to guide managers and teams in effectively managing AI to enhance CI, CR, and EI. It offers practical strategies for addressing AI-related uncertainties, fostering collaboration, trust, and adaptability. In doing so, it highlights AI's potential to strengthen both individual and collective capabilities, supporting a more resilient and intelligent workforce.

DOI: 10.4018/979-8-3693-7272-2.ch002

INTRODUCTION

The problem evaluated in this chapter centers on the increasing integration of Artificial Intelligence (AI) in the workplace and its impact on individuals, work groups, and organizational dynamics, particularly regarding Collective Intelligence (CI) and Collective Resilience (CR). The key issue is understanding how AI influences Experienced Integrity (EI)—the alignment between personal and organizational values—within individual and collective experiences.

The article "Collective Intelligence (CI) Synergizing into Collective Resilience (CR)" (Steggemann, 2023) did not consider AI technologies[1] as part of CI due to its lack of a social dimension. However, with AI's rapid workplace adoption, it is now essential to understand its influence on CI, CR, and EI.

The main objective of this chapter is to explore how AI can be effectively managed in the workplace to enhance Collective Intelligence (CI) and Collective Resilience (CR), with a specific focus on its impact on Experienced Integrity (EI) for both individuals and groups.

This chapter deals with personal and team experienced integrity, which involves comparing one's values to those of the organization rather than simply assimilating them into the environment.

The question guiding this exploration is: How can AI be managed in the Workplace to improve CI and RC, considering the significance of AI meaning for EI, both for individuals and groups and for the CI and CR? The premise is that using AI in the Workplace impacts the EI, which affects CI and CR, considering that an impact can be positive, negative, or neutral.

This document is inspired by Jordan B. Peterson's lectures on meaning (2017a) and personality (2017b) at the University of Toronto. The methodology for answering the questions is a conceptual approach to the problem under study enriched by the author's personal experience.

This chapter guides managers and team members in navigating the uncertainties of AI to foster trust, collaboration, and shared purpose. By understanding AI principles, individuals can enhance CI, CR, and creative reasoning. It highlights the importance of meaning-making for individuals and teams, shaped by past and present experiences, and establishes key concepts like EI, CI, CR, and AI.

This chapter is divided into five parts: Part one introduces the topic; Part two explores how meaning-making processes for individuals and groups within organizations link past and future experiences; Part three discusses AI's relevance to organizations and its relationship to CI, CR, and EI; Part four links to the practical side of the chapter's objective by offering theoretical insights and practical strategies for managing AI to improve CI, CR, and EI; and Part 5 concludes with recommendations for further research.

MEANING FOR THE INDIVIDUAL AND COLLECTIVE: CONNECTING PAST AND FUTURE

This part explores how individual and collective meaning-making processes, particularly within organizations, connect individual and collective experiences, bridging the past and future. It connects to the chapter's major objective by laying the foundation for understanding how personal and organizational values are aligned, a key component of Experienced Integrity (EI).

It explores the importance of meaning for individuals and groups as they navigate the integration of AI in the workplace. This section establishes the context for how individuals and teams can find purpose and cohesion, which are necessary for enhancing Collective Intelligence and Resilience in an AI-driven environment.

Talking about the meaning or nature of something in organizations is complex because it involves the mind's interpretation of reality. According to Atmanspacher (2023), meaning, in its two variants of reference relations and sense, provides a viable perspective to illuminate the deep structure of reality as it extends beyond physics and across its boundaries. In this sense, reference relations refer to the interpretation of conceptual terms in the mental domain concerning objects in the material domain of concrete and empirical facts, while meaning as sense corresponds to the interpretation or significance that people attach to a thing based on their experience and context; meaning as reference and meaning as sense are relational concepts that connect the physical world with the mental features of the human condition. (Atmansbacher, 2023) [2]

To simplify this complexity, in the context of this chapter, meaning refers to what it is for the individuals, meaning as a sense. It relates to the interpretation or understanding derived from the context, relationships, and mental models they generate. Models are a narrative about how it might work, involve abstractions and idealization, and can be understood as their representations of phenomena in the world (Morgan, 2023).

The way humans perceive the world is based on their experiences and senses (Peterson, 2017a). The author's model of how Collective Intelligence synergizes into Collective Resilience (Figure 1) gives a picture of the framework in which these concepts and their relationships are embedded. It forms the surroundings of AI use in a workplace.

The human capacity for rationality is nested within a metaphysical structure of thought and perception (Peterson, 2017a). In social interaction, our perceptions and reasoning become sharper, leading to a shared understanding of goals, vision, and values. Resulting motivation and emotions can inspire actions and support co-operation between individuals. This collaboration can create synergy and promote teamwork, resulting in a sense of integrity when comparing individual and team expectations and performance.

Figure 1. Collective Intelligence synergizes into collective resilience.

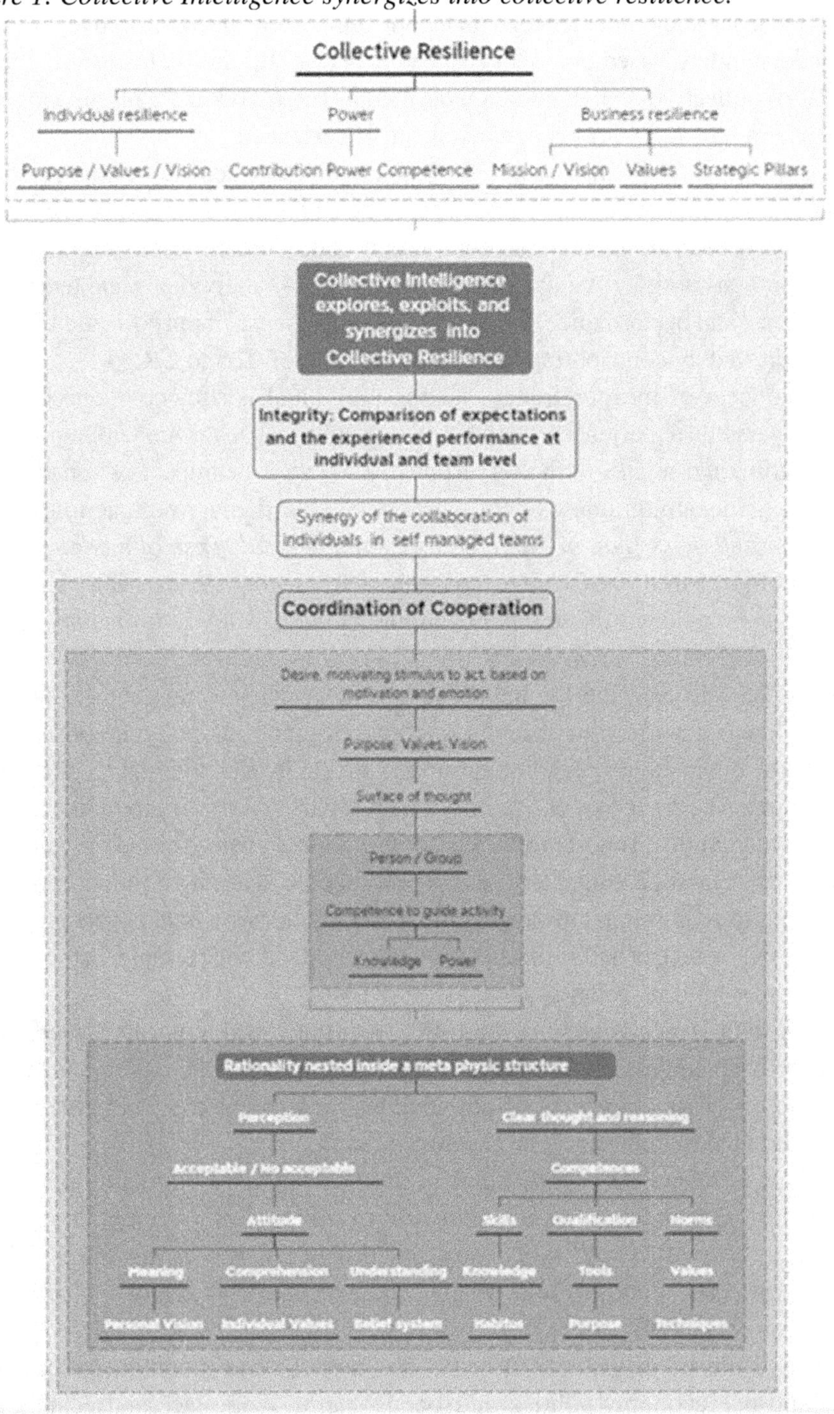

Source: Own elaboration.

A unit with a CI is established. This unit is strengthened by the individual and team's integrity and competence, which contributes to its power to convey meaning and understanding based on a set of values in action. It, in turn, leads to the development of collective resilience (CR), defined as the individual and the company's resilience in how the world is perceived and experienced.

These explanations illustrate how the collective experience in a workplace, shaped by individuals' perceptions and emotions, contributes to shared goals, visions, and values. This, in turn, fosters cooperation and collaboration, establishing synergy that strengthens both individual and team integrity. As individuals and teams align expectations and performance, they build a stronger sense of purpose and meaningfulness, ultimately contributing to the development of CI and CR.

The concept of meaningfulness for the individual is subjective and can vary based on personal experiences, knowledge, and cultural background. Its significance for the individual relates to the importance, relevance, or impact of something. It measures the meaningfulness or consequence of a particular event, action, or idea.

> *"Meaningfulness [can be] defined as a fundamental sense of meaning, based on an appraisal of one's life as coherent, significant, directed, and belonging. A judgment on one's life as empty, pointless, and lacking meaning amounts to a crisis of meaning." (Schnell, 2010)*

It is crucial to consider the individual's context when evaluating the situation. Humans live in a world with different surroundings, periods, and relationships. It is natural for humans to be born into groups and form groups to organize their lives.

The human being is part of a family, which is part of a social group like a village or city, which in turn is nested inside a socio-political society based on values like those of the Christian-Judea tradition. These people share a common experience and belong to professional groups within a local industry, which is part of a major economy in a state, in a nation, and altogether embedded, for example, in the western hemisphere within its belief system.

It is a multilayer dynamic relationship with the world, consciously organized and more frequently unconsciously organized by interest and desires, influenced by reflection of the past, present-day feelings, and future expectations(Peterson, 2017a). It is the manifestation of meaning as sense,

> *"Which is likewise an explication of implicit meaning. Meaning has a deep structure that plays a fundamental role in the very fabric of reality. On the surface, it is attributed to humans, but this attribution is constrained by its deep structure. It may appear partly subjective, but it is surely not arbitrary." (Atmanspacher, 2022)*

Figure 2 illustrates the deep structure and how the surroundings, including the global and local economy, political and social systems, Workplace, and technologies, impact individual and collective identity and integrity.

Figure 2. Individual and collective meaning between past and future[3]

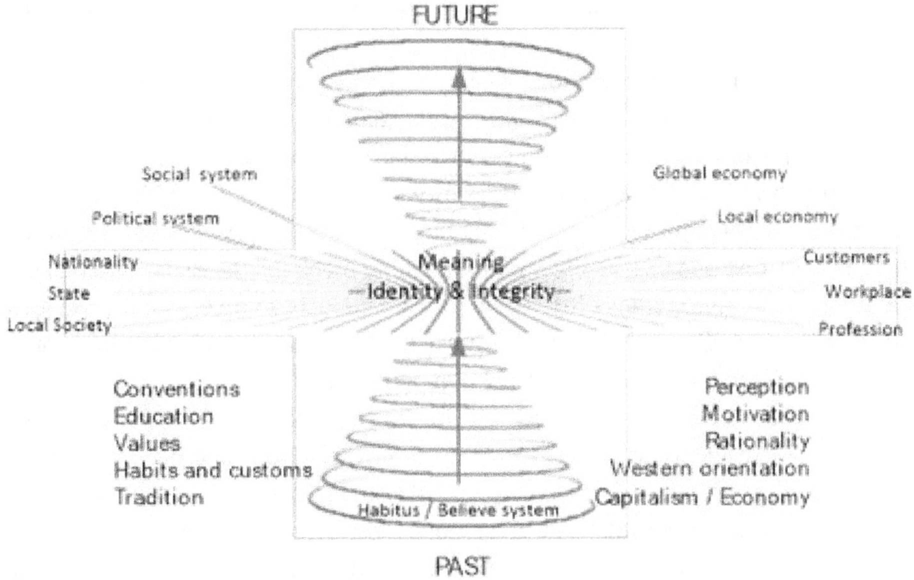

Source: Hyperbola plus double Helix pictures are taken from the next linkhttps://www.mathcurve.com/courbes2d.gb/hyperbole/hyperbole.shtml

The collective and individual meaning in organizations is influenced by both, past experiences and future aspirations. Their integration into the workplace framework strengthens collective resilience, making organizations more adaptable and robust in facing challenges.

Lately, a new actor, AI, has challenged the individual's balanced and often protected identity and integrity. The rapid advancement and integration of AI in the Workplace have raised concerns about their impact on the EI of individuals and work groups and the overall CI and CR within organizations.

Many organizations and nations are beginning to recognize the transformative power of AI. As the Danish Prime Minister Frederiksen (2023) noted: "AI is no longer the future. It is real. Moreover, it will change our society – on a scale we do not understand yet." AI will affect all areas of our lives, especially all business areas, including the ability of Large Language Models (LLM) like Chat GPT [4] to generate human-like responses at incredible speeds, though the quality of these responses is still not quite up to par (Peng, 2023).

AI technology has become a game-changing force, unprecedentedly transforming the world. It can simulate human dialogue and decision-making, making it more accessible to everyone (Accenture, 2023). Generative AI technology, which creates new content based on patterns and data (World Economic Forum, 2023a), is expected to automate many tasks over the next few years (World Economic Forum, 2023b). Recent studies have shown that LLM can automate up to 15% of tasks (Eloundou et al., 2023).

All this does not happen without causing fear and uncertainty. There are calls to govern artificial Intelligence in the public interest and assess the potential systemic harms from its under-governed application (Mazzucato et al., 2022).

The unknown and hidden generate reactions like “Pause Giant AI Experiments: An Open Letter” (Future of Life, 2023). The initiative is calling a halt to the deployment of LLM due to concerns about invisible mechanisms (Russell, 2023).

On the other hand, AI is being perceived by others as a universal purpose technology of the early 21st century, and countries are competing to lead in innovation capabilities and domestic technological competitiveness.

AI has been under research since the 1940s when Konrad Zuse built the first computer. The resulting industry faced elevated expectations and disappointments in the following decades. AI has encompassed a set of technologies with approaches and applications in various sub-areas, including human Intelligence, computer vision, machine translation, pattern recognition, and natural language processing (Mazzucato et al., 2022).

Undoubtedly, increasing the organizational use of AI technology will influence how people experience work (Bankins, 2023; World Economic Forum, 2018), the meaning of life in teams and projects, and the level of responsibility everyone takes on.

CONCLUSION

These interpretations illustrate how the collective experience in a workplace, shaped by individuals’ perceptions and emotions, contribute to shared goals, visions, and values. The integration of past experiences and future aspirations into the workplace framework strengthens collective resilience, making organizations more adaptable and robust in the face of challenges.

This promotes collaboration and synergy, strengthening individual and team integrity. As expectations align, a stronger sense of purpose develops, directly enhancing Collective Intelligence (CI) and Collective Resilience (CR).

The growing integration of AI in organizations will reshape individual and collective meaning at work. It will impact everything from how tasks are performed to how individuals find purpose and relevance in their roles, requiring a careful balance between innovation and experienced integrity (EI).

To fully understand the impacts of AI, we must consider its implications for concepts like EI, CI, and CR. The uncertainties AI provokes will affect not only how individuals and teams operate but also the broader organizational dynamics, making it essential to carefully manage its adoption and integration.

Before entering the main ideas of this chapter, it is essential to set conceptual boundaries for each concept. Some of the main concepts discussed include Artificial Intelligence (AI), experienced integrity (EI), the integrity of individuals and groups, Collective Intelligence (CI), and Collective Resilience (CR) in dynamic business environments. It is crucial to understand that uncertainties perceived by individuals working in teams that use AI technology can impact both the EI of individuals and the work group as a whole.

Artificial Intelligence (AI) In Context: Framework, Collective Intelligence, and Resilience

This part provides a framework for understanding AI's role within organizations and its impact on Collective Intelligence (CI) and Collective Resilience (CR). It explores how AI technologies can influence the dynamics of collaboration, cooperation, and coordination within teams and the broader organization. This section directly ties to the objective by discussing how AI can be utilized to strengthen or weaken the collective abilities of an organization. The emphasis is on how AI shapes workplace dynamics and its potential to either support or undermine the collective integrity and resilience required for organizational success.

Defining Artificial Intelligence (AI) has been a challenge due to its diverse technologies, goals, methods, approaches, and applications, as noted by Pei Wang[5] (2019) and Kristinn R. Thórrison (2020). Wang defines Intelligence as "the capacity of an information-processing system to adapt to its environment while operating with insufficient knowledge and resources," without referring to "artificial." His definition created public interest and prompted the Journal of Artificial General Intelligence to organize a special issue. (Monett et al., 2020)

The AI community's responses are research-oriented, with the development of Human-level AI or Artificial General Intelligence (AGI) being the main focus. However, estimates show that when truly agile and adaptable, AGI might emerge from 10 years to never (World Economic Forum, 2023a).

To simplify and summarize AI's definition, it can be described as "the ability of computers and other artificial entities to perform tasks typically classified as requiring human intelligence, such as reasoning, planning, problem-solving, and learning from experience" (Wang, 2019; cited in Bankins)

However, current AI technologies and tools need to meet the described requirements. They are examples of weak artificial Intelligence that can only perform intelligent functions in limited areas and cannot transfer learned skills to other areas. (Boden, 2016, cited in Bankins, 2023)

The fear of AI replacing humans with human-like capabilities is a fallacy, as we are talking about human-like artificial Intelligence that can automate rather than augment human labor (Brynjolfsson, 2022).

Brynjolfsson cautions against the Turing[6] Trap and argues that AI should focus on augmenting humans rather than mimicking them, generating new capabilities, products, and services that produce far more value than merely human-like AI (Figure 3). Understanding the meaning of AI's use in the Workplace is crucial for individuals, groups, and the integrity of CI and CR.

Figure 3. The Turing Trap: the promise and peril of human-like AI

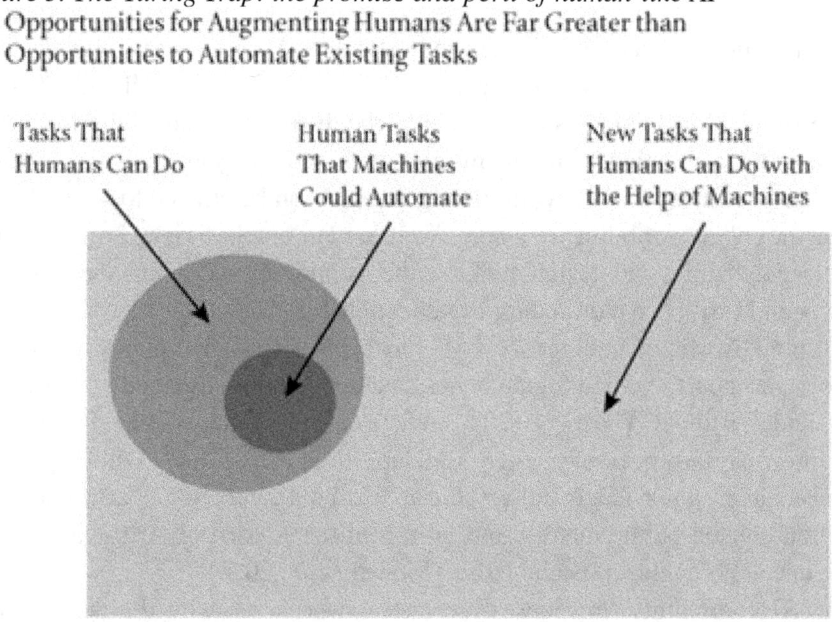

Source: Brynjolfsson (2022).

As highlighted by Brynjolfsson (2022), the opportunities for augmenting to improve humans are far greater than opportunities to automate existing tasks. AI is becoming the critical utility of the tech world, much like the way electricity revolutionized industries a century ago. Electricity is everywhere: electrical motors, heating systems, air conditioning transport systems, computer systems, digitization.

Now, everything that was formerly electrified has the potential to be enhanced with cognitive abilities through AI (Kolla, 2017).

Brynjolfsson (2023) explains that new technologies have the potential to be used not only for physical tasks but also for marketing and business process redesign. By providing these tools to a group, the combined capacity and capability of the team can be enhanced, even if they are not necessarily the best in their respective fields. It enables them to perform various tasks and solve diverse problems. Examples are prognostic analytics, which performs forecasting and predicting the future by looking at large amounts of data the companies process monthly from different approaches so that they can come up with findings to help run the company.

Figure 4 Industrial Revolutions 1.0 - 4.0

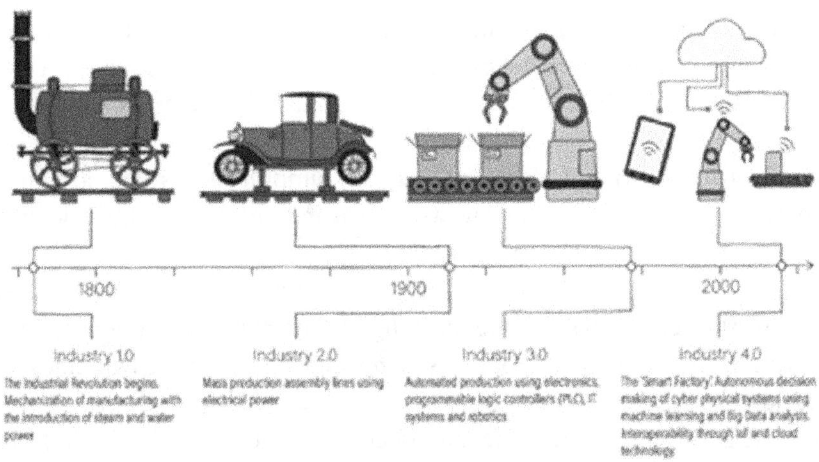

Source: Shutterstock (2023).

Much of the economy's value, throughout the different Industrial Revolutions, was generated from goods and services that did not exist before (Figure 4).

Accordingly, to move forward, Brynjolfsson (2022) recommends replacing the Turing Test and its associated mentality with practical benchmarks that guide progress toward AI-powered systems that surpass human capabilities. This shift towards AI-powered technology has the potential to benefit individuals greatly (Brynjolfsson, 2022).

In conclusion, defining AI remains complex due to its diverse technologies, goals, and applications, as noted by Wang and Thórrison. Wang's description of intelligence as an adaptable, information-processing system highlights the challenge of pinpointing AI's essence without focusing on its "artificial" nature. This ambiguity drives ongoing research, especially in the pursuit of Artificial General Intelligence (AGI), which experts believe may never fully materialize.

While AI is often simplified as the ability to perform tasks requiring human intelligence, today's systems are still "weak AI," limited to narrow tasks. This dispels fears of AI replacing humans, with real value, as Brynjolfsson suggests, lying in augmenting human abilities and creating new capabilities, products, and services.

As AI becomes integral to society and work, much like electricity in previous industrial revolutions, its true potential is to enhance human labor and innovation, shifting the focus from passing the Turing Test to developing AI that empowers human intelligence.

AI and Meaning

What is the known AI's meaning for the organization, the individual, and his surroundings? According to Peterson et al. (2013), the world makes itself known to us as meaning to be observed in three different manifestations:

- The first form consists of basic functional simplifications that structure the known, familiar, or determinate world and individual and social identity. – the known world.
- The second form challenges the integrity of our current known or determinate worlds, encompassing the meaning of the unknown, foreign, or indeterminate world, including anomalies or novelties. – the unknown, unexplored world.
- The third form arises from the integrated interaction of the first two forms of the known and the unknown, including meanings that emerge during voluntary exploratory behavior.

Open discussions address AI's ethical, social, economic, and data security practices. These discussions can contribute to a more informed and balanced perception of AI among individuals, organizations, and communities. While nations compete for leadership in AI innovation capabilities, there remains a perception of fear on a public and individual level. This fear is manifested when researchers and the public call for a halt on the deployment of LLM or speculate on the future of humanity with AI (Russell, 2023; Harari, 2023).

It may seem chaotic, but chaos can lead to new and valuable information. Our responsibility is to be on the border of order and chaos, looking for complementarities. Valuable information can arise from chaos; something new can be born from the pieces. It manifests a complementarity of the universal and the particular (Steggemann, 2015). What is meaningful depends on what is essential for the observer, what has significance and what is valued by the observer at a specific time and place.

The importance of something for the individual will lead the individual to take responsibility for it; meaning is to be founded in responsibility (Peterson, 2017a). What is essential for the individual depends on how the individual perceives (understands) its relationship with the different situations in the present time (Figure 1), projecting the future based on past experiences internalized in the habitus[7] and its belief system.

In contrast to the importance of something, a sensation of being meaningless or doing something meaningless leads, according to Victor Frankl (2006), to an "existential vacuum," causing aimlessness and disintegration in personal, social, and cultural dimensions. This leaves us mindless and disconnected from a world whose presence seems increasingly insensitive and indifferent to our touch (Mastropietro, 2023). In organizations, this leads to a disintegration of the individual and, consequently, of the group projects with its surroundings when working in teams.

Therefore, we need to get to the bottom by understanding the essence of the business using AI technology, the nucleus at the organization's core. Typically, an organization is embedded in a multilayer construct, and each organization consists of many layers, like an onion.

However, there is no nucleus in an onion. What happens if there is no essence, no meaning, and no "purpose" at the core of the business? Having a purpose is crucial because it gives the leader, the people, the staff, and the customers a firm understanding of the business they personify; it gives them, and the people involved significant convictions for the value proposition the business represents. It gives meaning, a sense of identity, self-awareness, and a collective understanding of supporting and managing a project for the customer, the company, and the staff. Remember, a project business is a people business.

To make AI technology meaningful and valued by individuals, it is crucial to have clarity about the purpose, mission, vision, and values of AI use. Individuals shape a company, and its mission declares the purpose of the business and its vision, the long-term goals, and a strategy developed and verified through CI and CR, ensuring that AI technologies are meaningful and valuable to the individual. For example, a Mission of AI use could be

1. to develop AI technologies and applications that enhance human capabilities, improve efficiency, and address complex societal challenges or
2. "to replicate, automate, and exceed human-level intelligence and capabilities." (Mazzucato et al., 2022)

A corresponding vision of AI use could be

1. an AI-driven world where technology empowers organizations, communities, and individuals and thrives and generates meaningful impact. Or
2. an AI focused on "augmenting humans to develop new capabilities and new products and services, ultimately generating far more value than merely human-like AI." (Brynjolfsson, 2022)

Values considered in AI development are context-dependent and should address individual needs for a meaningful life. For example, but not limited to:

- Adherence to ethical principles and responsible AI,
- Collaboration and knowledge sharing to boost a culture of collaboration,
- Culture of Innovation and continuous learning,
- Privacy and data security,
- Social Impact and Sustainability,
- Human needs-centered design.

The adherence of AI to the values described could enhance meaningful work, while nonadherence could diminish the perception of meaningful work (Bankins, 2023).

Perception and meaning of AI vary widely depending on personal experiences, knowledge, beliefs, and cultural backgrounds (Figure 1).

- Some people are enthusiastic about AI's potential and may see it as a powerful tool that could revolutionize distinct aspects of life.
- Others approach the AI with curiosity and interest or with a skeptical or fearful attitude and
- Others need more awareness of AI and perceive it as a distant, complex technology.
- Still, others are simply scared because they do not understand what is coming up.

It is important to reiterate that individual perceptions and meanings about AI can evolve as people gain more exposure to and knowledge about AI technologies. These meanings result from the conjunction of the known and the unknown, arising during voluntary exploratory behavior, as Peterson (2013) described it.

Having a collective agreement about the business (organization) using AI technologies, its potential, exploiting the existing competencies, and exploring the future ones is a convention generator. A convention is an evolutionarily stable element of regularity (Sugden, 1989) added to a business. It is the heart of creating value(s) in the multifaceted field of a company.

In conclusion, AI's meaning for organizations, individuals, and society lies in its ability to shape the known and unknown worlds. AI increases efficiency, automates tasks, and enhances innovation, contributing to a meaningful and purposeful work environment when aligned with a clear mission, vision, and values. However, the perception of AI varies, from enthusiasm to fear, depending on personal experiences and cultural contexts. For AI to be meaningful, it must promote ethical practices, collaboration, and human-centered design, while maintaining integrity and addressing societal challenges. In this way, AI can foster a sense of purpose, identity, and responsibility, driving meaningful progress for individuals and organizations alike.

AI and Experienced Integrity (EI)

Determining an individual's and a team's integrity involves comparing their expectations with their current performance, as shown in Figure 5. (Steggemann, 2023) It makes itself visible when a person and the team consistently act honestly and ethically, putting "their values into action" and earning them a reputation for trustworthiness, integrity, and reliability.

Figure 5. The Experienced Integrity (EI) of the person and the team

The integrity of the person and the team is the result of the comparison between

- **the individual's expectations and team levels of expectations**
    - based on individual and team level values and vision
- **and the experienced performance**
    - subjective and at team level as fulfillment of individual and team level requirements

→ Individual satisfaction includes opinions and evaluations
→ Individual satisfaction determines team performance

expectations

performance

Source: Steggemann (2023).

Integrity is critical for employees to perform well and behave ethically in the Workplace, requiring alignment between their principles, beliefs, and actions. On one hand, AI technology can boost the integrity of individuals by automating repetitive tasks, reducing human error, and freeing up time for more meaningful work. It can increase job satisfaction, motivation, and a sense of personal integrity. On the other hand, if individuals view AI as a threat to their job security or expertise, it can erode their EI and provoke conflicts. Furthermore, ethical concerns regarding AI's impact on privacy, bias, or transparency can challenge the EI of both individuals and the group (Bankins, 2023).

In conclusion, experienced integrity (EI) in the workplace is reflected in how well individuals and teams align their expectations with their actual performance, consistently acting in ways that uphold their values. This integrity is vital for maintaining trustworthiness and ethical behavior within an organization. AI can support EI by automating repetitive tasks, minimizing errors, and enabling employees to focus on more meaningful work, thereby enhancing job satisfaction and personal integrity. However, AI can also pose challenges to EI if perceived as a threat to job security or if it raises ethical issues related to privacy, bias, or transparency. Addressing these concerns is essential to ensure that AI integration drives rather than undermines integrity in the workplace.

AI and Collective Intelligence (CI) and Unity

Individual human Intelligence, or IQ, relates to the ability to think and reason logically. It has to do with cognitive ability and approaching problems from different perspectives. In short, it is about our brain's capacity to solve context-dependent issues. (Jänke et al., 2022) [8]

On the other hand, collective refers to social structures whose members are grouped indefinitely according to quite different points of view; this can be a religion, a state, a company, or a social class, as described in Figure 2. There are also action-oriented collectives whose members cooperate as a group or team in specific action communities in a purposeful and goal-oriented manner. [9]

With the advancement of communication and information technology, CI has become increasingly relevant in group and team dynamics. Genuine interaction and open-mindedness among people can lead to new insights and approaches that are exponentially more effective because of the differences in perspectives (Covey, 2023).

Like human Intelligence, there are various definitions of CI, each focused on a specific context and approached from different points of view, such as biological, social, or economic. Chikersal (2017) defines CI as the combined capacity and capability of a group or team, not necessarily consisting of the best individuals, to perform various tasks and solve diverse problems, which has been proven to consistently predict future group and team performance. Meanwhile, Pierre Levy (1997) describes CI as a type of Intelligence that is distributed everywhere, constantly developed, and coordinated in real-time, leading to an effective mobilization of competencies.

Morel et al. (2018) emphasize the networking of multiple types of Intelligence, the combination of knowledge and competencies, and collaboration and cooperation between community members. This type of Intelligence guarantees each member a unique place and contribution within the intelligent community, resulting in a new and effective social organization based on competencies and knowledge. Implementing agile and open-innovation project-management processes is essential to guide the information systems, technological systems, and human and managerial competencies required for collective Intelligence to thrive.

CI, involving all skills, knowledge, tools, and technologies such as AI, values unity over uniformity. The primary difference between IQ and CI is the social dimension and the ability of groups to achieve unity of purpose, action, and thought. Teams with high CI achieve a state of interdependence and flow while working together (Oxford Review, 2023), resulting in greater efficiency and productivity.

In the Workplace, AI technology can enhance CI by providing access to vast amounts of data, analyzing complex information, and offering insights that can nurture decision-making. AI-powered collaboration tools can facilitate knowledge sharing, cross-team collaboration, and collective problem-solving. However, if not well coordinated and implemented, AI can undermine CI by limiting creativity, innovation, and diversity of perspectives. Critical thinking, human input, and conflict resolution are essential for effective CI.

AI technology in the Workplace refers to coordinating and effectively mobilizing resources and competencies to define and adjust a company's business models and strategy, typically top-down by a smaller group, incorporating ideas bottom-up. Putting it into practice, like any project, involves various steps. For example:

- The assessments of needs of different areas where AI can be most beneficial include data analysis, customer support, and process automation.
- A top-down strategy led by a smaller group of decision-makers, such as top management or the IT department, to set up the goals and vision for AI integration.
- The allocation of resources and data preparation
- for developing and testing AI models tailored to the business needs.
- Training and educating employees to help them understand and use AI technologies.
- To encourage employees to contribute with ideas, insights, and opportunities bottom-up for AI implementation and to make improvements and adjustments.
- Effective change management strategies to ensure that employees are comfortable and preserve their integrity with the adoption of AI.
- The adherence to ethical and legal standards.
- The development of metrics to measure the AI initiatives' return on investment (ROI) to assess their impact on the organization's strategy and business models.

In the present context, CI integrating AI is understood as a part of a meta-meaning that involves unity, collaboration, and cooperation within the group organization. It includes common group principles and processes, a mass collaboration (Tapsott, 2008) visible as a self-managed team structure, where "the locus of authority has been transferred from the hierarchical system to the teams' and individuals' values, norms, and rules, which does not resemble the bureaucracy (Barker, 1993).

Self-managed teams are working based on roles rather than on positions. Roles are people's thinking, experience, and expertise, while positions are structures and authority vested in an office. Self-managed teams avoid authority over dynamics by eliminating the managerial role as it exists in the managerial hierarchy (Lee, 2017). Nevertheless, it is important to note that "within any group, diverging and conflicting interests make any kind of CI both a tool for cooperation and a site for competition, deception, and manipulation" (Mulgan, 2018).

Team conflicts are common, regardless of whether or not AI technologies are used. Some examples of conflicts include:

1. Unequal Skill Levels: Differences in team members' skill levels regarding working with AI technologies may cause conflict. Some members may feel overwhelmed or left behind, while others may feel their colleagues need to contribute more.
2. Resistance to Change: Introducing AI technologies to a team's workflow may cause resistance from individuals reluctant to embrace new tools or processes. They may fear job displacement or feel that AI undermines their expertise.
3. Trust and Reliability: Team members may experience conflicts related to trust and reliability in AI technologies. Doubts about the accuracy or bias of AI algorithms, concerns about data security, or skepticism about the value AI brings to the team's work can arise.
4. Loss of Human Interaction—Communication: The introduction of AI technologies in teamwork may impact human interaction. If certain tasks are automated, team members may feel detachment or reduced collaboration.
5. Ethical Considerations: AI technologies can raise ethical considerations within teams. Conflicts may evolve when team members hold differing opinions about the appropriate use of AI, potential algorithm biases, or the privacy implications of data collection.
6. Data Access and Ownership: AI often relies on data for training and decision-making, and conflicts can develop when team members disagree on data access, ownership, or sharing. Possible biases in algorithms, AI, and privacy implications should be considered.

Developing a culture of collaboration, empathy, and open communication is essential to defusing these conflicts. Encouraging team members to share their perspectives, providing training and support to improve AI skills, and encouraging a shared understanding of the team's goals and AI's role in the workflow can help teams use AI technologies effectively.

The focus should be on self-reflexivity and responsiveness and structural improvement measures such as less hierarchical organizing (Lee, 2017) by implementing a self-managing organization. Ultimately, CI rests fundamentally on relationships with and without AI. Promoting collaboration and resilience in the team requires the development of a psychologically safe[10] culture that values learning, exploration, appreciation (Edmondson, 2023; Edmondson et al., 2004), and dialogue (Gilan, 2021).

In conclusion, collective intelligence (CI) and AI work together to enhance unity, collaboration, and problem-solving in organizations. While individual intelligence focuses on cognitive abilities, CI emphasizes teamwork and diverse perspectives to achieve shared goals. AI amplifies CI by providing data-driven insights and enabling more efficient collaboration, but its success depends on thoughtful integration and maintaining creativity and human oversight. Fostering a culture of open communication, trust, and self-management ensures that AI and CI enhance unity and resilience, driving innovation and collective success.

AI and Collective Resilience (CR) and Unity

Resilient systems share many earlier characteristics and value unity over unity as CI. Resilience refers to “the capacity of a system, enterprise, or a person to maintain its core purpose and integrity in the face of dramatically changed circumstances” (Zolli, 2012).

Others refer to CR as the ability of the system to “absorb shocks and stressors while maintaining its essential structures and functions” (Wilson et al., 2020). These concepts are closely interrelated with CI, which is the capacity to mobilize competencies (including AI) in real-time effectively (Levy, 1997). In combination with CI, Resilient and robust systems undergo dynamic adaptation processes and have strategies that help avoid risky circumstances, detect disruptions early, and reorganize themselves through change processes.

AI technology can contribute to CR by improving operational efficiency, automating processes, and enabling faster response times. Predictive analytics can help with risk management and decision-making. However, reliance on AI can also introduce vulnerabilities. Technical failures, algorithm biases, or data breaches can disrupt operations and undermine resilience. Organizations must build a resilient culture integrating AI technologies while maintaining human oversight, continuous learning, and adaptability.

In combination with CI, resilience supports a business's most critical competitive advantage, its local and corporate organizational culture, and how things are done inside and outside the company. (Steggemann, 2015) Resilience and collective intelligence, combined with AI, mold an adaptable organizational culture and a competitive edge. AI enhances resilience by providing data-driven insights and automating processes. Collective Intelligence leverages AI for better decision-making. Together, they form a culture of adaptability and innovation, driving a competitive advantage by transforming internal and external operations.

Integrating resilience, collective Intelligence, and AI contributes to a better-equipped culture to navigate challenges and seize opportunities, whether at a local or corporate level. While the specific applications may differ, the overarching principles of promoting adaptability, innovation, and efficiency hold for local and corporate organizational cultures.

Planned action, keeping the overview, and designing a vision of one's activities and performance, coupled with psychological safety (Edmondson, 2023), are strategies that strengthen the unity and resilience of a company and its employees.

In conclusion, AI, collective intelligence (CI), and resilience are essential for adaptable and competitive organizational cultures. Resilience enables systems to absorb shocks and maintain core functions, while CI enhances real-time decision-making. When combined, AI enhances both by improving efficiency, automating processes, and offering predictive insights. However, reliance on AI also introduces risks that require human oversight and adaptability. By integrating AI with resilience and CI, organizations can cultivate innovation and unity, equipping themselves to navigate challenges and capitalize on opportunities at both local and corporate levels.

AI and Coordination: Cooperation - Collaboration

Buckley (2010) describes coordination as allocating resources so that someone is better and no one is worse off than before the assignment. Coordination is an appropriate basis for building cooperation (Buckley, 2010). Cooperation and coordination are a precondition for performance. It is based on the idea that cooperation benefits the parties directly involved. It synergizes the collaboration of individuals independent of physical, hierarchical, or geographical boundaries or the tools used, such as AI. It is teamwork, ideally in self-managed teams, open-mindedness, and the adventure of finding new solutions to old problems.

However, it does not happen on its own. It is a process; through that process, people bring their experience and expertise to the table (Figure 1). Valuing differences is what drives synergy (Covey, 2023).

Consequently, special attention must be paid to the coordination and the internal dynamics of less hierarchical organizations (Peerdom, 2019), mainly when working with AI tools. Team members must adopt a self-organization mindset, while managerial positions should no longer rely on traditional "command and control" approaches. Decision-making becomes more complicated, and the information flow requires special attention. While the process may take time and be frustrating for some team members, valuing differences and learning to work effectively together will ultimately drive synergy and improve performance. For many teams, an endeavor into self-organization will be the first time they explicitly consider how the organization works.

Cooperation in a business is essential for successful performance and requires proper coordination. Mintzberg (1983) explains that coordination is based on a power mechanism, which involves the ability to impact the organization's outcome. This power mechanism is similar to trust, where interpersonal trust is the expectation that others will act favorably toward one's interests (Bachmann, 2003). Both trust and coordination involve assuming a social actor's future behavior based on the perceived reality and rationality (Edmondson et al., 2004). The result of cooperation, based on coordination, is performance. Without proper coordination and cooperation, business performance will result from lucky accidents.

In a business setting, the professional habitus plays a significant role in shaping the identity and performance of the individual. Bourdieu (1996) describes habitus as the process through which professional performance is unconsciously internalized in individuals at the level of knowledge and professional practices. Cook et al. (2012) explain that professional habitus is "cultural capital made visible," its embodiment (Richardson, 1986), which shapes the identity of the group and generates a meta-meaning that engenders integrity, coordination, and cooperation in its field and business model.

In summary, proper coordination and cooperation, based on interpersonal trust and a well-adjusted professional habitus, are critical for successful performance in a business setting. Decisions for the future should not be solely based on a rational calculation of chances of success, as the acquired habitus also plays a significant role.

In summary, coordination, cooperation, and collaboration are essential for effective performance in business and organizations. Coordination lays the groundwork for cooperation, which is strengthened through collaboration, especially with AI tools. These processes require effort, valuing diversity, and embracing self-organization, moving away from traditional management styles. Trust, coordination, and professional habitus are key to generating synergy and driving innovation. Without these elements, performance risks are inconsistent and reliant on chance.

Part 3 has provided a comprehensive framework for understanding AI and its broader implications for organizations, individuals, and their environments. It highlighted how AI not only influences but also interacts with the concept of meaning at both personal and collective levels. It underscored the vital connection between AI and Experienced Integrity (EI), collective intelligence, and resilience, emphasizing the importance of ethical considerations, collaboration, and adaptive strategies when implementing AI technologies. By focusing on these aspects, this section laid the groundwork for managing AI effectively and ensuring environments where human-AI interactions can lead to meaningful, responsible, and innovative outcomes.

The application of AI in business settings is not just a technological advancement but a strategic approach to building resilient and intelligent systems. By comprehending AI's framework and its contribution to collective intelligence, we can fully unlock its potential.

Managing AI in the Workplace: Theoretical and Managerial Implications

This part connects directly to the practical side of the chapter's objective. It offers theoretical insights and managerial strategies for effectively managing AI in a way that improves Collective Intelligence and Resilience while maintaining or enhancing Experienced Integrity for individuals and teams. It provides actionable guidance on navigating the challenges and uncertainties AI introduces, ensuring that the organization can leverage AI for positive outcomes in trust, collaboration, and shared purpose. By addressing the implications of AI for management, this section helps bridge the conceptual understanding with real-world application, fulfilling the chapter's overall goal of enhancing workplace effectiveness in an AI-driven context.

Managing AI in the Workplace to enhance collective Intelligence and resilience involves several critical strategies based on the conceptual approach to the problem under study and the author's personal experience.

- It is essential to provide employees with training to promote a shared understanding of AI technologies' benefits and help them understand their potential impact on their roles. Meaning is the individual's interpretation of a situation based on context, relationships, and mental models. It is subjective and varies based on personal experiences, knowledge, and culture.
- To ensure that AI technology upholds the integrity of the individual, it is crucial to have a clear purpose, mission, vision, and values guiding its use.
- Integrity becomes visible when a person and the team consistently act honestly and ethically, putting "their values into action." Ethical AI use must be

promoted by setting guidelines for responsible AI deployment and addressing concerns about bias, fairness, and transparency.

- Moreover, strong data governance policies must be established to ensure data quality, privacy, and security. This will enable AI systems to work effectively and maintain trust among employees.
- Implementing a coordinated change management approach helps employees adapt to AI-driven changes and ensures a smooth transition, preferably using a project charter for follow-up and documentation. It should include AI conflict management and recovery strategies, such as resilience training, in case of system failures or unexpected disruptions. Maintaining open communication about AI's role and its impact in the Workplace reduces anxiety and promotes a shared understanding of its benefits.
- AI technology in the Workplace refers to coordinating and effectively mobilizing resources and competencies to define and adjust a company's business models and strategy. This involves a top-down
- approach by a smaller group incorporating ideas from the bottom up.
- Implementing AI collaborative tools like classical project management and platforms that facilitate information sharing is recommended. This will encourage employees to provide feedback on AI systems' performance, contribute ideas, insights, and opportunities bottom-up for AI implementation, and make improvements and adjustments.
- The focus should not only be on self-reflexivity and responsiveness but also on structural improvement measures, such as less hierarchical organizing and multi-functional teams that combine human and AI capabilities to solve complex problems, fostering collective Intelligence and resilience with the ability to maintain purpose and integrity in changing circumstances. Together, they support the way things are done, the corporate culture.

Effective coordination and cooperation are essential for business success. Collaboration between individuals, regardless of barriers or tools, is mutually beneficial. Flatter organizations require special attention to internal dynamics. A Professional habitus is critical for individual identity and performance.

Incorporating AI into the workplace requires a coordinated effort that balances top-down leadership with bottom-up input. By promoting transparency, ethical practices, and collaboration, organizations can enhance individual and collective capabilities, resulting in a more resilient, intelligent workforce.

CONCLUSION

The premise that AI impacts EI, which influences CI and CR, holds. Integrating AI in the workplace significantly reshapes individual and collective experiences, impacting Collective Intelligence (CI) and Collective Resilience (CR). Meaning-making, derived from past experiences and future aspirations, plays a crucial role in fostering collaboration, cooperation, and shared purpose, which strengthen the integrity of individuals and teams. AI can enhance these dynamics by automating tasks and providing valuable insights, but it also poses challenges related to ethical concerns, job security, and transparency.

Individual perceptions of AI evolve as people gain more exposure and knowledge about AI technologies and their impact on society. Engaging in open discussions, promoting education, addressing concerns, and ensuring ethical practices can contribute to a more informed and balanced perception of AI among individuals. By effectively managing AI, organizations can strike a balance between innovation and Experienced Integrity (EI), ensuring that AI supports, rather than undermines, human values and workplace ethics.

This chapter emphasizes the importance of proactively addressing the implications of AI in the Workplace by balancing the benefits and risks, building a culture of trust, empathy, collaboration, transparency, open communication, and prioritizing ethical considerations. By doing so, organizations can maximize the benefits of AI while preserving human values and promoting sustainable growth. of coordination, cooperation, and collaboration in AI implementation,

In conclusion, AI is not merely a tool but a transformative force that, when aligned with ethical principles and meaningful collaboration, can drive CI, CR, and organizational success.

Implications for Further Research

Different models and definitions of AI correspond to diverse ways of abstracting human Intelligence and distinct research expectations. As Alan Winfield (2020) stated, no general theory of Intelligence or learning unites the discipline, making it challenging to define Intelligence.

Further research on the interaction between humans and AI could focus on how users experience AI, including its potential long-term effects. It would be interesting to investigate the impact of AI on workforce dynamics, such as changes in job roles, skill requirements, and employment patterns, and their potential social and economic consequences. This impact may vary depending on specific industries or sectors and countries.

Research could also focus on how AI affects creativity and innovation in different industries and influences education and skill development. Additionally, research could explore the use of AI technology and its impact on IQ scores. Since the 1990s, IQ scores have declined, and the reasons behind this decline are unclear. However, the use of AI may impact its development.

REFERENCES

Accenture. (2023). A new era of generative AI for everyone. Accenture. https://www.accenture.com/content/dam/accenture/final/accenture-com/document/Accenture-A-New-Era-of-Generative-AI-for-Everyone.pdf

Aristoteles Nicomachean Ethics, b. (n.d.). Nicomachean Ethics. Retrieved march 15th, 2023, from http://classics.mit.edu/Aristotle/nicomachaen.2.ii.html

Atmanspacher, H. (2023). Why Physics Does Not Inform the Human Condition, But Its Boundaries Do. *Foundations of Science*. Advance online publication. DOI: 10.1007/s10699-023-09915-y

Atmanspacher, H., & Rickles, D. (2022). *Dual-Aspect Monism and the Deep Structure of Meaning*. Routledge., DOI: 10.4324/9781003270584

Bachmann, R. (2003). Trust and power as means of coordinating the internal relations of the organization: A conceptual framework. In *The trust process in organizations: Empirical studies of the determinants and the process of trust development* (pp. 58-74). DOI: 10.4337/9781843767350.00010

Bankins, S., & Formosa, P. (2023, February). The Ethical Implications of Artificial Intelligence (AI) For Meaningful Work. *Journal of Business Ethics*, 185(4), 725–740. Advance online publication. DOI: 10.1007/s10551-023-05339-7

Barker, J. (1993, September). Tightening the Iron Cage: Concertive Control in Self-Managing Teams. *Administrative Science Quarterly*, 38(3), 408–437. DOI: 10.2307/2393374

Beck, D. E., & Cowan, C. (2007/2014). *Spiral Dynamics: Leadership, Werte undWandel* (5th ed.). Inspire.

Boden, M. A. (2016). *AI*. Oxford University Press.

Bourdieu, P. (1990). The Logic of Practice (R. Nice, Trans.). Stanford University. DOI: 10.1515/9781503621749

Bourdieu, P., & Passero, J. (1996). *La reproducción*. Fontamara.

Brynjolfsson, E. (2022). The Turing Trap: The promise and peril of human-like artificial intelligence. *Daedalus*, 151(2), 272–287. DOI: 10.1162/daed_a_01915

Brynjolfsson, E., & Mac Afee, A. (2023). *The Impact of Generative AI on Workforce Productivity*. https://www.youtube.com/watch?v=4i1a-ApM00M

Buckley, P. J., & Casson, M. (2010). *The Multinational Enterprise Revisited.* Palgrave MacMillan. DOI: 10.1057/9780230250468

Chikersal, P., Tomprou, M., Yi, J., Williams, A., & Dabbish, L. (2017). Deep Structures of Collaboration: Physiological Correlates of Collective Intelligence and Group Satisfaction. *CSCW '17: Proceedings of the 2017 ACM Conference on Computer Supported Cooperative Work and Social Computing.* DOI: 10.1145/2998181.2998250

Cook, A., Faulconbridge, J., & Muzio, D. (2012). *Legal Elite: Recruitment Through Cultural Capital and the 'London's Reproduction of Social Exclusivity in City Professional Service Field.*

Covey, F. (2023). *The 7 Habits of Highly Effective People.* FranklinCovey.

Descartes, R. (1897). Meditationes de prima philosophia. In Adam, C., & Tannery, P. (Eds.), *Oevres de Descartes.* Cerf. DOI: 10.5962/bhl.title.39750

Dictionary.com Affect. (2023, March 15th). Retrieved from affect: https://www.dictionary.com/browse/affect

Edgington, U. (2017). *Emotional Labour and Lesson Observation: A Study of England's Further Education.* Springer. DOI: 10.1007/978-981-10-2991-2

Edmondson, A. (2023, March 24). Den richtigen Ton setzen. *Manager-magazin.* Link: https://www.manager-magazin.de/harvard/fuehrung/leadership-professorin-amy-edmondson-ueber-zusammenarbeit-a-00000000-0002-0001-0000-000174106563

Edmondson, A. C., Kramer, R. M., & Cook, K. S. (2004). Psychological safety, trust, and learning in organizations: A group-level lens. *Trust and distrust in organizations: Dilemmas and approaches*, 12(2004), 239-272.

Eloundou, T., Manning, S., Mishkin, P., & Rock, D. (2023). GPTs are GPTs: An Early Look at the Labor Market Impact Potential of Large Language Models. *arXiv.* https://doi.org/https://doi.org/10.48550/arXiv.2303.10130

Frankl, V. (2006). *Man's Search for Meaning.* Beacon Press.

Frederiksen, M. (2023). *Mette Frederiksen lässt Rede teilweise von KI schreiben, DER SPIEGEL.* Spiegel Online.

Future of Life. (2023). *Pause Giant AI Experiments: An Open Letter.* Future of Life.

Gilan, D. (2021). *Resilienz – die Kunst der Widerstandskraft.* Verlag Herder GmbH.

Harari, Y. N. (2023). AI and the future of humanity. *Frontiers Forum.*

Heidegger. (1993). *Sein und Zeit.* Tübingen: Max Niemeyer Verlag.

Jänke, L., Korte, M., & Stern, E. (2022). *The Answer to Almost Everything: Are we getting stupider?* (42). Retrieved from https://www.arte.tv/en/videos/104841-001-A/42-the-answer-to-almost-everything/

Jurt, J. (2010). Die Habitus-Theorie von Pierre Bourdieu. *Zeitschrift für Literaturund Theatersoziologie*, 3, 5–17.

Kolla, J. (2017). *How Artificial Intelligence benefits companies and ups their game*. MINT.

Leander, A. (2009). *Habitus and Field. Department of Intercultural Communication and Management*. Copenhagen Business School. DOI: 10.1093/acrefore/9780190846626.013.51

Lee, M. Y., & Edmondson, A. C. (2017). Self-managing organizations: Exploring the limits of less-hierarchical organizing. *Research in Organizational Behavior*, 37, 35–58. DOI: 10.1016/j.riob.2017.10.002

Levy, P. (1997). Vers L'intelligence Collective. *Sciences Humaines*, 59, 31.

Mastropietro, C., & Vervaeke, J. (2023). What is a Meaning Crisis? *The Side View*

Mazzucato, M., Schaake, M., Krier, S., & Entsminger, J. (2022). Governing artificial intelligence in the public interest. UCL Institute for Innovation and Public Purpose, *Working Paper Series* (IIPP WP 2022-12). https://www.ucl.ac.uk/bartlett/public-purpose/wp2022-12

Mintzberg, H. (1983). *Power in and around organizations*. Prentice Hall.

Monett, D., Lewis, C. W., Thórisson, K. R., Bach, J., Baldassarre, G., Granato, G., & Shevlin, H. (2020). Introduction to the JAGI special issue 'On defining artificial intelligence'–commentaries and author's response. *Journal of Artificial General Intelligence*, 11(2), 1–100. DOI: 10.2478/jagi-2020-0003

Morel, L., Dupont, L., & Boudarel, M.-R. (2018). Innovation spaces: new places for collective intelligence? In U. D (Ed.), *Collective Innovation Processes*. John Wiley & Sons. DOI: 10.1002/9781119557883.ch5

Morgan, M. (2023). *Model Narratives*. ICI Berlin. Retrieved from https://www.ici-berlin.org/events/mary-s-morgan/DOI: 10.25620/e230530

Mulgan, G. (2018). *Big Mind*. Princeton University Press. DOI: 10.1515/9781400888511

Nilsson, N. J. (2005). Human-Level Artificial Intelligence? Be Serious! *AI Magazine*. Advance online publication. DOI: 10.1609/aimag.v26i4.1850

Oxford-Review. (2023, March 21). *Collective Intelligence*. Oxford.

Peerdom. (2019). Discovering the dark side of self-organization: 7 common challenges. Peerdom. Link: https://peerdom.medium.com/discovering-the-dark-side-of-self-organisation-7-common-challenges-272fafe98927

Peng, B., Galley, M., He, P., Cheng, H., Xie, Y., Hu, Y., . . . Gao, J. (2023). Check your facts and try again: Improving large language models with external knowledge and automated feedback. arXiv preprint arXiv:2302.12813. https://doi.org//arXiv.2302.12813DOI: 10.48550

Peterson, J. (2017a). *Personality*. Toronto University.

Peterson, J. (2017b). *Maps of meaning*. Toronto University.

Peterson, J. B. (2013). Three forms of meaning and the management of complexity. In Markman, K. D., Proulx, T., & Lindberg, M. J. (Eds.), *The psychology of meaning* (pp. 17–48). American Psychological Association., DOI: 10.1037/14040-002

Reyes, R. (2009). Diccionario _ UCM. Retrieved from Habitus. De: https://webs.ucm. es/info/eurotheo/diccionario/H/habitus. htm

Richardson, J. (1986). 'The Forms of Capital. In Richardson (Ed.), *Handbook of Theory and Research for the Sociology of Education* (pp. 241-58). New York, Greenwood.

Russell, S. (2023). What AI Expert Prof Stuart J Russell: Said On Artificial Intelligence. Youtube. https://www.youtube.com/watch?v=Bzre5fWr6Ec

Schnell, T. (2010). Existential Indifference: Another Quality of Meaning in Life. *Journal of Humanistic Psychology*, 50(3), 351–373. DOI: 10.1177/0022167809360259

Shutterstock. (2023). Imágenes libres de regalías. Link: https://www.shutterstock.com/es/search/2023

Steggemann, M. (2015). *Complementarity between universalism and particularism in the filial of the German transnational located in Mexico*. Universidad La Salle. DOI: 10.13140/rg.2.1.3687.8564

Steggemann, M. (2023, May- August). Collective Intelligence synergizing into Collective Resilience. *Mercados y Negocios,* 65-82. DOI: 10.32870/myn.vi48.7686

Sugden, R. (1989). Spontaneous Order. *The Journal of Economic Perspectives*, 3(4), 85–97. DOI: 10.1257/jep.3.4.85

Tapsott, D., & Williams, A. (2008). *Wikinomics: How Mass Collaboration Changes Everything*. Penguin.

Thórrison, K. R. (2020). Discretionarily Constrained Adaptation under Insufficient Knowledge & Resources. *Journal of Artificial Intelligence*, 11(2), 7–12.

Wang, P. (2019). On Defining Artificial Intelligence. *Journal of Artificial General Intelligence*, 10(2), 1–37. DOI: 10.2478/jagi-2019-0002

Wang, P. (2023). *A General Theory of Intelligence*. A developing eBook. Link: https://cis.temple.edu/~pwang/GTI-book/index.html

Wilson, R., Herziger, A., & Hamilton, M. (2020). From incremental to transformative adaptation in individual responses to climate-exacerbated hazards. *Nature Climate Change. Nature*, 10(3), 200–208.

Winfield, A. (2020). Intelligence Is Not One Thing. *Journal of Artificial General Intelligence*, 11(2), 97–100. DOI: 10.2478/jagi-2020-0003

World Economic Forum. (2018). *The future of jobs report 2018*. Geneva, Switzerland: WEF.

World Economic Forum. (2023a). *Strategic Intelligence* Geneva, Switzerland: WEF.

World Economic Forum. (2023b). *The future of job reports*. Geneva, Switzerland: WEF.

Zolli, A., & Healy, A. (2012). *Resilience: Why things bounce back. Hachette UK*. Free Press.

ENDNOTES

1 This document uses the term "AI" to refer to both "AI technology" and "AI system". AI is the general field of study, research, and development focused on creating intelligent machines. AI technology includes the tools and techniques used to build AI systems. In contrast, AI systems are the specific implementations or applications that use AI technology to perform tasks or solve problems.

2 Cartesian Dualism is based on Descartes' proposal to distinguish reality's material and mental domains. "In Descartes' (1897) terminology, the Cartesian distinction splits the entirety of reality into a material component (res extensa) and non-material component (res cogitans)." (Atmanspacher, 2023).

4 ChatGPT is an AI-powered language model developed by OpenAI that can generate human-like text based on context and past conversations. https://chat.openai.com.

5 Pei Wang (2019): "there is no correct working definition of AI, as each of them has theoretical and practical values, so is not wrong."

6 A former test for human-like Intelligence: To pass the test, a machine must convince human participants in suitably staged anonymous dialogues that they are communicating with a human rather than with a machine (Nilsson, 205).

7 The concept of habitus goes back as far as Aristoteles. The habitus plays a vital role as an intermediate-term between the act and an effect, between the exterior and the interior, and how the external is internalized, thus linking the history and the experience to the present updates (Reyes, 2009). It is what we bring to every situation in our lives, such as past choices, experiences, hopes, and expectations, and we interact together to provide us with the opportunity of action or non-action (Edgington, 2017). Habitus (Bourdieu, 1990) is what makes us behave correctly or incorrectly, justified or unjustified (Aristoteles Nicomachean Ethics) living an authentic and inauthentic life (Heidegger,1983) concerning the affects. Habitus is the internalized experiences of the individual and his group, the norms, and conventions. It guides thinking, feeling, behavior, decision-making, and actions and frames the individual's choices. It is formed through people's accumulated experience in different fields, and each field is marked by its understanding of the world (Leander, 2009). Thus, forms of group practice may be consistent without an explicit agreement, with the agents not knowing or at least not intentionally doing so (Jurt, 2010).

8 According to the researchers, since 1930, the intellectual quotient (IQ) has increased by 4 points every ten years, known as the Flynn effect. Starting in the 1990s, the values of the intellectual quotient declined. The reasons behind the decline in IQ scores in recent years are not entirely clear, and researchers are still investigating this phenomenon. Several potential factors could contribute to this trend, such as changes in the environment, educational changes, changing demographics, and technological distractions such as smartphones and social media.

9 Kollektiv – Wikipedia.

10 Is understood as the absence of interpersonal fear (Edmondson, 2023). Edmondson distinguishes psychological safety from the related construct of interpersonal trust. Trust is the expectation that others' future actions will favor one's interests; psychological safety refers to a climate in which people are comfortable being (and expressing) themselves (Edmondson et al., 2004).

Chapter 3
Dynamic Capabilities Through Resilience and Ambidexterity

Juan Ramón Bravo
https://orcid.org/0009-0008-9509-8819
University of Guadalajara, Mexico

José Sánchez Gutiérrez
https://orcid.org/0000-0002-0120-7201
University of Guadalajara, Mexico

José Cabanelas Omil
https://orcid.org/0000-0003-3701-6076
University of Vigo, Spain

ABSTRACT

Changes in the environment and the speed with which many companies adapt to them lead to exploring the adaptation process. In other words, the authors question the development of dynamic capabilities and how it is linked to resilience and organizational ambidexterity. Companies that effectively address these challenges will be better positioned to thrive in the environment. This chapter attempts a detailed analysis of the interactions between dynamic capabilities, resilience, and ambidexterity.

DOI: 10.4018/979-8-3693-7272-2.ch003

INTRODUCTION

Changes in the environment and the speed with which many companies adapt to them lead to exploring the adaptation process (Sardesai & Klingebiel, 2023). In other words, we question the development of dynamic capabilities (Wu et al., 2023) and how it is linked to resilience (Buzzao & Rizzi, 2023) and organizational ambidexterity (Konlechner et al., 2023). This chapter attempts a detailed analysis of the interactions between dynamic capabilities, resilience, and ambidexterity.

The world is highly interconnected (Vina & Liu, 2023; Patel, 2023). People have become more dependent on technology (Stewart & Perren, 2023). We are witnessing the integration of advanced technologies such as the Internet of Things (IoT), artificial intelligence, robotics, and data analytics into manufacturing processes. This integration requires continuous innovation and digital transformation for organizational survival (Valentinov et al., 2023).

Global economic uncertainty generated by events such as pandemics, natural disasters, and financial crises requires companies to strengthen their resilience to navigate periods of volatility and recessions (Ramezani & Camarinha-Matos, 2020; Sheng et al., 2023).

These challenges demand a strategic approach that combines the ability to adapt quickly (dynamic capabilities) with the ability to withstand and recover from disruptive events (resilience) and the ability to balance exploration and exploitation (Ambidexterity). Companies that effectively address these challenges will be better positioned to thrive in the environment.

This chapter is divided into four parts. The first explores dynamic capabilities. The second discusses organizational resilience as a capability that allows the firm to recover from crises and shocks. The third defines organizational ambidexterity and how to manage both the exploitation of existing capabilities and the exploration of new opportunities. Finally, it discusses these interrelationships and their contribution to the firm's rapid adaptation.

DYNAMIC CAPABILITIES

An organization's dynamic capabilities are like a tree's adaptability in a forest (Vylobkova & Heintz, 2023). These capabilities enable the firm to identify new market conditions, adjust strategies, and respond to new environmental dynamics, learning from mistakes and innovating (Rhaiem & Halilem, 2023). Just like a tree flexing to adapt to changing winds to seek water or sunlight in this way, dynamic capabilities give the organization the flexibility to face challenges, adapt to new environmental conditions, and take advantage of emerging opportunities (Nie & Fan, 2023).

The theory of dynamic capabilities explains organizations' behavior in the face of increasingly dynamic and changing environments. A dynamic capability is a firm's ability to create, adjust, integrate, and refine its internal and external competencies, generating new ways of achieving value to adapt to rapidly changing environments (Teece,1997).

These capabilities are built through the organization's distinctive skills, processes, procedures, organizational structures, decision rules, and discipline, called micro foundations or components. According to Teece (2007), there are three components: absorptive, adaptive, and transformational.

These three components do not follow a linear sequence; a sequential cause-effect relationship is not established. Instead, interactions generate complex structures that build dynamic capabilities. In other words, addressing dynamic capabilities leads to a systemic and multidimensional approach.

The absorption component involves detecting and acquiring new knowledge from the environment. The organization interprets and evaluates its relevance, understanding how it can affect the organization and its position in the market.

The adaptation component is activated when potential impacts are identified. Strategies, processes, and operations are adjusted in response to the information acquired. Changes are implemented to take advantage of opportunities or mitigate identified threats.

If more significant changes are required, the transformation component enters the picture, actively reconfiguring its resources and competencies, even exploring new lines of business or strategic approaches (Cohen & Levinthal, 1990; Pérez, 2009; Miles et al., 1978; Helfat, 1997; Davies & Brady, 2016; Teece & Al-Aali, 2012; Teece et al., 1997; Teece, 2007).

Over the years, Amazon has exemplified the development of dynamic capabilities (Čirjevskis, 2023). In 1995, it started as an online bookstore. In 2000, it rapidly expanded to sell a wide range of products. In 2003, it offered unlimited free shipping through its affiliate program. The challenge from this was the speed of delivery, so to streamline and optimize its logistics processes in its warehouses, it integrated robots. In 2008, it identified an opportunity in the emerging Streaming market and launched Amazon Prime, thus demonstrating the company's capacity for continuous innovation and adaptation to changes in the business environment.

The Amazon case story is an example of dynamic capabilities in an organization. Amazon has adapted to the environment while influencing it to change (Vollero et al., 2023). There is no doubt about Amazon's dynamic capabilities or its linkage to the environment. However, because the capabilities are intangible and transforming, it takes work to evidence them sufficiently to measure them and to know how the organization's creative dynamics operate.

On the other hand, the impossibility of measuring does not prevent its understanding and applicability in organizations. However, developing dynamic capabilities for an organization represents an enormous challenge. Teece (2007) argues that developing and implementing the components of absorption, adaptation, and transformation is challenging. It requires substantial investments in technology (systems and equipment), ongoing talent development, constant organizational restructuring, and research and development activities. Regarding market or economics, organizations that focus on short-term results are unwilling to invest with a long-term return on investment and carry the implicit risk of not generating the expected results (Choi et al., 2010).

The implications of pursuing the development of dynamic capabilities are also not minor for the organization. Developing a culture of lifelong learning—collaboration and creativity—is necessary to create a work environment that fosters respect and transparent communication (Quayson et al., 2023). Effective change management enables adaptation to new practices and implementation of operational changes (Supriharyanti & Sukoco, 2023).

However, the most significant implication is having leadership with a long-term vision. Its authority goes beyond formal status; it is grounded in informal influence and cultural standing. When disruption occurs, the presence of such a leader has a profound impact (Zolli & Healy, 2012).

The theory of dynamic capabilities provides insight into what happens to organizations in the face of highly changing environments (Figure 1). However, the results are only positive for some organizations, and they are only sometimes positive for an organization. This situation leads to the question: What makes an organization adapt quickly? Why do some organizations manage to adapt and others do not? More than once, we have witnessed cases in which companies in the same line of business obtain different results in the same environment. These capabilities allow us to understand the various results. In other words, capabilities are not artifacts or tools to remedy specific organizational challenges. It is easier to explain how favorable results were obtained than to anticipate receiving them. These situations focus on two capabilities that, by their very nature, contribute to the answers to the questions posed above: organizational resilience and ambidexterity.

Figure 1. Dynamic capabilities

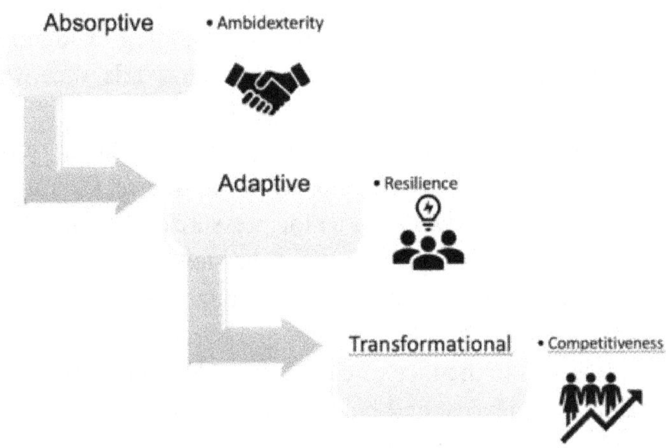

Source: own elaboration.

Organizational Resilience

Social distancing, confinement, and other measures taken in recent years increased online shopping and the use of social networks (Hamid & Azhar, 2023). According to the United Nations Conference on Trade and Development, UNCTAD (2021), the e-commerce sector experienced an enormous growth in retail sales from 16% to 19% in 2020.

The most significant percentage rise in retail sales occurred in South Korea, with the Asian country growing from 20.7% in 2019 to 25.9% in 2020. Other notable rises over the same period occurred in the United Kingdom, increasing from 15.8% to 23.3%; China from 20.7% to 24.9%; the United States from 11% to 14%; Australia from 6.3% to 9.4%; and Singapore from 5.9% to 11.7% (UNCTAD, 2021).

For example, Alibaba, Amazon, JD.com, and Pinduoduo maintained the top sales spots during 2019 and 2020. On the other hand, Shopify moved from 9th place to 5th place in 2020, and Walmart moved from 12th place to eighth place. These companies adapted quickly to the global environment (UNCTAD, 2021).

However, the main setbacks in sales occurred in companies dedicated to tourism or private transportation, with sharp reductions in the gross value of their goods. The following cases may exemplify this: the travel portal Expedia fell from fifth place in 2019 to eleventh in 2020, Booking Holdings fell from sixth to twelfth, and Airbnb, which launched its IPO in 2020, from eleventh to thirteenth. (UNCTAD, 2021)

In this context, the question arises: What did the companies that maintained or improved their place in global sales do differently? These technology companies developed innovative responses, taking advantage of the new needs created by the pandemic, demonstrating the industry's ability to adapt and maintain strong performance in challenging economic conditions. In other words, they were resilient organizations.

Like bamboo, known for its ability to bend rather than break during storms, resilient individuals and organizations resemble this strong yet flexible material. In challenging situations, bamboo bends under the pressure of the wind, but instead of breaking, it returns to its original position once the storm has passed.

Similarly, human resilience contributes to organizational resilience, involving adapting and recovering from adversity. Resilient people create resilient organizations by bending, not breaking, in the face of challenges (Holbeche, 2019). They adapt, learn from difficult experiences, and emerge more robust and better equipped to face future obstacles. Like bamboo, resilience lies in flexibility, adaptability, and finding strength through adversity.

Etymologically, the term resilience comes from the Latin root resilience, which means to bounce back and implies recoil (Russo & Ciancarini, 2017). Resilience represents the ability of systems to recover from sudden extreme events. The affected system can return to an acceptable state through absorption and adaptation, which is not necessarily the same as before (Dahlberg, 2015; Chroust et al., 2016).

Holling (1973) first introduced the term "resilience" in his seminal work Resilience and Stability of Ecological Systems, where he explored how ecosystems absorb disturbances and maintain their functions. Since then, resilience has evolved and expanded across various disciplines. It has been applied in ecology and fields such as biology, psychology, business and organizational studies, complex systems thinking, and supply chain management.

Each discipline offers a unique perspective on resilience, adapting the term to fit its particular context. For example, in psychology, resilience refers to an individual's capacity to recover from stress or adversity. At the same time, in business and organizations, it emphasizes the ability to adapt and thrive in the face of unexpected events. In complex systems thinking, resilience is viewed as an emergent property that enables systems to recover and return to dynamic stability following disruptions (Table 1).

Table 1. Concept of resilience based on different disciplines.

Discipline	Definition/Description	References
Biology	The capacity of the species that are part of them to return to the original state after a change has occurred due to natural disturbances or human activities is known as "resilience," or elasticity of ecosystems and communities.	Doak et al. (1998); Baert et al. (2016).
Psychology	It is a dynamic process that can be driven in any organism when exposed to adversity and the stress generated by this	Lucia (2016); Bhamra et al. (2011); Soni et al. (2014); Madni and Jackson (2009); Poseck (2006).
Administration	A company's ability to adapt to change and cope with unexpected events, exploiting opportunities to gain competitive advantages and growth in turbulent markets.	Parker (2023); Pettit et al. (2013); Murino et al. (2011); Vecchiola et al. (2013); Burnard & Bhamra, (2011); Ponomarov & Holcomb (2009); Tang (2006).
Organizational theory	Ability to adapt to and buffer the effects of abrupt environmental changes on the organization so that it recovers and strengthens dynamically reinventing itself for the future as that the surrounding environment changes.	Karman (2020); Jiang et al. (2019); Zhang (2021).
Complex Systems Thinking	Ability to recover to dynamic stability (acceptable state, even if not the same as before) after a disturbance.	Chroust and Aumayr (2017); Dahlberg (2015); Madni and Jackson (2009).
Supply Chain Management	Ability to prepare for, respond to, and recover from unexpected events, maintaining continuity of operation.	Carvalho et al. (2012); Ponomarov and Holcomb (2009); Jüttner and Maklan (2011); Barroso and Machado (2011).

Source: Modified from Ramezani & Camarinha-Matos (2020).

Resilience should be perceived as something other than a stable (static) state or a process that companies possess. It does not represent a good management practice (procedures, principles, and tools). Resilience is instead an emergent property rather than a qualification of the organization itself. It is attributed when unforeseeable adverse circumstances have been overcome due to the organization's ability to maintain its core purpose and integrity (González-Alvarado et al., 2021).

However, how much change can an organization absorb and retain its integrity and purpose? What characteristics make an organization adaptive to change? According to Zolli and Hoely (2012), virtually all resilient systems will exhibit the following patterns: effective feedback mechanisms, dynamic reorganization, built-in counter-mechanisms, decoupling, diversity, modularity, simplicity, and clustering.

Effective feedback mechanisms determine when abrupt change is approaching or a critical threshold has been passed. To ensure its continuity, the organization dynamically reorganizes itself regarding how it fulfills its purpose and the scale at which it operates. It does this reorganization through built-in counter-mechanisms, which are in a state of latency and act only when the crisis occurs, as do antibodies in the bloodstream to restore the body to health.

Organizations decrease or decouple their material requirements to continue a given activity during a crisis. They do so by diversifying their sources of energy (materials) to carry out that activity, thereby strengthening their resilience.

When an outage occurs in one part of the organization, the internal modular structure comes into action to prevent this failure from cascading to the rest and simplify connecting and disconnecting between components. It allows the organization to be reconfigured, ensuring the system can be grouped or regrouped correctly. These guidelines constitute a set of tools that enable the emergence of resilience in an organization.

During World War II, IBM developed and supplied Axis and Allied countries with tabulating machines and punch cards. These proved essential tools for processing and analyzing large amounts of data. IBM also manufactured parts for weapons operations, electrical systems for submarines, and aircraft engines (Campbell-Kelly et al., 2023).

It also provided logistical and strategic data analysis support. These were used in various applications, from personnel management to logistical routing analysis and decoding of encrypted messages. (Black, 2012)

IBM adapted to changing and extreme conditions, providing crucial technology. After World War II, it reinvented itself and distanced itself from war controversies. The company embarked on new initiatives and technologies, such as the first electronic computers, marking its transition into the computer age.

Implementing resilience strategies becomes a dilemma. Developing feedback mechanisms, organizing system components in a modular fashion, and seeking diverse energy sources to decouple and establish latent counter—mechanisms require significant investments. Doing so implies sacrificing the certainty of short-term efficiency gains to avoid or survive a hypothetical future emergency that may never materialize.

Another dilemma arises when resilience is sought to be strengthened in more than one part or level of the organization. It is possible that enhancing one part may introduce fragility in another, which in turn may trigger it in the rest. For this reason, a systemic vision is required (see the whole) so that the efforts made in one part can increase resilience in another.

A seemingly perfect system is often the most fragile, while a dynamic system, subject to occasional failure, can be the most robust. Resilience is, like life itself, messy, imperfect, and inefficient. However, it survives (Zolli & Haely, 2012). On the other hand, organizational decision-makers must decide what stays and changes. Part of the knowledge, key processes, or strategic personnel vital for change may be lost in adapting to the environment. The latter is due to erroneous decisions or actions in the race to adapt, so ambidexterity becomes essential for organizational adaptation.

Organizational Ambidexterity

The first Blockbuster opened in Dallas, Texas, on October 19, 1985. In late 1989, they opened their 1,000th location and decided to expand into other territories. Once a leader in the movie rental industry, Blockbuster was noted for its focus on physical stores and DVD rentals.

As online streaming and digital content distribution became increasingly popular, the company continued to exploit its traditional model. Not exploring new ways to offer its services made its business model obsolete. In 2010, Blockbuster filed for bankruptcy, and it was not until 2014 that they ceased operating most of their stores.

Research in Motion (RIM), in 1996, launched one of its first portable devices: an advanced browser, the Interactive Pager 900. In 1999, it was the turn of its first Blackberry, the first mobile device to integrate email. The company resisted change while the smartphone market evolved towards touch screens and applications.

RIM relied heavily on exploiting its existing model centered on the physical keyboard and messaging. Apple and Samsung, meanwhile, quickly innovated with devices that adapted to changing consumer preferences. In January 2022, Blackberry announced its exit from the market.

Why did successful companies like Blockbuster and RIM disappear from the market? The common denominator in both cases was resistance to change and the inability to adapt efficiently to emerging trends and technologies in their respective industries (Yeung & Ulrich, 2020).

Both companies continued to over-exploit their business models until they became obsolete. Exploring new opportunities resulted in an inability to adapt to market changes and a loss of competitiveness proactively.

Successful companies develop ambidexterity: They must optimize their existing operations (exploit), explore new opportunities, and adapt to emerging trends to ensure long-term relevance—explore and exploit simultaneously.

Imagine a skilled juggler holding two different objects in his hands, juggling in a fluid and coordinated manner. In this act, each object represents a critical dimension of organizational ambidexterity: one symbolizes the ability to 'explore,' i.e., to seek new opportunities and innovate, while the other represents the ability to 'exploit,' that is, to optimize and refine existing operations.

Similarly, in market environments, organizational ambidexterity implies a company's ability to skillfully balance efficient management of day-to-day operations skillfully, maximizing efficiency and quality in the short term (exploit) while simultaneously seeking new opportunities, innovating and adapting to changes in the long term (explore).

Just as the juggler must have precise control and balance to handle both tasks simultaneously, ambidextrous organizations must develop the ability to strategically juggle exploitation and exploration. This will enable them to thrive in the present and prepare for the future like a juggler who additionally walks a thin line (loop) well above the ground.

Duncan (1976) was the first to use ambidexterity to study organizational innovation processes. However, March's (1991) work develops a theoretical framework.

Organizational ambidexterity can be defined as the ability of a firm to simultaneously pursue incremental and discontinuous innovation through learning processes: experiential refinement, selection and reuse of existing routines, and planned experimentation using multiple structures and processes within the same firm (Baum et al, 2000; Benner & Tushman, 2003; Gupta et al., 2006; He & Wong, 2004; Tushman & O'Reilly, 1996; Ancona et al., 2001; Colbert, 2004).

Is it possible for companies to skillfully balance exploitation and exploration? The literature highlights three main approaches that foster ambidexterity within organizations: structural solutions, which involve separating exploitation and exploration activities into different units; leadership-based solutions, where the top management team is responsible for balancing and addressing tensions between these activities; and contextual solutions, which enable both exploitation and exploration to occur within the same unit (Raisch & Birkinshaw, 2008; Gibson & Birkinshaw, 2004; Adler et al., 1999; Lewis, 2000).

Minnesota Mining and Manufacturing Company (3M) is an example of organizational ambidexterity. This company has successfully balanced exploiting its established products and brands with exploring new opportunities. Its internal culture distinguishes 3M, which encourages innovation and exploration. Its "15% Culture" program allows employees to devote 15% of their time to projects of their choice.

R&D investments have enabled it to explore new technologies and applications for its products. 3M has made strategic acquisitions to broaden its portfolio of products and competencies. Operating in various industries, from healthcare to electronics to security, has facilitated exploring new opportunities in emerging markets.

3M illustrates how a company can succeed by balancing exploiting its existing successes and exploring new opportunities. Its organizational ambidexterity is fundamental to its ability to adapt to a dynamic and constantly changing business environment.

Most companies would find it challenging to become ambidextrous organizations. Benner and Tushman (2003) state that achieving a balance between exploration and exploitation can be difficult to achieve and maintain, and the inherent tensions can lead to compromises and challenges in practice.

When the organizational culture is managed, it favors optimizing existing processes. It generates an aversion to risk that inhibits innovation and exploration.

Another obstacle to overcome is financial; ambidexterity requires constant and long-term investments. Pressures for short-term results can discourage investment in long-term exploration and development. Adapting to environmental conditions becomes easier with leadership with a long-term strategic vision.

People generate collective knowledge by interacting with each other. This knowledge is the engine of innovation. Therefore, environments that foster creativity and mechanisms and structures that promote constant innovation are required.

Weaving Dynamic Capabilities

There are no single recipes or formulas for integrating dynamic capabilities, resilience, and ambidexterity. Their fabric is intricate and depends on each system's specific context. It is important to emphasize that these dimensions are interdependent. They do not follow a linear behavior (cause-effect); their interactions generate complex structures that allow them to adapt to the environment.

Feedback mechanisms constantly monitor the environment, look for sources of vulnerability (fragilities), and identify potential disruptive events, whether they are changes in the market, deterioration of the organizational climate, new government policies, climate change impacts, or supply chain risks.

The absorption component analyzes and interprets this information and determines whether it should be assimilated, integrated, and transformed into new organizational competencies.

When potential impacts are identified, the adaptation component comes into action to continue optimizing and optimizing existing operations (exploitation). The company dynamically reorganizes itself by adjusting organizational structures, strategies, and processes to adapt to the changing environment.

Structural adjustments are achieved by promoting the autonomy of different areas within the organization through modularity, which helps prevent the spread of crises from one location to another. Another critical measure is counter-mechanisms, which remain in a latent state and activate only when a crisis occurs. They function similarly to antibodies in the bloodstream that restore the body's health.

Adaptation strategies include reducing or decoupling material requirements, identifying diverse sources of supply to optimize existing operations (exploit), and strengthening resilience.

When faced with unexpected changes and events, organizations adapt and can identify and explore new opportunities, gaining competitive advantages and growing in turbulent markets while ensuring business continuity.

Exploring new opportunities requires more significant changes, giving way to the transformation component. It dynamically reconfigures resources and competencies, using the modular structure of the organization's areas to simplify connection and disconnection. This allows grouping or strategically regrouping to gain competitive advantages and grow in turbulent markets while maintaining operational continuity.

CONCLUSION

The integral development of dynamic capabilities, resilience, and ambidexterity represents a strategic response to address the challenges and capitalize on the environment's opportunities.

However, implementing these dimensions involves substantial investments in technology, talent, organizational restructuring, and a culture of continuous learning. These investments are sustained, and the fruits are harvested over the long term, generating tensions with short-term commitments to meet market and investor demands.

Dynamic capabilities, resilience, and ambidexterity are interdependent and create complex structures that facilitate environmental adaptation. These processes require trial and error, a continuous learning process, as no universal formulas exist for their development.

Some organizations, rooted in a culture that avoids risk and adheres to established practices, find it difficult to foster innovation and need more ability to adapt to unforeseen contingencies.

Addressing these dilemmas requires a strategic perspective and visionary leadership, a willingness to take risks, and an understanding of the organization's internal and external dynamics. This approach is crucial to success in this process, considering that each company will face unique challenges marked by its industry, culture, and market position.

REFERENCES

Adler, P. S., & Borys, B. (1996). Two types of bureaucracy: Enabling and coercive. *Administrative Science Quarterly*, 41(1), 61–89. DOI: 10.2307/2393986

Ancona, D. G., Goodman, P. S., Lawrence, B. S., & Tushman, M. L. (2001). Time: A new research lens. *Academy of Management Review*, 26(4), 645–663. DOI: 10.2307/3560246

Baert, J. M., De Laender, F., Sabbe, K., & Janssen, C. R. (2016). Biodiversity increases functional and compositional resistance, but decreases resilience in phytoplankton communities. *Ecology*, 97(12), 3433–3440. DOI: 10.1002/ecy.1601 PMID: 27912020

Barroso, A. P., Machado, V. H., & Machado, V. C. (2011). Supply chain resilience using the mapping approach. *Supply Chain Management*, 161–184.

Baum, J. A. C., Li, S. X., & Usher, J. M. (2000). Making the next move: How experiential and vicarious learning shape the locations of chains' acquisitions. *Administrative Science Quarterly*, 45(4), 766–801. DOI: 10.2307/2667019

Benner, M. J., & Tushman, M. L. (2003). Exploitation, exploration, and process management: The productivity dilemma revisited. *Academy of Management Review*, 28(2), 238–256. DOI: 10.2307/30040711

Bhamra, R., Dani, S., & Burnard, K. (2011). Resilience: The concept, a literature review, and future directions. *International Journal of Production Research*, 49(18), 5375–5393. DOI: 10.1080/00207543.2011.563826

Black, E. (2012). IBM and the Holocaust: The Strategic Alliance Between Nazi Germany and America's Most Powerful Corporation-Expanded Edition.

Burnard, K., & Bhamra, R. (2011). Organisational resilience: Development of a conceptual framework for organisational responses. *International Journal of Production Research*, 49(18), 5581–5599. DOI: 10.1080/00207543.2011.563827

Buzzao, G., & Rizzi, F. (2023). The role of dynamic capabilities for resilience in pursuing business continuity: An empirical study. *Total Quality Management & Business Excellence*, 34(11-12), 1–33. DOI: 10.1080/14783363.2023.2174427

Campbell-Kelly, M., Aspray, W. F., Yost, J. R., Tinn, H., & Díaz, G. C. (2023). *Computer: A history of the information machine*. Taylor & Francis. DOI: 10.4324/9781003263272

Carvalho, H., Azevedo, S. G., & Cruz-Machado, V. (2012). Agile and resilient approaches to supply chain management: Influence on performance and competitiveness. *Logistics Research*, 4(1-2), 49–62. DOI: 10.1007/s12159-012-0064-2

Charles, I. I., & Uford, I. C. (2023). Comparative analysis and evaluation of business and financial performance of Amazon. Com: A three-year period critical review of exceptional success. European Journal of Business. *Economics and Accountancy*, 11(2), 69–92.

Choi, J. N., Sung, S. Y., & Kim, M. U. (2010). How Do Groups React to Unexpected Threats? Crisis Management in Organizational Teams. *Social Behavior and Personality*, 38(6), 805–828. DOI: 10.2224/sbp.2010.38.6.805

Chroust, G., & Aumayr, G. (2017). Resilience 2.0: Computer-aided disaster management. *Journal of Systems Science and Systems Engineering*, 26(3), 321–335. DOI: 10.1007/s11518-017-5335-7

Čirjevskis, A. (2023). Measuring dynamic capabilities-based synergies using real options in M&A deals: Amazon's acquisition of Whole Foods. *International Journal of Applied Management Science*, 15(1), 73–85. DOI: 10.1504/IJAMS.2023.128296

Cohen, W., & Levinthal, D. (1990). Absorptive Capacity: A New Perspective on learning and innovation. *Administrative Science Quarterly*, 35(1), 128–152. DOI: 10.2307/2393553

Colbert, B. A. (2004). The complex resource-based view: Implications for theory and practice of strategic human resource management. *Academy of Management Review*, 29(3), 341–358. DOI: 10.2307/20159047

Dahlberg, R. (2015). Resilience and complexity: Conjoining the discourses of two contested concepts. *Culture Unbound*, 7(3), 541–557. DOI: 10.3384/cu.2000.1525.1572541

Davies, A., & Brady, T. (2016). Explicating the Dynamics of Project. *International Journal of Project Management*, 34(2), 314–327. DOI: 10.1016/j.ijproman.2015.04.006

Doak, D. F., Bigger, D., Harding, E. K., Marvier, M. A., O'malley, R. E., & Thomson, D. (1998). The statistical inevitability of stability-diversity relationships in community ecology. *American Naturalist*, 151(3), 264–276. DOI: 10.1086/286117 PMID: 18811357

Duncan, R. (1976). The ambidextrous organization: Designing dual structures for innovation. In Killman, R. H., Pondy, L. R., & Sleven, D. (Eds.), *The management of organization*. North Holland.

Gibson, C. B., & Birkinshaw, J. (2004). The antecedents, consequences, and mediating role of organizational ambidexterity. *Academy of Management Journal*, 47(2), 209–226. DOI: 10.2307/20159573

González, T., & Córdova, K. (2020). Capacidad dinámica y recursos para la resiliencia en empresas artesanales de cerámica en Jalisco, México. Cuadernos Latinoamericanos de Administración, 16(30).

González-Alvarado, T. E., Kubus, R., & Sánchez-Gutiérrez, J. (2021). Business Resilience and Complex Adaptive Systems. Business Resilience & Adaptive System, 7.

Gupta, A. K., Smith, K. G., & Shalley, C. E. (2006). The interplay between exploration and exploitation. *Academy of Management Journal*, 4(4), 693–706. DOI: 10.5465/amj.2006.22083026

Güttel, W. H., & Konlechner, S. W. (2023). *Strategic Change: Exploration, Exploitation & Ambidexterityi*. Successful in Turbulent Times.

Hamid, S., Azhar, M., & Sujood, . (2023). Behavioral intention to order food and beverage items using e-commerce during COVID-19: An integration of theory of planned behavior (TPB) with trust. *British Food Journal*, 125(1), 112–131. DOI: 10.1108/BFJ-03-2021-0338

He, Z. L., & Wong, P. K. (2004). Exploration vs. exploitation: An empirical test of the ambidexterity hypothesis. *Organization Science*, 15(4), 481–494. DOI: 10.1287/orsc.1040.0078

Helfat, C. (1997). Know-How and Asset Complementarity and Dynamic Capability Accumulation: Thee Case Of R&D. *Strategic Management Journal*, 18(5), 339–360. DOI: 10.1002/(SICI)1097-0266(199705)18:5<339::AID-SMJ883>3.0.CO;2-7

Holbeche, L. (2019). Designing sustainably agile and resilient organizations. *Systems Research and Behavioral Science*, 36(5), 668–677. DOI: 10.1002/sres.2624

Holling, C. S. (1973). Resilience and stability of ecological systems. *Annual Review of Ecology and Systematics*, 4(1), 1–23. DOI: 10.1146/annurev.es.04.110173.000245

Jiang, Y., Ritchie, B. W., & Verreynne, M. L. (2019). Building tourism organizational resilience to crises and disasters: A dynamic capabilities view. *International Journal of Tourism Research*, 21(6), 882–900. DOI: 10.1002/jtr.2312

Jüttner, U., & Maklan, S. (2011). Supply chain resilience in the global financial crisis: An empirical study. *Supply Chain Management*, 16(4), 246–259. DOI: 10.1108/13598541111139062

Karman, A. (2020). Flexibility, coping capacity and resilience of organizations: Between synergy and support. *Journal of Organizational Change Management*, 33(5), 883–907. DOI: 10.1108/JOCM-10-2019-0305

Konlechner, S., Güttel, W., & Keller, A. (2023). Ambidexterity for continuous change: Forms, operating conditions & organizational learning. In Güttel, W. (Ed.), *Successful in turbulent times. Leadership, change management and ambidexterity* (pp. 302–328). Nomos.

Lewis, M. W. (2000). Exploring paradox: Toward a more comprehensive guide. *Academy of Management Review*, 25(4), 760–777. DOI: 10.2307/259204

Lucia, S. (2016). Análisis de componentes y definición del concepto resiliencia: una revisión narrativa. Investig. psicol.

Madni, A. M., & Jackson, S. (2009). Towards a conceptual framework for resilience engineering. *IEEE Systems Journal*, 3(2), 181–191. DOI: 10.1109/JSYST.2009.2017397

March, J. G. (1991). Exploration and Exploitation in Organizational Learning. *Organization Science*, 2(1), 71–87. DOI: 10.1287/orsc.2.1.71

Miles, R., Snow, C., Meyer, A., & Coleman, H.Jr. (1978). Organizational Strategy, Structure, and Process. *Academy of Management Review*, 3(3), 546–562. https://www.jstor.org/stable/257544. DOI: 10.5465/amr.1978.4305755 PMID: 10238389

Murino, T., Romano, E., & Santillo, L. C. (2011, December). Supply chain performance sustainability through resilience function. In *Proceedings of the 2011 Winter Simulation Conference (WSC)* (pp. 1600-1611). IEEE. DOI: 10.1109/WSC.2011.6147877

Nie, S., & Fan, B. (2023). The Dynamics of Collaborative Emergency Capability: A Qualitative Comparative Analysis Based on Contingency Plans. *Natural Hazards Review*, 24(2), 05023002. DOI: 10.1061/NHREFO.NHENG-1645

Parker, L. D. (2023). Third sector crisis management and resilience: Reflections and directions. *Financial Accountability & Management*.

Patel, K. R. (2023). Enhancing Global Supply Chain Resilience: Effective Strategies for Mitigating Disruptions in an Interconnected World. *BULLET: Jurnal Multidisiplin Ilmu*, 2(1), 257–264.

Pérez, M. (2009) La relación entre la tecnología de la información, las prácticas de gestión de la calidad y el Desarrollo de las capacidades dinámicas: una aproximación empírica. Tesis Doctoral, Universidad de Granada, España.

Pettit, T. J., Croxton, K. L., & Fiksel, J. (2013). Ensuring supply chain resilience: Development and implementation of an assessment tool. *Journal of Business Logistics*, 34(1), 46–76. DOI: 10.1111/jbl.12009

Ponomarov, S. Y., & Holcomb, M. C. (2009). Understanding the concept of supply chain resilience. *International Journal of Logistics Management*, 20(1), 124–143. DOI: 10.1108/09574090910954873

Poseck, B. V., Baquero, B. C., & Jiménez, M. L. V. (2006). La experiencia traumática desde la psicología positiva: resiliencia y crecimiento postraumático. Papeles del Psicólogo, 27(1), 40-49.

Quayson, M., Bai, C., Sun, L., & Sarkis, J. (2023). Building blockchain-driven dynamic capabilities for developing circular supply chain: Rethinking the role of sensing, seizing, and reconfiguring. *Business Strategy and the Environment*, 32(7), 4821–4840. DOI: 10.1002/bse.3395

Raisch, S., & Birkinshaw, J. (2008). Organizational ambidexterity: Antecedents, outcomes, and moderators. *Journal of Management*, 34(3), 375–409. DOI: 10.1177/0149206308316058

Ramezani, J., & Camarinha-Matos, L. (2020). Approaches for Resilience and Antifragility in Collaborative Business Ecosystems. *Technological Forecasting and Social Change*, 151, 119846. Advance online publication. DOI: 10.1016/j.techfore.2019.119846

Rhaiem, K., & Halilem, N. (2023). The worst is not to fail, but to fail to learn from failure: A multi-method empirical validation of learning from innovation failure. *Technological Forecasting and Social Change*, 190, 122427. DOI: 10.1016/j.techfore.2023.122427

Russo, D., & Ciancarini, P. (2017). Towards antifragile software architectures. *Procedia Computer Science*, 109, 929–934. DOI: 10.1016/j.procs.2017.05.426

Sardesai, S., & Klingebiel, K. (2023). Maintaining viability by rapid supply chain adaptation using a process capability index. *Omega*, 115, 102778. DOI: 10.1016/j.omega.2022.102778

Sheng, X., Kim, W. J., Gupta, R., & Ji, Q. (2023). The impacts of oil price volatility on financial stress: Is the COVID-19 period different? *International Review of Economics & Finance*, 85, 520–532. DOI: 10.1016/j.iref.2023.02.006

Soni, U., Jain, V., & Kumar, S. (2014). Measuring supply chain resilience using a deterministic modeling approach. *Computers & Industrial Engineering*, 74, 11–25. DOI: 10.1016/j.cie.2014.04.019

Stewart, K., & Perren, R. (2023). Under the spell of your smartphone: How dependence evokes a halo of trust in advertising. *Journal of Promotion Management*, 29(1), 106–124. DOI: 10.1080/10496491.2022.2108188

Supriharyanti, E., & Sukoco, B. M. (2023). Organizational change capability: A systematic review and future research directions. *Management Research Review*, 46(1), 46–81. DOI: 10.1108/MRR-01-2021-0039

Tang, C. S. (2006). Robust strategies for mitigating supply chain disruptions. *International Journal of Logistics*, 9(1), 33–45. DOI: 10.1080/13675560500405584

Teece, D. (2007). Explicating dynamic capabilities: The nature and micro foundations of (sustainable) enterprise performance. *Strategic Management Journal*, 28(13), 1319–1350. DOI: 10.1002/smj.640

Teece, D. J., & Al-Aali, A. (2012). Knowledge assets, capabilities, and the theory of the firm. Handbook of organizational learning and knowledge management, 505-534.

Teece, D. J., Pisano, G., & Shuen, A. (1997). Dynamic capabilities and strategic management. *Strategic Management Journal*, 18(7), 509–533. DOI: 10.1002/(SICI)1097-0266(199708)18:7<509::AID-SMJ882>3.0.CO;2-Z

Tushamn, M. L., Smith, W. K., & Wood, R. C. (2010). *Organizational designs and innovation streams*. Industrial and Corporate Change. DOI: 10.1093/icc/dtq040

Tushman, M. L., & O'Reilly, C. A.III. (1996). Ambidextrous organizations: Managing evolutionary and revolutionary change. *California Management Review*, 38(4), 8–30. DOI: 10.2307/41165852

UNCTAD. (2021). El comercio electrónico mundial crece hasta los 26,7 billones de dólares, impulsado por la COVID-19. United Nations. https://news.un.org/es/story/2021/05/1491592

Valentinov, V., Van Assche, K., & Hermans, F. (2023). Toward a digital transformation of the theory of the firm: Emergence as framework for organizational sustainability. Canadian Journal of Administrative Sciences/Revue Canadienne des Sciences de l'Administration, 40(3), 270-282.

Vecchiola, C., Anjomshoa, H., Bernstein, Y., Dumitrescu, I., Garnavi, R., von Känel, J., & Wightwick, G. (2013). Engineering resilient information systems for emergency management. *IBM Journal of Research and Development*, 57(5), 2–1. DOI: 10.1147/JRD.2013.2259432

Vina, A., & Liu, J. (2023). Effects of global shocks on the evolution of an interconnected world. *Ambio*, 52(1), 95–106. DOI: 10.1007/s13280-022-01778-0 PMID: 35997989

Vollero, A., Sardanelli, D., & Siano, A. (2023). Exploring the role of the Amazon effect on customer expectations: An analysis of user-generated content in consumer electronics retailing. *Journal of Consumer Behaviour*, 22(5), 1062–1073. DOI: 10.1002/cb.1969

Vylobkova, V., & Heintz, S. (2023). A meeting of positive behaviors: The relations of three aspects of flexibility with character strengths. *Frontiers in Psychology*, 13, 1078764. DOI: 10.3389/fpsyg.2022.1078764 PMID: 36817377

Yeung, A., & Ulrich, D. (2020). *Reinventando la organización: Cómo crear mayor valor en mercados en constante evolución*. Editorial Almuzara.

Zhang, F. (2021). Evaluating public organization performance under extreme weather events: Does organizational adaptive capacity matter? *Journal of Environmental Management*, 296, 113388. DOI: 10.1016/j.jenvman.2021.113388 PMID: 34328864

Zolli, A., & Haely, A. M. (2012). Introduction. United Kingdom. In Resilience: Why Things Bounce Back (pp. 12-132). Free Press.

Chapter 4
Synergizing Success the Dynamics of Collaborative Business Ecosystems

Abhijit Chandratreya
https://orcid.org/0000-0001-9403-2094
SCES's Indira Institute of Management, Pune, India

ABSTRACT

The chapter explores the transformative impact of collaborative business ecosystems on organizational success and innovation. Collaborative business ecosystems, comprising interconnected organizations, suppliers, customers, and stakeholders, are reshaping traditional business models by fostering cooperation, co-creation, and shared value. This chapter delves into the key dynamics of these ecosystems, including trust-building, shared governance, resource integration, and digital connectivity, highlighting their role in enhancing competitiveness and resilience. It examines how businesses can leverage these ecosystems to drive innovation, reduce costs, and adapt to rapidly changing market conditions. The chapter addresses the challenges associated with managing collaborative ecosystems, such as balancing competition with collaboration and navigating complex stakeholder relationships.

INTRODUCTION

Collaborative business ecosystems represent a shift in how organizations interact, innovate, and compete in an increasingly interconnected global market. These ecosystems consist of diverse, interdependent entities—such as businesses, suppli-

DOI: 10.4018/979-8-3693-7272-2.ch004

ers, customers, and even competitors—that work together to create value that none could achieve independently (Adner, 2017). The rise of collaborative ecosystems reflects a growing recognition that success in the modern business landscape often hinges on the ability to build and sustain dynamic, cooperative relationships rather than operating in isolation.

The evolution of collaborative business ecosystems can be traced back to the emergence of networked organizational models in the late 20th century, driven by advances in information technology and globalization. These models challenged traditional, hierarchical forms of business organization by emphasizing flexibility, knowledge sharing, and co-creation of value (Moore, 1996). In this context, ecosystems are not merely strategic alliances or partnerships; they are complex, adaptive networks where participants continuously align their goals, resources, and capabilities to respond to changing market conditions (Iansiti & Levien, 2004).

Digital transformation has been a significant enabler of collaborative business ecosystems, providing the technological infrastructure that supports real-time communication, data sharing, and joint innovation. Platforms such as cloud computing, blockchain, and the Internet of Things (IoT) facilitate seamless collaboration among ecosystem participants, allowing them to share information, co-develop products, and coordinate activities more effectively (Jacobides, Cennamo, & Gawer, 2018). These technologies also help lower barriers to entry for new participants, fostering a more inclusive and dynamic ecosystem environment.

The collaborative approach inherent in business ecosystems offers numerous benefits, including enhanced innovation, improved efficiency, and access to new markets. By pooling resources and expertise, organizations within an ecosystem can accelerate research and development, shorten product development cycles, and respond more quickly to customer needs (Nambisan, 2018). Furthermore, ecosystems enable companies to leverage complementary capabilities, such as combining technological expertise with market access, which can result in innovative products and services that drive competitive advantage (Adner & Kapoor, 2010).

However, thriving within a collaborative ecosystem also presents challenges. Governance issues, such as managing intellectual property rights, aligning strategic objectives, and maintaining trust among participants, are critical to the ecosystem's success (Dhanaraj & Parkhe, 2006). Additionally, power dynamics can influence the balance of value capture, with dominant players potentially exerting disproportionate control over ecosystem decisions and outcomes (Gulati, Puranam, & Tushman, 2012). Effective management of these dynamics requires clear communication, transparent rules, and a shared commitment to the ecosystem's collective goals.

As collaborative business ecosystems continue to evolve, understanding their dynamics becomes essential for organizations seeking to navigate this complex environment. This chapter explores the factors that drive successful collaboration within business ecosystems, the challenges that participants face, and the strategies that can help foster a synergistic approach to value creation.

1. CBEs: AN OVERVIEW

1.1 Overview of Collaborative Business Ecosystems

Collaborative business ecosystems are networks of interdependent organizations—including companies, suppliers, customers, competitors, and other stakeholders—that work together to co-create value and achieve shared objectives. Unlike traditional linear supply chains or hierarchical business models, ecosystems are characterized by a high degree of interconnectedness, flexibility, and mutual reliance (Adner, 2017). These ecosystems thrive on collaboration, with each participant contributing unique resources, capabilities, and knowledge that collectively enhance the ecosystem's overall value proposition (Jacobides, Cennamo, & Gawer, 2018). The success of a business ecosystem depends on the ability of its members to align their goals, continuously adapt to market changes, and innovate in ways that benefit the entire network rather than just individual entities (Iansiti & Levien, 2004). This collaborative approach enables organizations to tackle complex challenges, accelerate innovation, and access new markets that would be difficult to penetrate independently.

The rise of digital technologies has further accelerated the development of collaborative business ecosystems, enabling real-time communication, data sharing, and joint innovation across geographical boundaries. Digital platforms such as cloud computing, blockchain, and artificial intelligence facilitate seamless interaction among ecosystem participants, lowering barriers to entry and fostering a more inclusive and dynamic environment (Nambisan, 2018). Moreover, ecosystems offer strategic advantages by allowing firms to leverage complementary assets, such as combining technological expertise with market access or integrating diverse skills to co-develop new products and services (Adner & Kapoor, 2010). However, managing these ecosystems requires careful orchestration, as the interdependencies among participants can lead to complex governance challenges, including maintaining trust, ensuring equitable value distribution, and managing power dynamics within the network (Dhanaraj & Parkhe, 2006).

1.2 Importance of Collaboration in Today's Competitive Business Landscape

Collaboration has become a critical driver of success in today's highly competitive and rapidly evolving business landscape. As globalization and technological advancements blur traditional industry boundaries, companies are increasingly recognizing that competitive advantage often lies in their ability to work collaboratively with other organizations rather than competing in isolation. Collaboration allows businesses to pool resources, share knowledge, and leverage complementary strengths to achieve outcomes that would be difficult or impossible to accomplish alone (Bouncken, Clauss, & Fredrich, 2016). Through strategic alliances, joint ventures, and ecosystem partnerships, firms can co-create innovative products and services, enter new markets more effectively, and respond more agilely to market changes and disruptions. This interconnected approach not only enhances individual company performance but also drives the overall competitiveness and adaptability of entire industries (Gulati, Wohlgezogen, & Zhelyazkov, 2012).

Collaboration fosters a culture of continuous learning and innovation, enabling companies to tap into diverse perspectives and expertise that fuel creativity and problem-solving. In an environment where the pace of technological change is accelerating, collaborative networks provide access to cutting-edge technologies, ideas, and capabilities that are essential for keeping up with market demands (Vanhaverbeke & Chesbrough, 2014). For example, collaborations in research and development (R&D) can significantly reduce the time and costs associated with bringing new products to market, as companies can share the risks and rewards of innovation. Additionally, collaboration enhances resilience by allowing companies to build more flexible and responsive supply chains, share critical information, and collectively address industry-wide challenges such as sustainability and regulatory compliance (Huxham & Vangen, 2013).

1.3 Objectives and Scope of the Chapter

The primary objective of this chapter is to explore the dynamics of collaborative business ecosystems and highlight their importance in fostering innovation, enhancing competitive advantage, and driving sustainable growth in today's interconnected business landscape. This chapter aims to provide a comprehensive understanding of how collaboration between diverse stakeholders—including businesses, suppliers, customers, and even competitors—can create value that extends beyond the capabilities of individual organizations. By examining key drivers, challenges, and best practices in managing collaborative ecosystems, the chapter seeks to equip readers with actionable insights and strategies for building and sustaining successful business partnerships.

The scope of the chapter encompasses several critical aspects of collaborative business ecosystems. It begins by defining collaborative business ecosystems and tracing their evolution, illustrating how technological advancements and shifting market dynamics have made collaboration a strategic imperative. The chapter then delves into the key drivers of collaboration, such as the need for innovation, access to new markets, and shared resources. Additionally, it addresses the challenges organizations face within ecosystems, including governance complexities, power imbalances, and trust issues. The chapter also explores various models of collaboration, such as strategic alliances, joint ventures, and digital platforms, and provides case studies that exemplify successful and unsuccessful ecosystem management.

It offers practical guidance on how organizations can effectively navigate the complexities of collaborative ecosystems, emphasizing the importance of governance, communication, and alignment of objectives among ecosystem participants. By the end of the chapter, readers will gain a holistic view of the role of collaboration in shaping modern business strategies and the tools needed to leverage these ecosystems for long-term success.

2. UNDERSTANDING COLLABORATIVE BUSINESS ECOSYSTEMS

2.1 Definition and Key Characteristics

Definition: Collaborative business ecosystems are dynamic networks of interdependent organizations, including businesses, suppliers, customers, competitors, and other stakeholders, that work together to create and share value through mutual collaboration. These ecosystems are characterized by open communication, shared goals, and cooperative strategies that leverage the collective strengths of each participant to achieve outcomes that would be unattainable individually (Adner, 2017). Unlike traditional business models, which often focus on competition and self-sufficiency, collaborative ecosystems emphasize co-creation, joint problem-solving, and synergistic partnerships, driving innovation and competitive advantage in a rapidly changing market environment (Jacobides, Cennamo, & Gawer, 2018).

Key Characteristics:

a) **Interdependence**: Collaborative ecosystems are built on the interdependence of participants, where each member relies on others to contribute complementary skills, resources, or capabilities. This interdependence fosters a culture of mutual support and shared responsibility, allowing organizations to achieve complex goals that are beyond their reach (Iansiti & Levien, 2004).
b) **Co-Creation of Value**: One of the core characteristics of collaborative business ecosystems is the co-creation of value. Participants jointly develop new products, services, and solutions by combining their expertise and resources, enhancing innovation, and creating value that benefits all members of the ecosystem (Nambisan & Sawhney, 2011). This collective approach enables faster adaptation to market changes and the ability to address customer needs more effectively.
c) **Diversity of Participants**: Ecosystems typically consist of a diverse range of participants, including large corporations, small and medium enterprises (SMEs), startups, and even non-profit organizations. This diversity brings a broad spectrum of ideas, technologies, and approaches, which can drive creativity and innovation within the ecosystem (Moore, 1996).
d) **Dynamic Adaptability**: Collaborative ecosystems are inherently dynamic, continuously evolving as market conditions, technologies, and participant roles change. This adaptability allows ecosystems to be resilient, quickly reorganizing resources and strategies in response to external pressures such as market shifts, technological disruptions, or regulatory changes (Jacobides et al., 2018).
e) **Shared Governance and Coordination**: Effective governance is crucial in managing collaborative business ecosystems. Governance structures define the rules of engagement, align incentives, and manage conflicts, ensuring that all participants are working towards shared objectives. Shared governance models facilitate coordination, enabling seamless interactions and decision-making processes across the ecosystem (Dhanaraj & Parkhe, 2006).
f) **Open Communication and Trust**: Successful collaborative ecosystems are underpinned by open communication and high levels of trust among participants. Transparent information sharing fosters collaboration reduces misunderstandings, and builds strong relationships, which are essential for long-term ecosystem sustainability (Gulati, Wohlgezogen, & Zhelyazkov, 2012).

2.2 Types of Business Ecosystems

Business ecosystems are diverse and can be categorized based on their structure, purpose, and the nature of interactions among participants. Understanding the different types of business ecosystems helps organizations identify suitable collaborative models that align with their strategic objectives.

a) **Innovation Ecosystems**: Innovation ecosystems are networks of organizations, including firms, universities, research institutions, and startups, that collaborate to drive technological advancements and develop new products and services. These ecosystems focus on fostering creativity, sharing knowledge, and leveraging diverse expertise to accelerate innovation processes (Adner & Kapoor, 2010). For example, Silicon Valley is a renowned innovation ecosystem where technology companies, venture capitalists, and research institutions collaborate to bring groundbreaking innovations to market.
b) **Platform Ecosystems**: Platform ecosystems revolve around a central platform that connects various participants, such as producers, consumers, developers, and service providers, facilitating interactions and transactions among them. These ecosystems create value by providing a common digital infrastructure that enables third-party participants to build and offer complementary products or services (Gawer & Cusumano, 2014). Examples include Apple's App Store, Google's Android ecosystem, and Amazon's marketplace, where independent developers, vendors, and service providers contribute to the overall ecosystem.
c) **Supply Chain Ecosystems**: Supply chain ecosystems consist of interconnected businesses that collaborate to manage the flow of goods, services, and information from raw materials to end consumers. These ecosystems emphasize coordination, efficiency, and resilience in managing complex supply chains. Collaboration within supply chain ecosystems helps participants optimize operations, reduce costs, and respond more effectively to market demands and disruptions (Kim, 2020). Automotive manufacturing, where car makers, suppliers, and logistics providers work closely together, is a prime example of a supply chain ecosystem.
d) **Customer-Centric Ecosystems**: Customer-centric ecosystems are designed to provide a seamless, integrated experience to customers by bringing together various services and products around a central customer need. These ecosystems leverage data analytics and digital platforms to tailor offerings, improve customer engagement, and enhance service delivery (Lusch & Nambisan, 2015). For instance, financial service ecosystems integrate banking, insurance, investment, and advisory services into a single platform, offering customers a comprehensive suite of financial solutions.

e) **Knowledge Ecosystems**: Knowledge ecosystems focus on the creation, sharing, and dissemination of knowledge and expertise among participants. These ecosystems are often found in academic and research settings, where universities, research centers, companies, and government entities collaborate to advance scientific research and innovation (Powell & Grodal, 2005). The biotechnology sector often operates within knowledge ecosystems, where academic researchers, pharmaceutical companies, and medical institutions work together to develop new drugs and treatments.

f) **Community Ecosystems**: Community ecosystems are networks of individuals and organizations that come together around shared values, interests, or social causes. These ecosystems often include non-profits, social enterprises, businesses, and government bodies working collaboratively to address societal challenges such as sustainability, healthcare, or education (Austin & Seitanidi, 2012). Community ecosystems focus on creating social impact through collective action and resource sharing, often facilitated by digital platforms and community networks.

2.3 The Role of Interconnected Stakeholders

Interconnected stakeholders play a crucial role in the functioning and success of collaborative business ecosystems. These ecosystems are not just collections of individual organizations but dynamic, interdependent networks where stakeholders work together to co-create value, drive innovation, and enhance competitive advantage. The involvement of diverse stakeholders—including businesses, suppliers, customers, regulators, and even competitors—enables ecosystems to leverage a wide range of resources, capabilities, and perspectives, fostering a collaborative environment that is adaptive, innovative, and resilient (Adner, 2017).

1) **Co-Creation of Value**: Stakeholders in collaborative ecosystems work together to co-create products, services, and solutions that provide value to the entire network. Each participant contributes unique expertise, technologies, or resources, enhancing the ecosystem's ability to innovate and respond to market needs. For example, technology firms, third-party developers, and end-users collaborate within platform ecosystems like Apple's App Store, where developers create apps that enhance the value of the platform for consumers and drive revenues for Apple and its partners (Jacobides, Cennamo, & Gawer, 2018).

    a) **Resource Sharing and Optimization**: In business ecosystems, interconnected stakeholders pool resources, including financial capital, technological capabilities, and market access, optimizing the use of these resources for mutual benefit. This shared approach reduces costs, speeds up time-to-market, and enables participants to undertake large-scale projects that would be challenging to manage independently (Gulati, Wohlgezogen, & Zhelyazkov, 2012).

b) **Knowledge Exchange and Innovation**: Stakeholders in collaborative ecosystems actively share knowledge, insights, and data, creating a culture of continuous learning and innovation. This open exchange allows organizations to stay ahead of market trends, rapidly prototype new ideas, and enhance their innovation capabilities (Nambisan, 2018). Knowledge ecosystems, such as those found in biotech or academic research networks, rely on universities, research institutions, and private companies sharing research findings and collaborating on development projects to push the frontiers of technology and science.

c) **Adaptability and Resilience**: Interconnected stakeholders enhance the adaptability and resilience of business ecosystems by enabling rapid responses to external disruptions, such as technological changes, market fluctuations, or supply chain disruptions. Ecosystem participants can reconfigure their roles, realign resources, and collectively develop solutions to emerging challenges, maintaining ecosystem stability (Iansiti & Levien, 2004). During the COVID-19 pandemic, for example, pharmaceutical companies, governments, and healthcare providers collaborated to accelerate vaccine development and distribution, demonstrating the resilience of collaborative ecosystems in crises.

d) **Governance and Trust Building**: Effective governance within ecosystems is facilitated by interconnected stakeholders who collaboratively establish rules, standards, and protocols that ensure smooth and fair interactions. Shared governance helps manage conflicts, align incentives, and maintain trust among participants, which is crucial for the ecosystem's long-term success (Dhanaraj & Parkhe, 2006). Trust and transparency are key factors that bind stakeholders together, fostering a cooperative atmosphere where stakeholders feel confident in sharing sensitive information and working towards common goals.

e) **Market Access and Expansion**: Through collaboration, stakeholders gain access to new markets and customer segments that would be difficult to reach individually. Ecosystems enable companies to leverage the market presence and distribution channels of their partners, facilitating quicker and more cost-effective market entry (Adner & Kapoor, 2010). For example, digital platforms often expand their reach by incorporating diverse third-party service providers who bring new customers and markets into the ecosystem.

f) **Government entities** play a crucial role in fostering collaborative business ecosystems by creating supportive policies, frameworks, and initiatives that encourage partnerships among businesses, academia, and other stakeholders. By providing regulatory clarity and incentives, such as tax breaks or grants, governments can stimulate innovation and collaboration across sectors (OECD, 2019). Furthermore, government entities often act as facilitators, bringing together diverse stakeholders to share knowledge, resources, and best practices, which can enhance the overall dynamism and resilience of business ecosystems (Nambisan, 2017). This collaborative approach not only drives economic growth but also addresses societal challenges by leveraging the strengths of various actors within the ecosystem (Bøllingtoft, 2019).

3. KEY DRIVERS OF COLLABORATIVE BUSINESS ECOSYSTEMS

3.1 Technological Advancements

Technological advancements are key drivers of collaborative business ecosystems, fundamentally reshaping how organizations interact, innovate, and create value together. Emerging technologies such as artificial intelligence (AI), blockchain, cloud computing, and the Internet of Things (IoT) have dramatically enhanced the connectivity, efficiency, and scalability of business ecosystems, enabling real-time data sharing, seamless communication, and more sophisticated coordination among participants (Iansiti & Lakhani, 2020).

Digital platforms, for instance, have revolutionized ecosystem dynamics by providing a common infrastructure where diverse stakeholders—including businesses, developers, and end-users—can collaborate effortlessly, co-create innovative solutions, and reach global markets with unprecedented speed and flexibility (Gawer & Cusumano, 2014).

AI and data analytics tools further empower ecosystem participants by providing actionable insights, predicting market trends, and optimizing decision-making processes, which fosters a more responsive and agile collaborative environment (Nambisan, 2018). Additionally, blockchain technology enhances trust and transparency within ecosystems by providing secure, tamper-proof records of transactions and interactions, thus reducing friction and enabling more efficient collaboration across organizational boundaries (Zhu & Zhou, 2016). These technological advancements not only lower the barriers to collaboration but also expand the potential for ecosystem growth, making technology a cornerstone of modern collaborative business strategies.

3.2 Globalization and the Need for Cross-Border Collaboration

Globalization is a major driver of collaborative business ecosystems, compelling organizations to engage in cross-border collaboration to remain competitive in a rapidly interconnected world. As businesses operate on a global scale, they encounter diverse markets, varied regulatory environments, and a broad spectrum of technological advancements and consumer preferences. This complexity necessitates collaboration beyond national boundaries to leverage global expertise, access new markets, and optimize operations (Madhok & Keyhani, 2012).

Cross-border partnerships enable companies to tap into international talent pools, share innovative technologies, and adapt to regional market conditions more effectively. For instance, multinational corporations often collaborate with local firms, research institutions, and government bodies in different countries to enhance their R&D capabilities, adapt products to local needs, and navigate complex regulatory landscapes (Gulati, 2007). Moreover, such collaborations facilitate the creation of global supply chains, where companies integrate suppliers and distributors across various regions to achieve cost efficiencies and enhance responsiveness to market changes (Contractor, Kumar, Kundu, & Pedersen, 2010). As globalization continues to reshape the business landscape, the need for cross-border collaboration becomes increasingly critical for firms aiming to innovate, expand their reach, and maintain a competitive edge in the global economy.

3.3 Digital Transformation and Data-Driven Decision-Making

Digital transformation involves integrating advanced technologies—such as cloud computing, artificial intelligence, and big data analytics—into business processes, enabling more efficient and agile operations (Westerman, Bonnet, & McAfee, 2014). This transformation facilitates seamless connectivity and collaboration among ecosystem participants by providing real-time data, automating processes, and enabling sophisticated communication channels.

Data-driven decision-making, on the other hand, relies on the analysis of large volumes of data to inform strategic choices, optimize operations, and enhance customer experiences (Davenport & Harris, 2007). By harnessing insights from data, organizations within a collaborative ecosystem can make informed decisions that drive innovation, personalize offerings, and identify new growth opportunities. The synergy between digital transformation and data-driven decision-making empowers ecosystem participants to collaborate more effectively, align their goals, and respond rapidly to market changes, thus enhancing the overall value and resilience of the ecosystem (Brynjolfsson & McElheran, 2016).

3.4 Consumer Demand for Personalized and Integrated Experiences

Consumer demand for personalized and integrated experiences is a significant driver of collaborative business ecosystems, compelling organizations to work together to meet evolving customer expectations. In today's digital age, consumers increasingly seek seamless and tailored interactions that cater to their individual preferences and needs. This heightened expectation for personalization and integration pushes companies to collaborate across various touchpoints and channels to deliver a cohesive and customized experience. For instance, in the financial services sector, customers demand integrated solutions that combine banking, investment, and insurance services into a single, user-friendly platform.

To meet these demands, banks, fintech companies, and insurance providers often collaborate within ecosystems to create comprehensive and interconnected offerings that enhance customer satisfaction and loyalty. This collaborative approach allows organizations to pool their expertise and resources, leveraging data and technology to deliver more accurate and relevant recommendations, streamline processes, and provide a unified experience that meets the diverse needs of consumers. As a result, businesses within these ecosystems are better positioned to attract and retain customers, gain a competitive edge, and drive innovation through the continuous evolution of their integrated solutions (Lusch & Nambisan, 2015).

3.5 Collective Intelligence

Collective intelligence, defined as the shared or group intelligence that emerges from collaboration and collective efforts, plays a crucial role in the dynamics of collaborative business ecosystems. This concept suggests that the aggregation of diverse perspectives, skills, and experiences can lead to enhanced problem-solving capabilities and innovative solutions (Levy, 1997). In collaborative environments, stakeholders can harness collective intelligence to create synergies that drive success, enabling organizations to adapt quickly to changing market conditions and leverage shared resources effectively (Benkler, 2006). As businesses increasingly operate within interconnected ecosystems, the ability to tap into collective intelligence becomes essential for fostering resilience, creativity, and sustainable growth (Whelan & Fink, 2020). Ultimately, understanding and harnessing the dynamics of collective intelligence is vital for organizations aiming to thrive in complex and collaborative landscapes.

4. BENEFITS OF COLLABORATIVE BUSINESS ECOSYSTEMS

Innovation acceleration through shared knowledge and resources

Collaborative Business Ecosystems (CBEs) are networks of organizations, including companies, suppliers, customers, academic institutions, and sometimes competitors, that work together to create shared value. These ecosystems benefit innovation acceleration through shared knowledge and resources in several keyways:

a) Enhanced Knowledge Sharing and Learning

Access to Expertise: CBEs bring together diverse expertise and perspectives, enabling participants to learn from each other and access specialized knowledge that would be difficult or expensive to develop independently.

Open Innovation: Participants can share insights, research findings, and best practices, facilitating open innovation. This collaborative approach helps identify new opportunities, refine ideas, and accelerate the development of innovative solutions.

b) Resource Pooling and Cost Reduction

Shared Resources: By pooling resources such as technology, data, R&D facilities, and human capital, CBEs reduce costs and barriers to entry, making innovation more accessible to all members.

Risk Sharing: Collaborative ecosystems allow companies to share the financial and operational risks associated with innovation. This risk-sharing model encourages bolder investments in new technologies and products.

c) Faster Time to Market

Accelerated Development: By leveraging shared resources and knowledge, businesses can speed up the innovation process, from ideation to prototyping to market launch. Joint efforts in research, development, and testing can significantly shorten the product development cycle.

Rapid Prototyping and Testing: Collaboration allows for quicker prototyping and feedback loops, as multiple partners can simultaneously test and refine new concepts, leading to faster iterations and improvements.

d) Increased Agility and Flexibility

Adaptability to Market Changes: CBEs enable companies to quickly adapt to changes in the market by leveraging collective insights and resources. This agility is crucial in industries where technology and customer preferences evolve rapidly.

Flexible Resource Allocation: Members can reallocate resources and capabilities within the ecosystem based on current needs and opportunities, enhancing overall innovation efficiency.

e) Access to New Markets and Technologies

Market Access: Collaborating with partners within the ecosystem can open up new markets and customer segments that individual companies might struggle to access on their own.

Technology Transfer: CBEs facilitate the exchange of cutting-edge technologies and tools, allowing members to adopt and integrate advanced solutions that drive innovation.

f) Enhanced Creativity and Idea Generation

Diverse Perspectives: Collaboration fosters a melting pot of ideas, driven by the diverse backgrounds of ecosystem participants. This diversity often leads to more creative and disruptive solutions.

Cross-Industry Innovation: Ecosystems that include partners from different industries can spark cross-industry innovation, where concepts from one sector are adapted and applied to another, leading to breakthrough products and services.

g) Strengthened Competitive Advantage

Collaborative Advantage: By working together, companies can build a competitive edge that is difficult for others to replicate. The collaborative advantage comes from the unique combination of shared knowledge, resources, and capabilities that drive superior innovation outcomes.

Faster Response to Competitors: CBEs enable faster collective responses to competitive threats, allowing member companies to innovate more rapidly and stay ahead in the market.

5. CHALLENGES IN BUILDING AND SUSTAINING COLLABORATIVE ECOSYSTEMS

Collaborative Business Ecosystems (CBEs) represent a strategic approach where organizations work together, sharing knowledge, resources, and capabilities to achieve common goals. Despite their potential benefits, building and sustaining these ecosystems come with significant challenges. The key challenges are discussed below:

a) Trust and Relationship Management

Building trust among partners is fundamental to the success of CBEs, yet it is often one of the most challenging aspects (Iansiti & Levien, 2004). Trust issues arise from the fear of intellectual property theft, conflicting interests, or uneven contributions by partners. Without a solid foundation of trust, open communication and the willingness to share valuable insights and resources are hindered, stalling innovation and collaborative efforts (Dyer & Singh, 1998).

b) **Governance and Decision-Making Complexity**

CBEs involve multiple stakeholders with diverse goals, making governance complex. Establishing decision-making frameworks that accommodate all participants can be challenging (Provan & Kenis, 2008). Disagreements on strategy, resource allocation, and risk management can slow down decision-making processes, leading to inefficiencies and potential conflicts that threaten the ecosystem's stability (Adner, 2017).

c) **Cultural and Organizational Differences**

Cultural and organizational diversity within ecosystems can hinder collaboration. Differences in corporate culture, management styles, and communication approaches can create friction among partners (Zeng, Xie, & Tam, 2010). Aligning these differences to achieve a shared vision requires significant effort in change management, training, and alignment of values, which can be time-consuming and costly.

d) **Resource Imbalances**

Resource imbalances among partners, such as differences in financial strength, technological capabilities, or market access, can lead to power dynamics that skew the benefits of collaboration (Williamson & De Meyer, 2012). Dominant partners may exert disproportionate influence, potentially sidelining smaller participants and undermining the collaborative spirit. Ensuring fair distribution of resources and influence is critical to sustaining a balanced and equitable ecosystem.

e) **Intellectual Property (IP) Management**

Managing IP within CBEs is a major challenge due to the need for open innovation and knowledge sharing (Bogers, Chesbrough, & Moedas, 2018). Partners must strike a delicate balance between protecting their proprietary technologies and being transparent enough to foster collaboration. Disputes over IP rights, ownership, and usage can disrupt collaborative efforts and erode trust among ecosystem members.

f) **Technological Integration and Compatibility**

Technological compatibility is essential for effective collaboration but can be a major obstacle. Integrating diverse systems, platforms, and data standards from various partners requires substantial investment and coordination (Gnyawali & Park, 2011). Disparate technologies can create silos, impede data sharing, and slow down the overall innovation process, making it harder to realize the full potential of the ecosystem.

g) **Sustaining Engagement and Commitment**

Sustaining long-term engagement from ecosystem participants is challenging, especially when initial enthusiasm wanes or when partners fail to see immediate returns (Adner, 2017). Continuous motivation, clear value propositions, and tangible benefits are necessary to keep partners committed to the ecosystem's goals. Misaligned expectations and perceived imbalances in benefits can lead to disengagement and the eventual breakdown of the ecosystem.

h) **External Environmental Factors**

External factors, such as regulatory changes, market dynamics, and economic shifts, can pose significant challenges to CBEs. Regulatory constraints may limit collaboration, particularly in industries with strict data privacy laws or antitrust regulations (Jacobides, Cennamo, & Gawer, 2018). Additionally, changes in market conditions, such as economic downturns or shifts in consumer behavior, can strain the resources and commitment of ecosystem participants.

6. DYNAMICS OF COLLABORATION: STRATEGIES AND BEST PRACTICES

The dynamics of collaboration within business ecosystems are complex, involving interactions among diverse entities such as companies, suppliers, customers, academic institutions, and sometimes competitors. Effective collaboration requires strategic alignment, mutual trust, shared resources, and continuous communication. Below, we explore key strategies and best practices that can enhance the dynamics of collaboration in business ecosystems.

a) Establish Clear Objectives and a Shared Vision

A successful collaborative ecosystem begins with a clear and shared vision among all participants. This vision serves as the guiding principle that aligns individual goals with the collective mission of the ecosystem (Gray & Stites, 2013). Establishing clear objectives helps partners understand their roles, contributions, and expectations, minimizing conflicts and ensuring that all efforts are directed towards common goals.

- **Best Practice**: Co-create the ecosystem's vision with input from all participants. This inclusive approach fosters commitment and ensures that the vision reflects the needs and ambitions of all stakeholders.

b) Foster Trust and Open Communication

Trust is the foundation of any collaborative effort. It enables open communication, knowledge sharing, and joint problem-solving (Ring & Van de Ven, 1994). Trust-building involves transparency, consistent behavior, and honoring commitments. Open communication channels allow for the free flow of information, reducing misunderstandings and enhancing decision-making.

- **Best Practice**: Regularly conduct meetings, workshops, and feedback sessions to maintain open lines of communication. Use collaborative tools and platforms that facilitate real-time information sharing among ecosystem participants.

c) Implement Effective Governance Structures

Governance structures define the roles, responsibilities, and decision-making processes within the ecosystem (Provan & Kenis, 2008). Effective governance ensures that the ecosystem operates smoothly, with clear mechanisms for conflict resolution, resource allocation, and accountability. A well-defined governance framework helps in managing the complexities of collaboration and ensures that decisions are made efficiently and equitably.

- **Best Practice**: Develop a governance model that includes representatives from all key stakeholders. Establish clear guidelines for decision-making, dispute resolution, and performance measurement.

d) Leverage Technology for Collaboration

Technology plays a crucial role in enabling collaboration by providing tools for communication, data sharing, and project management (Gnyawali & Park, 2011). Digital platforms, such as cloud-based collaboration tools, data analytics, and project management software, help streamline processes, enhance connectivity, and facilitate seamless collaboration across geographical boundaries.

- **Best Practice**: Invest in collaborative technologies that support ecosystem activities, such as shared databases, digital whiteboards, and virtual meeting platforms. Ensure all participants are trained and comfortable using these technologies.

e) Encourage Knowledge Sharing and Co-Creation

Knowledge sharing is vital for innovation and problem-solving within ecosystems. Collaborative ecosystems should create an environment where participants feel encouraged to share ideas, expertise, and resources (Nonaka & Takeuchi, 1995). Co-creation involves jointly developing products, services, or solutions, leveraging the collective intelligence of the ecosystem.

- **Best Practice**: Organize knowledge-sharing sessions, hackathons, and innovation workshops that bring together participants to brainstorm and co-create solutions. Establish incentive mechanisms that reward active participation and contribution.

f) Design Flexible Partnership Models

Flexibility in partnership arrangements allows ecosystems to adapt to changes in the market, technology, and participant needs (Jacobides, Cennamo, & Gawer, 2018). Collaborative agreements should be dynamic, enabling adjustments to roles, responsibilities, and contributions as the ecosystem evolves.

- **Best Practice**: Use modular partnership agreements that can be updated as conditions change. Allow for varying levels of participation and contribution to accommodate the diverse capabilities of ecosystem members.

g) Measure Performance and Impact

Regularly measuring the performance of the ecosystem is crucial to understanding its effectiveness and identifying areas for improvement (Adner, 2017). Key performance indicators (KPIs) should be established to track progress towards objectives, assess the health of partnerships, and evaluate the overall impact of the collaboration.

- **Best Practice**: Develop a set of KPIs that reflect the ecosystem's strategic goals, such as innovation outputs, time to market, and partner satisfaction. Use these metrics to guide decision-making and drive continuous improvement.

h) Manage Conflicts Proactively

Conflicts are inevitable in collaborative settings due to differing goals, resource constraints, and cultural differences (Linden, 2002). Effective conflict management involves proactive identification of potential issues, transparent communication, and structured resolution processes.

- **Best Practice**: Establish conflict resolution protocols that include mediation, negotiation, and escalation processes. Encourage an open environment where concerns can be voiced without fear of retribution.

i) Sustain Engagement and Motivation

Sustaining engagement over time requires continuous motivation and alignment of incentives. Partners need to see the value in their participation, both in terms of tangible benefits (e.g., financial returns) and intangible benefits (e.g., learning opportunities, reputation enhancement).

- **Best Practice**: Regularly communicate the ecosystem's achievements and the value generated for all participants. Recognize and celebrate contributions and ensure that benefits are distributed fairly.

7. CASE STUDIES OF SUCCESSFUL COLLABORATIVE ECOSYSTEMS

Case Study 1: Siemens' MindSphere – The Industrial IoT Ecosystem

Background: Siemens developed MindSphere, a cloud-based, open Industrial Internet of Things (IIoT) operating system designed to connect industrial devices and harness data for predictive maintenance, efficiency improvements, and other advanced analytics. Siemens realized that achieving the full potential of MindSphere would require collaboration with other technology providers, developers, and industry partners.

Collaborative Dynamics:

- **Shared Platform**: MindSphere serves as a shared platform where partners, including developers, software vendors, and industrial companies, can build, deploy, and scale IoT applications.

- **Open Ecosystem**: Siemens adopted an open innovation approach, allowing third-party developers to create apps and solutions on MindSphere, enhancing the system's capabilities and value proposition.
- **Partnerships with Industry Leaders**: Siemens formed strategic partnerships with companies like Microsoft, Amazon Web Services (AWS), and SAP to integrate advanced technologies such as AI, machine learning, and cloud computing into MindSphere.

Outcomes:

- **Accelerated Innovation**: The collaborative approach led to the rapid development of a diverse range of applications, enhancing the value of MindSphere for users.
- **Global Reach and Scale**: By partnering with global technology giants, Siemens was able to expand MindSphere's reach, making it accessible to a broader range of industries and markets.
- **Enhanced Customer Value**: The ecosystem's collaborative nature enabled Siemens to continuously evolve the platform, offering customers cutting-edge solutions tailored to their specific needs.

Success Factors:

- **Open Architecture**: Allowing third-party participation fostered a rich environment of innovation and co-creation.
- **Strategic Alliances**: Collaborating with industry leaders provided access to new technologies and global markets.
- **Clear Governance and Standards**: Siemens established clear guidelines for data security, intellectual property, and integration standards, ensuring a seamless and secure ecosystem.

Case Study 2: The Apple App Store – A Thriving Digital Ecosystem

Background: Apple's App Store, launched in 2008, is one of the most successful examples of a digital collaborative ecosystem. It brought together developers, users, and Apple's technology to create a dynamic platform that revolutionized the way software is distributed and consumed on mobile devices.

Collaborative Dynamics:

- **Developer Community**: Apple opened its ecosystem to millions of developers worldwide, providing tools, resources, and a marketplace to distribute their apps.

- **Shared Revenue Model**: Apple's revenue-sharing model incentivized developers to create high-quality apps, while Apple benefited from a consistent revenue stream.
- **Quality Assurance and Security**: Apple maintained stringent quality control and security protocols, ensuring that apps met high standards, which increased user trust and satisfaction.

Outcomes:

- **Massive Growth**: The App Store quickly became a major revenue generator, contributing billions to Apple's overall earnings while supporting the growth of a global developer community.
- **Innovation Hub**: The ecosystem facilitated the rapid development of innovative applications, from games to productivity tools, which have transformed user experiences and created entirely new market segments.
- **User Engagement and Loyalty**: By curating a diverse and high-quality app ecosystem, Apple enhanced the value of its devices, driving customer loyalty and engagement.

Success Factors:

- **Robust Developer Support**: Apple provided extensive documentation, development tools, and technical support, enabling developers to succeed.
- **Focus on User Experience**: Apple's commitment to user experience ensured that apps met high-quality standards, which reinforced the ecosystem's reputation.
- **Continuous Ecosystem Evolution**: Apple's iterative approach to evolving the App Store's policies, technology, and offerings kept the ecosystem relevant and competitive.

Case Study 3: Ecomagination by GE – Collaborative Innovation in Sustainability

Background: Ecomagination was launched by General Electric (GE) in 2005 as a business strategy to drive sustainable innovation. The initiative focused on developing environmentally friendly products while engaging partners, customers, and stakeholders in collaborative problem-solving to address global environmental challenges.

Collaborative Dynamics:

- **Public-Private Partnerships**: GE collaborated with governments, research institutions, and other corporations to co-develop technologies that reduced environmental impact.

- **Open Innovation Challenges**: Ecomagination included open innovation challenges that invited startups, researchers, and companies to contribute ideas and technologies, fostering a culture of co-creation.
- **Customer Co-Creation**: GE worked closely with its customers to identify sustainability needs and co-develop solutions, enhancing the alignment of its products with market demands.

Outcomes:

- **Product Innovation**: Ecomagination led to the development of over 140 sustainable products, generating billions in revenue and solidifying GE's reputation as a leader in green technology.
- **Sustainability Impact**: The initiative helped reduce GE's greenhouse gas emissions and water usage while contributing to significant environmental improvements across industries.
- **Enhanced Brand Value**: The collaborative approach and commitment to sustainability strengthened GE's brand, attracting partners and customers who prioritized environmental responsibility.

Success Factors:

- **Commitment to Open Innovation**: Ecomagination's success was driven by its willingness to engage external partners and leverage collective expertise.
- **Alignment of Business and Sustainability Goals**: GE's integration of sustainability into its core business strategy ensured that Ecomagination was not just a marketing initiative but a driver of growth.
- **Strong Leadership and Vision**: Clear leadership and a compelling vision for a sustainable future galvanized stakeholders and sustained the ecosystem's momentum.

7.1 Key Success Factors and Lessons Learned

The success of Collaborative Business Ecosystems (CBEs) hinges on several key factors that drive their effectiveness and sustainability. A major success factor is strategic alignment among partners, where shared goals and a common vision ensure that all participants work towards mutually beneficial outcomes. Open communication and trust are equally crucial, as they facilitate transparent knowledge sharing, foster innovation, and build strong, resilient relationships among stakeholders. Robust governance structures are necessary to define roles, streamline decision-making, and manage conflicts efficiently, while technological integration enhances collaboration by enabling seamless data sharing and coordination across the ecosystem. The emphasis on flexibility and adaptability allows ecosystems to respond dynamically to changes in market conditions and technological advancements. Lessons learned from successful CBEs highlight the importance of maintaining a balance of power and equitable distribution of benefits to sustain long-term engagement. Moreover, fostering a culture of continuous learning and innovation through open platforms and inclusive participation can drive the ecosystem's growth and adaptability. Ultimately, these factors underscore the need for deliberate planning, ongoing commitment, and an inclusive approach to collaboration, ensuring that ecosystems not only thrive but also deliver sustained value to all partners involved.

7.2 How These Ecosystems Have Reshaped Industries

Collaborative Business Ecosystems (CBEs) have significantly reshaped industries by fostering innovation, enhancing competitiveness, and driving new business models. In the technology sector, ecosystems like Apple's App Store and Google's Android platform have transformed the software distribution landscape, enabling developers worldwide to access global markets with minimal barriers. This democratization of app development has accelerated the pace of innovation, created new revenue streams, and disrupted traditional software and media industries by providing consumers with unprecedented access to diverse applications and content.

In manufacturing and industrial sectors, ecosystems such as Siemens' MindSphere and GE's Predix have revolutionized how companies approach the Industrial Internet of Things (IIoT). By leveraging collaborative platforms, businesses can integrate and analyze data from various sources, leading to improved operational efficiencies, predictive maintenance, and enhanced product innovation. These ecosystems enable firms to co-create solutions that were previously unattainable in siloed environments, thereby setting new industry standards for smart manufacturing.

The automotive industry has also been reshaped by collaborative ecosystems, particularly through alliances in electric and autonomous vehicle development. Companies like Tesla, BMW, and Toyota collaborate with technology firms, startups, and even competitors to share R&D costs, access cutting-edge technologies, and accelerate the deployment of next-generation mobility solutions. This collaborative approach has disrupted traditional automotive manufacturing, pushing the industry toward a future of connected, autonomous, shared, and electric (CASE) vehicles.

In the healthcare sector, collaborative ecosystems are transforming patient care and medical research. Initiatives like IBM Watson Health and the Medtronic-BioIntelliSense partnership use AI and data analytics to deliver personalized healthcare solutions, facilitate remote monitoring, and enhance clinical decision-making. These ecosystems bring together technology providers, healthcare institutions, and researchers, breaking down silos and enabling innovations that improve patient outcomes and reduce costs.

CBEs are reshaping industries by creating interconnected networks of companies that leverage shared knowledge, resources, and technologies. This collaborative approach accelerates innovation, enhances customer experiences, and redefines competitive dynamics, allowing companies to adapt rapidly to changing market conditions and technological advancements. As a result, industries are moving away from traditional, isolated business models towards more agile, customer-centric, and innovation-driven paradigms, fundamentally altering how value is created and delivered.

8. THE ROLE OF LEADERSHIP AND CULTURE IN COLLABORATIVE ECOSYSTEMS

Leadership and organizational culture play pivotal roles in the success of Collaborative Business Ecosystems (CBEs). These factors influence how effectively an ecosystem can harness the collective strengths of its participants, manage complexities, and drive sustainable innovation. Effective leadership and a supportive culture are essential in fostering trust, guiding strategic alignment, and enabling collaboration across diverse entities.

8.1 Leadership in Collaborative Ecosystems

Leadership in CBEs goes beyond traditional hierarchical roles, requiring a more facilitative and integrative approach. Leaders must act as connectors, visionaries, and enablers who bring together diverse stakeholders, align their interests, and drive the collective agenda of the ecosystem. According to Chesbrough and Appleyard (2007), open innovation ecosystems thrive under leadership that promotes inclusivity, transparency and shared decision-making. Such leaders create a clear vision that unites partners and provides direction, ensuring that all participants are motivated and committed to the ecosystem's goals.

Moreover, leaders in CBEs must excel in managing complex, networked relationships and be adept at navigating power dynamics within the ecosystem (Williamson & De Meyer, 2012). They need to balance the interests of multiple stakeholders while fostering a collaborative environment that encourages knowledge-sharing and co-creation. For example, the leadership in Siemens' MindSphere ecosystem played a critical role in establishing strategic partnerships and setting governance structures that facilitated open collaboration and innovation (Siemens, 2020).

8.2 Culture in Collaborative Ecosystems

The culture within a CBE significantly impacts how collaboration unfolds and sustains over time. A collaborative culture characterized by openness, trust, and a shared sense of purpose is crucial for the success of any ecosystem. A study by Schein (2010) emphasizes that organizational culture sets the norms and values that guide behavior, directly influencing how effectively partners work together. In collaborative ecosystems, a culture that values collective success over individual achievements promotes the sharing of resources, knowledge, and capabilities.

Trust is a cornerstone of a collaborative culture, as it reduces perceived risks and encourages deeper engagement among participants (Ring & Van de Ven, 1994). Ecosystems that cultivate a high-trust environment enable partners to contribute their best efforts without fear of exploitation, enhancing the ecosystem's overall performance. For instance, the culture of co-creation and mutual respect in GE's Ecomagination initiative allowed it to bring together diverse stakeholders, fostering innovation in sustainable technology (GE, 2016).

8.3 Leadership and Culture: Synergistic Effects

The interplay between leadership and culture creates a synergistic effect that amplifies the effectiveness of collaborative ecosystems. Leaders who embody the cultural values of openness, collaboration, and shared success can set the tone for the entire ecosystem, embedding these values into every interaction and decision-making process (Gnyawali & Park, 2011). Conversely, a collaborative culture can empower leaders by creating an environment that supports experimentation, risk-taking, and collective problem-solving.

8.4 Lessons Learned

Successful CBEs demonstrate that leadership and culture must be actively nurtured and aligned with the ecosystem's strategic objectives. Leaders need to be adaptable, culturally intelligent, and skilled in facilitating cross-boundary collaboration. At the same time, cultivating a culture that values transparency, trust, and shared learning is essential for maintaining the ecosystem's vibrancy and resilience. These elements are not just supportive but foundational to the success of collaborative ecosystems, as they enable the ecosystem to evolve, adapt, and thrive in a complex and interconnected business environment.

9. MEASURING THE IMPACT OF COLLABORATIVE ECOSYSTEMS

9.1 Key Performance Indicators (KPIs) for Ecosystem Success

Key Performance Indicators (KPIs) are essential for assessing the effectiveness and success of Collaborative Business Ecosystems (CBEs). These metrics provide a structured way to evaluate the performance of the ecosystem, guiding strategic decisions and helping stakeholders optimize their collaborative efforts. One of the most critical KPIs is innovation output, which measures the number of new products, services, or technological solutions developed within the ecosystem. This indicator reflects the ecosystem's ability to leverage shared resources and knowledge to drive innovation, which is a primary objective of most CBEs (Adner, 2017). Metrics such as the number of patents filed, new product launches, and the scale of collaborative projects initiated are often used to quantify innovation output. Additionally, participant engagement and satisfaction is a key KPI, as high levels of engagement indicate that ecosystem members are finding value and are motivated to contribute. Tools like partner satisfaction surveys, participation rates in co-creation sessions, and frequency of interactions help measure this aspect, which directly correlates with the ecosystem's health and sustainability (Jacobides, Cennamo, & Gawer, 2018).

Another critical KPI for ecosystem success is revenue and economic impact, which evaluates the financial performance generated through collaborative activities within the ecosystem. This KPI measures the total ecosystem revenue, revenue growth rate, and cost savings achieved through collaboration, providing insights into the economic value created for all participants (Teece, 2018). Furthermore, speed to market serves as an important performance indicator, reflecting how quickly new ideas can be developed and commercialized within the ecosystem. Reductions in development cycle times and faster market entries demonstrate the ecosystem's agility and responsiveness to market demands, which are crucial for maintaining a competitive edge (Iansiti & Levien, 2004). Finally, knowledge sharing and collaboration intensity are vital KPIs that assess the extent of knowledge exchange among participants, which drives collective problem-solving and innovation. By monitoring these KPIs, leaders can ensure that the ecosystem remains vibrant, adaptive, and aligned with its strategic goals, thereby maximizing its overall success.

9.2 Methods for Assessing Value Creation and Ecosystem Health

Assessing value creation and ecosystem health in Collaborative Business Ecosystems (CBEs) requires a multifaceted approach that captures both quantitative and qualitative dimensions. One commonly used method is the Balanced Scorecard, which evaluates ecosystem performance across financial, customer, internal processes, and learning and growth perspectives (Kaplan & Norton, 1996). This approach helps identify how well the ecosystem is meeting its strategic objectives and creating value for all stakeholders. In the context of CBEs, the Balanced Scorecard can be adapted to include ecosystem-specific metrics such as partner engagement, co-innovation outputs, and speed-to-market for new solutions. Another method is Network Analysis, which examines the structure, connections, and dynamics within the ecosystem to assess the intensity and quality of interactions among participants (Adner, 2017). Network Analysis provides insights into collaboration patterns, identifies key influencers within the ecosystem, and reveals potential bottlenecks or areas of underutilization, thus offering a clear view of ecosystem health and resilience.

In addition to quantitative methods, qualitative assessments play a crucial role in evaluating ecosystem value creation and health. Case Studies and Expert Evaluations are widely used to capture the nuances of collaboration, governance, and cultural alignment within ecosystems (Autio & Thomas, 2014). These methods involve in-depth interviews, surveys, and participatory observations, which provide rich insights into how value is co-created, shared, and perceived by participants. For example, ecosystem health can be gauged through Sentiment Analysis of stakeholder communications and feedback, which reveals underlying issues such as trust, satisfaction, and alignment with the ecosystem's goals (Rong et al., 2015). Furthermore, Ecosystem Maturity Models, which assess the lifecycle stage of the ecosystem based on criteria such as strategic alignment, technology integration, and participant diversity, can help identify growth opportunities and areas requiring strategic intervention (Moore, 2006). These combined assessment methods provide a comprehensive understanding of both the tangible and intangible aspects of value creation and the overall health of CBEs, guiding ecosystem leaders in making informed decisions for continuous improvement.

10. FUTURE TRENDS IN COLLABORATIVE BUSINESS ECOSYSTEMS

As Collaborative Business Ecosystems (CBEs) continue to evolve, several future trends are expected to significantly shape their development and impact. Increased Integration of Advanced Technologies is one such trend, with ecosystems increasingly leveraging artificial intelligence (AI), blockchain, and Internet of Things (IoT) to enhance data sharing, automation, and transparency (Bresciani et al., 2020). These technologies are expected to streamline operations, improve decision-making, and facilitate real-time collaboration across diverse participants. Sustainability and Social Impact will also become more central to ecosystem strategies, driven by growing environmental concerns and stakeholder expectations (Elkington, 2018). Ecosystems will likely prioritize initiatives that promote circular economies, resource efficiency, and social responsibility, aligning with broader global sustainability goals. Additionally, Decentralized and Distributed Models will gain traction as organizations seek more resilient and flexible structures. Decentralized ecosystems, supported by technologies such as blockchain, enable greater autonomy and reduce reliance on centralized entities, thereby enhancing the agility and security of collaborative efforts (Tapscott & Tapscott, 2016). These trends reflect a shift towards more technologically advanced, sustainable, and resilient ecosystems, positioning CBEs at the forefront of future business innovation and collaboration

11. CONCLUSION

As businesses navigate an increasingly complex and interconnected world, collaboration emerges as a cornerstone of future success. The ability to forge effective partnerships and engage in collaborative ecosystems not only enhances innovation but also drives resilience and adaptability. Future business landscapes will be shaped by the seamless integration of diverse technologies, which necessitates coordinated efforts among industry players, technology providers, and stakeholders. The rise of digital platforms, advanced analytics, and decentralized models underscores the importance of collaborative approaches in unlocking new opportunities and addressing complex challenges. Furthermore, as sustainability and social impact become integral to business strategies, collaboration will be crucial in developing solutions that meet both economic and environmental goals. In essence, collaboration fosters a synergistic environment where resources, knowledge, and capabilities are pooled to create greater value and drive progress. Organizations that embrace collaborative strategies and build robust partnerships will not only thrive in the dynamic business environment but also lead the way in shaping a more innovative, sustainable, and resilient future.

The dynamics of Collaborative Business Ecosystems (CBEs) reveal that synergistic success is deeply rooted in the art of collaboration. Throughout this chapter, we have explored how CBEs harness the collective strengths of diverse stakeholders to drive innovation, efficiency, and value creation. By fostering an environment where shared resources, knowledge, and expertise converge, organizations can achieve outcomes that are far greater than the sum of their efforts. The interplay of strategic leadership, a supportive culture, and advanced technologies exemplifies the power of synergy in overcoming challenges and seizing opportunities within these ecosystems.

The evolution of CBEs highlights the critical role of dynamic interactions and continuous adaptation in sustaining long-term success. As businesses increasingly operate in interconnected and rapidly changing environments, the principles of collaboration will become even more pivotal. Future trends, such as the integration of cutting-edge technologies and a heightened focus on sustainability, will further shape the landscape of CBEs, presenting both opportunities and challenges. Ultimately, the ability to effectively navigate and leverage collaborative dynamics will determine an organization's capacity to innovate, grow, and thrive in a complex global marketplace. Embracing these principles and fostering a culture of collaboration will be essential for organizations aiming to excel and lead in the future business environment.

REFERENCES

Adner, R. (2017). Ecosystem as structure: An actionable construct for strategy. *Journal of Management*, 43(1), 39–58. DOI: 10.1177/0149206316678451

Adner, R., & Kapoor, R. (2010). Value creation in innovation ecosystems: How the structure of technological interdependence affects firm performance in new technology generations. *Strategic Management Journal*, 31(3), 306–333. DOI: 10.1002/smj.821

Austin, J. E., & Seitanidi, M. M. (2012). Collaborative value creation: A review of partnering between nonprofits and businesses. Part I: Value creation spectrum and collaboration stages. *Nonprofit and Voluntary Sector Quarterly*, 41(5), 726–758. DOI: 10.1177/0899764012450777

Autio, E., & Thomas, L. D. W. (2014). Innovation ecosystems: Implications for innovation management. In Dodgson, M., Gann, D. M., & Phillips, N. (Eds.), *The Oxford Handbook of Innovation Management* (pp. 204–228). Oxford University Press.

Benkler, Y. (2006). *The wealth of networks: How social production transforms markets and freedom*. Yale University Press.

Bogers, M., Chesbrough, H., & Moedas, C. (2018). Open innovation: Research, practices, and policies. *California Management Review*, 60(2), 5–16. DOI: 10.1177/0008125617745086

Bøllingtoft, A. (2019). The role of government in fostering collaborative ecosystems: Lessons from practice. *The Journal of Business Strategy*, 40(2), 22–30.

Bouncken, R. B., Clauss, T., & Fredrich, V. (2016). Product innovation through coopetition in alliances: Singular or plural governance? *Industrial Marketing Management*, 53, 77–90. DOI: 10.1016/j.indmarman.2015.11.011

Bresciani, S., Ferraris, A., & Bresciani, S. (2020). Artificial intelligence in collaborative ecosystems: Implications for business model innovation. *Journal of Business Research*, 114, 30–39.

Brynjolfsson, E., & McElheran, K. (2016). The rapid evolution of digital businesses: Digital transformation and data-driven decision making. *MIT Sloan Management Review*, 57(3), 1–7.

Chesbrough, H., & Appleyard, M. M. (2007). Open innovation and strategy. *California Management Review*, 50(1), 57–76. DOI: 10.2307/41166416

Contractor, F. J., Kumar, V., Kundu, S. K., & Pedersen, T. (2010). Revisiting the role of culture in MNC performance: The case of management practices. *Journal of International Business Studies*, 41(5), 852–875.

Davenport, T. H., & Harris, J. G. (2007). *Competing on analytics: The new science of winning*. Harvard Business Review Press.

Dhanaraj, C., & Parkhe, A. (2006). Orchestrating innovation networks. *Academy of Management Review*, 31(3), 659–669. DOI: 10.5465/amr.2006.21318923

Dyer, J. H., & Singh, H. (1998). The relational view: Cooperative strategy and sources of inter-organizational competitive advantage. *Academy of Management Review*, 23(4), 660–679. DOI: 10.2307/259056

Elkington, J. (2018). *The triple bottom line: Does it all add up?* Routledge.

Gawer, A., & Cusumano, M. A. (2014). Industry platforms and ecosystem innovation. *Journal of Product Innovation Management*, 31(3), 417–433. DOI: 10.1111/jpim.12105

GE. (2016). *Ecomagination: Strategy and impact report*. General Electric.

Gnyawali, D. R., & Park, B. J. (2011). Co-opetition between giants: Collaboration with competitors for technological innovation. *Research Policy*, 40(5), 650–663. DOI: 10.1016/j.respol.2011.01.009

Gulati, R. (2007). *Managing network resources: Alliances, affiliations, and other relational assets*. Oxford University Press. DOI: 10.1093/oso/9780199299355.001.0001

Gulati, R., Puranam, P., & Tushman, M. (2012). Meta-organization design: Rethinking design in inter-organizational and community contexts. *Strategic Management Journal*, 33(6), 571–586. DOI: 10.1002/smj.1975

Gulati, R., Wohlgezogen, F., & Zhelyazkov, P. (2012). The two facets of collaboration are cooperation and coordination in strategic alliances. *The Academy of Management Annals*, 6(1), 531–583. DOI: 10.5465/19416520.2012.691646

Huxham, C., & Vangen, S. (2013). *Managing to collaborate: The theory and practice of collaborative advantage*. Routledge. DOI: 10.4324/9780203010167

Iansiti, M., & Levien, R. (2004). Strategy as ecology. *Harvard Business Review*, 82(3), 68–78. PMID: 15029791

Jacobides, M. G., Cennamo, C., & Gawer, A. (2018). Towards a theory of ecosystems. *Strategic Management Journal*, 39(9), 2255–2276. DOI: 10.1002/smj.2904

Kaplan, R. S., & Norton, D. P. (1996). *The balanced scorecard: Translating strategy into action*. Harvard Business School Press.

Kim, Y. (2020). Managing supply chain disruptions with resilience strategies: A review and future research directions. *Journal of Business Logistics*, 41(2), 123–137.

Levy, P. (1997). *Collective intelligence: Mankind's emerging world in cyberspace*. Plenum Press.

Lusch, R. F., & Nambisan, S. (2015). Service innovation: A service-dominant logic perspective. *Management Information Systems Quarterly*, 39(1), 155–175. DOI: 10.25300/MISQ/2015/39.1.07

Madhok, A., & Keyhani, M. (2012). Acquisitions as a strategy for globalization: A review and theoretical integration. *Journal of International Business Studies*, 43(3), 234–259.

Moore, J. F. (1996). *The death of competition: Leadership and strategy in the age of business ecosystems*. Harper Business.

Moore, J. F. (2006). Business ecosystems and the view from the firm. *Antitrust Bulletin*, 51(1), 31–75. DOI: 10.1177/0003603X0605100103

Nambisan, S. (2018). Digital innovation and dynamic capabilities: How digital transformation shapes firms' dynamic capabilities. *Information Systems Research*, 29(2), 461–475.

Powell, W. W., & Grodal, S. (2005). Networks of innovators. In Fagerberg, J., Mowery, D. C., & Nelson, R. R. (Eds.), *The Oxford Handbook of Innovation* (pp. 56–85). Oxford University Press.

Provan, K. G., & Kenis, P. (2008). Modes of network governance: Structure, management, and effectiveness. *Journal of Public Administration: Research and Theory*, 18(2), 229–252. DOI: 10.1093/jopart/mum015

Ring, P. S., & Van de Ven, A. H. (1994). Developmental processes of cooperative interorganizational relationships. *Academy of Management Review*, 19(1), 90–118. DOI: 10.2307/258836

Rong, K., Hu, G., Lin, Y., Shi, Y., & Guo, L. (2015). Understanding business ecosystem using a 6C framework in Internet-of-Things-based sectors. *International Journal of Production Economics*, 159, 41–55. DOI: 10.1016/j.ijpe.2014.09.003

Schein, E. H. (2010). *Organizational culture and leadership* (4th ed.). Jossey-Bass.

Siemens. (2020). *MindSphere: The Industrial IoT as a service solution*. Siemens AG.

Tapscott, D., & Tapscott, A. (2016). *Blockchain revolution: How the technology behind Bitcoin is changing money, business, and the world*. Penguin.

Teece, D. J. (2018). Profiting from innovation in the digital economy: Enabling technologies, standards, and licensing models in the wireless world. *Research Policy*, 47(8), 1367–1387. DOI: 10.1016/j.respol.2017.01.015

Vanhaverbeke, W., & Chesbrough, H. W. (2014). A classification of open innovation and open business models. In H. Chesbrough, W. Vanhaverbeke, & J. West (Eds.), *New Frontiers in Open Innovation* (pp. 50-68). Oxford University Press. DOI: 10.1093/acprof:oso/9780199682461.003.0003

Westerman, G., Bonnet, D., & McAfee, A. (2014). *Leading digital: Turning technology into business transformation*. Harvard Business Review Press.

Whelan, E., & Fink, L. (2020). Collaborative business ecosystems: The dynamics of collective intelligence. *Journal of Business Research*, 116, 1–12.

Williamson, P. J., & De Meyer, A. (2012). Ecosystem advantage: How to successfully harness the power of partners. *California Management Review*, 55(1), 24–46. DOI: 10.1525/cmr.2012.55.1.24

Zeng, M., Xie, X., & Tam, C. M. (2010). Relationship between cooperation networks and innovation performance of SMEs. *Technovation*, 30(3), 181–194. DOI: 10.1016/j.technovation.2009.08.003

Zhu, L., & Zhou, Z. (2016). Blockchain technology and trust relationships in business: A literature review. *Journal of Business and Technology*, 9(2), 155–168.

APPENDIX

For a chapter on *Synergizing Success: The Dynamics of Collaborative Business Ecosystems*, the dissemination elements can include a variety of stakeholders and channels that will help share the insights and findings effectively. Some potential dissemination elements:

1. Target Audience Identification
    - Business Leaders and Executives: Key decision-makers interested in collaborative strategies.
    - Entrepreneurs and Startups: Individuals seeking insights on building or joining business ecosystems.
    - Academics and Researchers: Scholars studying business ecosystems, collaboration, and innovation.
    - Policymakers: Government officials and regulators interested in fostering collaborative business environments.
    - Industry Associations: Organizations that represent business interests and can facilitate wider outreach.
2. Channels for Dissemination
    - Academic Journals: Publishing in journals focusing on business, management, and innovation.
    - Conferences and Workshops: Presenting findings at industry and academic conferences.
    - Webinars and Online Workshops: Hosting interactive sessions to discuss collaborative business strategies.
    - Social Media Platforms: Sharing insights through LinkedIn, Twitter, and industry-specific forums to reach a broader audience.
    - Industry Reports: Creating reports or white papers that can be distributed through professional associations or think tanks.

Chapter 5
The Synergy of Sustainability, Intelligent Methods, and Smart Grid Applications

Latifa Dekhici
https://orcid.org/0000-0002-9581-6488
University of Sciences and Technology of Oran, Algeria & LDREI, Higher School of Electrical Engineering and Energetic, Oran, Algeria

Khaled Guerraiche
https://orcid.org/0000-0002-5980-3647
LDREI, Higher School of Electrical Engineering and Energetic, Oran, Algeria

Karima Belmabrouk
https://orcid.org/0000-0003-1157-1274
University of Sciences and Technology of Oran, Algeria

ABSTRACT

This chapter explores the convergence of sustainability, intelligent methods, and smart grids as a solution to the escalating energy demands and environmental concerns of the 21st century. It investigates how smart grids, empowered by machine learning, artificial intelligence, and other advanced techniques, can create a more efficient and environmentally friendly energy ecosystem. Key applications in load forecasting, demand management, renewable integration, and grid optimization are examined. The chapter acknowledges challenges like resource intensity and data privacy, advocating for robust regulations and responsible development to ensure equitable access to smart grid benefits. Ultimately, it presents a comprehensive

DOI: 10.4018/979-8-3693-7272-2.ch005

analysis of this synergy, aiming to equip readers with the knowledge to navigate the complexities of the energy landscape and build a sustainable energy future.

1. INTRODUCTION

The burgeoning energy demand of the 21st century poses an unprecedented challenge, necessitating a paradigm shift in energy production and distribution. The traditional grid, characterized by its centralized and inflexible nature, struggles to keep pace with the escalating demand while simultaneously addressing the mounting concerns of environmental degradation and resource depletion. In this critical juncture, the convergence of sustainability principles, advanced intelligent methods, and the transformative potential of smart grids offers a promising solution.

This chapter aims to investigate the interplay between sustainability, intelligent methods, and the applications of smart grids. Through a detailed exploration of these synergies, our objective is to uncover innovative solutions that not only enhance the efficiency of energy systems but also foster environmental sustainability. By examining the intersections of sustainability principles with the intelligent implementation of machine learning, artificial intelligence, multi-agent systems, and metaheuristics within smart grid applications, this chapter offers insights into the evolving paradigm of a greener and more sustainable energy ecosystem. The discussions encompass key areas such as load forecasting, demand-side management, renewable energy integration, grid optimization, fault detection, and the overarching principles of resilience and self-healing.

However, the strategy towards a truly sustainable energy future is not without its hurdles. The potential roadblocks associated with smart grid implementation is critically examined, including resource intensity, data privacy concerns, and technological obsolescence. A comprehensive approach is advocated that prioritizes robust regulatory frameworks, responsible technology development, and inclusive access to ensure that the benefits of smart grids reach all segments of society.

Ultimately, this chapter serves as a comprehensive treatise on the synergistic relationship between sustainability, intelligent methods, and smart grid applications. By dissecting this nexus, a knowledge to navigate the complexities of the energy landscape and foster the development of a resilient and sustainable energy future for generations to come is given.

In the following section, the smart grids are defined by their elements and their applications. In the third section, we presented how intelligent methods can be applied to smart grid load forecasting, demand management and optimization. In the fourth section presents why the smart grid is considered as a sustainable solution with different aspects. The last section before the conclusion presents the challenge of sustainability and smart grids.

2. SMART GRID

A smart grid refers to an advanced and modernized electrical grid that incorporates digital communication technology, sensors, automation, and intelligent control systems to enhance the efficiency, reliability, and sustainability of the electricity distribution and management process. The primary goal of a smart grid is to optimize the generation, distribution, and consumption of electrical power by leveraging real-time data and communication capabilities.

2.1. Smart Grid Elements

A smart grid is characterized by the following elements (Figure 1):

Figure 1. Smart grid elements

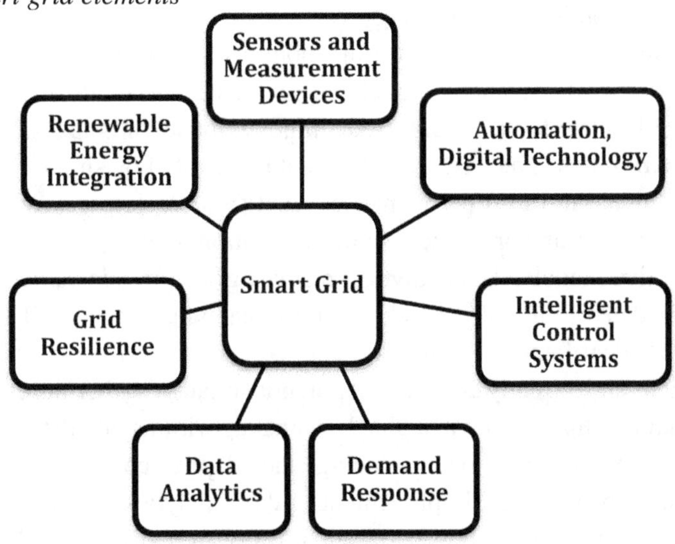

Digital Technology: Smart grids use digital communication technology to enable two-way communication between various components of the electrical grid, such as power plants, substations, and end-users.

Sensors and Measurement Devices: Smart grids are equipped with sensors and measurement devices that provide real-time data on electricity usage, system performance, and equipment status. This data helps in monitoring and managing the grid more efficiently.

Automation: Automation plays a crucial role in smart grids, allowing for the automated control and optimization of various grid functions. Automated systems can respond to changes in demand, detect and address faults, and reroute power to minimize disruptions.

Intelligent Control Systems: Smart grids utilize advanced control systems, often powered by artificial intelligence and machine learning, to make real-time decisions about grid operations. These systems can optimize energy distribution, predict potential issues, and adapt to changes in the grid environment.

Demand Response: Smart grids enable demand-response mechanisms, allowing consumers to adjust their electricity usage in response to real-time pricing or grid conditions. This helps in balancing supply and demand more effectively.

Renewable Energy Integration: Smart grids facilitate the integration of renewable energy sources, such as solar and wind power, by managing the variability and intermittency associated with these sources. This contributes to a more sustainable and environmentally friendly energy system.

Grid Resilience: Through real-time monitoring and automated response mechanisms, smart grids enhance the resilience of the electrical infrastructure. They can identify and isolate faults quickly, reducing the impact of outages.

Data Analytics: The vast amount of data generated by smart grids is analyzed to gain insights into grid performance, identify areas for improvement, enhance overall efficiency, and optimize resource allocation. Utilizing advanced algorithms and predictive models, data analytics in smart grids provide valuable information for informed decision-making and long-term planning. Additionally, data analytics enables the identification of trends, patterns, and anomalies, leading to proactive maintenance and the early detection of potential issues. Furthermore, the integration of artificial intelligence and machine learning algorithms into data analytics allows for advanced forecasting, load balancing, and adaptive control strategies. With the continuous expansion and improvement of data analytics capabilities, smart grids can unlock further operational efficiencies, enhance grid reliability, and enable effective utilization of renewable energy resources.

By incorporating these technologies and principles, smart grids aim to create a more adaptive, efficient, and sustainable electricity infrastructure that meets the evolving needs of modern society.

2.2. Smart Grid Applications

Smart grids have a wide range of applications that contribute to enhancing the efficiency, reliability, and sustainability of electrical power systems. Here are some key applications of smart grids:

Demand Response Management. Smart grids enable utilities to implement demand-response programs, allowing them to manage and control electricity consumption during peak demand periods. By incentivizing consumers to reduce or shift their electricity usage during peak times, demand response helps balance supply and demand, reducing the likelihood of blackouts and lowering operational costs.

Integration of Renewable Energy. Smart grids facilitate the integration of renewable energy sources, such as solar and wind power, by managing the variability and unpredictability of these sources. This application helps maximize the use of clean energy, reduces dependence on fossil fuels, and supports the transition to a more sustainable energy mix.

Grid Automation and Control. Smart grids employ automation and control systems to monitor and manage the electrical grid in real time. Automation improves grid reliability, identifies and isolates faults faster, and enables quicker responses to changes in grid conditions, ultimately reducing downtime and enhancing overall grid performance.

Advanced Metering Infrastructure (AMI). Smart grids incorporate AMI, which includes smart meters that provide real-time information on electricity consumption. AMI enhances billing accuracy, enables consumers to monitor and manage their energy usage, and supports dynamic pricing models to encourage efficient energy consumption.

Distribution System Monitoring and Optimization. Smart grids utilize sensors and monitoring devices to gather data on the performance of distribution systems. This application helps utilities identify and address issues in the distribution network proactively, optimizing the flow of electricity and minimizing losses.

Electric Vehicles (EV) Integration. Smart grids support the integration of electric vehicles by providing charging infrastructure and managing the increased demand for electricity. By coordinating the charging of electric vehicles during off-peak hours and optimizing grid resources, smart grids mitigate the impact of EV charging on the grid and support the growth of electric transportation.

Grid Resilience and Self-Healing. Smart grids enhance grid resilience by quickly detecting and isolating faults, minimizing the impact of disruptions. Self-healing capabilities reduce downtime, improve reliability, and contribute to the overall robustness of the electrical infrastructure.

Cybersecurity and Grid Security. Smart grids implement cybersecurity measures to protect against cyber threats and ensure the security of critical grid infrastructure. Robust cybersecurity safeguards the integrity and reliability of the grid, preventing unauthorized access and potential disruptions.

Data Analytics for Grid Optimization. Smart grids leverage data analytics to gain insights into grid performance, forecast demand, and optimize grid operations. Data-driven decision-making enhances efficiency, reduces operational costs, and supports continuous improvement in grid management.

Figure 2. Smart grid applications

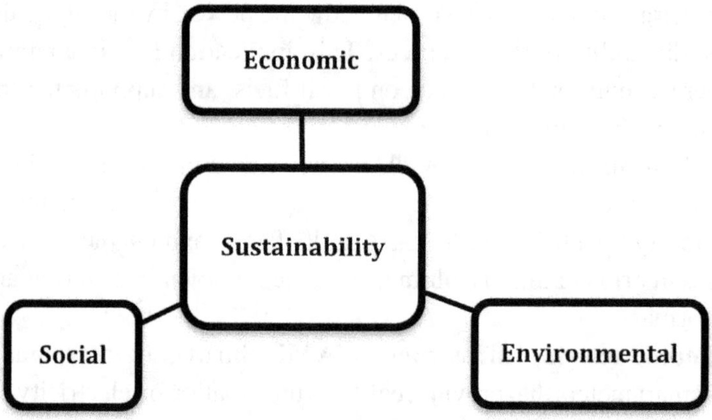

These applications (Figure 2) collectively contribute to the development of a more intelligent, responsive, and sustainable electrical grid system.

3. INTELLIGENT METHODS AND SMART GRID

Examining the connection between intelligent methods and smart grid applications, this section investigates how intelligent methods facilitate real-time data analysis, predictive modeling, and demand response in smart grid systems. By introducing intelligent methods, smart grid applications can enhance energy management and grid operations.

Enhancing smart grids with intelligent methods such as machine learning, multi-agent systems, and metaheuristics can significantly improve their efficiency, reliability, and overall performance. Here are several ways these intelligent methods can be applied to enhance smart grids:

3.1. Load Forecasting

Leveraging machine learning algorithms, specifically time-series forecasting models, enhances load forecasting within smart grids. This intelligent method allows utilities to predict electricity demand accurately. By doing so, they can optimize the allocation of resources, plan for peak demand periods, and ultimately improve the overall efficiency of the grid.

Many researchers were interested to this field(Ahmad et al. 2016, Hafeez et al. 2020, Li et al. 2020, Hong et al. 2020, Aly et al. 2020, Ibrahim et al. 2022). The integration of renewable energy sources and the increasing contribution of variable renewable energy to grid electricity have introduced unpredictable and variable load to the grid, posing challenges for load forecasting (De Santis & al. 2015), The traditional modeling, optimization, and control technologies have limitations in processing the data, highlighting the need for advanced artificial intelligence (AI) techniques in load forecasting for smart grids (Heider & al. 2022).

Khan et al.(2016) and Habbak et al. (2023) gave reviews of the application of machine learning in load forecasting. Haffez et al. (2021) proposed a dedicated framework.

3.2. Demand-Side Management

Smart grids benefit from the integration of AI and machine learning algorithms to analyze consumer behavior, predict load patterns, and optimize demand-side management strategies. These intelligent methods empower the implementation of efficient demand response programs, enabling better coordination and control of energy consumption. Consequently, this results in reduced peak demand, contributing to enhanced grid stability.

Demand-side management has become increasingly important for the stability of future smart grids, with the increasing development of communication infrastructure supporting the deployment of demand side management applications(Ronne, 2012). The proliferation of smart grid infrastructure, distributed generation, intermittent renewable energy sources, and energy storage devices has significantly affected DSM business models, emphasizing the need to create suitable business models for ensuring DSM sustainability(Kabeyi & al., 2022).The problem was also investigated by Jo et al.(2020),Wen et al. (2022), Puttamadappa et al.(2019), Mohamed et Mishra (2019) and khan et al. (2021).

Previous research can be found in some literature reviews of (Nasir et al.2021, Sarker et al. 2021, Iqbal et al.,2021).

3.3. Renewable Energy Integration

Machine learning, particularly for forecasting renewable energy production, coupled with AI-driven control systems, optimizes the integration of variable renewable sources into the grid. These intelligent methods enable accurate predictions of generation patterns, allowing for agile adjustments in grid operations to accommodate the variability inherent in renewable energy sources.

Tashtoush et al. (2023) performed a detailed review and comparison of methodologies for renewable energy integration in water desalination. Dang et al. (2023) extensively reviewed potential methodologies for integrating renewable energies with CO2 capture processes. Kataray et al. (2023) comprehensively reviewed methodologies and challenges associated with integrating smart grids and renewable energy sources.

3.4. Grid Optimization and Control

Utilizing multi-agent systems and AI-driven optimization algorithms enhances the coordination and optimization of various grid components. This includes generators, storage systems, and demand response programs. The application of these intelligent methods maximizes the efficiency and reliability of smart grid operations.

Many researchers were interested in optimizing energy flows and implementing robust control mechanisms, to improve operational efficiency of Grids. Lin et al. (2023) conducted stability analysis and optimization of control parameters for a multi-VSG parallel grid-connected system, emphasizing intelligent methods for enhanced system performance. Hasanien et al. (2023) employed the Gazelle optimization algorithm for optimal parameters estimation of lithium-ion batteries in smart grid applications, demonstrating the application of intelligent algorithms for battery management. Rahbari et al. (2024) focused on real-time modeling and optimization of molten salt storage using supercritical steam cycles, showcasing the integration of intelligent methods for sustainable power generation and grid support. Yin et al. (2023) utilized ensemble prediction and multi-objective co-design optimizations for grid-connected integrated renewables, showcasing the role of intelligent methods in optimizing green hydrogen production. Borin et al. (2024) introduced an automated test-driven design for robust optimized current control of GTIs, highlighting the application of intelligent methods for control optimization under varying grid conditions. Marlin and Jebaseelan (2024) conducted a comprehensive comparative study on intelligence-based optimization algorithms for maximum power tracking in grid-PV systems, offering insights into the effectiveness of different intelligent methods in solar energy systems.

3.5. Fault Detection and Diagnostics

Machine learning techniques for anomaly detection and fault diagnosis significantly improve the smart grid's resilience. By employing these intelligent methods, the system can detect abnormalities or faults in grid infrastructure early on, facilitating swift responses to minimize downtime and enhance overall grid reliability.

The application of artificial intelligence (AI) techniques, particularly machine learning, has been explored for fault detection in smart grids, demonstrating promising results in simulated environments (Behrangrad, 2015). Computational intelligence techniques, such as dissimilarity measure learning and clustering, have been successful in fault recognition in real-world power grids, offering a framework to aid human operators in understanding power grid status and making decisions on grid operations(Onu et al.,2023). In the literature, works show that diagnostics tools help in pinpointing the exact location and nature of a fault, facilitating faster and more accurate repairs. And in minimizing grids downtime.

Manservigi et al. (2022) proposed a diagnostic approach for fault detection and identification in district heating networks, emphasizing intelligent methods in fault diagnostics within energy systems. Similarly, Jose et al. (2023) addresse fault detection and diagnostics in the context of sparse multimodal data, specifically in hydrogenerators. Połok and Bilski's intelligent diagnostic system (2021) for rachet mechanism faults showcases the efficacy of acoustic analysis in fault detection. Kim and Braun (2020) developed a fault detection and diagnostics system based on integrated virtual sensors and fault impact models. Taheri et al. (2021) applied deep learning algorithms for fault detection and diagnostics in HVAC systems. Ogali and Orodu (2022) utilized capacitance-resistance models and diagnostic plots for fault characterization in flow barrier detection within petroleum engineering. Syed et al. (2020) worked on model-based fault detection and diagnostics in gas pipelines.

Singh et al (2022) and Zhang et al.(2021) presented reviews on fault detection, diagnostics, prognostics, and fault modeling in smart grid.

3.6. Energy Storage Optimization

AI algorithms play a crucial role in optimizing the charging and discharging cycles of energy storage systems. These intelligent methods maximize the effectiveness of energy storage solutions by dynamically managing storage operations based on real-time grid conditions and demand patterns. According to Pentakota and Kishore (2023), improving battery efficiency and lifespan involves optimizing charging cycles, and integrating AI and ML into battery management systems can enhance performance. Sensors collect data on voltage, current, and temperature, with AI focusing on battery health and ML on real-time optimization of charging and discharging. Evaluating the state of health (SOH) and state of charge (SOC) allows for proactive maintenance and extended battery life. These technologies promote sustainability, optimize energy use, and reduce costs, potentially revolutionizing energy storage systems.

3.7. Cybersecurity

Implementing AI-driven cybersecurity solutions, including machine learning for anomaly detection in network traffic, bolsters the security of smart grids. These intelligent methods actively detect and prevent cyber threats, ensuring the integrity and confidentiality of critical grid information.

Alaerjan et al (2024) propose a balanced integration of machine learning and deep learning algorithms to enhance SG stability. By using ensemble learning methods like voting and Dempster-Shafer, the study achieved 99.8% accuracy in predicting grid stability, outperforming other methods.

3.8. Predictive Maintenance

The utilization of machine learning in predicting equipment failures and maintenance requirements revolutionizes grid maintenance. It minimizes unavailability and prolongs grid component longevity by analyzing comprehensive data. This paradigm shift enhances grid reliability, optimizes performance, and saves costs. Utility companies can proactively address potential failures, preventing outages. Machine learning optimizes resource allocation, forecasts equipment conditions, and ensures uninterrupted operations.

Benefits include reduced costs, increased reliability, improved satisfaction, and reduced environmental impact (Mahmoud et al.2021)(Hoffmann et al.2020) .

3.9. Dynamic Pricing and Market Mechanisms

AI algorithms for dynamic pricing and multi-agent systems for market interactions revolutionize pricing strategies within smart grids. These intelligent methods facilitate dynamic pricing mechanisms based on real-time supply and demand conditions, encouraging efficient energy use and fostering dynamic market interactions.

Mahela et al (2022) review their applications in smart grid control, covering energy management, pricing, scheduling, reliability, security, fault handling, and communication, as well as integration with electrical vehicles and building energy systems.

3.10. Resilience and Self-Healing

Integrating AI-driven self-healing systems and multi-agent systems for adaptive responses enhances the resilience of smart grids. These intelligent methods automate responses to faults or disturbances, minimizing the impact on the overall system and contributing to a more resilient and reliable grid infrastructure.

Aziz et al. work (2023) introduced a self-healing restoration strategy for power grids, employing a two-stage adaptive decision-making approach to bolster grid resilience. AlKuwaiti et al. (2024) addressed power system resilience against climatic faults, utilizing conservative voltage reduction. Guo and Stan's study (2017) explored the implications of accelerated self-healing as a crucial design parameter for cross-layer resilience. Azizi et al. (2023) focused on robust island-mode operation in power distribution networks, utilizing game theory to reinforce power system resilience. Shittua et al. (2021) investigated meta-analysis offering a comprehensive overview of diverse methodologies and approaches to enhance overall power grid resilience.

In conclusion, the implementation of intelligent methods within smart grids marks a significant advancement in energy management, laying a strong foundation for sustainable practices. As smart grids evolve, integrating sustainability-focused strategies becomes essential to further enhance grid reliability while reducing environmental footprints. The following section will explore the intersection of sustainability and smart grids, emphasizing how intelligent methods contribute to a more eco-conscious and resource-efficient energy landscape.

4. THE SYNERGY BETWEEN SUSTAINABILITY AND SMART GRID APPLICATIONS

The applications of smart grids and their relationship with intelligent methods were seen in the previous sections. In this section, the sustainable aspects of these applications will be described.

4.1. Sustainability

Sustainability, in a general sense, refers to the ability of a system or process to endure and thrive over the long term while maintaining or improving its well-being and minimizing adverse environmental, social, and economic impacts (Khan et al., 2020). It encompasses a holistic approach to development that seeks to balance current needs with the preservation of resources and opportunities for future generations. Sustainability is often described in terms of three interconnected dimensions as shown in figure 3.

Figure 3. Sustainability in term of three interconnected dimensions

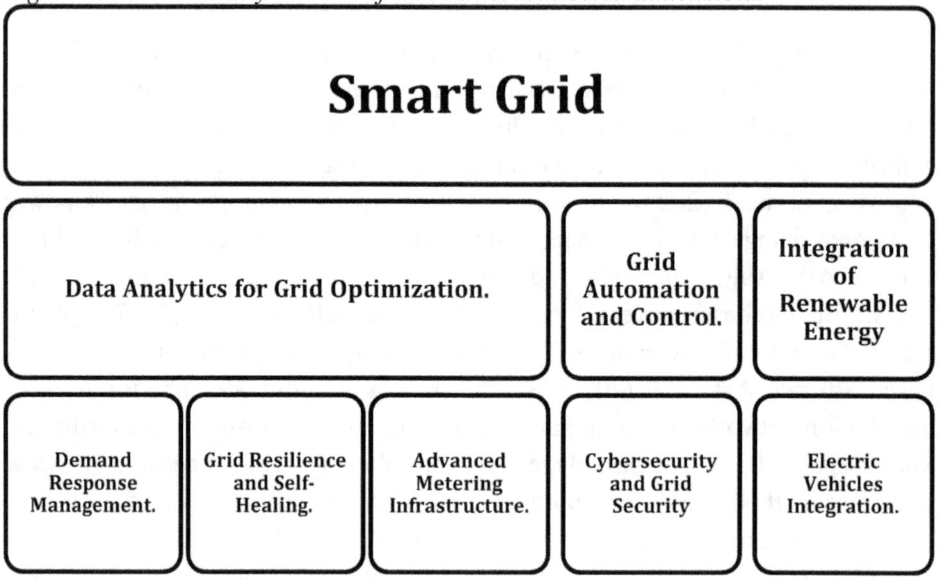

Environmental Sustainability. Focuses on the responsible management of natural resources and ecosystems to prevent environmental degradation. It involves practices that minimize pollution, reduce the consumption of non-renewable resources, and promote the use of renewable and clean energy sources. Environmental sustainability aims to maintain ecological balance and biodiversity (Jiaping Zhang et al., 2023; Dabbous et al., 2023).

Social Sustainability. Addresses the social aspects of development, ensuring that human well-being is prioritized (Schönborn et al., 2019). This includes promoting social equity, justice, and community resilience. Socially sustainable practices consider factors such as access to education, healthcare, and basic needs, as well as the preservation of cultural diversity and social cohesion.

Economic Sustainability. Involves creating economic systems that are viable in the long term, without depleting resources or causing harm to the environment. Economic sustainability includes fostering economic growth, creating jobs, and promoting fair trade practices. It aims to ensure that economic activities contribute to societal well-being without compromising future economic opportunities.

In addition to these three core dimensions, sustainability often involves the concept of the "triple bottom line," which considers economic, social, and environmental factors in decision-making. The idea is to achieve a balance that benefits people, the planet, and prosperity.

Principles and practices associated with sustainability include:

- Efficient Resource Use: Minimizing waste and optimizing the use of resources to reduce environmental impact.
- Renewable Energy: Promoting the use of clean and renewable energy sources to reduce dependence on finite fossil fuels.
- Social Equity: Ensuring fair and equitable distribution of resources, opportunities, and benefits within society.
- Conservation of Biodiversity: Preserving ecosystems and biodiversity to maintain the health of the planet.
- Resilience: Building systems that can withstand and recover from shocks, whether environmental, social, or economic.

Sustainability is a guiding principle in various fields (Xiaohui et al, 2023; Schaltegger et al, 2022), including environmental science, urban planning, business, and policymaking. The goal is to create a harmonious and balanced relationship between human activities (Zheng et al., 2021) and the natural environment, fostering a quality of life that is sustainable for current and future generations.

4.2. Sustainability in Smart Grid Context

In the context of smart grid applications, "sustainability" refers to the capacity of the energy practices and systems to endure and thrive over the long term while minimizing negative environmental impacts and supporting economic and social well-being. In the broader context of energy and the environment, sustainability involves balancing the current needs for energy with the preservation of resources and the ability of future generations to meet their own needs. Below is how sustainability is applied in the smart grid context:

- Minimizing negative impacts on the environment, such as reducing greenhouse gas emissions, minimizing pollution, and promoting the use of renewable energy sources. Smart grid applications aim to contribute to environmental sustainability by optimizing energy use and integrating cleaner, renewable energy into the grid.
- Ensuring the economic viability of energy systems in the long term. This includes optimizing resource utilization, reducing operational costs, and fostering economic growth through the development and implementation of smart grid technologies. Economic sustainability is closely tied to efficiency and cost-effectiveness in the energy sector.
- Addressing the social aspects of energy consumption, including equitable access to energy resources, job creation, and community well-being. Smart grid applications, by promoting efficient and reliable energy systems, can contrib-

ute to social sustainability by ensuring that energy resources are accessible to all and that the energy infrastructure supports the well-being of communities.

- Managing resources, such as fossil fuels and raw materials, in a manner that ensures their availability for future generations. Smart grid applications contribute to resource sustainability by optimizing energy use, reducing waste, and promoting the integration of renewable energy sources that are inherently more sustainable in the long run.
- Ensuring that the technologies used in energy systems are sustainable in terms of their lifecycle, energy efficiency, and environmental impact. Smart grid applications contribute to technological sustainability by leveraging advanced technologies for monitoring, control, and optimization, with a focus on long-term viability and efficiency.

Sustainability in the context of smart grids involves creating and maintaining energy systems that are environmentally responsible, economically viable, socially equitable, and technologically advanced, with a focus on meeting the needs of the present without compromising the ability of future generations to meet their own needs.

4.3. Smart Grid Contribution to Sustainability

Below the multifaceted contributions of smart grid applications in fostering sustainable energy practices are elucidated, emphasizing the pivotal roles of demand-side management, renewable energy integration, and grid optimization. The integration of sustainability principles with advanced smart grid applications serves as a foundational element for advocating the cultivation of a more environmentally conscientious and enduring energy ecosystem.

Additionally, smart grids support the development of a more decentralized energy system, empowering consumers to generate and sell their own electricity, thus fostering a more sustainable and participatory energy ecosystem. Ming et al. (2021) presented a critical review on sustainable techniques in electrical discharge machining offers insights into broader sustainable practices in electrical processes, potentially informing sustainable strategies within smart grid technologies. Jha (2023) addressed the intersection of cybersecurity and confidentiality in smart grids, emphasizing their role in enhancing sustainability and reliability. Pal and Shankar (2023) presented a hierarchical performance evaluation approach specifically designed for assessing the sustainability of smart grids, contributing to the ongoing discourse on optimizing the environmental impact of smart grid technologies. Rehan et al. (2023) focused on the sustainable use of biomass for electrical energy harvesting using distributed generation systems, providing a perspective on integrating renewable energy sources into smart grid frameworks. Ramprasad et al. (2022) explored strategies and options for the sustainable recovery of rare earth elements from electrical and electronic waste, contributing to the sustainable lifecycle management of components within smart grid systems. Nishat et al. (2023) presented the design and performance evaluation of an electrically heated concrete panel for sustainable winter maintenance. Trinh and Chung (2023) presented a review on renewable energy for sustainable electrical production and the global significance of integrating renewable sources into smart grids for achieving Sustainable Development Goal 7 (SDG-7) and promoting sustainable industrial applications.

Demand-Side Management and Renewable Energy Integration. Smart grid applications actively contribute to the realm of sustainability through Demand-Side Management and Renewable Energy Integration. By finely tuning energy consumption patterns through demand-side management and facilitating the harmonious integration of renewable sources, smart grid applications emerge as instrumental agents in the pursuit of sustainable energy practices. Smart grids enable the integration of renewable energy sources, such as solar and wind energy, for increased flexibility, resilience, and impact on grid stability and power quality (Omitaomu et al., 2021). The development of future smart grids requires the seamless integration of cutting-edge industrial advancements, flexible grid technologies, and sustainable energy infrastructure, emphasizing the role of smart grids in balancing energy supply and demand and the large-scale introduction of renewable energy sources(Mokhtari & al., 2024).

Together, Demand side management and renewable energy integration enable a more sustainable and resilient energy system. Karduri and Ananth (2023) contribute to the discourse on Sustainable Urban Energy, specifically integrating smart grids into smart cities. In a prior work (Karduri, 2018), Karduri investigated into the challenges and opportunities associated with integrating renewable energy into existing power systems. Oad et al.'s predictive analysis on green smart grids (2023) underscores the importance of intelligent methods in predicting and integrating sustainable energy, particularly emerging vehicle-to-grid (V2G) technologies, within the context of smart cities, showcasing for urban sustainability.

Grid Optimization for a Sustainable Energy Ecosystem. Building upon the antecedent discourse, this subsection accentuates the pivotal role of grid optimization as a linchpin in nurturing a more ecologically conscientious and sustainable energy ecosystem. Herein, the discussion expands on the intricacies of optimizing the electric grid, emphasizing its profound impact on minimizing environmental footprints and fostering sustainability. Through the meticulous optimization of grid operations, smart grid applications stand as architects of a greener, more resilient, and sustainable energy paradigm. Moreover, grid optimization facilitates the development of a more decentralized and flexible energy infrastructure, empowering consumers to actively participate in energy generation, storage, and consumption decisions. Renugadevi et al. (2023) contributed to the discourse on grid optimization for sustainability by introducing an IoT-based smart energy grid tailored for sustainable cities. Bandeiras et al. (2023) explored the energy trading markets within smart grid and microgrid systems.

5. SMART GRID AND SUSTAINABILITY CHALLENGE

While smart grids are designed to enhance sustainability by improving efficiency, reliability, and incorporating renewable energy, there can be situations or challenges that, if not addressed appropriately, might pose concerns or be perceived as contrary to sustainability principles. Here are a few situations where smart grids might face challenges in aligning with sustainability as shown in figure 4.

Figure 4. Smart grid and sustainability challenge

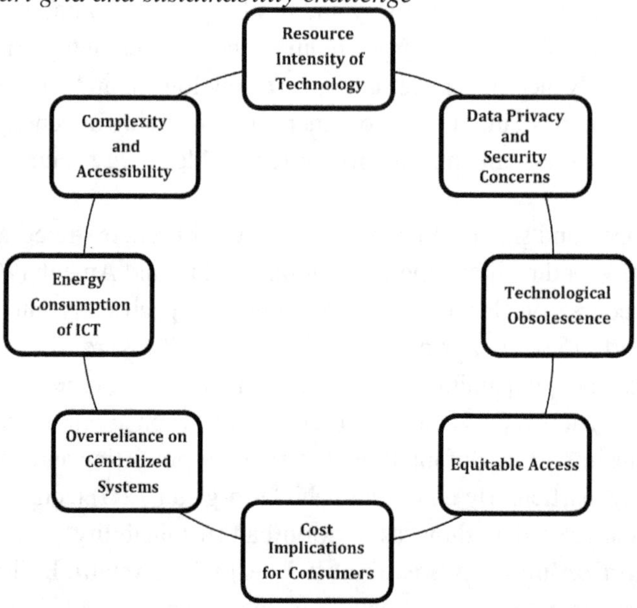

5.1. Resource Intensity of Technology

The production and disposal of smart grid technologies, including sensors, communication devices, and control systems, can have environmental impacts. If not managed sustainably, the resource intensity of these technologies may counteract their benefits.

5.2. Data Privacy and Security Concerns

Smart grids rely on extensive data collection and communication networks. If not adequately protected, there can be concerns about the privacy of consumer data and the vulnerability of the grid to cyber-attacks. Addressing these concerns is crucial for ensuring sustainability in terms of social and ethical considerations.

5.3. Technological Obsolescence

Rapid technological advancements may lead to the obsolescence of certain smart grid components, resulting in electronic waste. Managing electronic waste sustainably is essential to avoid environmental harm and maximize the lifecycle of technology.

5.4. Equitable Access

The deployment of smart grid technologies may initially concentrate in urban or affluent areas, potentially exacerbating existing social inequalities. Ensuring equitable access to the benefits of smart grids is essential for social sustainability.

5.5. Cost Implications for Consumers

The implementation costs of smart grid technologies may be significant. If the financial burden falls disproportionately on consumers, especially those with lower incomes, it could raise concerns about social and economic sustainability.

5.6. Complexity and Accessibility

The complexity of smart grid technologies may pose challenges for some communities or regions with limited resources or technical expertise. Ensuring accessibility and providing support for all users is critical for the inclusive and sustainable deployment of smart grids.

5.7. Energy Consumption of Information and Communication Technologies (ICT)

The energy consumption associated with the operation of communication networks, data centers, and other ICT infrastructure supporting smart grids may offset the energy savings achieved through grid optimization. Strategies to minimize the environmental impact of ICT components are essential for overall sustainability.

5.8. Overreliance on Centralized Systems

Some smart grid architectures may rely heavily on centralized control systems, which could be susceptible to systemic failures or attacks. Decentralized and distributed architectures might be more resilient and aligned with sustainability principles.

It's important to note that these challenges are not inherent to smart grids but represent potential pitfalls that need to be addressed through careful planning, regulation, and technology development. Proactive measures, including robust regulatory frameworks, stakeholder engagement, and ongoing assessment of environmental and social impacts, are crucial to ensure that smart grids contribute positively to sustainability.

6. CONCLUSION

The chapter summarizes key insights gained from exploring the link between sustainability, intelligent methods, and smart grid applications. In conclusion, it is clear that the smart grid, intelligent methods, and sustainability are interconnected in a remarkable and undeniable way. This harmonious relationship is of utmost importance and should be appreciated. This is due to the characteristics of smart grid as Digital Technology, Sensors and Measurement Devices, Automation and Grid Resilience.

However, it is vital to recognize that there are challenges that come with these innovative initiatives. For example, implementing smart grid technology in a way that is cost-effective and accessible for all communities is a significant challenge. Additionally, ensuring the security and privacy of data within the smart grid system is another obstacle that needs to be addressed.

Despite these challenges, the potential applications and benefits of these interconnected concepts are substantial and worth pursuing. It is essential to continue pushing forward with these initiatives while being mindful of the challenges and working to overcome them.

REFERENCES

Ahmad, A., Javaid, N., Guizani, M., Alrajeh, N., & Khan, Z. A. (2016). An accurate and fast converging short-term load forecasting model for industrial applications in a smart grid. *IEEE Transactions on Industrial Informatics*, 13(5), 2587–2596. DOI: 10.1109/TII.2016.2638322

Al-Emran, M. (2023). Beyond technology acceptance: Development and evaluation of technology-environmental, economic, and social sustainability theory. *Technology in Society*, 75, 102383. DOI: 10.1016/j.techsoc.2023.102383

Alaerjan, A., Jabeur, R., Ben Chikha, H., Karray, M., & Ksantini, M. (2024). Improvement of Smart Grid Stability Based on Artificial Intelligence with Fusion Methods. *Symmetry*, 2024(16), 459. DOI: 10.3390/sym16040459

AlKuwaiti, R. H., El-Sayed, W. T., Farag, H. E. Z., Al-Durra, A., & El-Saadany, E. F. (2024). Power system resilience against climatic faults: An optimized self-healing approach using conservative voltage reduction. *International Journal of Electrical Power & Energy Systems*, 155, 109519. DOI: 10.1016/j.ijepes.2023.109519

Aly, H. H. (2020). A proposed intelligent short-term load forecasting hybrid models of ANN, WNN and KF based on clustering techniques for smart grid. *Electric Power Systems Research*, 182, 106191. DOI: 10.1016/j.epsr.2019.106191

Arafat, M. Y., Hossain, M. J., & Alam, M. M. (2024). Machine learning scopes on microgrid predictive maintenance: Potential frameworks, challenges, and prospects. *Renewable & Sustainable Energy Reviews*, 190, 114088. DOI: 10.1016/j.rser.2023.114088

Aziz, T., Waseem, M., Liu, S., Ma, Y., Lin, Z., & Memon, Q.-U.-D. (2023). A self-healing restoration of power grid based on two-stage adaptive decision-making strategy to enhance grid resilience. *International Journal of Electrical Power & Energy Systems*, 154, 109435. DOI: 10.1016/j.ijepes.2023.109435

Azizi, A. A., Shamim, A. G., & Mosayebian, M. E. (2023). Robust island-mode operation of power distribution network using game theory for resilience enhancement, Sustainable Energy. *Grids and Networks*, 33, 100978.

Bandeiras, F., Gomes, Á., Gomes, M., & Coelho, P. (2023). Exploring Energy Trading Markets in Smart Grid and Microgrid Systems and Their Implications for Sustainability in Smart Cities. *Energies*, 16(2), 801. DOI: 10.3390/en16020801

Behrangrad, M. (2015). A review of demand side management business models in the electricity market. *Renewable & Sustainable Energy Reviews*, 47, 270–283. DOI: 10.1016/j.rser.2015.03.033

Borin, L. C., Hollweg, G. V., Osório, C. R. D., Carnielutti, F. M., Oliveira, R. C. L. F., & Montagner, V. F. (2024). Automated test-driven design for robust optimized current control of GTIs operating under normal and abnormal grid conditions. *Control Engineering Practice*, 143, 105790. DOI: 10.1016/j.conengprac.2023.105790

Chang, H.-W., Chang, T., Ling, Y. H., & Yang, Y.-L. (2023). Dynamical linkages between the Brent oil price and stock markets in BRICS using quantile connectedness approach. *Finance Research Letters*, 54, 103748. DOI: 10.1016/j.frl.2023.103748

Chen, J., & Zhang, J. (2023). Crude oil price shocks, volatility spillovers, and global systemic financial risk transmission mechanisms: Evidence from the stock and foreign exchange markets. *Resources Policy*, 85, 103875. DOI: 10.1016/j.resourpol.2023.103875

Dabbous, A., & Barakat, K. A. (2023). The road towards environmental sustainability: Investigating the role of information and communication technologies and green technology innovations. *Journal of Cleaner Production*, 432, 139826. DOI: 10.1016/j.jclepro.2023.139826

Dayo-Olupona, O., Genc, B., Celik, T., & Bada, S. (2023). Adoptable approaches to predictive maintenance in mining industry: An overview. *Resources Policy*, 86, 104291. DOI: 10.1016/j.resourpol.2023.104291

De Santis, E., Rizzi, A., Sadeghian, A., & Mascioli, F. M. F. (2015). A learning intelligent system for fault detection in Smart Grid by a One-Class Classification approach. Proceedings of the International Joint Conference on Neural Networks, 2015-September, Article 7280756. DOI: 10.1109/IJCNN.2015.7280756

Deng, H., Wang, J., Shao, Y., Zhou, Y., Cao, Y., Zhang, X., & Li, W. (2023). Optimization of configurations and scheduling of shared hybrid electric-hydrogen energy storages supporting to multi-microgrid system. *Journal of Energy Storage*, 74, 109420. DOI: 10.1016/j.est.2023.109420

Faquir, D., Chouliaras, N., Sofia, V., Olga, K., & Maglaras, L. (2021). Cybersecurity in smart grids, challenges and solutions. *AIMS Electronics and Electrical Engineering*, 5(1), 24–37.

Gong, Wong, Peng, Khamdamov, Albasher, Hoa, & Nhan. (2023). Exploring an interdisciplinary approach to sustainable economic development in resource-rich regions: An investigation of resource productivity, technological innovation, and ecosystem resilience, 87, 104294.

Gunduz, M. Z., & Das, R. (2020). Cyber-security on smart grid: Threats and potential solutions. *Computer Networks*, 169, 107094. DOI: 10.1016/j.comnet.2019.107094

Guo & Stan. (2017). Implications of accelerated self-healing as a key design knob for cross-layer resilience. Integration, the VLSI Journal, 56, 167-180.

Habbak, H., Mahmoud, M., Metwally, K., Fouda, M. M., & Ibrahem, M. I. (2023). Load forecasting techniques and their applications in smart grids. *Energies*, 16(3), 1480. DOI: 10.3390/en16031480

Hafeez, G., Alimgeer, K. S., & Khan, I. (2020). Electric load forecasting based on deep learning and optimized by heuristic algorithm in smart grid. *Applied Energy*, 269, 114915. DOI: 10.1016/j.apenergy.2020.114915

Hafeez, G., Khan, I., Jan, S., Shah, I. A., Khan, F. A., & Derhab, A. (2021). A novel hybrid load forecasting framework with intelligent feature engineering and optimization algorithm in smart grid. *Applied Energy*, 299, 117178. DOI: 10.1016/j.apenergy.2021.117178

Han, X., Li, J., & Zhang, Z. (2023). Dynamic game optimization control for shared energy storage in multiple application scenarios considering energy storage economy. *Applied Energy*, 350, 121801. DOI: 10.1016/j.apenergy.2023.121801

Hao, J., Yuan, J., Wu, D., Xu, W., & Li, J. (2023). A dynamic ensemble approach for multi-step price prediction: Empirical evidence from crude oil and shipping market. *Expert Systems with Applications*, 234, 121117. DOI: 10.1016/j.eswa.2023.121117

Hasanien, H. M., Alsaleh, I., Tostado-V'eliz, M., Alassaf, A., Alateeq, A., & Jurado, F. (2023). Optimal parameters estimation of lithium-ion battery in smart grid applications based on gazelle optimization algorithm. *Energy*, 285, 129509. DOI: 10.1016/j.energy.2023.129509

Heider, F., Jahic, A., Plenz, M., & Schulz, D. (2022). Extended residential power management interface for flexibility communication and uncertainty reduction for flexibility system operators. *Energies*, 15(4), 1257. Advance online publication. DOI: 10.3390/en15041257

Hoffmann, M. W., Wildermuth, S., Gitzel, R., Boyaci, A., Gebhardt, J., Kaul, H., Amihai, I., Forg, B., Suriyah, M., Leibfried, T., Stich, V., Hicking, J., Bremer, M., Kaminski, L., Beverungen, D., zur Heiden, P., & Tornede, T. (2020). Integration of novel sensors and machine learning for predictive maintenance in medium voltage switchgear to enable the energy and mobility revolutions. *Sensors (Basel)*, 20(7), 2099. DOI: 10.3390/s20072099 PMID: 32276442

Hong, Y., Zhou, Y., Li, Q., Xu, W., & Zheng, X. (2020). A deep learning method for short-term residential load forecasting in smart grid. *IEEE Access : Practical Innovations, Open Solutions*, 8, 55785–55797. DOI: 10.1109/ACCESS.2020.2981817

Hu, Y., Lang, C., Corbet, S., Hou, Y. G., & Oxley, L. (2023). Exploring the dynamic behaviour of commodity market tail risk connectedness during the negative WTI pricing event. *Energy Economics*, 125, 106829. DOI: 10.1016/j.eneco.2023.106829

Humbert, G., & Sciacovelli, A. (2024). Design of effective heat transfer structures for performance maximization of a closed thermochemical energy storage reactor through topology optimization. *Applied Thermal Engineering*, 239, 122146. DOI: 10.1016/j.applthermaleng.2023.122146

Hurtado, J., Salvati, D., Semola, R., Bosio, M., & Lomonaco, V. (2023). Continual learning for predictive maintenance: Overview and challenges. *Intelligent Systems with Applications*, 19, 200251. DOI: 10.1016/j.iswa.2023.200251

Ibrahim, B., Rabelo, L., Gutierrez-Franco, E., & Clavijo-Buritica, N. (2022). Machine learning for short-term load forecasting in smart grids. *Energies*, 15(21), 8079. DOI: 10.3390/en15218079

Iqbal, S., Sarfraz, M., Ayyub, M., Tariq, M., Chakrabortty, R. K., Ryan, M. J., & Alamri, B. (2021). A comprehensive review on residential demand side management strategies in smart grid environment. *Sustainability (Basel)*, 13(13), 7170. DOI: 10.3390/su13137170

Jha, R. K.Rahul Kumar Jha. (2023). Cybersecurity and Confidentiality in Smart Grid for Enhancing Sustainability and Reliability. *Recent Research Reviews Journal*, 2(2), 215–241. DOI: 10.36548/rrrj.2023.2.001

Jo, J., & Park, J. (2020). Demand-side management with shared energy storage system in smart grid. *IEEE Transactions on Smart Grid*, 11(5), 4466–4476. DOI: 10.1109/TSG.2020.2980318

Jose, S., Nguyen, K. T. P., Medjaher, K., Zemouri, R., Lévesque, M., & Tahan, A. (2023). Fault detection and diagnostics in the context of sparse multimodal data and expert knowledge assistance: Application to hydrogenerators. *Computers in Industry*, 151, 103983. DOI: 10.1016/j.compind.2023.103983

Kabeyi, M. J. B., & Olanrewaju, O. A. (2022). The use of smart grids in the energy transition. Proceedings - 30th Southern African Universities Power Engineering Conference, SAUPEC 2022. DOI: 10.1109/SAUPEC55179.2022.9730635

Karduri, R. K. (2018). Integrating Renewable Energy into Existing Power Systems: Challenges and Opportunities. International Journal of Advanced Research in Management Architecture Technology & Engineering.

Karduri, R. K. R., & Ananth, C. (2023). Sustainable Urban Energy: Integrating Smart Grids into Smart Cities. International Journal of Advanced Research In Basic Engineering Sciences and Technology, 10.

Khan, A. R., Mahmood, A., Safdar, A., Khan, Z. A., & Khan, N. A. (2016). Load forecasting, dynamic pricing and DSM in smart grid: A review. *Renewable & Sustainable Energy Reviews*, 54, 1311–1322. DOI: 10.1016/j.rser.2015.10.117

Khan, H. W., Usman, M., Hafeez, G., Albogamy, F. R., Khan, I., Shafiq, Z., & Alkhammash, H. I. (2021). Intelligent optimization framework for efficient demand-side management in renewable energy integrated smart grid. *IEEE Access : Practical Innovations, Open Solutions*, 9, 124235–124252. DOI: 10.1109/ACCESS.2021.3109136

Khan, S. A. R., Zhang, Y., Kumar, A., Zavadskas, E., & Streimikiene, D. (2020). Measuring the impact of renewable energy, public health expenditure, logistics, and environmental performance on sustainable economic growth. *Sustainable Development (Bradford)*, 28(4), 833–843. DOI: 10.1002/sd.2034

Kim, W., & Braun, J. E. (2020). Development, implementation, and evaluation of a fault detection and diagnostics system based on integrated virtual sensors and fault impact models. *Energy and Building*, 226, 110368. DOI: 10.1016/j.enbuild.2020.110368

Konstantinou, C., & Mohanty, S. P. (2020). Cybersecurity for the smart grid. *Computer*, 53(5), 10–12. DOI: 10.1109/MC.2020.2975901

Li, J., Deng, D., Zhao, J., Cai, D., Hu, W., Zhang, M., & Huang, Q. (2020). A novel hybrid short-term load forecasting method of smart grid using MLR and LSTM neural network. *IEEE Transactions on Industrial Informatics*, 17(4), 2443–2452. DOI: 10.1109/TII.2020.3000184

Lin, J., Liu, S., & Wang, G. (2023). Stability analysis and control parameter optimization of multi-VSG parallel grid-connected system. *Electric Power Systems Research*, 221, 109478. DOI: 10.1016/j.epsr.2023.109478

Lu, X., & Zhou, K. (2024). A distributionally robust optimization approach for optimal load dispatch of energy hub considering multiple energy storage units and demand response programs. *Journal of Energy Storage*, 78, 110085. DOI: 10.1016/j.est.2023.110085

Mahela, O. P., Khosravy, M., & Gupta, N. (2022). Comprehensive Overview of Multi-agent Systems for Controlling Smart Grids. *CSEE Journal of Power and Energy Systems*, 8(1), 115–131. DOI: 10.17775/CSEEJPES.2020.03390

Mahmoud, M. A., Md Nasir, N. R., Gurunathan, M., Raj, P., & Mostafa, S. A. (2021). The current state of the art in research on predictive maintenance in smart grid distribution network: Fault's types, causes, and prediction methods—A systematic review. *Energies*, 14(16), 5078. DOI: 10.3390/en14165078

Manservigi, L., Bahlawan, H., Losi, E., Morini, M., Spina, P. R., & Venturini, M. (2022). A diagnostic approach for fault detection and identification in district heating networks. *Energy*, 251, 123988. DOI: 10.1016/j.energy.2022.123988

Marlin, S. (2024). A comprehensive comparative study on intelligence based optimization algorithms used for maximum power tracking in grid-PV systems. *Sustainable Computing : Informatics and Systems*, 41, 100946. DOI: 10.1016/j.suscom.2023.100946

Mei, S., Tan, Q., Liu, Y., Trivedi, A., & Srinivasan, D. (2023). Optimal bidding strategy for virtual power plant participating in combined electricity and ancillary services market considering dynamic demand response price and integrated consumption satisfaction. *Energy*, 284, 128592. DOI: 10.1016/j.energy.2023.128592

Ming, W., Xie, Z., Ma, J., Du, J., Zhang, G., Cao, C., & Zhang, Y. (2021). Critical review on sustainable techniques in electrical discharge machining. *Journal of Manufacturing Processes*, 72, 375–399. DOI: 10.1016/j.jmapro.2021.10.035

Mohammad, N., & Mishra, Y. (2019). Demand-side management and demand response for smart grid. Smart grids and their communication systems, 197-231.

Mohammadi, F. (2021). Emerging challenges in smart grid cybersecurity enhancement: A review. *Energies*, 14(5), 1380. DOI: 10.3390/en14051380

Mokhtari, S., & Yen, K. K. (2024). False data injection attack detection, isolation, and identification in industrial control systems based on machine learning: Application in load frequency control. *Electronics (Basel)*, 13(16), 3239. Advance online publication. DOI: 10.3390/electronics13163239

Nasir, T., Bukhari, S. S. H., Raza, S., Munir, H. M., Abrar, M., Muqeet, H. A. U., Bhatti, K. L., Ro, J.-S., & Masroor, R. (2021). Recent challenges and methodologies in smart grid demand side management: State-of-the-art literature review. *Mathematical Problems in Engineering*, 2021, 1–16. DOI: 10.1155/2021/5821301

Nguyen, T. N., Liu, B. H., Nguyen, N. P., & Chou, J. T. (2020, June). Cyber security of smart grid: attacks and defenses. In ICC 2020-2020 IEEE International Conference on Communications (ICC) (pp. 1-6). IEEE. DOI: 10.1109/ICC40277.2020.9148850

Nishat, F. M., Chakraborty, R., Oh, H.-J., Yoo, D.-Y., Mohapoo, R., & Yeon, J. H. (2023). Design and performance evaluation of an electrically heated concrete panel for sustainable winter maintenance. *Developments in the Built Environment*, 16, 100259. DOI: 10.1016/j.dibe.2023.100259

Oad, A., Ahmad, H. G., Talpur, M. S. H., Zhao, C., & Pervez, A. (2023). Green smart grid predictive analysis to integrate sustainable energy of emerging V2G in smart city technologies. *Optik (Stuttgart)*, 272, 170146. DOI: 10.1016/j.ijleo.2022.170146

Ogali, O. I. O., & Orodu, O. D. (2022). Fault characterization and flow barrier detection using capacitance-resistance model and diagnostic plots. *Journal of Petroleum Science Engineering*, 209, 109817. DOI: 10.1016/j.petrol.2021.109817

Omitaomu, O. A., & Niu, H. (2021). Artificial intelligence techniques in smart grid: A survey. *Smart Cities*, 4(2), 548–568. DOI: 10.3390/smartcities4020029

Onu, P., Mbohwa, C., & Pradhan, A. (2023). Advancements, challenges, and recommendations for resilient and decarbonized future smart grids. International Conference on Electrical, Computer and Energy Technologies, ICECET 2023. . 2023.10389344DOI: 10.1109/ICECET58911.2023.10389344

Pal, C., & Shankar, R. (2023). A hierarchical performance evaluation approach for the sustainability of smart grid. *International Journal of Energy Sector Management*, 17(3), 569–594. DOI: 10.1108/IJESM-02-2022-0011

Połok, B., & Bilski, P. (2021). Intelligent diagnostic system for the rachet mechanism faults detection using acoustic analysis. *Measurement*, 183, 109637. DOI: 10.1016/j.measurement.2021.109637

Poyyamozhi, N., Senthil Kumar, S., & Ashok Kumar, R. (2024). An investigation into enhancing energy storage capacity of solar ponds integrated with nanoparticles through PCM coupling and RSM optimization. *Renewable Energy*, 221, 119733. DOI: 10.1016/j.renene.2023.119733

Puttamadappa, C., & Parameshachari, B. D. (2019). Demand side management of small scale loads in a smart grid using glow-worm swarm optimization technique. *Microprocessors and Microsystems*, 71, 102886. DOI: 10.1016/j.micpro.2019.102886

Qing, L., Abbas, J., Najam, H., Ma, X., & Dagestani, A. A. (2024). Investment in renewable energy and green financing and their role in achieving carbon-neutrality and economic sustainability: Insights from Asian region. *Renewable Energy*, 221, 119830. DOI: 10.1016/j.renene.2023.119830

Quang, D. V., Milani, D., & Abu Zahra, M. (2023). A review of potential routes to zero and negative emission technologies via the integration of renewable energies with CO2 capture processes. *International Journal of Greenhouse Gas Control*, 124, 103862. DOI: 10.1016/j.ijggc.2023.103862

Rahbari, H. R., Mando, M., & Arabkoohsar, A. (2024). Real-time modeling and optimization of molten salt storage with supercritical steam cycle for sustainable power generation and grid support. *Process Safety and Environmental Protection*, 182, 866–879. DOI: 10.1016/j.psep.2023.12.024

Ramprasad, C., Gwenzi, W., Chaukura, N., Izyan Wan Azelee, N., Upamali Rajapaksha, A., Naushad, M., & Rangabhashiyam, S. (2022). Strategies and options for the sustainable recovery of rare earth elements from electrical and electronic waste. *Chemical Engineering Journal*, 442, 135992. DOI: 10.1016/j.cej.2022.135992

Rehan, M., Raza, M. A., & Abro, A. G. (2023). A sustainable use of biomass for electrical energy harvesting using distributed generation systems. *Energy*, 278, 128036. DOI: 10.1016/j.energy.2023.128036

Ren, H., Gao, D., Ma, Z., Zhang, S., & Sun, Y. (2024). Data-driven surrogate optimization for deploying heterogeneous multi-energy storage to improve demand response performance at building cluster level. *Applied Energy*, 356, 122312. DOI: 10.1016/j.apenergy.2023.122312

Renugadevi, N., Saravanan, S., & Sudha, C. N. (2023). IoT based smart energy grid for sustainable cites. *Materials Today: Proceedings*, 81, 98–104. DOI: 10.1016/j.matpr.2021.02.270

Rønne, A. (2012). Smart grids and intelligent energy systems: A European perspective. In *Energy Networks and the Law*. Innovative Solutions in Changing Markets. DOI: 10.1093/acprof:oso/9780199645039.003.0008

Sarker, E., Halder, P., Seyedmahmoudian, M., Jamei, E., Horan, B., Mekhilef, S., & Stojcevski, A. (2021). Progress on the demand side management in smart grid and optimization approaches. *International Journal of Energy Research*, 45(1), 36–64. DOI: 10.1002/er.5631

Satish & Kishore. (2023). AI and ML for Intelligent Battery Management in the Age of Energy Efficiency. International Journal for Recent Developments in Science & Technology, 134-140.

Schaltegger, S., Christ, K. L., Wenzig, J., & Burritt, R. L. (2022). Corporate sustainability management accounting and multi-level links for sustainability–A systematic review. *International Journal of Management Reviews*, 24(4), 480–500. DOI: 10.1111/ijmr.12288

Schönborn, G., Berlin, C., Pinzone, M., Hanisch, C., Georgoulias, K., & Lanz, M. (2019). Why social sustainability counts: The impact of corporate social sustainability culture on financial success. *Sustainable Production and Consumption*, 17, 1–10. DOI: 10.1016/j.spc.2018.08.008

Shittua, E., Tibrewala, A., Kalla, S., & Wang, X. (2021). Meta-analysis of the strategies for self-healing and resilience in power systems. *Advances in Applied Energy*, 4, 100036. DOI: 10.1016/j.adapen.2021.100036

Singh, V., Mathur, J., & Bhatia, A. (2022). A comprehensive review: Fault detection, diagnostics, prognostics, and fault modeling in HVAC systems. *International Journal of Refrigeration*, 144, 283–295. DOI: 10.1016/j.ijrefrig.2022.08.017

Subhan, M., Irfan, M., Pan, X., Ahmad, G., Naeem, M. H., & Zamir, M. N. (2024). Unveiling the dynamic impact of energy generation on economic sustainability in Canada: A roadmap towards sustainable development. *Journal of Cleaner Production*, 434, 139783. DOI: 10.1016/j.jclepro.2023.139783

Syed, M. M., Lemma, T. A., Vandrangi, S. K., & Ofei, T. N. (2020). Recent developments in model-based fault detection and diagnostics of gas pipelines under transient conditions. *Journal of Natural Gas Science and Engineering*, 83, 103550. DOI: 10.1016/j.jngse.2020.103550

Taheri, S., Ahmadi, A., Mohammadi-Ivatloo, B., & Asadi, S. (2021). Fault detection diagnostic for HVAC systems via deep learning algorithms. *Energy and Building*, 250, 111275. DOI: 10.1016/j.enbuild.2021.111275

Tarun Kataray, B. (2023). Integration of smart grid with renewable energy sources: Opportunities and challenges – A comprehensive review. *Sustainable Energy Technologies and Assessments*, 58, 103363. DOI: 10.1016/j.seta.2023.103363

Tashtoush, B., Wa'ed, A., Al Ghadi, M., Al-Omari, J., & Morosuk, T. (2023). Renewable energy integration in water desalination: State-of-the-art review and comparative analysis. *Applied Energy*, 352, 121950. DOI: 10.1016/j.apenergy.2023.121950

Trinh, V. L., & Chung, C. K. (2023). Renewable energy for SDG-7 and sustainable electrical production, integration, industrial application, and globalization. *Cleaner Engineering and Technology*, 15, 100657. DOI: 10.1016/j.clet.2023.100657

Tufail, S., Parvez, I., Batool, S., & Sarwat, A. (2021). A survey on cybersecurity challenges, detection, and mitigation techniques for the smart grid. *Energies*, 14(18), 5894. DOI: 10.3390/en14185894

Ustun, T. S., & Hussain, S. S. (2019, November). A review of cybersecurity issues in smartgrid communication networks. In *2019 International Conference on Power Electronics, Control and Automation (ICPECA)* (pp. 1-6). IEEE. DOI: 10.1109/ICPECA47973.2019.8975629

Wang, W., Kang, K., Sun, G., & Xiao, L. (2023). Configuration optimization of energy storage and economic improvement for household photovoltaic system considering multiple scenarios. *Journal of Energy Storage*, 67, 107631. DOI: 10.1016/j.est.2023.107631

Wang, X., Wang, X., Shi, Y., Wu, D., Ma, L., & Huang, M. (2023). Core-selecting auction-based mechanisms for service function chain provisioning and pricing in NFV markets. *Computer Networks*, 222, 109557. DOI: 10.1016/j.comnet.2023.109557

Wen, L., Zhou, K., Feng, W., & Yang, S. (2022). Demand side management in smart grid: A dynamic-price-based demand response model. *IEEE Transactions on Engineering Management*.

Yan, W., Shi, Y., Ji, Z., Sui, Y., Tian, Z., Wang, W., & Cao, Q. (2023). Intelligent predictive maintenance of hydraulic systems based on virtual knowledge graph. *Engineering Applications of Artificial Intelligence*, 126, 106798. DOI: 10.1016/j.engappai.2023.106798

Yin, X., Zhao, Z., & Yang, W. (2023). Ensemble prediction aided multi-objective co-design optimizations of grid-connected integrated renewables for green hydrogen production. *Journal of Cleaner Production*, 425, 138585. DOI: 10.1016/j.jclepro.2023.138585

Zhang, J., & Gong, X. (2023). From clicks to change: The role of Internet use in fostering environmental sustainability awareness. *Journal of Environmental Management*, 348, 119275. DOI: 10.1016/j.jenvman.2023.119275 PMID: 37827071

Zhang, L., Leach, M., Bae, Y., Cui, B., Bhattacharya, S., Lee, S., Im, P., Adetola, V., Vrabie, D., & Kuruganti, T. (2021). Sensor impact evaluation and verification for fault detection and diagnostics in building energy systems: A review. *Advances in Applied Energy*, 3, 100055. DOI: 10.1016/j.adapen.2021.100055

Zhang, Z., Cheng, X., Xing, Z., & Wang, Z. (2024). Energy management strategy optimization for hybrid energy storage system of tram based on competitive particle swarm algorithms. *Journal of Energy Storage*, 75, 109698. DOI: 10.1016/j.est.2023.109698

Zheng, X., Wang, R., Hoekstra, A. Y., Krol, M. S., Zhang, Y., Guo, K., & Wang, C. (2021). Consideration of culture is vital if we are to achieve the Sustainable Development Goals. *One Earth*, 4(2), 307–319. DOI: 10.1016/j.oneear.2021.01.012

Zhong, D., Xia, Z., Zhu, Y., & Duan, J. (2023). Overview of predictive maintenance based on digital twin technology. *Heliyon*, 9(4), e14534. DOI: 10.1016/j.heliyon.2023.e14534 PMID: 37025897

Zhuang, P., Zamir, T., & Liang, H. (2020). Blockchain for cybersecurity in smart grid: A comprehensive survey. *IEEE Transactions on Industrial Informatics*, 17(1), 3–19. DOI: 10.1109/TII.2020.2998479

Chapter 6
Collective Intelligence Approach for New Mobility

Hugo Pérez-Moure
https://orcid.org/0000-0002-2233-0057
University of Vigo, Spain

Jesus F. Lampón
https://orcid.org/0000-0001-9267-4448
University of Vigo, Spain

Pablo Cabanelas
https://orcid.org/0000-0002-4661-0141
University of Vigo, Spain

ABSTRACT

This chapter examines how collective intelligence is transforming the mobility industry into the era of "new mobility." Collective intelligence—the collaborative problem-solving and knowledge-sharing of groups—is reshaping traditional paradigms, business models, and global value chains (GVCs). Furthermore, this explores new business models emerging from digitalization and collective intelligence, such as mobility as a service (MaaS) and car-sharing platforms. The shift from traditional mobility to new mobility that emphasizes alternative energy sources, sustainability, connectivity, and user-centric services, is driven by advancements in electric vehicles (EVs), connected and autonomous vehicles (CAVs), digital platforms, big data, and artificial intelligence. Collective intelligence is redefining relationships within the mobility value chain, moving from OEM-dominated hierarchies to collaborative networks involving diverse stakeholders like tech companies and public entities.

DOI: 10.4018/979-8-3693-7272-2.ch006

This necessitates shared knowledge, data exchange, and cooperative innovation.

INTRODUCTION

As highlighted in the preceding chapters, the burgeoning significance of collective intelligence permeates various sectors, profoundly influencing their dynamics. Among these sectors, the mobility domain emerged as a focal point, warranting dedicated consideration within the pages of this book. The mobility industry, a linchpin of numerous countries, has received attention because of its strategic importance. It attracts substantial investments and is a primary arena for research and development endeavors. Remarkably, it has ascended to the pinnacle as the foremost sector in Europe and claims a significant standing globally, ranking second and, in some instances, third, depending on the country. However, delving into discussions concerning the interplay of collective intelligence within this industry needs nuanced comprehension. Thus, a comprehensive exploration of the underlying dynamics is imperative to unravel the intricacies shaping the nexus between the mobility industry, resilience and collective intelligence.

Resilience plays a critical role in the ongoing transformation of the mobility industry. In an environment characterized by rapid technological advancements, shifting business models, and the increasing integration of digital solutions, companies must demonstrate the ability to adapt and thrive amid constant change (Dahles & Susilowati, 2015). Resilience in this context refers to the capacity of businesses, especially traditional OEMs, to adjust their strategies, operations, and collaborations in response to disruptions while maintaining their competitiveness (Saad et al., 2021). The collective intelligence fostered through collaboration within the mobility sector not only drives innovation but also enhances resilience by enabling companies to pool resources, knowledge, and expertise. This collective approach allows businesses to respond more flexibly to market shifts and challenges, ensuring they can withstand and recover from potential disruptions, while continuing to evolve in line with the demands of the new mobility paradigm (Adekola & Clelland, 2019).

Collective intelligence is understood as the ability of a group, community, or ref to solve problems, make decisions, share and create knowledge by working together. That is, collective intelligence focuses on how different members (in this case companies) of a group (in this case industry) contribute to achieving a common goal by taking advantage of the different skills, knowledge, and experiences of each one, allowing for results: more creativeness, efficiency, and flexibility (Leimester, 2010). Therefore, it is based on relationships and collaboration between different members. Applied to a business context, members do not have to be companies. However, they can also be public agents if they focus on the same context and collaborate with the idea of a common goal by getting actively involved (Boder, 2006).

The mobility Industry and its intricate context constitute a multifaceted landscape comprising various interconnected components, each of which deserves meticulous attention. The term "new mobility" is pivotal in comprehending this industry's contemporary horizon and elucidating the profound relevance of collective intelligence within its framework (Kamargianni et al., 2016). Contrary to the conventional imagery associated with the mobility industry, typified by assembly lines, the present landscape is notably more complex and characterized by what is now recognized as the Global Value Chain (GVC) (Yi, 2003).

The GVC paradigm signifies a transformative shift, delineating a scenario where diverse segments and activities in the vehicle manufacturing process are dispersed, with distinct entities overseeing specific facets in different geographical locations. This intricate interplay has given rise to elaborate interactions and ecosystems that necessitate collaborative efforts among companies (Boder, 2006; Lampón, 2020). Furthermore, the confluence of new Mobility, GVC, and the escalating wave of digitalization has catalyzed the emergence of innovative and collective new business models. These business models are driven by increasing digitalization and the irruption of newcomers from other industries for its development, generating different streams of collective intelligence within this industry (Jung & Gómez-Bengoechea, 2022).

Previously, a singular company, the Original Equipment Manufacturer (OEM), traditionally spearheaded and controlled all facets of manufacturing and development processes. This centralized governance model underwent a significant transformation. By leveraging the power of collective intelligence, numerous enterprises now collaborate with OEMs to craft and generate new business models (Sturgeon et al., 2008; Yi, 2003). Consequently, understanding the paradigm shift in new Mobility, extended to encompass new business models, the Global Value Chain, and overarching mobility ecosystems, becomes complete with a robust comprehension of the intricate dynamics introduced by collective intelligence (Lampón et al., 2024).

This chapter embarks on an exploratory examination of the relationship between collective intelligence and the mobility landscape. It presents a structured narrative that commences with a thorough definition and evolution of the new Mobility concept, followed by an analysis of its transformative journey and projections. Subsequently, an in-depth examination of the mobility value chain is conducted, employing a dual perspective of traditional and emerging sectors and the impact of collective intelligence on them.

The chapter then delves into the wide-ranging implications of collective intelligence for various stakeholders in the mobility ecosystem, highlighting its transformative effects on established players and new entrants. Subsequently, the exploration extends to the complex interplay between collective intelligence and emerging business models, elucidating how this dynamic force alters conventional paradigms and stimulates innovation. The chapter concludes with two instructive case studies illustrating how collective intelligence shapes leading automakers' strategies, operations, and future trajectories. Overall, this chapter serves as an academic investigation of the intersection between collective intelligence and Mobility, providing an empirically informed understanding of the profound changes occurring in the mobility landscape.

THE NEW MOBILITY

The field of Mobility is undergoing a period of disruptive change, characterized by the emergence of new power structures, business models, and alliances that were once considered unthinkable. It is essential to understand what "new mobility" represents to navigate this dynamic landscape and comprehend the role of collective intelligence in shaping the future of Mobility. It involves exploring its origins, foundations, and growing importance. Therefore, before delving into the broader paradigm of "new mobility," it is necessary to examine the fundamental concept of "mobility" (Pérez-Moure et al., 2023a)

Firstly, it is essential to acknowledge the diverse forms that the concept of Mobility takes today. While traditional transportation-related Mobility has been a constant for centuries, the term now encompasses dimensions such as labor, social, human, digital, and spatial Mobility. However, in the context of this chapter, the focus is specifically on Mobility from a transportation perspective. Secondly, despite the relative recentness of some forms of Mobility, transportation-related Mobility has been a consistent feature throughout history. Therefore, Mobility refers to the ability of people or goods to move from one place to another using transportation.

This concept encompasses many modalities, including public transport, air mobility, micro-mobility (bicycles or scooters), pedestrians, and urban planning. Despite the diverse forms of Mobility and recognizing its importance in social and technological evolution, this chapter will primarily focus on automotive Mobility (Medina et al., 2022). Due to its prominent position as a leading sector where significant innovations occur, collective intelligence plays a key role.

Mobility is defined by the need to move, which has been fulfilled throughout history and has evolved. As a result, the concept of Mobility is highly dynamic and reaches its pinnacle with the advent of the combustion engine and the mass production of vehicles. Initially, large manufacturers (e.g., Stellantis, Toyota, Volkswagen, and Honda), known as Original Equipment Manufacturers (OEMs), met the need for transportation through innovation. However, recent disruptive changes have the potential to alter the mobility landscape, primarily driven by two significant phenomena: the emergence of alternative energy sources for vehicle propulsion and the growing digitalization that has impacted all industries, especially in the field of Mobility (Lampón et al., 2022). This digitalization extends beyond the production of vehicles and profoundly impacts collective intelligence, which is a critical enabler in the transformation of the current mobility paradigm.

The traditional paradigm of Mobility, characterized by internal combustion engines, places a secondary emphasis on accessibility and sustainability. This approach is limited regarding vehicle connectivity and focuses primarily on the vehicle itself rather than the people or services it could provide.

This paradigm has significant implications for infrastructure and the fundamental perception of Mobility. In contrast, the new paradigm of Mobility emphasizes a diversity of energy sources, including electricity, hydrogen, and gas, and places a greater focus on sustainability and accessibility. Technology is fundamental in this approach, enabling real-time vehicle connectivity and facilitating interaction between vehicles and other infrastructures.

This shift in perspective places people and services at the center of Mobility, giving rise to new forms of economy, such as the sharing economy, in which more accessible and shared models replace traditional vehicle ownership. In this new context, Mobility is no longer defined by individual vehicle ownership. However, it is transformed into a dynamic service that adapts to the changing needs of people (Pérez-Moure et al., 2023b).

Table 1. Comparison between traditional Mobility and New Mobility.

	Traditional mobility	New mobility
Fuel type	Based on fossil fuels and internal combustion engines.	Based on alternative energies such as electricity or hydrogen.
Focus	On the vehicle (product).	On the user (service).
Sustainability	Low importance.	It plays a fundamental role and influences other aspects of our business.
Technology	Traditional product/process production technology.	Inclusion of new mobility technologies, i.e.: apps, intelligent traffic management...
Connectivity	Vehicle not connected.	Highly connected vehicle that generates, captures and processes data.
Ownership	Own car.	Gradually the car as a personal asset disappears.
Accessibility	Privatized and less accessible mobility.	Increased accessibility through multi-modality and carpooling.
Infrastructures	They are not key.	They are key; connected to all elements of mobility.
Types of economy	Traditional economy.	Emergence of new types of economy such as the share-economy.

Source: Own elaboration.

The realm of New Mobility, characterized by its high degree of innovation, encompasses cutting-edge technologies such as artificial intelligence, big data, autonomous driving, data management platforms, and in-vehicle communication. The substantial data traffic generated by vehicles across diverse industries requires collective intelligence through higher coordination among value chain participants, detailed knowledge transfer processes, and ex-ante-defined procedures. This dynamic gives rise to novel business models and engages a spectrum of new stakeholders, integrating new perspectives and approaches to problems.

Concepts integral to this paradigm, including Electric Vehicles (EVs), Connected and Autonomous Vehicles (CAVs), over-the-air updates, and vehicle-to-everything communication (V2X, encompassing V2V for vehicle-to-vehicle, V2I for vehicle-to-infrastructure, and V2P for vehicle-to-pedestrian), have assumed paramount importance in shaping this new mobility landscape. Within this milieu, collective intelligence emerges as a critical force, orchestrating the convergence of these technological advancements and shaping the future trajectory of Mobility (Leminen et al., 2022).

THE GLOBAL VALUE CHAIN

The GVC encompasses all the various activities different parties undertake to bring a product or service from its inception to its final consumption. The GVC can be studied from two different perspectives. On the one hand, the relationship view. On the other hand, the unique distribution view. Therefore, the configuration of the GVC in a particular industry is determined by two main components: the allocation of value across the chain and the key actors who execute those activities (Sturgeon et al., 2008). So, the GVC approach examines the connections and interactions among specialized actors in various segments of a global value chain (Yi, 2003; Sturgeon et al., 2008) and the distribution of the critical activities. Concepts such as subcontracting, cooperation, and fragmentation of the value chain have become central elements in GVC analysis, involving specialized actors and how they cooperate and exchange knowledge.

The GVC approach has mainly been employed to examine the conventional value chain of the automotive industry (Sturgeon et al., 2008; Lampón et al., 2018). Studies have mainly focused on the product (vehicle) and scrutinized the structure of its associated production network, including components, modules, and systems, as well as the manufacturing processes utilized in building the vehicle (Sturgeon et al., 2008). The connections between OEMs and their suppliers are also assessed (Lampón et al., 2022).

The GVC concept, when considered within the context of collective intelligence, gains a collaborative dimension. The diverse activities involved in bringing a product to market are interconnected and depend on specialized actors' collective knowledge and cooperation throughout the chain. Both the relationship and spatial distribution views within the GVC adhere to the principles of collective intelligence, where actors collaborate, share information, and contribute their expertise to optimize the entire value-creation process.

The emphasis on subcontracting, cooperation, and value chain segmentation in GVC analysis aligns with the idea that collective intelligence flourishes when various actors bring their unique skills and knowledge to the collaborative setting, resulting in a more efficient and innovative global value chain. Although the GVC approach has been widely used for analyzing value chains in the automotive industry, it can also be applied to examine collective intelligence.

In the conventional value chain, the OEMs significantly influence critical value-added activities, such as vehicle design and motorization. They also manage their suppliers through unequal power dynamics, setting the terms for various process aspects, including location, quality standards, and product design (Sturgeon et al., 2008). Then, the concentration of control and knowledge related to production and technology activities is high among a few leading multinational firms, including automobile manufacturers and Tier-1 suppliers (Lampón et al., 2016).

These leading firms have exercised control over an extended network of suppliers, with the capacity to decide upon the conditions of supply (Lampón et al., 2022). The value chain for this product (vehicle) is structured and focused on the vehicle itself and its modules, systems, and components. This arrangement has emerged from vertical disintegration and outsourcing, where component suppliers carry out a substantial portion of the activities organized hierarchically across different supply levels. So, as the vehicle was not connected and most of the added value was focused on the product, the concept of collective intelligence was limited, as a single company decided and organized the activities and efforts over the others. Therefore, the GVC is a dynamic structure that must be analyzed from different approaches to understand how it is evolving and how collective intelligence impacts and transforms it.

From Locals to Beyond Borders: The Importance and Evolution of the Mobility's GVC Spatial Organization

The focus of the new mobility value chain lies not only in the traditional product, i.e., the vehicle but on services related to digitalization and connectivity that require higher levels of collective intelligence, specifically in the post-production stage when the customer takes possession of the vehicle and when services can be offered. GVC approach demands a re-examination of the new mobility value chain, which includes an identification of the elements comprising the value chain (activities and actors), the dominant types of relationships in terms of control and dependence, and the distribution of power among actors (Yi, 2003; Sturgeon et al., 2008). Regarding activities, the GVC approach requires identifying those determining the value distribution along the chain (Sturgeon et al., 2008).

In this context, the primary activities would be the critical services and associated business models linked to digitalization and connectivity that provide value-added services to customers in the realm of new Mobility through collective intelligence processes. Relevant services mentioned in prior works include mobility solutions for connected, electric, and autonomous vehicles (Cabanelas et al., 2023), services based on digital platforms, services related to connectivity and data exchange, and car-sharing services (Athanaspoulou et al., 2019; Cabanelas et al., 2023; Mahmood, 2020). All these services are crucial to future scenarios and require higher levels of collective intelligence in new Mobility due to the interdisciplinary nature of the industry, as highlighted in the literature (Leminen et al., 2022; You et al., 2022).

Therefore, the current technological, economic, and social changes have driven the automotive industry to incorporate new technologies and non-traditional companies, raising questions about global value chains (You et al., 2022). Actors involved in these value chains are confronted with a multitude of challenges across various domains, particularly regarding leveraging the wealth of new knowledge, intelligence, and data, adapting to disruptive technologies related to them, and transparently sharing information (Leminen et al., 2022; You et al., 2022). Among these challenges is a focus on digitalization's profound transformation and the need to integrate knowledge and technologies to create customer value (You et al., 2022).

These changes encompass the increasing significance of collective intelligence in various fields such as information and communication technologies (e.g., connectivity and autonomous vehicles), responses to social trends (e.g., “peak car”), and customer preferences (e.g., on-demand Mobility). The OEM can no longer manage and coordinate the GVC as they need to control the core activities.

As previously indicated, the rise of collective intelligence has led to the emergence of new players in the industry to meet the needs resulting from advancements in connectivity, autonomous and electric vehicles, and shared Mobility. The products, technologies, and activities of firms engaged in connected, autonomous, electric, and shared Mobility tend to differ significantly from traditional automotive industry production processes, giving rise to new technologies, products, and activities related to vehicle automation (e.g., telematic control units) (Athanasopoulou et al., 2019), connectivity (e.g., data-exchange systems) (Mahmood, 2020), and shared mobility systems (e.g., digital platforms) (Leminen et al., 2022).

The interplay of various factors is having a transformative impact on the automotive industry, fostering collaboration, the sharing of knowledge, and a shift away from conventional hierarchical arrangements. As a result, the influence of collective intelligence is emerging as a crucial driving force, guiding the industry toward a more interconnected, innovative, and customer-focused future.

Regarding the actors involved, the new mobility value chain comprises traditional OEMs and various non-traditional automotive companies (Cabanelas et al., 2023). The GVC definition encompasses all entities involved in bringing a product from conception to end use, and the new mobility value chain must extend to include entities offering related services (e.g., car-sharing firms, digital platform service providers) as well as those concerned in the development of technologies that support such services (e.g., vehicle connectivity software, positioning, and localization technologies). Moreover, collaboration between OEMs and new actors is essential in this context (Pérez-Moure et al., 2023a).

From a product/service perspective, the emergence of new market entrants has given rise to a new value chain that, while partially retaining the structure of the traditional value chain where automobile manufacturers coordinate a network of component suppliers focused on the production of vehicles, this circumstance is provoking a reconfiguration of the GVC.

The focus of these new players is on services rather than production, and activities related to sharing and generating data, knowledge, and intelligence have become crucial to the operation of vehicles. It aligns with the requirements of new mobility technologies, which necessitate physical components to create the automation needed for vehicles.

A Story of Power and Control: Relationships Within the New Mobility Value Chain

In addition to analyzing chain configuration, examining the types of relationships among actors within a value chain is essential. Traditionally, relationships have been considered in terms of control, dependence, and decision-making power (Sturgeon et al., 2008).

Previous research on the traditional automotive industry indicated that OEMs exercised significant control over value-added activities, possessing considerable decision-making power within the value chain and being relatively independent of suppliers due to their possession of all relevant intelligence within the value chain. However, as demonstrated by the GVC approach in the case of the new Mobility, this traditional dynamic of low dependency and high decision-making power only applies to an increasing number of digital activities and services; this is because sharing objectives, data, and knowledge which are crucial in the new mobility value chain, requires OEMs to relinquish some of their power.

New players have gained significant importance, particularly in decision-making along the value chain. These new players come from industries other than automotive, such as information and communication technology (ICT). The activities undertaken by these new players are not a result of a prior vertical disintegration process or outsourcing compelled by automobile manufacturers, suggesting a lack of dependence on traditional leading automotive firms. Consequently, leading firms need to improve their ability to control new players, unlike the traditional value chain (Sturgeon et al., 2008).

The impact of the necessity of collective intelligence is apparent in the automotive industry, as new players with a background in the ICT industry contribute through diverse knowledge and expertise. The collaboration between traditional and new players exemplifies a more cooperative and interconnected value chain driven by the tenets of collective intelligence. As a result, conventional automobile manufacturers must engage in partnerships with these emerging entities (Pérez-Moure et al., 2023b).

Decision-making power is closely connected to positioning in the top echelons of the value chain (Lampón et al., 2018). In a vehicle's product architecture context, most firms specializing in new mobility technologies directly provide their physical components for modules to automobile manufacturers, thus being classified as Tier-1 suppliers. Furthermore, and more significantly, the services offered by new players are typically based on collective intelligence processes, with these players managing data to develop functions for automation, connectivity, and vehicle sharing. Software and applications for managing and exchanging data are crucial in performing these functions. It is worth noting that many new players are involved in these specific activities (Mahmood, 2020).

In terms of added value, the new players in the market have introduced knowledge-based activities with increased technological requirements. Research has shown that ICT firms operating in the mobility industry require their personnel to possess strong engineering skills and high qualifications. While traditional innovations related to product and manufacturing processes (e.g., processing of new materials) remain relevant (Lampón et al., 2016), emerging technologies in electric, autonomous, connected, and shared Mobility are undergoing accelerated innovation. This technological development is not limited to automobile manufacturers but is undertaken by new market players.

The current configuration of the new mobility value chain is thus characterized by close collaboration among various actors, resulting in the erosion of traditional boundaries of control and a more equitable distribution of knowledge. This fundamental shift necessitates collaboration among participants to chart the course toward the future of Mobility. The proliferation of business models that foster collaboration marks a departure from the hierarchical structures of the past. Integrating collective intelligence into the value chain has been significant and has become a crucial component of innovation and decision-making. This transformation is particularly evident in new entrants to the new mobility scene and in OEMs, who are challenged to share power and collaborate with other participants to adapt to the demands of an ever-evolving mobility landscape. In summary, collective intelligence has moved beyond being a peripheral option to becoming an essential component that defines the very nature of the new mobility value chain.

Implications for deploying collective intelligence within the mobility value chain. It is crucial to incorporate the concept of collective intelligence into the theoretical framework to adequately capture the ongoing transformation of the traditional automotive industry value chain. It is necessary to incorporate elements from the traditional model to develop a theoretical framework encompassing the new mobility value chain. Recent studies that have adopted the GVC approach have explored various aspects of the new mobility value chain, including digital business models adopted by automakers, shifts in value-added and innovation activities, and the relationships fostered by sustainable mobility firms within this evolving landscape (Lampón & Muñoz-Dueñas, 2023; Pérez-Moure et al., 2023b). By augmenting the GVC approach with a focus on collective intelligence, a more nuanced analysis can be conducted, shedding light on the dynamic interplay of decision-making power and the strategic positioning of firms along the chain. This integration of collective intelligence into the theoretical framework highlights its essential role in shaping the form of the new mobility value chain.

On the other hand, the spatial division of labor related to the activities required to produce a vehicle (Lampón et al., 2015) has lost relevance in favor of the spatial division of value-added and innovation activities linked to collective intelligence and, therefore, to digitalization and autonomous and connected technologies. The new mobility value chain is focused mainly on digital mobility services and on the technologies that support those services (Pérez-Moure et al., 2023a), diminishing the importance of traditional production processes related to vehicle manufacture and where knowledge (as value-added activities) plays a central role.

In this context, the critical actors linked to autonomous, electric, connected, and shared Mobility now wield significant control, decision-making power, and the capacity to develop value-added activities around new mobility technologies. Instead of being controlled by traditional manufacturers, they are companies that work together, sharing objectives, skills, and knowledge. Thus, the model that has been worked on until now is changing with the introduction of collective intelligence throughout the value chain. The fact that the activities that generate, process, and share information are no longer in traditional manufacturers' hands suggests a new way of conceiving the new mobility value chain.

At the forefront of the automotive industry's revolution, collective intelligence emerges as a driving force that facilitates the redefinition of the value chain. OEMs recognize the limitations of their internal capabilities in embracing new technologies driven by digitization, automation, and connectivity.

This acknowledgment has led to a significant transition towards strategic alliances, shifting from the traditional leadership paradigm to a more collaborative and inclusive model. In the realm of autonomous and electric vehicles and connectivity, the convergence of efforts is evident, where OEMs actively collaborate with various entities. However, this dynamic extends beyond, creating a complex network of relationships that transcends the traditional boundaries between OEMs and local companies. This change regarding space and power dynamics places collective intelligence at the epicenter of this transformation.

The key to this redefinition lies in understanding that efficiency and the economy of innovation are maximized when knowledge and resources are shared. In this context, collective intelligence ceases to be an abstract concept to become a driving force behind creating a more accessible and inclusive global value chain. Once maintained as an exclusive asset of OEMs, the decentralization of knowledge becomes a fundamental pillar for effective collaboration among industry players. This transformation not only brings a shift in the focus of power, where the possession of knowledge becomes more relevant than ever but also moves the attention from the product to services and Mobility as a Service (MaaS). Consequently, OEMs, far from maintaining centralized control, are compelled to incorporate new actors into their ecosystem to offer a more diversified range of services that respond to the changing market demands (Pérez-Moure et al., 2023b).

In summary, collective intelligence is increasingly recognized as a critical component of a versatile value chain, where cooperation among diverse stakeholders is essential for success. By embracing this new paradigm, the automotive industry can reshape its current landscape and establish a more agile, innovative, and adaptive ecosystem.

BUSINESS MODELS LINKED TO COLLECTIVE INTELLIGENCE. THE ROLE OF DIGITALIZATION

Using business models that prioritize value creation (Medina et al., 2022) is essential for structuring innovative value propositions, pinpointing market opportunities, and incorporating customer-centric approaches (Osterwalder & Pigneur, 2010). Due to new mobility technologies associated with digitalization, the automotive industry is undergoing a transformative period; novel business models (Cabanelas et al., 2023) present challenges and opportunities. In the realm of new Mobility, digitalization's profound impact underscores the need to integrate knowledge and technologies to enhance customer value (You et al., 2022).

Although business models have been examined in scholarly literature since the 1950s, their significance has recently increased (Medina et al., 2022). A well-implemented business model focusing on value creation enables the structuring of innovative value propositions and the identification of market segments and contributes to defining the structure of the relevant value chain (Athanaspoulou et al., 2019). Contemporary business models emphasize collective intelligence, which enhances cooperative efforts within the value chain, fostering innovation and responsiveness to dynamic customer needs.

Digitalization fundamentally transforms conventional mobility business paradigms, compelling automotive manufacturers to extend their offerings to address evolving mobility needs (Cabanelas et al., 2023). In this era of transformative technological advancements, integrating digital tools into business models is not merely functional; it represents a profound shift towards harnessing collective intelligence. Collaborative synergies fostered by collective intelligence become paramount as industry stakeholders navigate the complexities of digitalization.

Simultaneously, the pervasive influence of digitalization is fostering the prevailing trend of servitization in new mobility business models (Cabanelas et al., 2023). Businesses, cognizant of the need for strategic adaptation, adjust their value propositions and recognize collective intelligence's crucial role in navigating this digital terrain. The centrality of digitalization in modern business models is carving out novel avenues for value creation (Pérez-Moure et al., 2023b), with a noteworthy emphasis on the collaborative aspect of intelligence. Integrating digital tools into business models is not just about providing diverse service options; it is a strategic move to tap into the collective insights and innovations emerging from interconnected ecosystems.

Digitalization has led to new business models that leverage advanced ICT capabilities to recalibrate customer value propositions (Athanaspoulou, 2019). The intertwined concepts of collective intelligence and digital transformation facilitate this process. As businesses adapt to customers' evolving needs, the collaborative intelligence embedded in these models becomes a powerful force reshaping the value chain dynamics (Berman, 2012). In this context, the collaboration facilitated by digitalization is not merely a byproduct but part of a cooperative and interconnected value creation essence.

The emergence of these digital business models is not only a response to current market trends but a strategic imperative for anticipating and navigating future contexts (Cabanelas et al., 2023). As digitalization unfolds, these models offer a lens into the future and serve as critical instruments for understanding, responding to, and capitalizing on emerging market landscapes. Within this transformation, the fusion of digitalization and collective intelligence emerges as the linchpin, reshaping business models and the entire fabric of the automotive industry.

Examples of the Impact of Digitalization

This growing digitalization with the collective intelligence in new Mobility is reinforced and influenced by EVs, digital platforms, connectivity, big data, Artificial Intelligence, and AVs (Leminen et al., 2022; Medina et al., 2022; You et al., 2022). First, The situation that EVs are currently experiencing forces multiple actors to work together, cooperate, and believe in the same purpose because EVs need different infrastructures, such as charging points, and a substantial improvement in battery life. On the one hand, public agents must work together by sharing knowledge with OEMs and vice versa to deploy a charging infrastructure appropriate to the current battery levels of EVs and work together for adequate urban planning.

On the other hand, OEMs are developing different battery solutions with other companies or providing other types of services to users. In this context, digitalization plays a fundamental and enabling role, reflected in aspects such as a third party offering digital services related to charging stations (Medina et al., 2022), where a navigation system selects the best charging station location. Another example may be the Companies that have introduced electric vehicle parking and routing systems that use control algorithms. An optimized navigation system can improve the efficiency of electric car rental systems by decreasing the average travel time and reducing energy consumption (Lampón & Muñoz-Dueñas, 2023).

Second, incorporating digital platforms, connectivity, and big data is intimately intertwined with the sharing and collaborative exchange of data among vehicles, individuals, and new mobility infrastructures. Within this digital ecosystem, collective intelligence becomes increasingly prominent as it underpins the collaborative dynamics inherent in data sharing and utilization. A wide array of digital services is interconnected with connectivity, encompassing aspects such as data exchange, digital platforms that serve as collaborative hubs, and the essential infrastructure for car-sharing initiatives (Pérez-Moure et al., 2023b).

The collaborative nature of intelligence is particularly evident in the development of personalized connected services and enhanced user experiences driven by digitalization. Examples range from optimizing car usage through real-time information on vehicle condition and remote maintenance services to enhancing in-car entertainment with diverse content and seamless access to social media platforms. Additionally, the subscription-based model for software updates, chosen by customers and collectively funded, exemplifies the collaborative approach to service improvement (Athanasopoulou et al., 2019).

Third, the evolution of autonomous driving technologies and artificial intelligence presents a new realm of possibilities in transportation services, marking a paradigm shift in the utilization of vehicles (Athanasopoulou et al., 2019). The early stage of autonomous vehicle development is characterized by its infancy, and the landscape is marked by collaboration and shared intelligence necessitated by the complexity of these technologies. Unlike conventional automotive advancements, the progression of autonomous vehicles is not solely reliant on the capabilities of the OEMs but significantly hinges on the collective evolution of an intricate network of collaborators and partners (Mahmood, 2020).

The collaborative nature of the autonomous vehicle ecosystem accentuates its distinctiveness as stakeholders, including technology firms, data analysts, and mobility service providers, converge to contribute to the expansive pool of knowledge (Leminen et al., 2022; You et al., 2022). In this shared pursuit of developing and refining autonomous driving capabilities, the collective intelligence of the entire network plays a pivotal role. Unlike traditional automotive models, the trajectory of autonomous vehicles is intertwined with a broader array of contributors, emphasizing a dynamic and collaborative approach to knowledge generation.

Recent research has underscored the pivotal role of servitization in contemporary business models, illustrating its significance in navigating the evolving market landscape. Amidst this shifting business terrain characterized by heightened competition, companies, particularly those at the forefront of innovation, strategically orient their value propositions towards servitization, leveraging collective intelligence (You et al., 2022).

Within the realm of new Mobility, these transformative forces converge in the concept of MaaS, representing a user-centric paradigm for mobility solutions that integrates a diverse range of personalized and customized services primarily driven by ICTs (Lampón, 2023; Medina et al., 2022; Pérez-Moure et al., 2023a). This paradigm shift emphasizes the centrality of digitalization and collective intelligence in shaping contemporary business models, where the convergence of technological capabilities and cooperative networks propel the evolution of MaaS. As companies deal with this dynamic landscape, the emphasis on servitization becomes not merely an operational choice but a strategic imperative to align with the emerging trends and customer preferences in the new mobility industry where collective intelligence can play a fundamental role (Mahmood, 2020).

Study Cases of How Automobile Manufacturers Are Implementing Collective Intelligence

Having grasped how collective intelligence alters the value chain and observing the alterations to business models resulting from this collective intelligence, it is imperative to apply the knowledge acquired from the case studies. In the latter portion of this chapter, we will delve into the instances of Toyota and Stellantis, two OEMs that rank among the top investors in innovation and boast the highest revenues. Furthermore, Stellantis is one of the OEMs encompassing the most extensive array of brands. The following case studies illustrate the various points discussed in the chapter, specifically those about applying collective intelligence across the value chain and new business models. These areas include autonomous and electric vehicles, digitalization as platforms and connectivity, data generation, and car-sharing.

Stellantis

At the level of CAVs, Stellantis is working on it and, with the common goal of meeting customer demands, has signed a collaboration agreement with Waymo exclusively for light commercial vehicles. Although Waymo has agreements on autonomous driving with other OEMs, it has opted to put into service a fleet of autonomous light commercial vehicles with Stellantis to offer Deliver as a Service. The horizon for launching the service using SAE Level 3 automated driving is 2025. It is an example of how collective intelligence works in the basics. In this case, it involves two companies collaborating toward a common objective to reach new knowledge and bring new services to a community, sharing information, resources, and data.

EVs remain important to Stellantis and are another example of collective intelligence. In this case, not only with other companies but with public actors, too. On the one hand, by working with TheF Charging, Stellantis can offer its customers access to a vast network of electric charging stations, totaling over 2 million locations in city centers and spanning more than 15,000 locations, with a specially developed app. This network includes exclusive conditions for Stellantis customers. In addition, the company has established a new subsidiary called Free2Move Charge in the United States, with plans to expand to Europe. This subsidiary is designed to provide seamless charging and energy management solutions to meet the needs of electric vehicle customers, regardless of where or how they charge their vehicles. To achieve this goal, Stellantis must collaborate with private companies and public entities, such as local governments, to create a city map that allows for the installation of charging stations.

On the other hand, and by its dedication to electric vehicles, Stellantis has partnered with Kiri to establish a program that rewards drivers for adopting sustainable practices. This program utilizes eCoins, which can be redeemed in Kiri's marketplace. These eCoins are earned through the Uconnect services tool app, which features an eco: Score section that evaluates driving efficiency and assigns scores on a scale of 0 to 100; with this, data about how drivers drive is generated. This data is shared within both companies.

Nevertheless, in the case of Stellantis, the peak of collective intelligence is around digital platforms, connectivity, and data generation. After several initiatives and different technological partners, Stellantis has collaborated with Amazon Web Services, the multinational American corporation, to support its various digital platform business models jointly. By partnering with Amazon Web Services, Stellantis has established a marketplace where it can directly provide its customers with various offerings, including warranty services, accessories, on-demand insurance, maintenance, and vehicle rental.

This collaboration represents a significant step forward in Stellantis' efforts to enhance its digital capabilities and better serve its customers. The collaboration extends beyond the consumer domain, with Stellantis developing a B2B platform to support and assist other companies and businesses transitioning to electric Mobility, covering aspects such as subsidies, taxes, and technologies.

This collaboration allows Stellantis to offer customer-centric services based on increased connectivity. The collaboration between Amazon and Stellantis is focused on delivering customer-centric connected experiences across the brand's vehicles. To this end, the STLA SmartCockpit will become operational in 2024 and serve as the leading platform for these experiences. This platform will offer various applications with features and services such as trip planning, voice assistance, and payment services. Additionally, Alexa, Amazon's virtual assistant, will be integrated into Stellantis vehicles to enhance the user experience. The drivers themselves can choose these apps, which are offered via connectivity, and can also pay for the subscription.

This strategic alliance between Stellantis and Amazon Web Services is a compelling illustration of collective intelligence within the automotive industry. The seamless integration of digital platforms, connectivity, and data utilization exemplifies the shared determination to harness diverse expertise for innovative and customer-focused solutions. By forming a partnership with a technological powerhouse like Amazon, Stellantis not only accesses an extensive array of knowledge and capabilities but also embodies the spirit of collective intelligence. This interconnected ecosystem, in which consumers can select and subscribe to services, symbolizes the democratization of information and the collective endeavor to reshape mobility experiences. This collaboration emphasizes that intelligence can no longer be attributed to individual entities but flourishes within collaborative networks.

In car-sharing, Stellantis presents a multifaceted approach that embodies the tenets of collective intelligence. The possession of Free2Move, a company that furnishes a comprehensive array of Stellantis-branded vehicles solely for professionals, illustrates an autonomous endeavor to develop mobility solutions. Free2Move, a dedicated application offered by Stellantis, provides car-sharing and on-demand mobility services and incorporates features such as parking space reservations. These services are currently limited to the cities of Paris and Madrid. Hence, implementing this new business model necessitates the coordination of numerous actors, including cities, developers, and other businesses. Concurrently, the data generated throughout the process can be utilized to determine distances and the most frequently utilized parking areas.

Toyota

The situation regarding Toyota differs from that of Stellantis in several respects. About EVs, Toyota has not entered into any partnerships or collaborations. This decision can be attributed to the fact that the company has only recently produced EVs. However, regarding CAVs, Toyota has made significant strides through its subsidiaries and alliances with other companies, leveraging collective intelligence and transcending sectorial boundaries. Toyota has developed the e-palette for the movement of both people and goods in an autonomous manner.

The development of this project involves multiple entities, as it requires a collaborative effort to function effectively. It is due to its integration with the Autonomous Mobility Management System, which is augmented by a mobile application that facilitates the distribution of tasks, such as door-to-door deliveries.

The autonomous vehicle for these deliveries has already been circulated in one city in Japan (Woven City). However, it is expected to be deployed in the country's main cities by 2025 and established door-to-door service partners with various corporations, including Amazon, Uber, and Pizza Hut. One of the most cutting-edge examples of collective intelligence is the "door-to-door doctor" service, which utilizes the e-palette model and its corresponding app. Users can request medical services via the e-Palette Task Assignment Platform (e-TAP) application, and the vehicle will navigate autonomously to their location. Additionally, the e-palette model accommodates a medical room within the vehicle, enabling patients to receive medical care conveniently and comfortably. In collaboration with Pony.ai, the development of a virtual assistant, Guardian, was facilitated, alongside testing in Beijing and Shanghai, paving the way for the launch of this autonomous vehicle.

Regarding digital platforms, connectivity, and data generation, since 2016, Toyota has been developing its own digital Mobility Service Platform. However, in 2020, the company recognized that this endeavor could only be pursued in collaboration. Consequently, Toyota collaborated with Amazon as a technology partner while maintaining ownership of its Mobility Service Platform.

This platform employs multiple devices to store data, which Toyota subsequently processes to provide a range of services to customers. These services extend beyond direct offerings to customers and enable third parties to offer them via the platform. The services include personalized maintenance plans, adaptable leasing options, and on-demand insurance (in collaboration with the MS&AD Insurance Group's Aioi Nissay Dowa Insurance Company). Toyota prioritizes constructing mobility solutions for society as a central tenet of its mission.

Consequently, it is crucial to establish connectivity through the integration of its services within the Toyota Smart Center. This multifaceted hub encompasses various connectivity services, including over-the-air software updates, authentication systems, maps, virtual assistant functionality, and the ability to adjust the vehicle's interior conditions automatically. Likewise, Toyota established the 'Early detection, Early resolution system' that employs various devices, including the Trans-Log and Smart Key Box, to facilitate key encryption via smartphone and provide continuous emergency services with route and driving recommendations.

The interconnected nature of the services within the Toyota Smart Center exemplifies a collaborative and collective intelligence-driven initiative in which various technologies seamlessly work together to elevate the overall driving experience. It also implies the involvement of other companies, such as garages or mobile companies, in successfully implementing this initiative.

Finally, for Toyota, car-sharing is a fundamental business model and is one of the best representations of collective intelligence. Toyota has established various subsidiary companies to offer these services: Toyota Share, Hui, and Kinto, where the most developed are Hui and Kinto, where collective intelligence has a significant impact. Toyota owns the vehicles in question, yet variations exist between them. Hui has partnered with Servco Pacific in the United States since 2018, adopting a B2C model that utilizes an app for on-demand services. However, it is currently only available in Hawaii.

Kinto, a company with a presence in Europe since 2020, operates with a dual focus on both B2B and B2C markets. It offers vehicles to businesses for car-sharing purposes. Also, it connects individual users through its mobile application, developed in collaboration with Ridecell, which is currently accessible in Dublin, Venice, Copenhagen, Madrid, Santiago de Chile, and Buenos Aires. Therefore, Toyota develops collective intelligence in car-sharing to boost its business model thanks to the help of technology companies and agreements with local governments. In addition,

Toyota has made significant investments in other car-sharing companies, such as Grab (1 billion US dollars since 2018) and Didi (600 million dollars since 2019).

It is important to note that the fleet in question does not belong to Toyota, nor does the company manage it; instead, data is obtained from the service. So, the purpose of these investments is not only to have the company's vehicle brands represented in the carsharing fleets operated by Grab in Southeast Asia (which spans 218 cities and is the leading company with 6 million trips per day) and Didi Chuxing in the Chinese market in the medium term but to work jointly to develop new car-sharing apps, to share data obtained by the vehicles during the trip and then use that data to upgrade and develop better services, new business models and to attach population's demands. These investments embody a collaborative exchange of ideas, technologies, and market knowledge, thereby fostering the collective growth of shared mobility ecosystems. Toyota's aim to incorporate its vehicle brands into external fleets reflects a shared vision for a harmonized future in shared Mobility.

CONCLUSION

The traditional mode of transportation is being replaced by a new form of Mobility, which has fundamentally altered how society moves and redefined the concept of Mobility. Present-day new Mobility is primarily centered on services, with the vehicle as a product taking a backseat. The emergence of autonomous, electric, connected, and shared vehicles has essentially rendered traditional vehicles obsolete. The resulting complexity in the new mobility landscape has necessitated collaboration between traditional manufacturers and companies outside the sector. This partnership involves sharing data and developing creative, adaptable, and flexible solutions while generating new knowledge with a common goal. Traditional automobile manufacturers have had to become part of a collective intelligence to survive in this new environment.

It has been demonstrated that collective intelligence is present in all forms of Mobility and is responsible for configuring value chains. In order to effectively and quickly adapt to unfamiliar business models, traditional companies must include other members. This inclusion leads to various consequences. Firstly, the added value is perceived in new Mobility services, particularly in high-tech services such as digitization and connectivity. Secondly, including high-added value activities implies that OEMs now have a dependency they did not previously have, losing power and control over the value chain and the companies they previously held. This shift in power and control favors technology companies, modifying relationships along the value chain. Therefore, collective intelligence contributes spatially and relationally to reconfiguring value chains, serving to analyze the changes produced.

Collective intelligence is a phenomenon that not only affects value chains but also has a significant impact on business models. Digitalization plays a crucial role in enabling collective intelligence, and without new technologies, collaboration levels would be significantly lower. New business models predict the importance of collective intelligence in upcoming innovations. Incorporating digital platforms, connectivity, and big data emphasizes the sharing and collaborative data exchange among vehicles, individuals, and mobility infrastructures.

The collaborative dynamics inherent in data sharing align with the principles of collective intelligence, making it a central aspect of this digital ecosystem. From data exchange to collaborative platforms and car-sharing initiatives, the interconnectivity of digital services relies on collective intelligence to drive enhanced user experiences and personalized services. Autonomous driving technologies and artificial intelligence usher in a new era of transportation services marked by collaboration and shared intelligence.

The development of autonomous vehicles depends significantly on the collective evolution of a network of collaborators and partners, making the collaborative approach to knowledge generation in the autonomous vehicle ecosystem exemplifying the transformative potential of collective intelligence in the automotive industry. Servitization, a vital aspect of contemporary business models, is gaining prominence as companies strategically align their value propositions with this evolving market landscape.

The emphasis on servitization becomes a strategic imperative, leveraging collective intelligence to navigate the dynamic shifts in the new mobility industry. It is particularly evident in the concept of MaaS, which represents a user-centric paradigm shaped by digitalization and collective intelligence.

The integration of collective intelligence can be observed in the business models of Stellantis and Toyota. It includes various companies and public entities not previously associated with this concept. Specific business models rely heavily on collective intelligence, such as developing CAVs or digital platforms. However, the rapidly changing nature of Mobility, value chains, and business models suggests that collective intelligence may have an even more significant impact in the future and continue to intensify within the sector.

The resilience shown by traditional automobile manufacturers is crucial to their survival and continued competitiveness in this rapidly changing environment. With the shift away from traditional vehicles and the emergence of autonomous, electric, connected, and shared vehicles, these companies have had to adapt by forming new collaborations and embracing digitalization. This ability to adapt demonstrates their resilience as they transition from traditional manufacturing models to ones focused on services and collective intelligence. By partnering with technology companies and other external actors, traditional manufacturers are not only maintaining their presence but also reshaping their business models to stay competitive. Their resilience is evident in their capacity to innovate and adjust to the new demands of the mobility sector, which requires flexibility, collaboration, and the integration of new technologies.

REFERENCES

Adekola, J., & Clelland, D. (2020). Two sides of the same coin: Business resilience and community resilience. *Journal of Contingencies and Crisis Management*, 28(1), 50–60. DOI: 10.1111/1468-5973.12275

Athanasopoulou, A., de Reuver, M., Nikou, S., & Bouwman, H. (2019). What technology enabled services impact business models in the automotive industry? An exploratory study. *Futures*, 109, 73–83. DOI: 10.1016/j.futures.2019.04.001

Berman, S. J. (2012). Digital transformation: Opportunities to create new business models. *Strategy and Leadership*, 40(2), 16–24. DOI: 10.1108/10878571211209314

Boder, A. (2006). Collective intelligence: A keystone in knowledge management. *Journal of Knowledge Management*, 10(1), 81–93. DOI: 10.1108/13673270610650120

Cabanelas, P., Parkhurst, G., Thomopoulos, N., & Lampón, J. F. (2023). A dynamic capability evaluation of emerging business models for new mobility. *Research in Transportation Business & Management*, 47, 100964. DOI: 10.1016/j.rtbm.2023.100964

Dahles, H., & Susilowati, T. P. (2015). Business resilience in times of growth and crisis. *Annals of Tourism Research*, 51, 34–50. DOI: 10.1016/j.annals.2015.01.002

Jung, J., & Gómez-Bengoechea, G. (2022). A literature review on firm digitalization: drivers and impacts. *Estudios sobre la Economía Española*.

Kamargianni, M., Li, W., Matyas, M., & Schäfer, A. (2016). A critical review of new mobility services for urban transport. *Transportation Research Procedia*, 14, 3294–3303. DOI: 10.1016/j.trpro.2016.05.277

Lampón, J. F. (2020). The impact of uncertainty on production relocation: Implications from a regional perspective. *Papers in Regional Science*, 99(3), 427–446. DOI: 10.1111/pirs.12493

Lampón, J. F. (2023). Efficiency in design and production to achieve sustainable development challenges in the automobile industry: Modular electric vehicle platforms. *Sustainable Development (Bradford)*, 31(1), 26–38. DOI: 10.1002/sd.2370

Lampón, J. F., Cabanelas, P., & Delgado-Guzmán, J. A. (2018). Keys in the evolution of Mexico within the global value chain in the automobile components industry: The case of Bajio. *El Trimestre Economico*, 85(3), 483–514.

Lampón, J. F., Lago-Peñas, S., & Cabanelas, P. (2016). Can the periphery achieve core? The Case of the automobile components industry in Spain. *Papers in Regional Science*, 95(3), 595–612. DOI: 10.1111/pirs.12146

Lampón, J. F., Lago-Peñas, S., & González-Benito, J. (2015). International relocation and production geography in the European automobile components sector: The case of Spain. *International Journal of Production Research*, 53(5), 1409–1424. DOI: 10.1080/00207543.2014.942757

Lampón, J. F., & Muñoz-Dueñas, P. (2023). Are sustainable mobility firms reshaping the traditional relationships in the automotive industry value chain? *Journal of Cleaner Production*, 413, 137522. DOI: 10.1016/j.jclepro.2023.137522

Lampón, J. F., Pérez-Moure, H., Carballo-Cruz, F., & Velando-Rodríguez, M. E. (2024). New mobility technologies and regional status in the automotive industry value chain: The case of Spain and Portugal. *Technology in Society*, 78, 102624. DOI: 10.1016/j.techsoc.2024.102624

Lampón, J. F., Rodríguez-De La Fuente, M., & Fraiz-Brea, J. A. (2022). The dilemma of domestic suppliers on the periphery of the automotive industry global value chain. *Kybernetes*, 51(12), 3637–3655. DOI: 10.1108/K-01-2021-0073

Leimeister, J. M. (2010). Collective intelligence. *Business & Information Systems Engineering*, 2(4), 245–248. DOI: 10.1007/s12599-010-0114-8

Leminen, S., Rajahonka, M., Wendelin, R., Westerlund, M., & Nyström, A. (2022). Autonomous vehicle solutions and their digital servitization business models. *Technological Forecasting and Social Change*, 185, 122070. DOI: 10.1016/j.techfore.2022.122070

Mahmood, Z. (2020). *Connected vehicles in the Internet of Things*. Springer. DOI: 10.1007/978-3-030-36167-9

Medina, E., Mazaira, A., & Alén, E. (2022). Innovation in the broadcasters' business model: A bibliometric and review approach. *European Research on Management and Business Economics*, 28(3), 100202. DOI: 10.1016/j.iedeen.2022.100202

Osterwalder, A., & Pigneur, Y. (2010). *Business model generation: a handbook for visionaries, game changers, and challengers*. Wiley.

Pérez-Moure, H., Lampón, J. F., & Cabanelas, P. (2023a). Mobility business models toward a digital tomorrow: Challenges for automotive manufacturers. *Futures*, 103309. Advance online publication. DOI: 10.1016/j.futures.2023.103309

Pérez-Moure, H., Lampón, J. F., Velando-Rodríguez, M. E., & Rodríguez-Comesaña, L. (2023b). Revolutionizing the road: How sustainable, autonomous, and connected vehicles are changing digital mobility business models. *European Research on Management and Business Economics*, 29(3), 100230. Advance online publication. DOI: 10.1016/j.iedeen.2023.100230

Saad, M. H., Hagelaar, G., Van Der Velde, G., & Omta, S. W. F. (2021). Conceptualization of SMEs' business resilience: A systematic literature review. *Cogent Business & Management*, 8(1), 1938347. DOI: 10.1080/23311975.2021.1938347

Sturgeon, T. J., Van Biesebroeck, J., & Gereffi, G. (2008). Value chains, networks and clusters: Reframing the global automotive industry. *Journal of Economic Geography*, 8(3), 297–321. DOI: 10.1093/jeg/lbn007

Yi, K. (2003). Can vertical specialization explain the growth of world trade? *Journal of Political Economy*, 111(1), 52–102. DOI: 10.1086/344805

You, W., Sarpong, D., & O'Regan, N. (2022). Global value chains in a digitalized era. *Strategic Change*, 31(1), 5–8. DOI: 10.1002/jsc.2476

Chapter 7
Adaptive Capacity in the Tourism System:
Resilience and Collective Intelligence

Pilar Morales Valdez
https://orcid.org/0000-0001-5401-4297
University of Guadalajara, Mexico

Tania Elena González Alvarado
https://orcid.org/0000-0002-3062-9665
University of Guadalajara, Mexico

Orly Manjarrez Salazar
La Salle University, Mexico

ABSTRACT

This chapter analyzes the role of adaptive capacity in the tourism system, specifically examining the interplay between resilience and collective intelligence. It argues that understanding how businesses adapt to unpredictable environments requires a systemic approach that considers the interconnectedness of individual companies within their broader economic and social contexts. The chapter explores the concept of business resilience as a crucial factor in navigating change and uncertainty, proposing that it stems from the collective intelligence of an organization's members. By analyzing examples of collective intelligence in nature and human societies, the chapter highlights its importance for survival, self-organization, and creative problem-solving within the tourism industry. The chapter concludes by emphasizing the need for further research on the specific mechanisms through which collective intelligence enhances adaptive capacity in tourism destinations.

DOI: 10.4018/979-8-3693-7272-2.ch007

INTRODUCTION

The environment is highly unpredictable for companies. What makes companies prevail and adapt to continuous change? Only sometimes do individual decisions determine the existence of these companies. Sometimes, it is the environment that allows them to exist rather than the strategies that are taken internally. Enterprises are open systems that are linked to other economic agents located in a specific territory.

Firms are made up of individuals who are also part of other organizations, making the system highly dynamic. Determining a line isolating the enterprise from the environment or other organizations is challenging. The enterprise is immersed in its environment. The local, national, and even international systems affect the enterprise (van der Straate et al., 2023). What changes are the degree and speed of impact?

Understanding how business adapts to different scenarios requires a systemic approach to this understanding (Zhakupov et al., 2023). Explaining or giving possible reasons for the success of firms (Müller et al., 2023), even under unfavorable circumstances, leads to considering business resilience (Shepherd & Williams, 2023) as part of the explanation. In the same way, understanding business resilience as being caused by the resilience of each company member opens the way to the discussion on collective intelligence[1].

Collective intelligence in nature, and even in humanity, is linked to moments of survival, self-organization, and creativity that would not have been possible individually (Galesic et al., 2023; Watson & Levin, 2023; Zeren et al., 2023). This chapter aims to analyze the adaptive capacity of a tourism system based on its enterprises. It aims to discuss how collective intelligence contributes to the resilience of both the enterprise and the locality to which it belongs. Panarchy is considered to help understand how the system favors resilience (Qiao et al., 2024; Galderisi & Limongi, 2024), making the best use of collective intelligence. To this end, the case of entrepreneurs in the tourism system in Tapalpa, Jalisco, is analyzed. The relationship between collective intelligence and tourism is evidenced by the cooperation between the local community and travelers to improve the tourist experience. Some actions are sharing information, tourism resource management, service innovation, community creation, resilience, and adaptation. Online platforms, such as social networks and travel forums, allow travelers to share experiences, tips and recommendations. Collective intelligence encourages the creation of communities of travelers who share similar interests. These communities promote lesser-known destinations, thus diversifying the tourist offer and better distributing the flow of visitors. In times of crisis, such as pandemics or natural disasters, collective intelligence allows tourism communities to adapt and find creative solutions to attract visitors and maintain economic activity.

This chapter is divided into three parts: the first part deals with the Hierarchy in complex adaptive systems and explains how each part contributes to the system's adaptation to the environment; the second part deals with resilience and its role in complex adaptive systems; and the third part presents the case of Tapalpa, which allows us to exemplify the above and derive the conclusions.

Tourism is one of the most important economic activities in the world. The income it generates has become a critical factor in the balance of payments of many countries and regions (Wang et al., 2024). However, the emerging scenarios expose the financial precariousness of social, ecological, and economic systems, including tourism. For this reason, resilience becomes important and attractive because it provides insight into the relationships and dynamics of the system.

A tourism system is a group of three interrelated, interdependent, and interacting essential elements: tourists, geographical elements (traveler generating region, tourist destination region, and transit route region), and the tourism industry. Together, these elements form a single functional structure (Tardivo et al., 2014).

PANARCHY AND COMPLEX ADAPTIVE SYSTEMS

The application of the theory of complex adaptive systems (CAS)[2] for the analysis of tourism destinations helps to delve deeper into the mechanisms responsible for their development and survival, contributing to their adaptation in times of change (Hartman, 2018; Hartman, 2020) and in a rural[3] environment, paying attention to the interactions in all aspects of the environment, economy, and society, analyzing them in general (An & Alarcón, 2020). For this reason, we seek to answer the question: What is the adaptive capacity of a tourism destination through its businesses?

The complex adaptive systems are represented based on an adaptive cycle that consists of four stages (Nkhata et al., 2008): exploitation, conservation, release, and reorganization. Exploitation represents the initial stages of a system when resources are abundant, and the system undergoes rapid expansion. It is characterized by innovation, exploration, and accumulation of resources and connections. As the system matures, it becomes more stable and efficient in the conservation phase. The focus shifts from exploration to exploitation of existing resources. The system becomes more resistant to external disturbances and reinforces existing structures and patterns. Release: At some point, the system reaches a threshold where it can no longer adapt or respond effectively to changing conditions. A breakdown or release of accumulated structures, resources, or relationships characterizes this phase. Internal or external shocks, disturbances, or crises can trigger it. After the release phase, the system enters a reorganization period. This phase allows the emergence of new structures, relationships, and strategies that allow the system to adapt and evolve. It represents a moment of opportunity for innovation, learning, and transformation.

Holling, Gunderson, and Lance (2002) introduced the concept of Panarchy. This concept presents a social-ecological system as an interactive set of adaptive cycles[4] produced by dynamic tensions between novelty and efficiency at multiple scales. Initially considered a conceptual framework, Panarchy has grown beyond a concept to give meaning to the different levels of hierarchy where an adaptive system develops.

Each system can only be understood and managed by focusing on a single scale. All systems, especially ecological and social systems, exist and function simultaneously at multiple scales of space, organization, and time. The interactions (Figure 1) between these scales are fundamental in determining the dynamics of a system at whatever level it is focused, and these hierarchical interactions are represented by the Panarchy (Gunderson & Holling, 2002).

Figure 1. Panarchy of interconnected adaptive cycles.

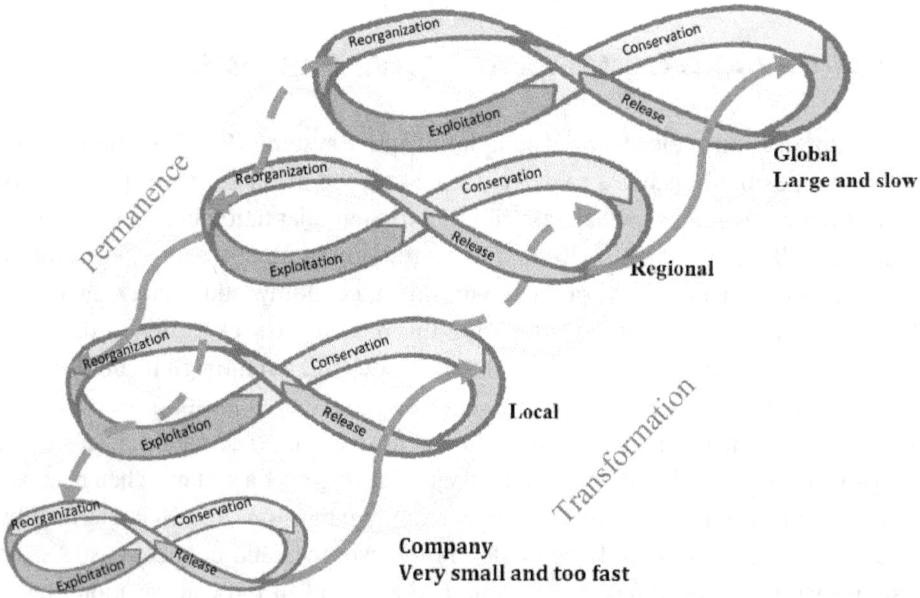

Source: Modified from Extremadura (2022).

A social system operates at different geographical scales (Figure 1). Here, the enterprise is considered to adapt faster with shorter cycles. At each level, changes coincide, providing feedback between the outside and inside of these scales. Changes and impacts between systems at the global level take much longer, considering that more agents are needed, corresponding to a larger geographical space. On the other hand, in local systems, it is the opposite; changes and impacts occur in very short periods because individual agents exert significant influence, and the territory is also smaller.

All systems have an adaptive cycle, which Holling studied in 1986. This cycle consists of four phases commonly occurring in systems' change processes. These processes result from their internal dynamics and external influence: growth, conservation, release, or creative destruction and reorganization.

Systems operating at global scales establish or achieve the permanence of long-term changes for regional and local systems. Meanwhile, smaller systems (firms) generally establish the properties of larger ones through their interactions (Pendall et al., 2009).

This model makes it possible to understand the contribution of the business to the resilience of the local tourism system. The contribution is not individual but rather the contribution of the collective of businesses operating in the territory to construct resilient territories.

A tourism system is essentially a complex socioeconomic system whose interaction is based on information and communication, open, susceptible to variations in the environment that serves as context, which is in a dynamic equilibrium, with continuous adaptive adjustments of the system (Moreira et al., 2021).

RESILIENCE AND COLLECTIVE INTELLIGENCE IN A TOURIST COMPLEX ADAPTIVE SYSTEM

Like many other concepts, resilience has evolved and been explained by different disciplines. A relatively general definition of resilience states that it is the ability of a system to function while disturbed (static resilience) or the ability and speed of a system to recover (dynamic resilience) (Rose, 2017).

In the territory context, it implies the capacity to generate organizational ways based on learning[5] that arises from disturbances, i.e., innovation in the face of unpredictable situations that allow for adaptation (Holling, 1973;1996).

The entire flow of matter, energy, and information in complex socio-ecological systems generates feedback loops through which the system can generate knowledge and use it to its advantage to adapt (collective intelligence). This idea leads to the second idea: collective resilience is closely linked to collective intelligence. Behind a resilient system is collective intelligence, and in the same way, behind a resilient company is collective intelligence.

This concept is entirely related to the Complex Adaptive Systems (CAS) theory. CAS serves as a basis for understanding the adaptive success of these systems, so resilience is intrinsic to the level of adaptation. Resilience can only be considered by considering collective intelligence.

The CAS represents a type of system made up of diverse elements working at different levels. These elements are part of an extensive interconnected network that can change its structure and behavior based on learning experience, eventually leading to the whole system's evolution (Carmichael & Hadžikadić, 2019; Ma et al., 2020). Collective intelligence is the driver of evolution in complex adaptive systems. These systems do not change simply for change; they react to the environment based on their learning, creativity, and collective knowledge.

Therefore, this model shows (Figure 2) the existence of interdependence and non-linearity in social systems and the capacity of self-organization to achieve their adaptation to changes. In a tourism system, the CAS allows its structure to be classified into four elements for study: agent system, external environment system, tourism service facility system, and tourism attraction system (Yang et al., 2019).

Figure 2. Complex adaptive rural tourism system

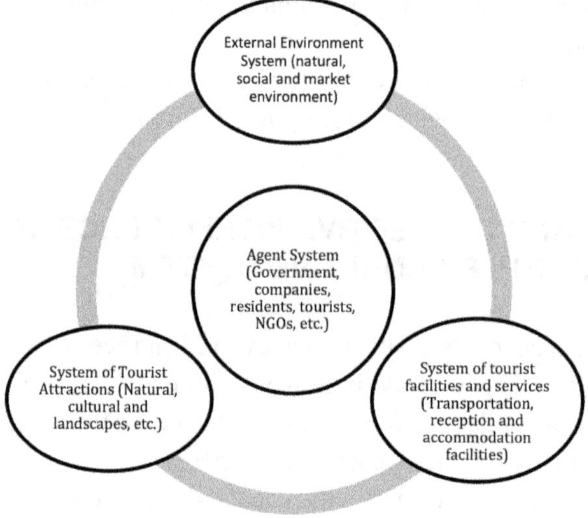

Source: Own elaboration.

Yang et al. (2019) identify that these microscopic agents promote the hierarchical differentiation and diversity of macroscopic systems, as well as their spatial structure, level of development, and adaptability. This ultimately allows for understanding the evolution of tourism destination systems. Evolution allows for the adaptation of both system elements and the whole system, and innovations are the main evolutionary features in socioeconomic systems (González & Martin, 2016).

Understanding both vertical and horizontal interactions and feedback and amplification movements in tourism systems is essential to achieving their resilience (Figure 2). Within a tourism destination (which can be considered a system in itself), the leader is the system of agents who make decisions based on what they learn from the perturbations and conditions of the external environment.

This system of agents promotes the dynamics, self-organization, and adaptation of everything. It achieves this by exchanging materials, information, and energies with the two sub-systems: tourist service facilities and tourist attractions. Finally, it achieves the development and evolution of tourist destinations. Panarchy explains how all these systems work at different scales vertically and horizontally simultaneously and experience different levels of influence on each other (Figure 3); if we talk about tourism systems, the same principle applies.

Figure 3. Scales of complex systems and panarchy.

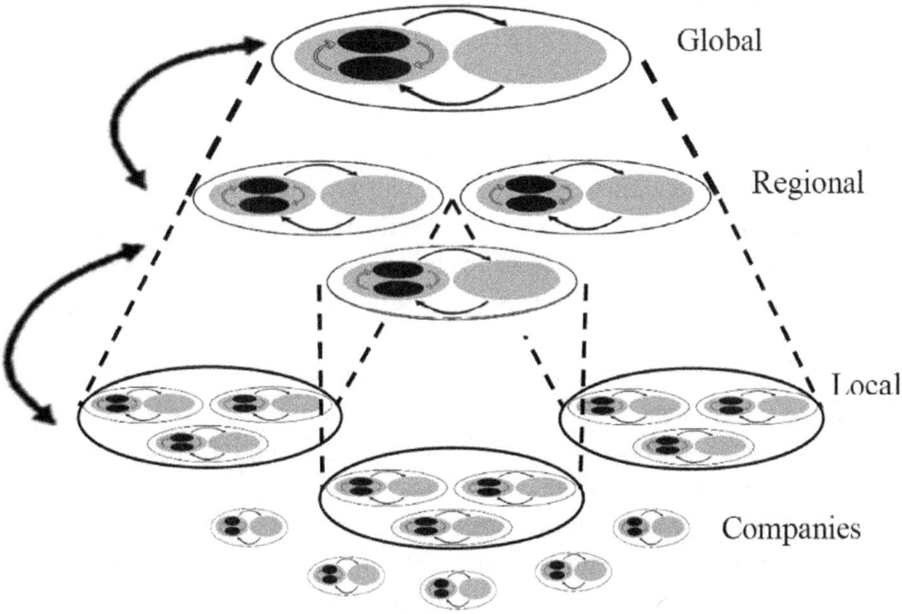

Source: Raskin, 2006.

What happens inside the company? The company is made up of individuals who do not act in isolation. Staff members act based on their experience, the norms and rules of the company, and the influence of those around them, and they are socially constructed within the company. Individuals are part of a whole, and their actions contribute to the collective. Management capabilities within a firm based on CAS theory are identified by four fundamental characteristics (Anderson, 1999):

1. The firms (agents) that make up the system do not follow the same knowledge schema, which determines their decisions.

2. Firms are interconnected through feedback loops, so agents' behavior is dictated not by the individual actions of one but by the interactions between all. They collaborate.
3. Companies evolve from one to another depending on the decisions taken. These decisions are always based on the actions already taken by the companies.

Although the evolution of all firms is connected, the relationship between them is different. As a consequence of successful recombination, new actors may emerge. This leads to a change in the pattern of interconnections, levels, and connection strength. On the other hand, the survival of A social system in a capitalist environment has economic aspects inherent in the social ones. Thus, systems that survive, adapt, and obtain favorable results are considered competitive. Analyzing a tourism system implies approaching it from a perspective in which resilience, adaptive capacity, and competitiveness are intertwined in the same phenomenon under study.

Rural tourism is an open system. It is continuously exposed to the relatively autonomous pressures of its dynamic environment (Hartman, 2020) and has numerous interactions between the sectors operating within the territory. The territory has multiple stakeholders with varied and often conflicting interests. The diverse interests of the different actors and the dynamic and non-linear nature of the interactions between the different components add further complexity to rural tourism systems (Sedarati et al., 2018).

Therefore, a comprehensive and systematic understanding (Hulland & Houston, 2020) of the elements that affect or enhance adaptive capacity is necessary to broaden and deepen knowledge on this topic. By adapting, they not only survive but also become more competitive.

The following are the models that function as references and are widely accepted within the academic community for analyzing the adaptation of tourism systems. These models consider the main factors for the adaptation of enterprises to the environment.

1. Toledo, Valdez, and Polero (1998) created the Integrated Interfunctional System Model of Competitiveness in Tourism Destinations (SIIC). SIIC seeks to develop a tourism cluster's competitive advantage based on "a holistic approach and from the general theory of systems. It is considered that the tourism sector, specifically a tourism cluster, is a homeostatic open system with equifinality, configured to achieve sustainable competitiveness" (Toledo et al., 1998, p. 14).
2. Ritchie and Crouch's (2003) Calgary Model was first presented in 1993. Its conceptual structure was further developed and refined until 2003, becoming one of the most comprehensive models of tourism competitiveness. It is based on the functioning of tourism within an open system, which is constantly being

influenced by continuous changes in the wider environment, which considers that interactions at both global and local scales affect competitiveness performance as either threats or opportunities (Ritchie & Crouch, 2003). Therefore, the analysis focuses on identifying these opportunities and threats to favor the competitive success of these tourism products, identifying six categories in the macro-environment: economic, technological, ecological, political and legal, socio-cultural, and demographic.

3. Based on the model proposed by Ritchie and Crouch (2003), the Integrated model of tourism destination competitiveness is generated (Dwyer & Kim, 2003). This model is based on the search for closer and more real relationships between its factors through two components: first, the resources represented by the "raw material" with which they must develop the activity, in turn, are inherited and/or created; second, the environment that provides the scenarios for development, policy and management and demand conditions.
4. The fourth is The Premier-ranked Tourist Destination, created by Genest and Legg (2003). It presents a methodology for assessing a tourism destination's market situation. This model identifies failures and competitive advantages because the basis of the evaluation is the observation of the destination's performance in each area where the tourism product is developed, as well as the opinion and satisfaction levels of the tourists. The above generates tools for strategic planning and tourism development as a sustainable economic activity in a locality. As a tool, its structure is expected to allow:
    - Capture the attributes, factors, or conditions necessary for a tourism destination to be perceived as a privileged competitive area.
    - Identify weaknesses and gaps that need to be addressed.
    - Identify strengths and opportunities that could be used to create a sustainable competitive advantage.
    - Enable consistent measurement of destinations to assess whether they are among the best ranked (Genest & Legg, 2003, p.9).
5. In their tourism competitiveness analysis model, Jiménez and Aquino (2012) propose to analyze a destination's competitiveness by grouping factors for analysis. This clustering is done based on the relationships between the destination and the tourist in different time slices. These authors also analyze the results found from these relationships regarding tourist satisfaction, environmental care, equity, and economic efficiency (Jiménez & Aquino, 2012). This model differs from others because it provides relevance to the outcomes of tourism activity, manifested in the tourist, the level of responsible use of natural and cultural resources, and the socioeconomic effects (Garcés et al., 2018).

Table 1 shows the purpose and objective of each model, as well as their relationship with the factors for environmental adaptation. It should be noted that the models that emphasize economic development include cultural and natural conservation in their evaluative considerations to achieve the long-term competitiveness of the tourism product and contribute to social welfare.

Table 1. Main models for tourism competitiveness

Model	Purpose	Sustainability dimensions	Adaptation factors
Integrated Interfunctional System of Competitiveness in Tourist Destinations IISC (Toledo et al., 1998)	It analyzes and studies elements of the tourism system within a cluster.	Emphasis on long-term economic development.	Critical mass and nature of demand, Cluster, competitive, cooperative and consumer relationship strategies.
Crouch and Ritchie's Calgary Model (2003)	It conceptualizes the relationship between sustainability and competitiveness through a model for tourism destinations	The balance between economic and governmental development, as well as environmental and cultural preservation.	Innate resources and essential attractions, supporting resources, destination management, policy, approach, and development. Determining qualifiers and enhancers
Integrated Model of Tourism Destination Competitiveness (Dwyer & Kim, 2003)	Define competitiveness through the search for genuine relationships between its factors.	Economic emphasis with developmental, cultural, and developmental, cultural, and environmental implications.	It is divided into three elements: resources, environment, management, and demand conditions, and one more, the synthesis of the destination's competitiveness.
The Premier-ranked Tourist Destinations (Genest & Legg, 2003)	Development of a self-assessment model for destinations to identify competitive advantages and disadvantages.	Economic emphasis with developmental, cultural and environmental implications	Dimension product, product performance, and future dimension (long-term investment planning).
Tourism competitiveness analysis model (Jiménez & Aquino, 2012))	Increase competitive advantage over competitors while maintaining comparative advantage.	Emphasis on long-term economic development.	It is evaluated as a value chain on the relationship of four blocks: accessibility, amplifiers or reducers, destination conditions, and finally, results.

Source. Own elaboration based on Mazaro and Varsin (2008).

THE CASE OF A RURAL TOURISM SYSTEM

Smaller enterprises (SMEs) predominate in a tourism system (UNWTO, 2021). In rural tourism, clusters stand out for their small size and the familiarity of their formation with the environment (Bastakis et al., 2004). It is no exception for Tapalpa.

Tapalpa is a mountain village the Mexican government has promoted as a tourism system. The closure due to the pandemic, physical distancing, and other health measures made it easier to understand the level of adaptation of the economic agents to the environmental changes. The study showed that individual decisions prevented the company from adapting to the new scenario. However, the isolated decisions taken by the entrepreneur were never individual. Other system elements and other economic agents in Tapalpa influenced these decisions. In the same way, the decisions that each enterprise made affected the system.

The companies have maintained links with each other, the local government, and international service providers. They have also used technology to promote the services offered in this part of the country, attract new clients, and manage some of their activities.

The study's field observations, preliminary survey results, and interviews led to the conclusion that the rural tourism system was sustained as a whole and that the businesses within it were preserved until after the pandemic. Social isolation contributed to rural tourism's taking on greater significance at the global level.

The results can be explained in collective intelligence, in the expanded capacity for learning, decision-making, and problem-solving that societies can achieve when they use technology appropriately. It happens when a structure is created that helps society assimilate more perspectives and use them to make decisions more participatory and pluralistically in favor of the common good (Cervantes, 2023).

In the tourism system of Tapalpa, 122 businesses were registered as tourism businesses at the beginning of 2020. These businesses were surveyed in 2021 to find out how they were integrated into the tourism system and their capacity to adapt to changes in service (Table 2). The questions aimed to determine the extent to which business decisions had contributed to the business's adaptation. The pandemic was over, and the businesses remained in business; therefore, they all had adapted (only 22 businesses had closed).

Table 2. Adaptability of enterprises in the rural tourism system

Question	Q1. Did the company adapt quickly to the new reality?	Q2. Is the company to be performing well despite challenging market situations?	Q3. Does the company work closely with the local government?
Authors	Teece et al. (1997), the originators of the Dynamic Capabilities Theory, argue that the concept of dynamic capabilities "involves the firm's ability to integrate, build and reconfigure internal competencies to cope with highly changing environments" (p.516).	Dynamic capabilities and their study, assume resilience as the maximum achievement and competitive advantage, and in combination with CRT, it is not only the latter element but the highest levels of the three variables that control the adaptive cycle (Teece et al., 1997; Rodríguez & Ricárdez, 2020, Bakti, Lew & Kim, 2017).	It speaks of an ability to adapt through organization and collaboration with other actors within a Panarchy (Bui et al., 2020; Yang et al. 2019)

Source: Own elaboration.

Out of 100 active companies, 50 entrepreneurs responded to the survey. The results were as follows: 68.62% perceived that the company adapted quickly to the new reality; 54.90% considered that the company achieved good results despite the difficult situation for the tourism market; and only 39.21% acknowledged close collaboration with the government. The results led to grouping the companies into three study groups:

1. Critical cases (17) include eleven companies that adapted quickly, made a profit, and worked closely with the local government. The entrepreneurs answered all three questions affirmatively, supporting the theoretical framework. In addition, six companies adapted quickly but did not make a profit and needed to work closely with the local government.
2. Atypical cases (9) are nine companies that adapted to change but feel that they could have adapted more quickly, have not made a profit and have not worked closely with local government.
3. Mixed cases (22) are 15 companies that have adapted quickly but responded that they need to work more closely with local government. In addition, four companies worked closely with local government but did not perceive rapid adaptation, nor did they perceive benefits during the change process, while three companies relate close collaboration with local government to rapid adaptation, with no benefits.

CONCLUSION

The system itself causes adaptability in enterprises. This capacity does not depend on the decisions of the entrepreneur. Instead, the elements of the system contribute to adaptation. However, the entrepreneurs' decisions contributed to the tourism system. Therefore, it is essential to consider all system elements within a Panarchy and their adaptive properties. In this way, actions and changes can be implemented that enable a higher level of resilience.

Collective intelligence played a predominant role in the changing scenario. The self-organization of agents within the tourism system was not an accident but a lucky coincidence. The intelligence of individuals creates synergies within a collective. The research finds that at the local level, most tourism enterprises perceived little adaptive capacity derived from measures imposed or implemented by higher levels of the Panarchy system and environmental conditions (short-term events). Despite their perception, the reality shows that all these enterprises adapted and managed to maintain their activities despite the challenges imposed. More research is required to understand local dynamics. Each tourist destination has unique characteristics, and collective intelligence can manifest differently. Understanding how knowledge is organized and shared in a community helps optimize natural and cultural resources, minimizing environmental impact and maximizing economic benefits. It also helps identify effective ways to involve the local community in decision-making.

The conclusion is that adaptability is achieved by the system rather than on an individual basis. This analysis found that critical cases confirm the theory, outlier cases give new evidence by contradicting it, and mixed cases allow nuances to be made in understanding the differences between critics and outliers. The majority of tourism enterprises within Tapalpa, Jalisco, perceived positively at least one of the three indicators of adaptive capacity; very few responded negatively to all three questions (9), indicating that overall, there is resilience (at different levels) in the destination of Tapalpa, Jalisco.

These entrepreneurs perceive that they were able to adapt to the new reality and assimilate the changes established from the systems operating at global scales, and ultimately, they are the ones who achieve permanence in the changes.

In this case, the 2020 situation forced both global and regional systems to impose health measures and economic cutbacks, which deeply affected the local systems, of which these rural tourism destinations are a part. It forced them to make drastic changes in order to survive.

Adaptation comes at a time when the negative impacts are less. It should be considered that this adaptation process is dictated not only by societal behaviours, but by events or in this case by the pandemic situation.

Another critical point is that very few responded positively to all the questions, but a majority perceived that they adapted quickly to the pandemic. The latter is a global unforeseen event; it demanded speed, and therefore, there needed to be more accumulated capital to cope with it. They needed to have business knowledge to adapt in the best way. That is why the complex adaptive systems theory offers exciting contributions to business resilience, collective intelligence, and competitiveness in rural areas.

These enterprises are part of the same system. They do not follow or apply the same pattern of actions. Therefore, the capacities of the actors in each enterprise and their relationship with the level of resilience are different. The resilience of these enterprises was due to their connection and how they were integrated into the tourism system, which is, therefore, the result of a collective phenomenon rather than an individual one.

The constantly changing global scenario (natural disasters, wars, health emergencies, and climate change) affects every economic and social system. The challenge is for local systems, not just tourism systems, to become robust enough to withstand these shocks and flexible enough to recover, reinvent, or diversify to achieve resilience. Doing so implies putting any mechanisms that incentivize collective intelligence at the centre of attention in order to have adaptive systems in place. Taking this perspective allows us to identify the conditions that contribute to the ability of systems to adapt, evolve, and build resilience (Hartman, 2018).

REFERENCES

Ambrosio, M. (2017). Ciclo adaptativo y cambio rural: El enfoque territorial en la gestión de la resiliencia rural. *Revista de Fomento Social*, 72(3-4), 665–682. DOI: 10.32418/rfs.2017.287-288.1470

An, W., & Alarcón, S. (2020). How Can Rural Tourism Be Sustainable? A Systematic Review. *Sustainability (Basel)*, 12(18), 7758. DOI: 10.3390/su12187758

Anderson, P. (1999). Complexity Theory and Organization Science. *Organization Science*, 10(3), 216–232. DOI: 10.1287/orsc.10.3.216

Bakti, L., Lew, A., & Kim, Y. (2017). A Resilient Approach to Collaborative Coral Reef Conservation on Gili Trawangan, Indonesia. In Lew, A., & Cheer, J. (Eds.), *Understanding Tourism Resilience: Adapting to Environmental Change*. Routledge. DOI: 10.4324/9781315463971-12

Bastakis, C., Buhalis, D., & Butler, R. (2004). The Perception of Small and Medium-Sized Tourism Accommodation Providers on the Impacts of the Tour Operator's Power in Easter Mediterranean. *Tourism Management*, 25(2), 151–170. DOI: 10.1016/S0261-5177(03)00098-0

Bui, H., Jones, T., Weaver, D., & Le, A. (2020). The adaptive resilience of living cultural heritage in a tourism destination. *Journal of Sustainable Tourism*, 28(7), 1022–1040. DOI: 10.1080/09669582.2020.1717503

Carmichael, T., & Hadžikadić, M. (2019). The fundamentals of complex adaptive systems. In *Complex Adaptive Systems*. Springer. DOI: 10.1007/978-3-030-20309-2_1

Cervantes, F. (2023). *Del algoritmo a la inteligencia colectiva. Un experimento con el potencial de ayudar a la mejora continua de los programas públicos*. PNUD.

Colella, V., Klopfer, E., & Resnick, M. (2001). *Adventures in modeling: Exploring complex, dynamic systems with StarLogo*. Teachers College Press.

Díaz de Rada, V., & Portilla, I. (2015). Encuestas telefónicas: Estrategias para mejorar la colaboración. *Perspectiva Empresarial*, 2(1), 97–115. DOI: 10.16967/rpe.v2n1a7

Dwyer, L., & Kim, C. (2003). Destination Competitiveness: Determinants and Indicators. *Current Issues in Tourism*, 6(5), 369–414. DOI: 10.1080/13683500308667962

Extremadura. (2022). *Estructura de actuación: ecosistema 2030*. Extremadura 2030. Link: https://extremadura2030.com/ecosistema-extremadura-2030/

Galderisi, A., & Limongi, G. (2024). A methodological path to foster inner peripheries' sustainable and resilient futures: A research experience from Southern Italy. *Futures*, 156, 103320. DOI: 10.1016/j.futures.2024.103320

Galesic, M., Barkoczi, D., Berdahl, A., Biro, D., Carbone, G., Giannoccaro, I., Goldstone, R. L., Gonzalez, C., Kandler, A., Kao, A. B., Kendal, R., Kline, M., Lee, E., Massari, G. F., Mesoudi, A., Olsson, H., Pescetelli, N., Sloman, S. J., Smaldino, P. E., & Stein, D. L. (2023). Beyond collective intelligence: Collective adaptation. *Journal of the Royal Society, Interface*, 20(200), 20220736. DOI: 10.1098/rsif.2022.0736 PMID: 36946092

Garcês, S., Pocinho, M., Jesus, S., & Rieber, M. (2018). Positive psychology and tourism: A systematic literature review. *Tourism & Management Studies*, 14(3), 41–51. DOI: 10.18089/tms.2018.14304

García, M. (2019). Del riesgo a la resiliencia. Hacia el diseño y gestión adaptativo del paisaje. *Estudios del Hábitat*, 17(1), 1–15.

Genest, J., & Legg, D. (2003). *Premier-ranked tourist destinations: development of a framework for analysis and its self-guided workbook.* Ontario. Link: http://www.tourism.gov.on.ca/english/research/pdf/self-guidedworkbook.pdf

González, T., & Martin, V. (2016). *Emprendimiento e innovación para el desarrollo local.* México UNAM FCA.

Gunderson, L., & Holding, C. (2002). *Panarchy: Understanding Transformations in Human and Natural Systems.* Island Press.

Hartman, S. (2018). Resilient tourism destinations? Governance implications of bringing theories of resilience and adaptive capacity to tourism practice. In Innerhofer, Fontanari, & Pechlaner (Eds.). *Destination resilience – Challenges and opportunities for destination management and governance* (pp. 66–75). Abingdon: Routledge. DOI: 10.4324/9780203701904-5

Hartman, S. (2020). Adaptative tourism areas in times of change. *Annals of Tourism Research*, 87, 102987. Advance online publication. DOI: 10.1016/j.annals.2020.102987 PMID: 32836568

Holling, C. (1973). Resilience and Stability of Ecological Systems. *Annual Review of Ecology and Systematics*, 4(1), 1–23. DOI: 10.1146/annurev.es.04.110173.000245

Holling, C. (1996). *Engineering Resilience versus Ecological Resilience.* Engineering Within Ecological Constraints, National Academy of Engineering, National Academy Press.

Holling, C., Gunderson, L., & Peterson, G. (2002). Sustainability and Panarchies. In *Panarchy: understanding transformations in human and natural systems*. Island Press.

Hulland, J., & Houston, M. (2020). Why Systematic Review Papers and Meta-Analyses Matter: An Introduction to the Special Issue on Generalizations in Marketing. *Journal of the Academy of Marketing Science*, 48(3), 351–359. DOI: 10.1007/s11747-020-00721-7

Jiménez, P., & Aquino, F. (2012). Propuesta de un modelo de competitividad de destinos turísticos. *Estudios y Perspectivas en Turismo*, 21(4), 977–995.

Lévy, P. (1997). *Collective Intelligence*. Perseus Books.

Ma, F., Xue, T., & Huang, S. (2020). On the Conceptual Framework of Tourism Complex Research from the Perspective of the Theory of Complex Adaptive System. *Tourism Management and Technology Economy*, 3, 1–15.

Mazaro, R., & Varzin, G. (2008). Modelos de Competitividad para Destinos Turísticos en el Marco de la Sostenibilidad. *Revista de Administração contemporánea,* 12, 789-809.

Moreira, C., Ferreira, R., & Santos, T. (2021). Smart Tourism and Local Heritage: Phygital Experiences and the Development of Geotourism Routes. In Oliveira, L., Amaro, A., & Melro, A. (Eds.), *Handbook of Research on Cultural Heritage and Its Impact on Territory Innovation and Development* (pp. 206–232). IGI Global. DOI: 10.4018/978-1-7998-6701-2.ch012

Müller, S., Kirst, A., Bergmann, H., & Bird, B. (2023). Entrepreneurs' actions and venture success: A structured literature review and suggestions for future research. *Small Business Economics*, 60(1), 199–226. DOI: 10.1007/s11187-022-00644-3

Nkhata, A., Breen, C., & Freimund, W. (2008). Resilient social relationships and collaboration in the management of social–ecological systems. *Ecology and Society*, 13(1), art2. DOI: 10.5751/ES-02164-130102

Pendall, R., Foster, A., & Cowell, M. (2009). Resilience and regions: Building understanding of the metaphor. *Cambridge Journal of Regions, Economy and Society*, 3(1), 71–84. DOI: 10.1093/cjres/rsp028

Qiao, D., Yuan, W., & Li, H. (2024). Regulation and resilience: Panarchy analysis in forest socio-ecosystem of Northeast National Forest Region, China. *Journal of Environmental Management*, 353, 120295. DOI: 10.1016/j.jenvman.2024.120295 PMID: 38330839

Raskin, P. (2006). *World Lines. Pathways, Pivots, and the Global Future*. Tellus Institute.

Ritchie, J., & Crouch, G. (2003). *The competitive destination*. CAB International Publishing.

Rodríguez, R., & Ricárdez, J. (2020). Aproximación a la gestión ambiental proactiva como capacidad dinámica en el sector turístico hotelero mexicano. Elementos determinantes para su desarrollo. *El Periplo Sustentable*, (38), 194–218. DOI: 10.36677/elperiplo.v0i38.7029

Rose, A. (2017). *Defining and measuring economic resilience from a societal, environmental and security perspective*. Springer Singapore., DOI: 10.1007/978-981-10-1533-5

Sedarati, P., Santos, S., & Pintassilgo, P. (2018). System Dynamics in Tourism Planning and Development. *Tourism Planning & Development*, 1–25. DOI: 10.1080/21568316.2018.1436586

Shepherd, D., & Williams, T. (2023). Different response paths to organizational resilience. *Small Business Economics*, 61(1), 23–58. DOI: 10.1007/s11187-022-00689-4 PMID: 38625189

Tardivo, G., Scilla, A., & Viassone, M. (2014). A New Frontier in the Satisfaction of the Cultural Tourist: The QR Code. In Aiello, L. (Ed.), *Handbook of Research on Management of Cultural Products: E-Relationship Marketing and Accessibility Perspectives* (pp. 348–366). IGI Global. DOI: 10.4018/978-1-4666-5007-7.ch017

Teece, D., Pisano, G., & Shuen, A. (1997). Dynamic Capabilities and Strategic Management. *Strategic Management Journal*, 18(7), 509–533. DOI: 10.1002/(SICI)1097-0266(199708)18:7<509::AID-SMJ882>3.0.CO;2-Z

Toledo, G., Valdés, J., & Pollero, A. (1998). *Empresas turísticas en ambiente globalizado: marketing y competitividad. Estudio de casos de clústeres turísticos*. FEA/USP.

UNWTO. (2021). *The Importance of SMEs in the Tourism Industry*. UNWTO. Link https://www.unwto.org/es/node/12378

van der Straaten, K., Narula, R., & Giuliani, E. (2023). The multinational enterprise, development, and the inequality of opportunities: A research agenda. *Journal of International Business Studies*, 54(9), 1623–1640. DOI: 10.1057/s41267-023-00625-y

Wang, T., Yang, Z., Han, F., Yu, J., Ma, X., & Han, J. (2024). Assessment of tourism socio-ecological system resilience in arid areas: A case study of Xinjiang, China. *Ecological Indicators*, 159, 111748. DOI: 10.1016/j.ecolind.2024.111748

Watson, R., & Levin, M. (2023). The collective intelligence of evolution and development. *Collective Intelligence*, 2(2). DOI: 10.1177/26339137231168355

Yang, Z., Yin, M., Xu, J., & Lin, W. (2019). Spatial evolution model of tourist destinations based on complex adaptive system theory: A case study of Southern Anhui, China. *Journal of Geographical Sciences*, 29(8), 1411–1434. DOI: 10.1007/s11442-019-1669-z

Zeren, G., Tan, J., Zhang, Q., & Qiuying, B. (2023). Rebuilding rural community cooperative institutions and their role in herder adaptation to climate change. *Climate Policy*, 23(4), 522–537. DOI: 10.1080/14693062.2023.2184763

Zhakupov, A., Yessilov, A., Yelemessov, A., & Ismailova, N. (2023). The Impact of the Pandemic on the Economic Development about Small and Medium Sized Businesses. *Theoretical and Practical Research in Economic Fields*, 14(1), 146–163. DOI: 10.14505/tpref.v14.1(27).12

ENDNOTES

1 Collective adaptation can be seen as an emergent property of a complex socio-cognitive system driven by dynamic interactions of social integration strategies, social environments and problem structures collectives face (Galesic et al., 2023).

2 CAS is a third-generation systems theory, developed based on first-generation system theories (represented by general system theory and cybernetics) and second-generation system theories (represented by dissipative structure theory and synergy theory) (Yang et al., 2019), which arose from the biological study of complex lifestyles, as a system that aims to evidence the existence of large, interconnected networks (Carmichael & Hadžikadić, 2019). Complex = challenging to understand or difficult to predict. Dynamic = moving, changing. Adaptive = changing to adapt to an environment or condition. Complex systems are collections of simple units or agents interacting in a system. A complex system is a large-scale system whose behaviors may change, evolve, or adapt (Colella et al., 2001).

3 Traditionally, rural areas are associated with agricultural activities, and the people there are seen as mere physical support. Beyond a territory, when approached from a systemic perspective, rural areas are an open system, as they are seen as an environment in which agents and resources have close interactions. As a subset of social systems, some interdependent relationships between beings and resources are "mediated" through biophysical and non-human biological units (Ambrosio, 2017).

4 An essential part of studying a CAS is understanding cycles, which were initially proposed for studying natural systems (Gunderson & Holling, 2002). However, as time went on and new research was conducted, it was found that the dynamics of other complex and non-linear systems could also be explained by adaptive cycles, such as in the.

5 Economic networks and territorial power depend on humankind's capacity to acquire knowledge and develop collective imagination rapidly, as does survival (Lévy, 1997).

Chapter 8
Building Resilient Companies Through Internal Marketing

Tania Elena González Alvarado
https://orcid.org/0000-0002-3062-9665
University of Guadalajara, Mexico

Francia Contreras García
https://orcid.org/0000-0002-5096-6415
Instituto Tecnológico y de Estudios Superiores de Monterrey, Mexico

Pablo Cabanelas
https://orcid.org/0000-0002-4661-0141
University of Vigo, Spain

ABSTRACT

This chapter describes the relationship between talent attraction, internal communication, and empowerment as crucial elements of company resilience. The transnational company under study operates globally and has business units in thirty countries. The chapter is divided into three sections: the first section explains internal marketing and its relation to business resilience; the second section describes the actions that the transnational company carried out from 2020 to 2021; the third part presents the research results obtained by applying a questionnaire to the company's employees at two different times in order to derive conclusions on the elements that have contributed to business resilience.

DOI: 10.4018/979-8-3693-7272-2.ch008

INTRODUCTION

Resilience is a quality that every individual possesses (Lu et al., 2023). It is the ability to cope with and adapt to change (Duchek, 2020) to consider the new situation better than the previous one. Humans are resilient (Kuldas & Foody, 2022); however, resilience is not homogeneous (Duro et al., 2023). Each person has different degrees of resilience and ways of achieving it (Denckla et al., 2020).

This individual resilience contributes to collective resilience (Saul, 2020). Human beings are social beings, not isolated entities. In the same way, resilience interpreted in isolation for each individual is biased. Resilience is a collective phenomenon. Therefore, an organization also has a degree of resilience if each individual is resilient.

What makes one organization more resilient than another? In principle, this depends on how the members of an organization cope with change, integrate into the collective, and commit themselves to the organization's goals. High organizational resilience may be the spontaneous result of organizational leadership rather than a deliberate instrument or policy to manage resilience (Karman, 2020).

The world events of the last few years made this clear. The pandemic changed the world radically. Markets were affected. Businesses, too, were forced to transform their strategies from one day to the next. These changes made it possible to observe and understand how individuals acted collectively. Some organizations were found to be more resilient than others.

Resilience is essential for businesses to survive and remain competitive (Conz & Magnani, 2020). The least resilient companies disappeared, while the most resilient companies remained in the market and increased their profits or were little affected. A study of a transnational company that successfully adapted to the new reality identified that internal communication, empowerment, and talent attraction were essential for the company to adjust to changes in the global environment, which was observed during and after the pandemic (Contreras & González, 2021).

This chapter describes the relationship between talent attraction, internal communication, and empowerment as crucial elements of company resilience. The transnational company under study operates globally and has business units in thirty countries.

The chapter is divided into three sections: the first explains internal marketing and its relation to business resilience; the second describes the actions that the transnational company carried out from 2020 to 2021; and the third presents the research results obtained by applying a questionnaire to the company's employees at two different times to derive conclusions on the elements that have contributed to business resilience.

INTERNAL MARKETING AND ITS RELATIONSHIP TO BUSINESS RESILIENCE

A characteristic of the transnational organization is empowering employees, which increases human development and quality of life despite the significant challenges that economic inequality, the global crisis, and climate change have brought about.

Research shows that aligning employee and organizational interests leads to higher productivity, engagement, and well-being (Ibrahim et al., 2020). It even reduces work-related stress (Garrosa & Carmona, 2011). Unfortunately, the models applied to achieve this reconciliation in recent decades have focused only on productivity, sometimes sacrificing employee well-being (Drucker, 1999).

Decreased production costs have led to falling wages and job insecurity (Borderías & Martini, 2020). This situation allows stating that the top management technique has led to the tool delivering results far from the employee's well-being, also affecting the organization's resilience in times of more significant environmental change. An employee who sees the company as an organization unlikely to engage with their well-being is unlikely to engage with the company in unfavorable times so that it does not close down. Even if the company's closure leads to unemployment, employees who have recognized the company's lack of commitment to them will not act in favor of the company in difficult times.

Therefore, the employee represents a substantial investment of effort, cost, and time (Bavdaž et al., 2023). Turnover, job abandonment, change of company, and bad reputation negatively affect the company and the employees in situations that require collaboration, teamwork, trust, leadership, communication, and organizational culture, among other things.

The logic driven by further production cost reduction through labor flexibility and outsourcing (Mukherjee et al., 2023) has contributed to the erosion of the global economic system, which no longer guarantees the long-term sustainability of global business (Martín & González, 2016).

Given the current challenges and the quest to create more inclusive workplaces that guarantee employees' well-being while making the company more resilient, internal marketing is considered to provide a theoretical model that, in practice, offers particularly appropriate tools (Contreras & González, 2021).

Internal marketing means (1) employee satisfaction and motivation (Yi et al., 2023) to (2) focus on customer and customer satisfaction (Hidayat & Idrus, 2023) through (3) cross-functional coordination and integration (Pradono et al., 2024), (4) with a market focus (Yi et al., 2023), and (5) the implementation of corporate strategies and specific actions (Sutaguna et al., 2023). Under this perspective, job satisfaction is granted through customer satisfaction (Lings, 2004). Employees are more likely to engage in collaborative behaviors (Chun et al., 2018) that contribute to collective intelligence when satisfied and motivated.

This resilience within the workforce helps them adapt to challenges and maintain high performance. Motivated employees care about the customer and improve their experience, increasing their satisfaction. Resilient staff respond effectively to customer needs, demonstrating collective intelligence because they work as a team and share knowledge. Internal marketing encourages collaboration between departments, achieving more significant use of collective intelligence. This coordination allows organizations to respond quickly to market changes, showing resilience in a dynamic environment.

Companies can harness collective intelligence to innovate and adapt by aligning employee efforts with market demands. Resilience here is reflected in the organization's ability to pivot strategies based on customer feedback and market trends. The actions taken to implement strategies depend on a motivated and knowledgeable workforce. Resilience is vital for overcoming obstacles, while collective intelligence ensures that diverse perspectives contribute to strategic decisions.

From an internal marketing point of view, the employee is an internal customer. It is a more humanistic view of the company's results because it includes the different perceptions of employees and the multiple realities that coexist in their work area. By operating as an internal market, the company is diluted between the labor and goods and services markets, being more congruent in its actions and adapting to changes more quickly. Diluting between the two markets does not mean disappearing; it means acting with the same logic and speed and becoming more resilient (Contreras & González, 2021).

Based on previous studies (Contreras & González, 2021), the elements of internal marketing that facilitate the dynamics described above are Empowerment, Internal Communication, and Talent Attraction. These factors make the company's capabilities dynamic and respond equally quickly and accurately to external changes (Figure 1).

Figure 1. Internal marketing

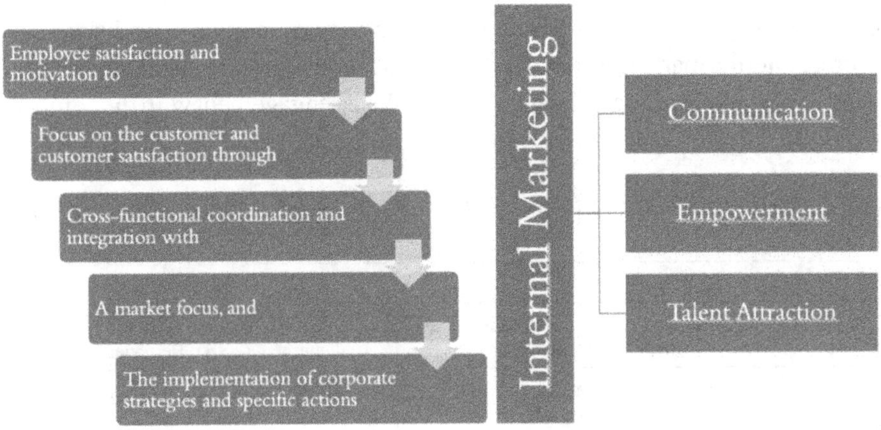

Source: Own elaboration based on Contreras & González (2021).

Internal marketing facilitates labor flexibility for the benefit of employees. A company with labor flexibility is a constantly assembled puzzle (Sisto, 2009). In this puzzle, the employee becomes the true protagonist of business performance in unstable situations, resulting in long-term permanence, professional growth, and talent development.

The human element connects and imparts meaning to all other components. Table 1 presents the questionnaire, detailing each question's theoretical foundations linking internal marketing to resilience. Internal marketing brings speed and congruence between the company's internal elements and those external to it, increases its capacity to respond to changes, and even turns it into an agent of change (Contreras & González, 2021).

Internal marketing is the recognition of employees as the company's first market; therefore, managers need to identify and satisfy their needs (Qaisar & Muhamad, 2021). The marketing mix focuses on job satisfaction. The product is the job; the price is the cost of providing the employee with what is necessary for their activities; the place is the work environment; the promotion refers to positive communication that incentivizes productivity and strategic and operational activities that facilitate work (Qaisar & Muhamad, 2021). Collective intelligence is significant for collaboration, co-creation value, and make-decision.

Resilience is important because investing in the right resources helps employees perform their jobs better and enables them to adapt to challenges. Resilient employees can handle setbacks, bounce back from difficulties, and continuously grow with the support provided.

In short, this marketing mix approach to job satisfaction recognizes that a holistic focus on job design, resources, communication, and environment can enhance collective intelligence and resilience, leading to a more motivated and successful workforce. Internal marketing includes communication, empowerment, talent attraction, and development, directly influencing employee engagement with the company.

Table 1. Theoretical underpinning of internal marketing and its relationship to resilience

Item	Empowerment	Authors
EM1	Fixed protocols and standards are established in work procedures.	Wang et al. (2023); Stufflebeam (1994); Fetterman (2001); Bernauer (1999)
EM2	I am allowed to solve problems at my discretion.	Purkarthofer & Mäntysalo (2022); Makrooni (2020)
EM3	My supervisor encourages me to try harder.	de la Rosa-Navarro & Carmona-Lavado (2010)
EM4	I feel free to develop my work	Moriano *et al.* (2009); Moriano *et al.* (2014)
	Talent Attraction and Development	
TA1	I am proud to tell others that work here.	Handy (1995); Kimberly & Bouchikhi (1995)
TA2	I want to work here for a long time	Derrida (2005); Bailey & Kurland (1999); Smite *et al.* (2023)
TA3	Job opportunities are inclusive, flexible, and suited to my personal and professional needs.	Zhang, Hu & Lin (2023); Kumar (2023)
TA4	The company's values are aligned with my own.	Lu *et al.* (2023); Cooper *et al.* (2019)
TA5	My career plan is achievable.	Morando, Zehnter & Platania (2023); Batta, Bandameeda & Parayitam (2023)
	Internal communication	
IC1	I feel free to develop my work	Vieira (2023); Ridley (2020); Bennett & Strange (2014).
IC2	I am informed about my employee benefits and entitlements.	Mannix, Neale & Northcraft (1995)
IC3	I received the information I needed to do my job on time.	Bassanino, Fernando & Wu (2014); Kurtzberg (2014).
IC4	Information is shared openly in my team	de Vreede (2016); Shah & González (2011); Anaya & Boticario (2009)
IC5	I feel comfortable sharing my opinion	Swart *et al.* (2012); Edwards (2020)

Source: Own elaboration.

Internal Communication

Communication strategy is often defined as planned actions to achieve desired results, as it is considered the basis of a well-functioning organization (Mokhtar et al., 2019). However, strategies emerge independently of the strategist's intention. An organization with a highly changing environment must adapt at the same speed as the environment (Abaid, Cordera & Pasco, 2021). This situation leads to the emergence of strategies that transform communication structures, causing internal communication to diminish because other forms of communication are constructed at the time of change (Boromisza-Habashi, 2015).

Internal communication helps to focus on the problem, reduce uncertainty, and foster relationships between employees and the organization. It is imperative in periods that require rapid adaptation (Li et al., 2021). Communication directed at employees from the perspective of internal customers makes them feel free to do their job, keeps them informed about their benefits, and provides them with the information they need to do their job. Information is shared openly with all members, and they are encouraged to share their opinions.

A communication system with these characteristics integrates administrative functions (planning, organization, management, and control); additionally, it integrates people and links the company with its culture and environment. Communication is a fundamental instrument for creating organizational culture, communicating values to individuals that comprise the organization's body and the outside world (Sánchez, 2016).

It applies to both formal and informal communication. Both provide the basis for 1) developing the organizational culture[1] as unique and 2) developing and maintaining the group members' bond.

Organizational communication occurs within an organizational culture; it constitutes the system of pathways through which patterns of interaction between members of the organization are established. It weaves together formality and informality. Otherwise, it would be challenging to share information openly and the freedom to express personal, different, and creative points of view. Situations that make it easier to meet the company's objectives while adapting to external changes.

Communication may encourage employees to seek more feedback from different interpersonal sources, including supervisors, co-workers, and peers in other departments, enhancing creativity (Lee & Kim, 2021). Interpersonal sources contribute to performance improvements.; creativity results in new solutions to problems, the construction of different channels and forms of communication, and rapid adaptation to change.

Job satisfaction is associated with many organizational variables and is often a central consideration in organizational theory. Internal marketing variables impact job satisfaction and strengthen employee-company relationships by providing a desirable work situation. A satisfied employee values communication between co-workers.

Communication, like any system, involves technical and interpersonal subsystems. These subsystems are interrelated and interdependent and send information to the people who communicate with each other directly.

Many variables simultaneously influence an organization's communication climate. Technical and interpersonal interactions are not a function of linear, direct cause-effect relationships; they are complex processes (Martin, 1995).

The greater the interdependence through communication, the greater the integration and satisfaction. It leads to loyalty and permanent employee retention towards the company. At the same time, others will want to work for the company that offers this to its employees.

Talent Attraction and Development

The employee is satisfied (Verčič, 2021) rather than fearful of change, increasing the organization's attraction and development of talent. Relational communication is prioritized over informational communication. Relational communication has a more significant influence on affective commitment, which strengthens work engagement (Einwiller et al., 2021).

When working for the company, the external employee feels a sense of pride in the community. They want to stay with the company long-term because they consider the work opportunities inclusive, flexible, and appropriate to their personal and professional needs. The company's values align with their own, making their career plan achievable. Therefore, training, recognition, and trust are evident.

In internal marketing, training is a priority tool for adapting to change. Training someone from within the company is more accessible than bringing in a new person. Hiring someone with the desired profile can take several months due to the process of identifying and hiring the right talent.[2]. It ultimately becomes an obstacle to company growth due to the slowness experienced in the selection processes.

Retaining people due to their professional development within the company also becomes a tool to attract the best talent. Who does not want to work in a place where they are highly valued, listened to, and supported to grow professionally? A satisfied employee in this respect is the best letter of introduction. This valued employee is the one who will give the best publicity and will spontaneously enthuse others.

Employees satisfied with their professional growth will be the best magnet for attracting new talent. If it is not one employee but hundreds or thousands of employees, then the company will have such prestige in the labor market that it can guarantee it will obtain the best talent. Attracting talent is directly related to the company's image and its employees' valuation. Talent attraction and retention are linked and a widespread need. Companies go to great lengths to improve employees' image of the company they work for or would like to work for (Edwards, 2020; Sargeant & Asif, 2000).

Bearing that the most critical asset of any organization is its people, organizations that want to adapt to change successfully without sacrificing their objectives have strategies for attracting and retaining human talent. They incorporate and maintain the right people to integrate the different levels of the organization and thus guarantee the satisfaction of its needs. These companies have plans based not only on supplying the basic needs of their workers with an economic remuneration that is in line with their training and experience but also on increasing their motivation and fulfilling their expectations of growth, making a career in the company, seeking to enhance their capabilities for the benefit of both them and the organization itself (Figueroa, 2014).

Empowerment

Empowerment contributes to higher-quality results and better work performance. It is an essential element in adapting the company to new scenarios. It contributes to organizational resilience; the more empowered an employee is, the more they will contribute to the company in terms of competitiveness, productivity, resilience, and innovation.

An empowered employee enjoys a certain degree of authority and discretion to act autonomously in achieving the company's goals. This autonomy does not mean that he or she will act in isolation and opposition to his or her team. Instead, it will be a means to carry out complementary activities that reinforce the activities of the team and the company. It means acting individually with collective thinking and using autonomy without forgetting that individual decisions and actions always affect others. This way, the empowered employee will make decisions that improve the company and its members. In addition, employee satisfaction will increase when employees recognize their performance and value as a critical part of the company.

Empowerment is a dynamic, highly individualistic, and contextually stratified process (Foster et al., 1998). When the individual is empowered, communication with others is expected to be more agile and proactive. If empowerment implies the ability to mobilize resources and institutions to achieve goals (Coy et al., 2021), informal communication becomes important, while formal communication becomes less critical for achieving results.

Empowerment depends partly on organizational culture (Foster & Keys, 1997). On the other hand, the cultural background of each individual makes differences in the level and form of Empowerment (Eylon & Au, 1999). People with higher levels of empowerment are more individualistic, participate in community and organizational activities more frequently, and have a stronger sense of community than people with lower levels of Empowerment (Speer, 2000). Empowerment involves the internal customer in decision-making to better fulfill their responsibilities. It fosters a sense of belonging and creativity that strengthens leadership through fair and equitable treatment within the work team.

Organizational empowerment is a facilitation that aims to bring decision-making as close as possible to the place and time where the events occur. Alles (2002) refers to two dimensions of the concept: the first is a work method for which a change of work routines is necessary, and the second is a competence that contemplates the design of new work routines, levels of responsibility, and respective controls. Empowerment allows the organization to emerge in an environment of resilience, positioning, and social recognition.

Empowerment is an effective tool within organizations that seeks to make their work teams perform well. However, it is not a process that is implemented and works alone; the collaboration of all institution members is necessary for the benefits to be favorable for each party. (Prieto, 2015) To empower employees, fixed protocols and standards are expected to be established in the work procedures. These protocols and standards make it possible to know the scope of action and degrees of freedom the employee has.

Empowerment does not mean simply being free to do whatever comes to the employee's mind. It implies improving what is possible, overcoming or adapting to obstacles creatively to achieve the proposed objectives, and communicating new ideas or alternative measures to others. Protocols and standards are the maps that map where employees are and where they want to go in the process involved. In this way, the empowered employee knows that he or she can solve problems according to his or her judgment. It is then a reasonable judgment based on specific knowledge of the problem to be dealt with. They do not simply act; their supervisor (superior) stimulates them to try harder, making them feel free to develop their work. It makes an empowered employee satisfied with his work.

Job satisfaction affects workers' attitudes toward their duties. It arises from the correspondence between the actual work and the employee's expectations. Any self-respecting company that aims to increase its performance must consider both the motivation and satisfaction aspects of its employees. It should not be forgotten that a company's greatest asset is its human capital (Sáenz, 2013).

This dynamic and uncertain view may also facilitate a greater understanding of productivity and allow the rediscovery of why one employee is more productive than another under the same conditions, or what causes one employee to be more productive in different periods or circumstances, or even in adverse circumstances.

The framework outlined directly aligns job satisfaction with both collective intelligence and resilience. By ensuring that the product (the job), the price (the resources), the place (the work environment), and the promotion (communication and strategic activities) are aligned with these two concepts, employers can create an ecosystem where employees feel supported, engaged, and capable of facing challenges together.

Collective intelligence allows a transnational company to exploit employees' diverse experiences and skills from different cultures and regions. Resilient and intelligent teams can better identify and respond to customer needs, improving the customer experience and fostering brand loyalty. Internal marketing is considered essential to achieve all this.

Internal marketing identifies the differences between what the employer perceives about the employee's view of the company and the employee's actual perception of himself/herself in and for the company, thus reinstating his/her job, the working climate, and the employer-employee-customer relations. In this way, the company will be better able to adapt to external changes. This was the case for the transnational[3] companies under study from 2020 to 2023.

ACTIONS FROM 2020 TO 2021

The transnational company under analysis focuses on the automotive and telecommunications industries. It is worth USD 25 billion, has over 100 plants in 30 countries, and has approximately 160,000 employees. In 2019 (GPTW, 2019), Cisco recognized it as a Great Place to Work (GPTW) and in 2022 (MarthenSeries, 2022) as a sustainable company.

GPTW (2019) is a model of Internal Marketing that provides feedback to the company regarding the internal work environment and the external labor market. Companies look beyond productivity and profitability; they seek a distinction from the competition. The feedback and the distinction of GPTW contribute to the company operations in unity with the three markets: internal, labor, and goods and services. The main elements considered by this prescriptive model are comparative measurement and analysis of workplace competitiveness, Intellectual Capital for Leadership Development, and Human Capital Best Practices and Knowledge Sharing (GPTW, 2019). In the business environment, there is a lot of optimism and credibility towards this model (Contreras & González, 2021).

In this way, those who make decisions based on their beliefs lead the practice to transform the business reality; in turn, the new business reality transforms the theory (explanation of reality). The GPTW model is an essential link between practical reality and the theory of Internal Marketing (GPTW, 2019). GPTW strengthens the phenomenon (Internal Marketing) and gives it continuity in such a way that practices of Internal Marketing focused initially on the service sector have transferred to the industrial sector, with more and more companies in the industry interested in obtaining the distinction and in carrying out the necessary practices to improve employee welfare (Contreras & González, 2021).

In the early months of the pandemic, it had to quickly identify and address the shortage of facemasks in its operations in all three regions: Asia, the Americas, and Europe. These circumstances affecting the global economic system tested empowerment. Mask manufacturing was mobilized in ten countries. At least one million weekly masks were needed to secure employees and maintain operations. So, the ability to respond to challenges and embrace change in activities and processes tested the entire workforce in these ten countries.

The crucial and most complex element was mobilizing production equipment (machinery) to manufacture face masks and deliver them to their operations in ten countries when conventional freight routes were limited. Experts within the organization solved this problem collectively, with the operations team being the first to devise a solution.

To identify the right solution for getting the mask-making machines to the different sites, the team considered all the logistical options available from the first mile to the last mile, spanning air, sea, and land. In addition to this complexity, export and import guidelines and restrictions must be understood. In the end, a coordinated effort between operations and legal affairs identified how to resolve the logistical complexity.

The GPTW model that incentivizes internal marketing elements was crucial for the company's adaptation to the new global reality. This work was achieved by human and artificial intelligence and the international community (employees of different nationalities, experiences, and backgrounds located in various cities and countries) with a common goal: to manufacture millions of masks quickly to keep themselves, other employees, and their communities safe. A group of people who needed to gain the knowledge and equipment to produce this type of product had to identify how to do so without affecting the supply of face masks to the frontline healthcare sector.

Ultimately, the team considered a phased approach that involved securing materials from three different regions in the quickest and least risky way. The best solution was to supply the mask manufacturing material for all sites outside China in the initial phase. Once supply was secured, the team moved to the next phase and worked with regional suppliers to safeguard future supply.

Securing commitments from these regional suppliers required skill and creative thinking because materials from traditional suppliers were in short supply. Since good filtration is a crucial requirement for mask materials, the company closed the deal with a world-leading energy company, an example of resilience and innovative thinking. In a parallel effort (Flex, 2023), the supply chain team navigated the procurement maze to secure high-quality materials in suitable regions.

Success was executing on three key business dimensions: operational excellence and resilience, a sustainable supply chain, and internal marketing. The goal of making face masks was largely successful due to the bond between employees because of their shared values. Employees (individuals) and teams (collectives) had a clear purpose by sharing ideas and learning. As a result, they learned and generated new knowledge. They went from never making a mask to producing 30 million in just 22 weeks, exceeding expectations and managing to supply employees in three shifts. Employees had to change masks three times a day. There was an oversupply, so the masks were donated to employees' families, local charities, and frontline healthcare workers (Baldassari, 2020).

The business challenge focusing on collective intelligence is to capture the value of employee contributions, both individually and in aggregate. Organizations should use common mechanisms and practices to capture employee value and create complementarities between contributions. This will turn the crowd into ambassadors for the company and encourage entrepreneurial behavior to manage risks.

WHAT HAPPENS IN THE TRANSNATIONAL AT TWO DIFFERENT POINTS IN TIME

Under this scenario, 2021, a questionnaire[4] (Table 1) was applied to a statistically representative sample[5] of 0.45% of the total universe for a single country. A descriptive statistical analysis[6] of the different study variables and an inferential analysis of the information obtained from the sample were carried out to get valuable conclusions that can be transferred to the universe of companies in Mexico, specifically in the state of Jalisco.

Table 2 of the Pearson correlation coefficient analysis shows whether any study variables are related. The independent variables analyzed are Empowerment (EM), Organizational Culture (OC), Internal Communication (IC), and Talent Attraction and Development (TA).

Table 2. Pearson's correlation coefficient analysis

		EM	OC	IC	TA
EM	*Pearson Correlation*	1	.016	.389**	.518**
	Sig. (2-tailed)		.649	.000	.000
OC	*Pearson Correlation*	.016	1	-.119**	.040
	Sig. (2-tailed)	.649		.001	.259
IC	*Pearson Correlation*	.389**	-.119**	1	.230**
	Sig. (2-tailed)	.000	.001		.000
TA	*Pearson Correlation*	.518**	.040	.230**	1
	Sig. (2-tailed)	.000	.259	.000	

**. *Correlation is significant at the 0.01 level (2-tailed).*
N=802
Source: Own elaboration.

The significance values closest to zero, below .050, for the Empowerment variable were concerning Internal Communication, which is moderately significant at .389, and Talent Attraction and Development, which is highly significant at .518. It is interpreted as a direct relationship: the more significant the empowerment, the better the Talent Attraction and Development and the better the internal communication. The relationship between empowerment and organizational culture was shallow (0.016).

The significance values of the Internal Communication variable are minimally related, with a value of .389 for empowerment, a value of .230 for talent attraction, and a negative value of -.119 for organizational culture. It indicates that Internal Communication was transformed. The items show internal communication through the company's formal channels. Telecommuting and organizational changes led to the construction of new communication strategies that differed from traditional ones. Empowerment, talent attraction, and organizational culture could have been negatively affected if the company had forced the internal customer to maintain and prioritize formal communication channels. The implementation of emerging communication strategies needs to be reflected in the items.

The indicators (talent attraction and development, empowerment, and internal communication) showed high internal customer satisfaction, which prepared and sustained the transnational with high resilience during the most critical months of COVID-19 and allowed it to continue operating with new strategies to adapt to the environment.

Based on the analysis of the results, the questions posed in the introduction are answered: Was internal communication more excellent during the pandemic? From the traditional perspective and as per theoretical models, it was not. The significance values of the variable Internal Communication are minimally related, with a value of .389 with empowerment. The emerging communication strategies resulting from empowerment may have played a more critical role. The questions in the questionnaire were constructed based on theoretical models before the pandemic.

The statistical results show that the minority, only 18%, considered communication to be poor. How did internal communication relate to empowerment? The greater the empowerment in times of change, the different the communication. It may explain why the majority, over 50%, rated the information as inclusive, transparent, and engaging. It is a high percentage. There are also 84% of the sample who consider that they receive the information they need to do their job. What role did organizational culture play? 92% consider that it can bring about changes in the work environment. Organizational culture fosters Talent Attraction and Development. This leads to the last question: Was talent attraction and development maintained? Yes, 93% were proud to work for the company; 92% wanted to work for the organization for a long time.

Based on these results, the study was expanded in terms of the sample, discarding Organizational Culture, and focusing the Research on Internal Communication, Empowerment, and Talent Attraction. The questionnaire was emailed to 48,000 transnational employees. It represents 30% of the universe. Below are the comparative results for 2021 versus 2022.

A second questionnaire was applied in 2022, allowing comparisons of company employee perceptions. A Likert scale questionnaire, comprising 14 items based on empowerment, Talent Attraction and Development, and Internal Communication, was used in both stages.

The definition of each question was mutually exclusive, taking into account the language of the target audience. At most, 20 items (14 items) were considered per questionnaire, and easy and short questions were drafted. The questions were neutrally worded (no negative, no positive), logically categorized and ordered, and Likert scale closed questions. Closed questions are preferable when the researcher's objective is to obtain an opinion (agreement or disagreement) with a particular point of view (Lazarsfeld, 1994).

The Empowerment items were maintained following the first questionnaire; for the Talent Attraction and Development and Internal Communication constructs, the original items were maintained, and two more were added, respectively, making a total of 14 items for the final questionnaire. The three constructs incorporated belong to the Trust Index™, the primary diagnostic tool of the GPTW, used by thousands of companies worldwide and providing insight into the company's work climate (GPTW, 2019).

Table 3. Comparison of results for the three study variables between 2021 and 2022

		2021		2022	
	Empowerment	**Agreed**	**Disagreement**	**Agreed**	**Disagreement**
EM1	Fixed protocols and standards are established in work procedures.	67%	33%	93%	7%
EM2	I am allowed to solve problems at my discretion	83%	17%	76%	24%
EM3	My supervisor encourages me to try harder	87%	13%	71%	29%
EM4	I feel free to develop my work	90%	10%	95%	5%
	Talent Attraction and Development	**Agreed**	**Disagreement**	**Agreed**	**Disagreement**
TA1	I am proud to tell others that work here	93%	7%	89%	11%
TA2	I want to work here for a long time	92%	8%	78%	22%
TA3	Job opportunities are inclusive, flexible, and suited to personal and professional needs.	74%	26%	94%	6%
TA4	The company's values are aligned with my own.	___	_____	91%	9%
TA5	My career plan is achievable	_____	_____	79%	21%
	Internal communication	**Agreed**	**Disagreement**	**Agreed**	**Disagreement**
IC1	I feel free to develop my work	85%	15%	58%	42%
IC2	I am informed about my employee benefits and entitlements	81	19	87%	13%
IC3	I received the information I needed to do my job on time	78	22	84%	16%
IC4	Information is shared openly in my team	------	------	89%	11%
IC5	I feel comfortable sharing my opinion	------	------	85%	15%

Source: Own elaboration.

The responses that increased the percentage of employees who agreed with the statement are shown in grey (Table 3). The statements that increased in percentage are: EM1, fixed protocols, and standards are established in work procedures; EM4, I feel entirely free to develop my work; TA3, work opportunities are inclusive, flexible, and adequate to my personal and professional needs; CI2, I am informed about the benefits and perks I have as an employee; and CI3, I receive the necessary information to do my job in time.

Item TA3 shows a 20% increase, which shows that the company improved talent attraction. Organizational change aimed at workplace inclusion and adaptation contributes to collective intelligence. Employees feel more supported, so they are more resilient. Item CI3 indicates timely communication contributes to productivity, effective decision-making, and collective intelligence.

The questions that increased in percentage possibly owe this increase to two or one of the following situations: 1) after the pandemic, the transnational maintained and reinforced these actions that allowed it to adapt successfully; and 2) in the UNEs located in other countries, these actions have been practiced with greater emphasis, therefore, extending the sample contributed to an increase in the percentages.

The same situations apply in reverse for the statements that decreased the percentage of employees who agree with them. The statements that decreased are EM2, I am allowed to solve problems at my discretion (decreased by seven percentage points); M3, my supervisor stimulates me to try harder (16 points); TA1, I am proud to tell others that I work here (4 points); TA2, I want to work here for a long time (14 points); CI1, I feel entirely free to do my job (27 points).

The significant decrease in CI1 indicates more centralized control or micromanagement post-pandemic, reducing employees' ability to make decisions autonomously. This also reflects a potential decline in resilience and empowerment, as employees may feel constrained in their approach.

The new statements (items) added in the second stage of Research obtained the following percentages: TA4, I feel that my company's values align with my own (91 percent of employees surveyed agreed); TA5, my career plan is achievable (79 percent agreed); CI4, information is shared openly in my team (89 percent agreed); and CI5, I feel comfortable sharing my opinion (85 percent agreed).

The results of item TA4 show a strong alignment of the employee with the company's values. This translates into high collective intelligence. Shared values foster integration, trust, and a unified organizational culture. CI5 shows that expressing opinions fosters a sense of security, which is essential for resilience and collective intelligence. All of this ensures that employees feel heard and valued.

In the first research stage (Jalisco, Mexico only), the statement with the fewest employees agreeing compared to the others was EM1, fixed protocols, and standards established in work procedures (67%). This statement obtained a high percentage (93%) in the second research stage.

The positive change (5%) in EM4 reflects a stronger sense of autonomy and ownership over work. In terms of collective intelligence, this could indicate an increased trust in employees to make decisions and innovate, contributing to a more collaborative and empowered workforce.

In the second research stage (all UNEs at the global level), the statement with the fewest employees agreeing compared to the other statements is CI1: I feel entirely free to do my job (58%). This same statement was agreed upon by 85 percent of employees in the first research stage agreed upon this same statement.

The notable decrease (16%) in EM3 suggests that the leadership style might have shifted or that employees' leadership expectations have evolved, possibly due to stress or burnout due to the pandemic. This could point to a challenge in resilience, as employees may feel less motivated to push beyond their limits if they need more support or recognition.

The changes in employee perceptions between 2021 and 2022 reflect several broader collective intelligence and resilience trends. Increased structured protocols, inclusive job opportunities, and open information sharing align with collective intelligence by promoting clarity, trust, and collaboration. These factors support organizational resilience by helping employees adapt to new challenges more effectively. The declines in areas like autonomy and long-term commitment suggest a reduction in employee empowerment and a potential decrease in resilience. This could be due to post-pandemic challenges, such as increased workload, uncertainty, or a shift in organizational priorities.

The new items introduced in the second survey, particularly around value alignment and career growth, reflect the organization's attempt to strengthen its support systems and improve employee engagement, which is vital for resilience and collective intelligence.

The results show that the organization is moving positively in some key areas. However, there are still challenges, especially in autonomy, leadership support, and long-term commitment. These issues must be addressed to enhance employee resilience further and leverage collective intelligence for organizational success.

CONCLUSION

The comparative results between 2021 and 2022 provide a better understanding of the relationship between Talent Attraction, Internal Communication, and Empowerment. These three elements are essential for organizational transformation in constant change. At the same time, these factors contribute to the growth of employees on a human scale.

Resilience starts with change and intensifies when an organization considers the employee essential. Change is constant because the company is in a dynamic environment. Therefore, companies' actions and practices on empowerment, talent attraction, and internal communication are expected to transform. Some practices tend to strengthen, and others to weaken.

These practices must be congruent with the historical moment that determines the environment to which the transnational must adapt. The results show that some practices are more generalized and reinforced in all three dimensions, while some have been weakened. It would be a mistake to say that all practices should be reinforced and generalized because they are prescribed in theory. Practices are carried out depending on the local culture, the economic actors in the territory, and how each individual contributes to the organization.

What is very accurate is that when an employee can grow professionally and is in an organization that prioritizes such growth, even in times of uncertainty, he or she becomes an actor of change for the locality in which he or she lives. An actor with this profile is expected to act favorably in the community of residence and positively impact that locality.

The findings have several important implications for practices within transnational enterprises. Encouraging autonomy by allowing employees more discretion in problem-solving fosters a culture of empowerment essential for resilience and innovation. Implementing regular feedback loops to ensure employees feel their input is valued helps improve perceptions of supervisor support and overall empowerment. Create personalized career development plans and mentorship programs that align with employee aspirations. This addresses concerns about career achievability and commitment. Ensure flexible and inclusive job opportunities, catering to diverse employee needs and enhancing attraction and retention, particularly in a global workforce. Develop clear communication strategies that keep employees informed about company benefits, organizational changes, and performance expectations. Invest in platforms that facilitate open information sharing and collaboration within teams, reinforcing collective intelligence and promoting a sense of community.

Regularly assess and communicate how company values align with employee values to enhance job pride and long-term commitment. Transnational enterprises should consider cultural differences and local practices when implementing policies, ensuring strategies resonate with local employees. Provide mental health and well-being resources, helping employees cope with stress and adapt to change enhance overall resilience within the workforce.

Offer resilience training programs that equip employees with skills to manage change effectively, promoting a culture of adaptability and problem-solving. Use insights from various regions to identify best practices and tailor strategies that can be implemented across different locations, enhancing overall organizational effectiveness. Utilize data analytics to monitor employee engagement and satisfaction in real-time, enabling proactive practice adjustments. Invest in technology that supports remote work and collaboration, which are crucial for maintaining communication and connection in a global workforce.

Transnational enterprises must adapt their practices proactively to foster empowerment, enhance talent development, improve communication, align values, and build resilience. By implementing these strategies, organizations can create a supportive work environment that leverages collective intelligence, ultimately driving productivity and employee satisfaction across diverse cultural contexts.

REFERENCES

Abaid, E. A., Cordera, A., & Pasco, A. (2021). Resiliencia organizacional en una microempresa: Estudio preliminar. *RILCO: Revista de Investigación Latinoamericana en Competitividad Organizacional*, (12), 52–59.

Adams, J., & DeFleur, M. (2005). The Acceptability of a Doctoral Degree Earned Online as Credential for Obtaining a Faculty Position. *The American Journal of Distance Education*, 19(2), 71-85.

Alles, M. (2002*). Dirección Estratégica de Recursos Humanos*. Gestión por competencias: El Direccionario. Editorial Garnica, 1-86.

Anaya, A., & Boticario, J. (2009, April). Clustering learners according to their collaboration. In *2009 13th International Conference on Computer Supported Cooperative Work in Design* (pp. 540-545). IEEE. DOI: 10.1109/CSCWD.2009.4968115

Ansorena, Á. (1996). *15 pasos para la selección de personal con éxito: Método e instrumentos* (41). *Grupo Planeta.*

Bailey, N., & Kurland, N. (1999). The advantages and challenges of working here, there, anywhere, and anytime. *Organizational Dynamics*, 28(2), 53–68. DOI: 10.1016/S0090-2616(00)80016-9

Bassanino, M., Fernando, T., & Wu, K. (2014). Can virtual workspaces enhance team communication and collaboration in design review meetings? *Architectural Engineering and Design Management*, 10(3-4), 200–217. DOI: 10.1080/17452007.2013.775102

Batta, A., Bandameeda, G., & Parayitam, S. (2023). Human Resource Management Practices, Job Satisfaction and Performance: Evidence from Transportation Sector in India. *Asia-Pacific Journal of Management Research and Innovation*, 19(1), 47–62. DOI: 10.1177/2319510X231166800

Bavdaž, M., Bounfour, A., Martin, J., Nonnis, A., Perani, G., & Redek, T. (2023). Measuring investment in intangible assets. *Advances in Business Statistics, Methods and Data Collection*, 79-103.

Bennett, J., & Strange, N. (Eds.). (2014). *Media independence: Working with freedom or working for free?* Routledge. DOI: 10.4324/9781315776392

Bernauer, J. (1999). Emerging standards: Empowerment with purpose. *Kappa Delta Pi Record*, 35(2), 68–74. DOI: 10.1080/00228958.1999.10518419

Borderías, C., & Martini, M. (2020). En las fronteras de la precariedad. Trabajo feme-nino y estrategias de subsistencia (XVIII-XXI). *Historia y Sociedad (Rio Piedras, San Juan, P.R.)*, (96), 63–78.

Boromisza-Habashi, D. (2015). *Speaking hatefully: Culture, communication, and political action in Hungary*. Penn State University Press.

Chun, Y. H., Choi, S., & Song, M. (2018). Analyzing the Link Between Job Satisfaction and Performance in Educational Institutions. *International Journal of Public Administration*. Advance online publication. DOI: 10.1080/01900692.2018.1498101

Contreras, F., & González, T. (2021). Business Resilience and Social Inclusion: A Critical Reflection on Internal Marketing. *Mercados y negocios*, 22(43), 77-96.

Conz, E., & Magnani, G. (2020). A dynamic perspective on the resilience of firms: A systematic literature review and a framework for future research. *European Management Journal*, 38(3), 400–412. DOI: 10.1016/j.emj.2019.12.004

Cooper, B., Wang, J., Bartram, T., & Cooke, F. L. (2019). Well-being-oriented human resource management practices and employee performance in the Chinese banking sector: The role of social climate and resilience. *Human Resource Management*, 58(1), 85–97. DOI: 10.1002/hrm.21934

Coy, D., Malekpour, S., Saeri, A. K., & Dargaville, R. (2021). Rethinking community empowerment in the energy transformation: A critical review of the definitions, drivers and outcomes. *Energy Research & Social Science*, 72, 101871. DOI: 10.1016/j.erss.2020.101871

de la Rosa-Navarro, M., & Carmona-Lavado, A. (2010). Cómo afecta la relación del empleado con el líder a su compromiso con la organización. *Universia Business Review*, (26), 112–132.

de Vreede, G., Antunes, P., Vassileva, J., Gerosa, M., & Wu, K. (2016). Collaboration technology in teams and organizations: Introduction to the special issue. *Information Systems Frontiers*, 18(1), 1–6. DOI: 10.1007/s10796-016-9632-3

Denckla, C., Cicchetti, D., Kubzansky, L., Seedat, S., Teicher, M., Williams, D., & Koenen, K. (2020). Psychological resilience: An update on definitions, a critical appraisal, and research recommendations. *European Journal of Psychotraumatology*, 11(1), 1822064. DOI: 10.1080/20008198.2020.1822064 PMID: 33244362

Derrida, J. (2005). At This Very Moment in This Work Here I Am. *Emmanuel Levinas: Levinas, phenomenology and his critics, 1*, 174.

Drucker, P. (1999). Knowledge-Worker Productivity. *California Management Review*, 41(2), 79–94. DOI: 10.2307/41165987

Duchek, S. (2020). Organizational resilience: a capability-based conceptualization. *Business research*, 13(1), 215-246.

Duro, J., Perez, A., & Fernandez, M. (2022). Territorial tourism resilience in the COVID-19 summer. *Annals of Tourism Research Empirical Insights*, 3(1), 100039. DOI: 10.1016/j.annale.2022.100039

Edwards, S. (2020). How to encourage collaboration and break down silos in remote teams? *Strategic HR Review*, 19(4), 157–158. DOI: 10.1108/SHR-05-2020-0043

Einwiller, S., Ruppel, C., & Stranzl, J. (2021). Achieving employee support during the COVID-19 pandemic–the role of relational and informational crisis communication in Austrian organizations. *Journal of Communication Management (London)*, 25(3), 233–255. DOI: 10.1108/JCOM-10-2020-0107

Eylon, D., & Au, K. (1999). Exploring empowerment cross-cultural differences along the power distance dimension. *International Journal of Intercultural Relations*, 23(3), 373–385. DOI: 10.1016/S0147-1767(99)00002-4

Fetterman, D. (2001). Foundations of empowerment evaluation. *Sage (Atlanta, Ga.)*.

Figueroa, H. (2014). *Estrategias de Atracción y Retención de Talento Humano en la Industria Minera Colombiana*. Económicas CUC, 61-77.

Flex. (2023). Our mask-making journey | Flex. Link: https://flex.com/resources/our-mask-making-journey-three-dimensions-of-success

Foster, P., Salem, D., Chibnall, S., Legler, R., & Yapchai, C. (1998). Empirical support for the critical assumptions of empowerment theory. *American Journal of Community Psychology*, 26(4), 507–536. DOI: 10.1023/A:1022188805083

Foster, & Keys, C. (1997). The person/environment dynamics of employee empowerment: An organizational culture analysis. *American Journal of Community Psychology,* 25(3), 345-369.

Garrosa, E., & Carmona, I. (2011). Salud laboral y bienestar: Incorporación de modelos positivos a la comprensión y prevención de los riesgos psicosociales del trabajo. *Medicina y Seguridad del Trabajo*, 57, 224–238. DOI: 10.4321/S0465-546X2011000500014

GPTW. (2019). Que es el trust index: Diagnóstico de la experiencia del empleado. *Great place to work.* http://greatpacetowork.es/que-es-trust-index/

Handy, C. (1995). *Gods of management: The changing work of organizations.* Oxford University Press.

Hidayat, K., & Idrus, M. (2023). The effect of relationship marketing towards switching barrier, customer satisfaction, and customer trust on bank customers. *Journal of Innovation and Entrepreneurship*, 12(1), 29. DOI: 10.1186/s13731-023-00270-7 PMID: 37193581

Ibrahim, N., Said, A., Abas, N., & Shahreki, J. (2020). Relationship between well-being perspectives, employee engagement and intrinsic outcomes: A literature review. *Journal of Critical Reviews*, 7(12), 69–74.

Karman, A. (2020). Flexibility, coping capacity and resilience of organizations: Between synergy and support. *Journal of Organizational Change Management*, 33(5), 883–907. DOI: 10.1108/JOCM-10-2019-0305

Kimberly, J., & Bouchikhi, H. (1995). The dynamics of organizational development and change: How the past shapes the present and constrains the future. *Organization Science*, 6(1), 9–18. DOI: 10.1287/orsc.6.1.9

Kuldas, S., & Foody, M. (2022). Neither resiliency-trait nor resilience-state: Transactional Resiliency/e. *Youth & Society*, 54(8), 1352–1376. DOI: 10.1177/0044118X211029309

Kumar, P. (2023). Gig Workers in Chhattisgarh: Emerging Opportunities in the New Economy. *Central Asian Journal of Innovations on Tourism Management and Finance*, 4(6), 140–148.

Kurtzberg, T. (2014). *Virtual teams: Mastering communication and collaboration in the digital age*. Bloomsbury Publishing USA. DOI: 10.5040/9798216032564

Lazarsfeld, P. (1994). The controversy over detailed interviews. *Public Opinion Quarterly*, 38–60.

Lee, Y., & Kim, J. (2021). Cultivating employee creativity through strategic internal communication: The role of leadership, symmetry, and feedback seeking behaviors. *Public Relations Review*, 47(1), 101998. DOI: 10.1016/j.pubrev.2020.101998

Li, J. Y., Sun, R., Tao, W., & Lee, Y. (2021). Employee coping with organizational change in the face of a pandemic: The role of transparent internal communication. *Public Relations Review*, 47(1), 101984. DOI: 10.1016/j.pubrev.2020.101984 PMID: 36568504

Lin, M., Xie, M., & Li, Z. (2023). Organizational error tolerance and change-oriented organizational citizenship behavior: Mediating role of psychological empowerment and moderating role of public service motivation. *Psychology Research and Behavior Management*, 16, 4133–4153. DOI: 10.2147/PRBM.S431373 PMID: 37850190

Lings, I. (2004). Internal market orientation: Construct and consequences. *Journal of Business Research*, 57(4), 405–413. DOI: 10.1016/S0148-2963(02)00274-6

Lu, Y., Zhang, M., Yang, M., & Wang, Y. (2023). Sustainable human resource management practices, employee resilience, and employee outcomes: Toward common good values. *Human Resource Management*, 62(3), 331–353. DOI: 10.1002/hrm.22153

Makrooni, G. (2020). From Challenge to Empowerment. *Journal of Ethnic and Cultural Studies*, 7(3), 112–128. DOI: 10.29333/ejecs/522

Mannix, E., Neale, M., & Northcraft, G. (1995). Equity, equality, or need? The effects of organizational culture on the allocation of benefits and burdens. *Organizational Behavior and Human Decision Processes*, 63(3), 276–286. DOI: 10.1006/obhd.1995.1079

Martin, F. (1995). *Comunicación en Empresas e Instituciones: de la Consultora a la Dirección de Comunicación*. Universidad de Salamanca.

Martín, M., & González, T. (2016). *Negocios internacionales y estrategias empresariales para la sustentabilidad*. UNAM.

Mokhtar, I., Abdullah, N., Ismael, D., Othman, B., & Ali, R. (2019). The Development of training participation conceptual framework among academic staff: A qualitative study based on training officers perception at Malaysian public universities. *International Journal of Psychosocial Rehabilitation*, 23(3), 544–572. DOI: 10.37200/IJPR/V23I3/PR190346

Morando, M., Zehnter, M., & Platania, S. (2023). Reverse Sexism and Its Impact on Job Satisfaction and Career Planning: Italian Validation of the "Belief in Sexism Shift Scale". *Social Sciences (Basel, Switzerland)*, 12(6), 357. DOI: 10.3390/socsci12060357

Moriano, J., Molero, F., Topa, G., & Lévy Mangin, J. (2014). The influence of transformational leadership and organizational identification on intrapreneurship. *The International Entrepreneurship and Management Journal*, 10(1), 103–119. DOI: 10.1007/s11365-011-0196-x

Moriano, J., Topa, G., Valero, E., & Lévy, J. (2009). Identificación organizacional y conducta "intraemprendedora". *Anales de Psicología/Annals of Psychology, 25*(2), 277-287.

Mukherjee, D., Nuruzzaman, N., Gaur, A., & Singh, D. (2023). Pro-market reforms and the outsourcing tradeoffs: Evidence from the transition economies. *International Business Review*, 32(4), 102105. DOI: 10.1016/j.ibusrev.2023.102105

Pradono, N., Sulistyo, H., & Zulfa, M. (2024). Waqi'iyah networking power based on cross-function integration on marketing performance. *Quality - Access to Success*, 25(198).

Prieto, J. (2015). *Gestión Estratégica Organizacional*. ECOE Ediciones, 1-8.

Purkarthofer, E., & Mäntysalo, R. (2022). Enhancing Knowledge, Skills, and Identity Development Through Collaborative Student-Led Learning: Experiences With the Gradual Empowerment of Students in a Planning Studio Course. *Journal of Planning Education and Research*.

Qaisar, F., & Muhamad, N. (2021). Internal marketing: A review and future research agenda. *Asia Pacific Business Review*, 27(2), 267–300. DOI: 10.1080/13602381.2021.1858590

Ridley, M. (2020). *How innovation works: And why it flourishes in freedom*. Harper.

Sánchez, M. (2016). Cultura y Comunicación Organizacional. In *Comunicación institucional y cambio social. Claves para la comprensión de los factores relacionales de la comunicación estratégica y el nuevo ecosistema comunicacional* (pp. 15-38).

Sargeant, A., & Asif, S. (2000). Modelling internal communications in the financial services sector. *European Journal of Marketing*, 34(3/4), 299–317. DOI: 10.1108/03090560010311867

Saul, J. (2022). *Collective trauma, collective healing: Promoting community resilience in the aftermath of disaster*. Routledge.

Shah, C., & González, R. (2011). Evaluating the synergic effect of collaboration in information seeking. In *Proceedings of the 34th international ACM SIGIR conference on Research and Development in Information Retrieval* (pp. 913-922). DOI: 10.1145/2009916.2010038

Sisto, V. (2009). Cambios en el trabajo, identidad e inclusión social en Chile: Desafíos para la investigación. [Talca]. *Universum (Talca)*, 24(2), 192–216. DOI: 10.4067/S0718-23762009000200011

Smite, D., Moe, N., Hildrum, J., Gonzalez, J., & Mendez, D. (2023). Work-from-home is here to stay: Call for flexibility in post-pandemic work policies. *Journal of Systems and Software*, 195, 111552. DOI: 10.1016/j.jss.2022.111552 PMID: 36320721

Speer, P. (2000). Intrapersonal and interactional empowerment: Implications for theory. *Journal of Community Psychology*, 28(1), 51–61. DOI: 10.1002/(SICI)1520-6629(200001)28:1<51::AID-JCOP6>3.0.CO;2-6

Stufflebeam, D. (1994). Empowerment evaluation, objectivist evaluation, and evaluation standards: Where the future of evaluation should not go and where it needs to go. *Evaluation Practice*, 15(3), 321–338. DOI: 10.1177/109821409401500313

Sutaguna, I., Achmad, G., Risdwiyanto, A., & Yusuf, M. (2023). Marketing Strategy For Increasing Sales Of Cooking Oil Shoes In Barokah Trading Business. *International Journal of Economics and Management Research*, 2(1), 132–152. DOI: 10.55606/ijemr.v2i1.73

Swart, K., Bond, T., & Chugh, R. (2022). Challenges and critical success factors of digital communication, collaboration and knowledge sharing in project management virtual teams: A review. *International Journal of Information Systems and Project Management*, 10(4), 84–103. DOI: 10.12821/ijispm100404

Verčič, A. (2021). The impact of employee engagement, organisational support and employer branding on internal communication satisfaction. *Public Relations Review*, 47(1), 102009. DOI: 10.1016/j.pubrev.2021.102009

Vieira, T. (2023). The unbearable precarity of pursuing freedom: A critical overview of the Spanish Sí soy autónomo movement. *Sociological Research Online*, 28(1), 244–260. DOI: 10.1177/13607804211040090

Wang, S., & Sun, C. (2023). Blockchain empowered dynamic spectrum sharing: Standards, state of research and road ahead. *IEEE Communications Standards Magazine*, 7(3), 72–80. DOI: 10.1109/MCOMSTD.0010.2200026

Yi, H., Cho, Y., & Amenuvor, F. (2023). Internal marketing and salespeople's out-of-role behaviour: The mediating role of job satisfaction. *European Research on Management and Business Economics*, 29(2), 100216. DOI: 10.1016/j.iedeen.2023.100216

Yi, H., Cho, Y., & Amenuvor, F. (2023). Internal marketing and salespeople's out-of-role behaviour: The mediating role of job satisfaction. *European Research on Management and Business Economics*, 29(2), 100216. DOI: 10.1016/j.iedeen.2023.100216

Zhang, M., Hu, E., & Lin, Y. (2023). The impact of flexibility-oriented HRM systems on innovative behaviour in China: A moderated mediation model of dualistic passion and inclusive leadership. *Asia Pacific Business Review*, 29(1), 114–135. DOI: 10.1080/13602381.2022.2076446

ENDNOTES

1 Specialized organizational culture comprises shared beliefs, values, and behavior patterns within some segment of society, which distinguishes it from society's general culture (Adams & DeFleur, 2005).

2 The selection process is defined as the structured and planned activity that makes it possible to attract, evaluate, and identify the personal characteristics of a set of subjects that differentiate them from others and make them more suitable to a set of characteristics and capacities determined for the effective and efficient performance of a specific professional task (Ansorena, 1996).

3 The name of the transnational company is anonymous. For this analysis, the characteristics that contribute to understanding the studied phenomenon are offered.

4 A questionnaire is designed based on the Likert scale, and the relevant validity and reliability indicators are applied in an analysis of variance (ANOVA), clusters, and principal components analysis. The validation and reduction of factors can be consulted in Contreras (2022).

5 The representative sample is made up of a total of 827 employees: men and women in operational and administrative positions, aged between 25 and 55 years, who work in the transnational company in the electronics industry.

6 It is research with mixed design, for which multivariate methods of clusters and principal components, as well as descriptive analysis, were used.

Chapter 9
Khadi, Arts, and Handicrafts as India's Symbol of Freedom and Fashion in Today's Internet and Circular Economy

Balaji Gopalan
https://orcid.org/0000-0002-1082-5597
Faculty of Management Studies, CMS Business School, Jain University, India

ABSTRACT

This chapter focuses on a relevant topic, an element of India's freedom struggle called Khadi or the homespun cloth made of cotton on spinning wheels as an example of product stewardship in terms of ethics and environmental impact. Product stewardship is identified as businesses with commitments to a healthy, safe, and environmentally friendly society. This closely aligns with the philosophy of a circular economy that adheres to lean production principles of manufacturing and business processes that are eco-friendly and sustainable. Textile industries around the world are integrating manufacturing towards a circular economy and green practices due to an increasing need to reduce the environmental impact. Social entrepreneurship as an alternative has been in focus as a sustainable business model and the popularity of Khadi, arts, crafts, and cottage industries in India is growing in today's internet economy. This study has explored how social entrepreneurship is providing numerous opportunities for growth and sustainability and a solution to social problems.

DOI: 10.4018/979-8-3693-7272-2.ch009

1. INTRODUCTION

Textile industries around the world are integrating manufacturing towards a circular economy and green practices due to an increasing need to reduce the environmental impact. The main principles of a circular economy (CE) are to sustain businesses with the practice of saving and recycling resources, reducing waste with the help of a closed loop production (Dziubaniuk et al. 2024). For small and medium industries, 'Circular by Design', is a concept devised to incorporate environment friendly closed-loop systems for the most suitable sustainable designs for textile industries (Ballie and Woods 2018). A holistic comprehension of CE explains it as responsible and sustainable economics requiring a new way of thinking (Kirchherr et al., 2023), where materials and products are valued and maintained for a long time, and the option for reuse, recycle, and refurbishment and repair are preferred and disposal in landfills or incineration or burning of waste is considered as the last option (Korhonen et al., 2018). Recycled textile fibres are only 8.9% of textiles produced globally in 2021, while polyester constitutes 14.8% compared to recycled cotton that is 1% of global production (Textile Exchange, 2022).

The apparel industry is considered as a 2 trillion-dollar business that accounts for 2% of the world's gross domestic product (GDP) (Khanna et al., 2020) and in India alone it is a $100 bn industry (Aggarwal. et al., 2023). The growth is expected between $5bn to $7bn at the annual rate of 3.6%. The waste generated from the textile industry adds 90 million tons of waste annually and may increase to 130 million tons by the year 2030 (Beall 2020). The environmental pollution amounts to biotic, abiotic, water, air and erosion. Even, most consumer goods packaging employs plastic materials that contributes to waste and may end up in dumps. The role of climate change has brought scientific problem solving towards sustainability and environment friendly products. There is also an urgent need for environmental compliance and focus on energy efficiency and pollution control from industries.

There are also calls and actions for ocean and land preservation and a circular economy to prioritize the recycling of plastics and other polluting materials. Combining the approaches of popular brands, priorities include stakeholder engagement, human rights and social compliance, climate change control and environmental regulations compliance, sustainable and responsible materials management, environmental profit and loss account, health and safety compliance, better governance with ethics training and compliance across the supply chain. Studies on the fast-fashion industry have even discussed the needs for integrating customers and addressing their activism with regards to expectations and concerns on environmental sustainability, and the negative environmental impact of such industries (Martínez-Martínez et al. 2023).

The fashion industry is considered as one of the most polluting in the world and India alone is the third largest producer of waste accounting for 8% of the world's total waste and around 50% of textile waste is resourced into supply chains for recycling and production (Mohan et al., 2022). The Ministry of textiles has passed regulations such as the national textile policy to support environment friendly products. In a circular economy, the waste fabric is resourced and then organized and sorted. It then goes through a process of treatment and shredding and converted into raw material for production to produce shopping tote bags, packaging materials, and are also used in home furnishings (Aggarwal et al., 2023).

How can textile industries, cottage industries and online shopping move towards a circular economy and green practices?

How can the disorganized sector of weavers and artisans from India be integrated into the collective intelligence of the Internet economy?

In this regard, we discuss the role of sustainable economics of the Khadi movement that popularized homespun cloth during India's freedom struggle and other sustainable industries such as cottage industries that have supported arts and crafts for centuries in India and environment friendly practices that may add value to industries. Process innovation for sustainable and environment friendly businesses can build on this philosophy. Studies have discussed how process innovation in the textile industry can transform the circular economy in terms of reducing environmental impact, improve raw material and textile waste traceability, water conservation and chemical use minimization. This has resulted in entrepreneurial communities of collective intelligence, agency and action (Rae and Blenker, 2023). The collective intelligence of the internet economy can benefit from the cognitive diversity, individualism, knowledge diversity and its aggregation (Matzler et al. 2016).

2. SCOPE, RESEARCH PROBLEM, AND PROBLEM STATEMENT

2.1 Scope

To identify sustainability needs of small and medium industries and entrepreneurs in the global and the collective intelligence of the Internet economy.

2.2 Objectives

a) To study the stakeholders, business models and success of small and medium industries that support traditional arts and crafts and entrepreneurship.

b) To study the challenges faced by small and medium industries.
c) To study successful business models that support traditional arts and crafts with the collective intelligence of the internet economy.

2.3 Research Questions Identified

1) What is the online shopping experience of customers purchasing ethnic and traditional products such as Khadi or products made of homespun cloth?
2) What is the customer opinion regarding the promotion of traditional arts and crafts and products such as Khadi?
3) How popular are ethnic and traditional products in online shopping portals?
4) How can supply chain resilience and the collective intelligence of the internet economy affect the craft sector?
5) How can innovation improve the craft sector for the new economy and entrepreneurs?

3. RESEARCH, LITERATURE REVIEW AND BACKGROUND

This paper focuses on a relevant topic, an element of India's freedom and independence struggle called Khadi or the homespun cloth made of cotton on spinning wheels as an example of product stewardship in terms of ethics and environmental impact. Product stewardship is identified as businesses with commitments to a healthy, safe and environment friendly society (Pinto 2023). The philosophy of a circular economy adheres to lean production principles of manufacturing and business processes that are eco-friendly and sustainable (Hazen et al. 2021). Even natural dyes are being utilized in the designing of fabrics (Perera and Ranaweera, 2023). Some examples of natural dyes include bougainvillaea flowers for pink, flat bean leaves for green, turmeric powder for yellow, butterfly pea flowers for blue, and rice powder for white (Singh et al. 2024). An exergy analysis of an industry helps audit the energy or fuel consumption and waste generated. It enables identifying the location, types and quantity of wastes (contained exergy) and losses (exergy irreversibly lost) for industries (Morris 1991; Wall 2010) including the processing of non-biodegradable wastes.

Industrial biopolymers made from biowaste as a raw material manufactured as a substitute for plastic for industrial use in the European Union (EU) is stated to reach almost 3 metric tonnes by 2025 and is expected to reach 360 metric tonnes in market demand (European Bioplastics 2022). Biopolymer based crops are even cultivated to meet the demands of the cosmetics industry, biogas production, tanning and processing using environment friendly methods and the recycling of vegetable and fruit waste. Studies have also found that textile industry waste recycled generated US $11 million in savings and reduced the raw material consumption to about 31 billion kgs (de oliveira Neto et al., 2022). Natural dyes that are sourced from nature are being used in the design of contemporary accessories, heritage artworks, interior décor and apparel fabrics (Singh et al. 2024).

Enzymatic hydrolysis of turning fabric waste grind into a fibre and then chemically treating it using an alkaline solution to be recycled and mixed with fabrics including polyester and cotton is suitable for industrial use (Piribauer et al. 2021). The environmental impact from pretreatment was reduced to 60% while that from enzymatic hydrolysis and melt spinning reduced the environmental impact on the ecosystem and human health to 30%. Textile industries that recycled denim fabric waste were able to recover 53% of the raw material for industrial use. Energy requirement costs were optimized at 40% for every metre of fabric. A circular economy for the textile industry would require optimizing the costs of mechanical recycling, energy consumption and lubricant use in recycling (Fidan et al. 2021). This requires an enormous amount of effort.

Social business ecosystems of small and medium industries such as the Khadi and cottage industries has been in focus as a sustainable economic business model. Khadi or the homespun cloth in India is a three-billion-dollar industry (Swain and Patoju 2022). Small and medium industries that are part of a social ecosystem are considered as opportunities for growth and sustainability (Kabbaj et al., 2018) and a solution to social problems. A few other examples of successful cooperative businesses from India are FabIndia, Guthali, Arvind Eye Care Hospital, Dabbawala or The Tiffin Carrier business and Amul. The European Research Network defines such cooperatives as an act of producing goods or services, legitimate paid work, an autonomous community initiative and a self-deciding community (Defourny and Nyssens, 2010).

4. METHODOLOGY AND ANALYSIS

India's Khadi or Homespun Cloth

This research paper starts with the review of literature on the textile industry and its environmental impact and a brief discussion on sustainable economic models such as the Khadi movement in India and other cottage industries that became a symbol of freedom and environmental sustainability that is relevant even today. A survey of more than 100 respondents of internet users in India was completed to study how and whether ethnic and sustainable products are being promoted and what needs to be done in today's internet economy of online shopping. A literature review of how customers have co-created value with firms through the collective intelligence of the Internet economy provides a valuable discussion of how value co-creation can contribute to sustainable businesses and reduced environmental impact. The brand in focus for this study is "Khadi" or homespun cloth made from cotton in India along with cottage industries that have promoted sustainability and environment friendly products. The idea of the Khadi movement and the cottage industries can contribute significantly to process innovations of not just the textile industry but also various other industries in terms of sustainability and their impact on the environment.

The politico economic environment during the period of India's freedom movement resulted in the creation of a brand called "Khadi" or homespun cloth that became iconic. This became a symbol of self-sufficiency and national identity. Many of the khadi clothing products made in India are homespun and are made with a spinning wheel. Many Indians trained themselves to learn how to spin the wheel and make their own cloth (Shah 2018). There is a lot of information that relate to the circular economy by reading the historical research on marketing of such products as brands. However, it so happened that in this case, history created India's brand called "Khadi", its institutionalization and the economy that we still use today continues this tradition. In turn "Khadi" or homespun cloth became a symbol of nationalism. As it was a sign of sustenance and being closer to being an environmental practice, it soon became a national icon and is now marketed as a fashionable brand in clothing across the world with the ethnic look and feel.

In the history of the freedom struggle in India, the idea of spinning cloth and handweaving became popular with people from all walks of life including the rich and the poor. Homespun cotton was promoted as a symbol of independence and a sustainable way of making clothes with no use of chemicals and processes with no harm to the environment. The table indicates that online shopping portals can promote the sales and exports of ethnic products, arts and crafts.

Table 1. t-Test statistic. Online shopping and the promotion of ethnic and traditional products

	Do you think that more regional, local, arts and crafts need to be promoted in online shopping portals in multiple languages?	*Do you think that there is more export potential for local arts and crafts and small and medium business in online shopping portals?*
Mean	0.82300885	0.85840708
Variance	0.146965866	0.122629583
Observations	113	113
Pooled Variance	0.134797724	

continued on following page

Table 1. Continued

	Do you think that more regional, local, arts and crafts need to be promoted in online shopping portals in multiple languages?	*Do you think that there is more export potential for local arts and crafts and small and medium business in online shopping portals?*
Hypothesized Mean Difference	0	
Df	224	

The table shown indicates that customers are comfortable browsing online shopping portals in English.

Table 2. t-Test statistic. Customer response to online shopping

	Do you browse E-Commerce websites in English?	*Do you prefer to browse the product catalogue in English?*
Mean	0.991150442	0.991150442
Variance	0.008849558	0.008849558
Observations	113	113
Pooled Variance	0.008849558	
Hypothesized Mean Difference	0	
Df	224	

The Table shows that multilingual customer support improves the online shopping experience of customers

Table 3. t-Test statistic. Customer support while online shopping for ethnic products

	Do you get adequate customer support in your local language while browsing on Amazon, Flipkart or Myntra?	*Do you face challenges while browsing in your own native language during your online shopping experience?*
Mean	0.513274336	0.654867257
Variance	0.252054362	0.228034134
Observations	113	113
Pooled Variance	0.240044248	
Hypothesized Mean Difference	0	
Df	224	

The table shows that customers desire that local arts and crafts can be significantly promoted in online shopping portals.

Table 4. t-Test statistic. Online shopping and support for ethnic and traditional products

t-Test: Two-Sample Assuming Equal Variances		
	Do you think websites like Flipkart, Amazon, Myntra and others can support local arts and crafts and small and medium businesses? Do you agree?	*Do you think that more regional, local, arts and crafts need to be promoted in online shopping portals in multiple languages?*
Mean	0.778761062	0.82300885
Variance	0.173830594	0.146965866
Observations	113	113
Pooled Variance	0.16039823	
Hypothesized Mean Difference	0	
Df	224	

Today's Relevance From Contention and Reconciliation

Due to the contention started by the excessive exploitation of resources during India's freedom struggle, the Khadi movement of making the homespun cloth was a show of self-reliance and promotion of a skill that suited an unskilled rural workforce (Ghosh 2009). There was contention in the choice between clothing manufactured by mills and those that were made in handlooms or were homespun. During the Khadi movement and India's freedom struggle, the market of clothing had to depend on homespun cloth and reduced dependence on expensive factory equipment and cost. Many years before independence, the Indian spinners' Association had placed the employment figures at somewhere around 240,000 people. Small workshops could even produce customized and personalized designs.

The Khadi or homespun cloth has become an industry and has created a network of producers, distributors, and sales agents (McGowan 2016). Even curtains are being made of Khadi. Personalizing it with design and embroidery made it more aesthetic and appealing for homes. The handloom sector today accounts for home items such as pillow and cushion covers, bedsheets, table mats and other accessories such as tote bags and handbags and apparels including suits, sarees, shawls, scarves and casual wear, handicrafts and even office items (Attri & Bairagi, 2022; Singh et al. 2024).

The independence movement focused on two ideologies, one called "Swaraj" that stood for independence and other was called "Swadeshi" or homegrown products. The "Charkha" or spinning wheel that made homespun cloth became a symbol of the movement. The whole act of spinning yarns made from cotton was labour intensive, requiring very little capital and became economically viable for the poor (Bhattacharya and Roy, 2017). This promoted socio-team effectiveness and income. Today, the handloom Industry in India, considered as a disorganized sector employs about 4.3 million weavers and 7 million artisans and craftsman from rural areas and towns (Attri & Bairagi, 2022). The Ministry of Textiles in India has initiated many programs such as the National Handloom Development Program, Handloom Cluster's Program and the Weaver's Welfare Scheme to provide support to this sector.

The industry of handlooms, handicrafts and khadi and cottage industries and other agro products constitute the second largest employment share as private owned businesses at 32% in comparison to agriculture (Swain & Patoju, 2022). A few of the products from this sector in India include home and interior décor, upholstery, embroidery, textile and mirror work from Gujarat; block printed textiles from Rajasthan; pashmina shawls from Kashmir; chikankari and brocades from Uttar Pradesh (Attri & Bairagi, 2022; Fibre2Fashion, 2011); Mysore, Banarasi and Kanjivaram silks from Karnataka, Varanasi and Tamil Nadu and Kantha and Jamdhani from West Bengal.

From this perspective, studies identified that there is an immense opportunity for employment in this sector across India due to the organizational climate, cultural values, overall team effectiveness and a sense of responsibility (McClelland 1961). New concepts such as redesigned products based on fashion and accessories, customer experience, nature, eco and adventure tourism, sports and event tourism, urban life, spirituality, food and dining are getting popular (Costa and Buhalis, 2006; Teixeira and Ferreira, 2019). Local cultural heritage is considered integral to social business ecosystems and has benefits of integrating business knowledge of shared community values (Sammatavet and Raudsaar, 2015) that support individual businesses in not so well off and poor communities.

Local fashion business ecosystems have sustained themselves more efficiently because of maintaining "tight feedback loops" ensuring a close affinity between consumers, manufacturing and eco-friendliness, facilitating a business based on continuous feedback and sustainability (Perera and Ranaweera, 2023). In the internet economy, localization and collective intelligence of the fashion industry involves entrepreneurs and small-scale businesses, government support, online shopping, social networks, local designers, community employment, labour ethics, youth support, exports and sustainability (Perera and Ranaweera, 2023)

Other product categories considered as works of artisans (Teixeira and Ferreira, 2019):

- Tiles and ceramics
- Utensils and wooden objects
- Embroidered products, synthetic materials, clothing accessories, glass working, wax working, rag doll making, jewellery, leather working, stained glass works
- Brass works, tiles, knitted products, art of gilding, wool felting, paper works, wood sculptures
- Production of clothing accessories, home fabrics, basket weaving, textile weaving

The table shows the value co-creation contexts for small and medium businesses, entrepreneurs, job design, circular economies, product portfolio management, digitization, value centric networks and governance.

Table 5. Value co-creation for small and medium businesses as a collective intelligence of the Internet Economy (Source: Gopalan 2022)

Value co-creation Contexts for the Craft industry	**Industry learning systems and research**	**Business process Improvement**	**Service Management**
1. New products and services, start-ups and new business creation, Employability. Distributed craftsmanship, workmanship and ecosystems	(Rathore et al. 2016; Romero et al. 2011; Costa and Buhalis, 2006). (Singh et al. 2024) (Perera and Ranaweera 2023) (Attri and Bairagi 2022)	(Rathore et al. 2016; Romero et al. 2011) (Singh et al. 2024) (Perera and Ranaweera 2023) (Attri and Bairagi 2022)	
4. Eco-friendly, Green practices, circular economy	(Hazen 2021), (Aggarwal and Krishna 2023), (de Oliveira Neto et al. 2022), (Khanna et al. 2020) (Perera and Ranaweera 2023)	(Hazen 2021) (de Oliveira Neto et al. 2022) (Perera and Ranaweera 2023)	
5. IT support services	(Ramaswamy and Ozcan, 2018) (Singh et al. 2024)	(Singh et al. 2024)	
6. Product portfolio management, Geographies, Cultures, New markets	(Ramaswamy and Ozcan, 2018; Teixeira and Ferreira 2019) (Singh et al. 2024) (Perera and Ranaweera 2023) (Attri and Bairagi 2022)	(Ramaswamy and Ozcan, 2018) (Singh et al. 2024) (Perera and Ranaweera 2023) (Attri and Bairagi 2022)	

continued on following page

Table 5. Continued

Value co-creation Contexts for the Craft industry	Industry learning systems and research	Business process Improvement	Service Management
7. Product and service discussion social networks	(Chan and Li 2010; de Valck et al., 2009; Dennis et al., 2017; Stephen and Toubia, 2010) (Gnyawali 2010) (Singh et al. 2024)	(Chan and Li 2010; de Valck et al., 2009; Dennis et al., 2017; Stephen and Toubia, 2010) (Gnyawali 2010) (Singh et al. 2024)	(Chan and Li 2010; de Valck et al., 2009; Dennis et al., 2017; Stephen and Toubia, 2010) (Gnyawali 2010)
8. Digitization of business processes for products and services	(Rai et al. 2012) (Singh et al. 2024)	(Rai et al. 2012) (Singh et al. 2024)	(Rai et al. 2012)
9. Service model management	(Verma et al., 2012)	(Verma et al., 2012)	(Verma et al., 2012)
10. Value centric networks	(Stephen and Toubia 2010) (Singh et al. 2024)	(Stephen and Toubia 2010) (Singh et al. 2024)	(Stephen and Toubia 2010)
11. Governance, IT support and logistics, multichannel businesses, Intra and Inter firm business processes, circular economy	(Rai et al. 2012) (Hazen et al. 2021), (Aggarwal and Krishna 2023), (de Oliveira Neto et al. 2022), (Khanna et al. 2020) (Singh et al. 2024)	(Sarker et al. 2012) (Rai et al. 2012) (Hazen et al. 2021) (de Oliveira Neto et al. 2022) (Singh et al. 2024)	(Sarker et al. 2012) (Rai et al. 2012) (Hazen et al. 2021)
12. Job design, employment, economic growth and task variety	(Gray et al. 2011) (Zomerdijk and Voss, 2010) (Singh et al. 2024)	(Gray et al. 2011) (Zomerdijk and Voss, 2010) (Singh et al. 2024)	(Zomerdijk and Voss, 2010)

In this regard, proper training, skill development and rewards and recognition improves the working conditions and morale of workers. During India's freedom struggle, newspaper classifieds became popular during the young India movement and promoted napkins, blankets, nets, dusters and towels and other home-made products. Local artisans began using the block printing techniques for designs that adorned furniture that became very fashionable. Woven khadi became popular catering to a wide variety of tastes. The marketing of Khadi as a product that suited various market segments created a sustainable ecosystem for business and livelihood of the needy. Eventually, it portrays Khadi as a traditional product, sustainable and became a visual symbol (Trivedi 2003, Parel and Trivedi 2009). Exhibitions held over the past century have popularized Khadi as a brand.

Today, this brand is being given a new modern image to identify with a younger generation of Indians. This fits into the context of the circular economy in a way that it eliminates the ills seen with the manufacturing of clothing and the exploitation of resources such as material, water, labour and also the issues dealing with recycling and consumerism. It had promoted a sense of patriotism during India's Independence struggle. Khadi is now seen as a brand that identifies itself with a whole new generation, right from the old to the young who identify and have a sense of belonging.

Last but not the least, it also suits the climatic conditions in India. Research also shows that Khadi cloth has higher air permeability or ventilation (Soundri et al., 2023). It may be used even as a sports fabric. Blended fabrics are also gaining popularity instead of pure wool or polyester due to the desired moisture management capability and water vapor transmission rate. The Indian government also promotes Khadi products with the Khadi and Village Industries Commission. Many brands have promoted Khadi and Indian products that are ethnic and environment friendly.

4.1 Online Shopping and the Success of the Internet Economy

Online shopping portals have recognized the increasing significance of integrating brands into the collective intelligence of social networks in the internet economy to sell their products to customers and increase the outreach for markets for existing and new products and services. The collective intelligence of the internet economy has generated profits, sales and expanded markets beyond the physical store for businesses with a wide-ranging portfolio of products and services. IT business logic supporting online business processes now engage large, small and medium businesses, makers, start-ups, banking services, online shopping and regional services adding economic and social value for customers and have transactions more convenient and environment friendly, that has improved financial performance and has facilitated customer loyalty and trust (Meinardes et al. 2017; Grover and Kohli, 2012; Rai et al., 2012). Social commerce networks that discuss about brands provide additional information to businesses on markets, market performance and economic growth.

Online businesses now facilitate and multiply online co-shopping, digital-payment conveniences and services. Authenticated secure transactions, rich online web content depicting geography, cultures, themes, affordability, incentives, increased outreach of product and service promotions have increased the value of the brand. (Grover and Kohli 2012; Ketonen-Oksi and Valkokari 2019; Kohler et al. 2011; Messinger et al. 2009; Rai et al. 2012). Guthali, FabIndia, Pepper Fry, Myntra, World Art Community, Zwende and Urban ladder are a few examples of businesses and their online web portals in India that sell home and interior décor, arts and crafts, upholstery, handcrafted items, embroidery, textiles, sarees, fashion accessories for men and ladies from all over India (Attri & Bairagi, 2022; Fibre2Fashion, 2011) that have made their presence popular in both physical stores and online portals such as on Facebook, Instagram, Etsy and other channels. Many of these online portals are popular with sellers who may be makers, boutiques and creative self-employed people. The popularity of adding quality product listings, content and storylines have supported artisans and craftspeople from all around the world. Figure 1 explains the relevance of value co-creation between customers and firms during the product and service life cycle. The analysis was completed using NVivo.

Figure 1. Analysis using NVivo to observe customers and firms during the product and service life cycle

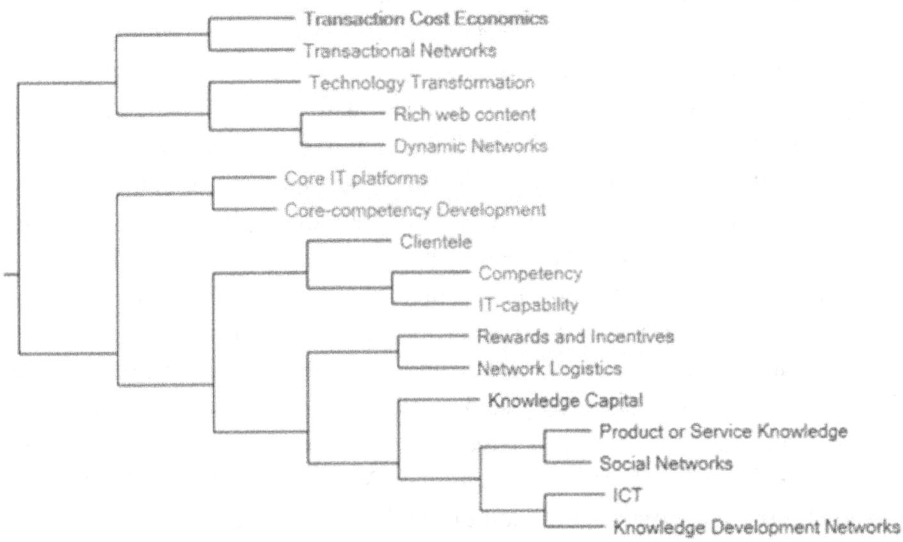

Electronic-commerce has created efficient service models incorporating the best practices and principles for the collective intelligence of the Internet economy. Studies have shown that hyper-linking sellers in online-marketplaces creates considerable economic value in social commerce networks (Stephen and Toubia 2010) that may add value to small and medium industries. Online shopping firms today and the collective intelligence of the internet economy multiply the interactivity between consumers and online-businesses by enabling multi-channel communication via chats, emails, hyperlinks and context searches that facilitate a greater tele-presence. In this regard, the personalization/customizability of technologies and social networks, networked interactivity, and customer value creation constitute Web 2.0 functionality that align a firm's business processes during upgrades and transitions towards Web 2.0 (Wirtz et al. 2010).

Supply chain resilience (SCR) for the craft and cottage industries, depend on mobilizing employees towards innovative practices and the use of information and communication technologies in production and operations for the needs of businesses add value to the collective intelligence of the internet economy. Individual and organisational focus on business practices and priorities, adherence to market supply demand, and effectively communicating with the team with the help of information management and reporting targets, plans, and progress along with capacity planning and material requirements planning becomes necessary for the daily conduct of business without interruptions. Implementation of problem-solving methods such as employee and workplace management, project management, forecasting, process mapping, production planning and control, time management, accounting, invoice and cost management, production and operations management, quality management, capacity planning, transportation planning for efficient logistics and supply chain management becomes crucial. Furthermore, information management, business regulations and governance and timely training programmes are crucial for enhancing business governance (Yadav and Tripathi 2024) and aligning with the needs of a circular economy and green practices for environmental compliance. This establishes a basis for efficient coordination of various organisational functions to communicate, plan, and manage information for finance, marketing and operations and continuous improvement of processes to better manage businesses. Studies have also discussed the significance of growing markets, human capital and financial support are very relevant to the entrepreneurial ecosystem. External economies of scale emerge when production increase by one firm augments the production and optimizes the unit costs of other firms in a shared business system (Montes and Olleros 2020) in terms of assembly lines, equipment and facilities and reduce imitations.

In organizations, rhetorical practices of using information and communication technologies (ICT) by senior managers across departments for interactivity and improving work life co-ordination with co-workers and stakeholders facilitates work life balance (Huang et al. 2013) and enhance organizational learning practices. In today's internet economy, studies on social network service (SNS) firms demonstrate that alliances of inter-firm software development that support business processes as collective intelligence enhance value cocreation (Gnyawali et al. 2010) in terms of product and service innovation. A research study (Grover and Kohli 2012) from the IT industry summarises that the cocreation of IT value maximizes into positive cocreation routines when inter-firm businesses integrate (1) proficiency and resources; (2) business process routines; (3) complementary resources and skills; and (4) effective governance.

In a time-series study of social networking service (SNS) firms, it was found that competing businesses improve product innovation; software development across business ecosystems and efficient management of human resources and IT alliances accounting for 85% of all competitive actions (Gnyawali et al. 2010). In this regard, the different levels of a firm's innovativeness in terms of patenting and asset management can elicit a favourable market reaction from investors. The ability of the World Wide Web to facilitate crowd-sourced knowledge development 24/7 around the world facilitates cross network interactivity multiplying economic growth.

Prahalad and Ramaswamy (2003) when referring to the value co-creation between firms and customers have focused on the singular experience involving – namely, the locus of proficiencies and skills (i.e. firms' resources; inter-firm business processes and the networked consumer community). Further, social networks were found to enhance the experience and knowledge diversity of customer motivation towards value co-creation in virtual worlds for crowd-sourced problem-solving in terms of innovativeness and economics. Research on customer participation that enhances substantial creativity in projects integrates the extrinsic/intrinsic motivation of individual proficiencies, performance requirements and broadcast search (Frey et al., 2011).

During online shopping, the customer experiences dependent on information quality, information access and order fulfilment constitute the service convenience of hybrid commerce service-delivery systems (Oh and Teo, 2010) in the online economy. In today's internet economy and social networks, the collective intelligence involving celebrities, the rewards or incentives, fairness or ethics and social intentions for customers have demonstrated enthusiastic participation, value co-creation across networks and knowledge creation. Also, customers find the incentives for online shopping and the quality of product or service reviews that enhance consumer knowledge and self-efficacy to be rewarding. In social networks, the networked interactivity promotes growth in subscriptions, networked marketing (Trusov et al. 2009) and an opportunity to promote brands on economies of scale. In logistics and supply chain management firms, numerous control variables are responsible for the cocreation of business value – namely (1) firm size, (2) logistics spending, (3) supplier dependence, (4) IT management, (5) contracts, (6) problem solving, (7) customer satisfaction, (8) IT utilization and (9) industry size (Rai et al. 2012).

In the collective intelligence of the internet economy, inter-firm IT networks of ICT improve customer efficacy, knowledge capital and support for online shopping, co-shopping, markets and marketing routines (Lechner and Hummel, 2002; Attri and Bairagi 2022; Chan and Li 2010, Dennis et al. 2017, de Valck et al. 2009). Popularizing co-shopping of quality products and services with referrals across social networks has enhanced the online shopping experience through networked consumer activism, awareness and product communities. Thus, structuring online shopping portals and social networks integrating the structural, cognitive and relational aspects of conversations improves the experience for customers. In terms of decision support during online shopping, active social commerce networks, archived knowledge of products and services provide decision support for customers across geographies and facilitates customer self-efficacy towards purchases (Teixeira and Ferreira 2019; Singh et al. 2024; Perera and Ranaweera 2023). Online shopping purchases supported by networked recommendations, networked discussions and archived knowledge tend to be more effective at communication. Online wikis, blogs and social networks facilitates knowledge growth through a process and curation of knowledge creation, knowledge retention and archiving. Companies have further capitalized on utilizing the collective intelligence of internet portals in co-designing products and services with customers for improved experiences in empowerment, engagement, interactivity, mobility, networking, product portfolio management, optimization of costs and greater profitability (Zhu and Zhang 2010; Holzwarth et al. 2006; Rapp et al. 2013).

4.2 Advertising and Research

IT-based inter-firm alliances create significant wealth through the networking of greater innovation types and offer a greater degree of cooperation between firms for service model management, improved management practices and contextualization of products and services for markets and new projects (Grover and Kohli 2012; Oh and Teo 2010; Rai et al. 2012; Rathore et al. 2016; Romero and Molina 2011). This enhances problem solving, new business creation across geographies, demography and themes. In the collective intelligence of the internet economy, the multidimensionality of knowledge, customer-centricity and the online experience of sociability has facilitated socio-technological innovation (Gnyawali et al. 2010; Kohler et al. 2011). IT-based alliances of industries in projects have demonstrated increased market value for competing firms operating in similar portfolios (Han et al. 2012). During initial stock market listings, alliances of firms engaged in new projects gain significant investments due to the shared recognition of derived or invented value between investors.

4.3 Business Research, Decision Support Systems and Electronic Commerce

Networked meaning, multidimensionality, tacit intelligence, tele-presence and economic or social value definitions are outcomes or concepts of archived product or service knowledge created in networked communities (Gnyawali et al. 2010; Gray et al. 2011; Messinger et al. 2009). Consumer efficacy with online shopping is enhanced by archived information in blogs, websites (Colliander and Dahlen 2011) and online magazines. Online shopping experiences that offer customized products and services is becoming more common. Virtual spaces such as MySpace, Facebook and blogs were seen to become a focus of continuous knowledge creation, brand evaluations and learning through expected reciprocal benefits. Firms today are integrating networked consumers into new projects, entrepreneurship and empowering customers for problem solving (Rathore et al. 2016; Attri and Bairagi 2022). Further, social networks are providing decision support to customers depending on product and service ratings (Cheung and Lee 2010; Kim et al. 2008; Moran and Gossieaux 2010; Shen et al. 2010) and shopping needs. Social networks as a collective intelligence in the internet economy have facilitated sociability in the customer experience of co-shopping, recreation, decision support, market typologies, global market outreach and inclusiveness for brands.

The collective intelligence of the internet economy now facilitates new markets, improved portfolio management, technology ecosystems, investments, subscriptions for utilities and services. International logistics and supply chain management firms supported by IT now provide and expedite deliveries, enhance warehouse and inventory management, and business process efficiency. In today's global economy, the costs of operating international logistics and supply chain management depend on service management of deliveries, costing, commissions, accounts and invoicing, subscriptions and memberships, transportation costs, tariffs and company insurance. Online shopping and improved logistic support have facilitated growing customer subscriptions, new services, customer service centres, enhanced business processes, transport businesses and shipping.

4.4 Mobile Subscriptions and Economics and Services Value Add

Many businesses in the collective intelligence of the internet economy today have members and subscribers that are supported by IT and various portfolio of services. The collective intelligence of the internet economy facilitates greater customer loyalty, growing subscriptions, accurate invoice management, sales and rewards. Online services such as banking provide secure payment conveniences and incentives by partnering with numerous banks and facilitates transactions (Mainardes et al., 2017) and consumer protection. The value co-creation between customers and firms in the collective intelligence of the internet economy has enhanced the value of brands resulting in innovations, improved efficacy, proficiencies and skills, co-branding, co-shopping, discounts and rewards (Gummesson and Mele 2010; Yang et al. 2017; Zomerdijk and Voss 2010). Social networks supporting professions and vocations have grown in subscriptions exponentially due to the value creation, service conveniences, and economic benefits such as rewards and incentives. Logistics and supply management firms that support online shopping and transportation of goods depend on business growth, infrastructure management, warehouse and vendor management (Hazen et al. 2021) and circular economies. Further, IT support services, branding, multichannel business process management, automation, accurate invoice management, time management and incentives create value for both the firm and the customer (Dennis et al. 2017; Lechner and Hummel 2002). Business models in the internet economy are easily configurable and firms calibrate their brands and adjust with uncertainties in forecast and demand in markets and growing clientele.

In today's collective intelligence of the internet economy, the core-business processes and IT business logic have created new firms, professions and IT logic supporting various industry sectors. Customers' improved efficacy, creativity and learning have enhanced businesses and transformed brands. In this regard, today's brands selling in the internet economy have gained from customer loyalty, increasing subscribers, online billing and invoice management, and growing sales. Online shopping and sales now measure customer experiences and interactivity, satisfaction, reach and financial performance enhancing customer relationship management (CRM) for firms (Sigala 2018). Further, businesses are inviting and investing in integrating creative customers in the co-design and co-creation of brands. Online shopping now facilitates multi-firm business process management, multichannel sales, logistics and supply chain management and portfolio management across geographies (O'Hern and Rindfleisch, 2010). Firms that depend on production and operations management, logistics and supply management coordinate intensive business processes for decision making and support (Ramaswamy and Ozcan, 2018; Grover and Kohli 2012; Rai et al. 2012, de Koster et al. 2021; Faccia and Petratos 2021; Sarker et al. 2012). Small and medium industries supported by the collective intelligence of the internet economy have facilitated the growth of professions, makers, entrepreneurs and startups in growing business ecosystems (Gopalan 2022; Grover and Kohli 2012; Romero and Molina 2011). Logistics and supply chain management that supports today's internet economy is dependent on efficient product portfolio management, trading, invoice and credit management, inventory management, transportation (Rai et al. 2012) and the growing needs for green practices and circular economies (Hazen et al. 2021). There are many challenges for businesses expanding in the internet economy. These businesses depend on asset deployment, lead time transport logistics and revenue. Further, IT support services are required for managing intensive business processes such as vendor management, invoice accuracy and multichannel business transactions.

4.5 Quality Content, Networks and Technology

In the collective intelligence of the internet economy, IT support and CRM for brands have improved the value of products and services. Online shopping has provided secure internet payment conveniences, and benefits such as incentives for a range of businesses and services (Oh et al., 2010; Shen et al., 2010) in the collective intelligence of the internet economy. Customers reviewers in social commerce networks and online shopping portals have creatively and innovatively raised the value of brands (Kim et al. 2008; Moran and Gossieaux 2010; Romero and Molina

2011; Lechner and Hummel 2002; Nambisan and Watt 2011). Online shopping has succeeded due to customer incentives, inclusiveness, customer efficacy, product and service ratings, subscriptions and economies of scale, privacy management, conveniences, and dependable internet services such as billing, transactions, invoice management and deliveries (Grover and Kohli 2012; Gummesson 2008; Colliander and Dahlén 2011; Oh and Teo 2010). Social rewards, incentives and cost benefits, aesthetic content management across social commerce networks and multichannel shopping have resulted in value creation for brands and customers (Stephen and Toubia 2010; Lechner and Hummel 2002; Dennis et al. 2017). The effectiveness of social networks and a positive work-life balance has resulted in productivity at work and improved customer efficacy with completing tasks. Technology enhancement of customer efficacy, proficiency and skills, co-branding, referral shopping, discounts, coupons and incentives are steering the collective intelligence of the internet economy resulting in new markets, portfolio expansion, investments and personalized subscription-based services (Kim et al., 2008; Oh and Teo 2010; Rapp et al., 2013; Schlosser et al., 2006). This has led to the globalization of businesses. With reference to the internet economy and its support for entrepreneurs, network utility, professional connections, market expansion, social networking and participation in international trade fairs were identified to facilitate entrepreneur internationalization (Tiwari and Korneliussen 2022).

5. ANALYSIS AND CONCLUSION

The most important aspect of this topic is to focus on an ecosystem that involves businesses and makers to integrate traditions that have sustained themselves for centuries in a responsible manner in terms of being affordable, environment friendly, cultural, ethnic and sophisticated at the same time in today's world of online shopping and the collective intelligence of the internet economy. Studies have discussed cultural capital existing in three forms: (1) objectified as pieces of art, craft, handicraft; (2) institutionalised into formal education, accreditations for professions and vocations; (3) Cultural way of doing business. Social capital refers to an individual's network of social culture. Symbolic capital denotes reputational assets that individuals can draw on to position themselves. Personalized experiences, proficiency, knowledge, skills, enhanced decision making and individualism are rarely considered (Hill 2021; Bourdieu, 1986, 1990).

Traditional Artwork and Craftsmanship for Mass Markets

Most of the arts and crafts have focused on mass market demands such as exports and the new trend of increasing popularity of traditional products in local markets. A good example is how Fabindia over the past 60 years supported and employed over 15000 local weavers and artisans from rural India and established a successful exports business and local market (Gopalan 2022). Partnerships in handicraft exports have significantly improved profits of small sized firms through marketing practices, international experience in exporting (Dassouli et al. 2024) taking into consideration the product portfolio, pricing, promotion, export sales profitability and destination. The most commonly exported handicraft products are cashmere shawls, sweaters, handmade knit apparel, fashion accessories, jewellery, handmade paper products, metallic and wooden craft items, money bags, money belts, essential oils and paintings (Tiwari and Korneliussen 2022). Customers who are knowledgeable about artistic work are willing to pay a premium for authentic handcrafted work (Singh et al. 2024). Traditional arts and crafts in India that use mastery and motifs from cultures passed on from generation to generation over many centuries is spread across all regions of India giving a uniqueness to the products made and have formed clusters of makers. It became necessary to preserve this knowledge and impart design education to the next generation of makers. Handicraft industries that include small and medium businesses improve performance, succeed and become competitive by integrating supply chains and become more digital, adaptive, agile, and innovative to gain strategic advantage (Yadav and Tripathi 2024). The same study concludes that entrepreneurial leaders and their business orientation that includes innovativeness, risk-taking, proactiveness along with market orientation, technology utilization, supply chain orientation enhances supply chain resilience.

Design Training in Arts and Crafts

Kalaraksha Vidyalaya in Gujarat, works with established designers to impart training (Pathak & Mukherjee, 2020). Another example is how Fabindia sends its executives to learn how weavers and artisans lived and worked. At Sewagram in Gujarat, a place known for Gandhi's charkha or spinning wheel movement instrumental in the making of khadi, women self-help groups (SHG) are trained to become highly skilled makers based on the same principles (Swain and Patoju 2022). This initiative is taken by 'Sewagram Khadi', an organization of small and medium businesses. In the state of Jharkand in India, initiatives such as Jharkraft arrange training programs are organized for skilled artisans and classify them into semi-skilled, medium-skilled and highly skilled professionals to improve their managerial skills (Singh and Chaudhary, 2023). The objective is to provide sustainable livelihood to artisans, employable youth and cotton farmers; and making khadi cloths more fashionable by integrating new designs and patterns for the new generation. This genre of artists and craftsman cater to an exclusive market of customers and connoisseurs of the arts and combines traditional crafts in designer wear.

The study recommends:

- Identification of self-help groups (SHG) of working artisans.
- Low interest bank investments for SHG
- Collaborating with design institutes and training semi-skilled, middle level and advanced skill level professionals and providing international certifications.
- Job support in rural areas to prevent outmigration
- Support for the cottage industry and weavers in terms of new looms, infrastructure, best raw materials that produce arts and crafts, jewellery, terracotta, jute, metalworks and other products and support for emporiums.

Governments have provided support and subsidies in making the livelihood of handlooms that have focused on sustainable business models.

The Government of India has partnered with the Handloom communities of India through initiatives such as the Khadi (homespun cloth) and village industries commission of India. https://www.kviconline.gov.in/

The emphasis with partnerships has prioritized

- Use of naturally occurring resources such as dyes and fibre
- Small and medium business promotion
- Cottage industries support
- Training
- Awareness creation
- Incentives and financing
- Recycle management
- Environment friendly technology
- Promotion of environment friendly goods as brands

These can be integrated with the collective intelligence of the internet economy for the promotion of goods and products that are sustainable and environment friendly in the world of online shopping.

REFERENCES

Aggarwal, R., Singh, H., & Krishna, V. (2023). Doodlage: Contributing to circular economy in fashion. *CASE Journal*, 20(3), 747–756. DOI: 10.1108/TCJ-05-2023-0117

Albright, S., & Winston, W. (2003). *Business Analytics: Data Analysis and Decision Making* (6th ed.). Cengage Learning.

Attri, R., & Bairagi, R. (2022). Guthali – challenges in marketing Indian handicrafts and handloom. *Emerald Emerging Markets Case Studies*, 12(1), 1–23. DOI: 10.1108/EEMCS-09-2021-0298

Ballie, J., & Woods, M. (2018). Circular by Design: A Model for Engaging Fashion/Textile SMEs with Strategies for Designed Reuse. In *Unmaking Waste in Production and Consumption: Towards the Circular Economy.* Emerald Publishing Limited. DOI: 10.1108/978-1-78714-619-820181010

Beall, A. (2020). Why clothes are so hard to recycle. BBC Future. Available at: www.bbc.com/future/article/20200710-why-clothes-are-so-hard-to-recycle

Bhattacharya, S., & Roy, P. (2017). Organisational climate and team effectiveness – A study on small scale industries. ASBM Journal of Management, 10(2), 17-24. Retrieved from https://search.proquest.com/docview/1963102034?accountid=177896

Bourdieu, P. (1986). The forms of capital. In Richardson, J. (Ed.), *Handbook of Theory and Research for the Sociology of Education, Greenwood, New York* (pp. 241–258).

Bourdieu, P. (1990). *The Logic of Practice*. Stanford University Press. DOI: 10.1515/9781503621749

Chan, K. W., & Li, S. Y. (2010). Understanding consumer-to-consumer interactions in virtual communities: The salience of reciprocity. *Journal of Business Research*, 63(9/10), 1033–1040. DOI: 10.1016/j.jbusres.2008.08.009

Cheung, C. M. K., & Lee, M. K. O. (2010). A theoretical model of intentional social action in online social networks. *Decision Support Systems*, 49(1), 24–30. DOI: 10.1016/j.dss.2009.12.006

Colliander, J., & Dahlén, M. (2011). Following the Fashionable Friend: The Power of Social Media - Weighing the Publicity Effectiveness of Blogs Versus Online Magazines. *Journal of Advertising Research*, 51(1), 313–320. DOI: 10.2501/JAR-51-1-313-320

Costa, C., & Buhalis, D. (2006). *Tourism Business Frontiers: Consumers, Products and Industry*. Elsevier.

Dassouli, S., Bodolica, V., Satt, H., & M'hamdi, M. (2024). Adaptation strategy, international experience and export performance of Moroccan handicraft firms: The mediating role of partnerships. *International Journal of Emerging Markets*, 19(2), 412–434. DOI: 10.1108/IJOEM-01-2021-0127

de Koster, R., Roy, D., Yun, F. L., & Kumar, S. (2021). Special Issue of Production and Operations Management Journal "Managing Autonomous and IoT-driven Intralogistics Operations". *Production and Operations Management*, 30(1), 293–294. DOI: 10.1111/poms.13372

de Oliveira Neto, G. C., Teixeira, M. M., Souza, G. L. V., Arns, V. D., Tucci, H. N. P., & Amorim, M. (2022). Assessment of the Eco-Efficiency of the Circular Economy in the Recovery of Cellulose from the Shredding of Textile Waste. Polymers, 14(7), 1317. DOI: 10.3390/polym14071317

de Valck, K., van Bruggen, G. H., & Wierenga, B. (2009). Virtual communities: A marketing perspective. *Decision Support Systems*, 47(3), 185–203. DOI: 10.1016/j.dss.2009.02.008

Defourny, J., & Nyssens, M. (2010). Conceptions of social enterprises and social entrepreneurship in Europe and the United States: Convergences and divergences. *Journal of Social Entrepreneurship*, 1(1), 32–53. DOI: 10.1080/19420670903442053

Dennis, C., Bourlakis, M., Alamanos, E., Papagiannidis, S., & Brakus, J. (2017). 'Value Co-Creation Through Multiple Shopping Channels: The Interconnections with Social Exclusion and Well-Being', International Journal of Electronic Commerce, 21(4), 517-547.

Dziubaniuk, O., Ivanova-Gongne, M., Kaipainen, J., & Nyholm, M. (2024), Exploring the heuristics behind the transition to a circular economy in the textile industry. Management Decision. DOI: 10.1108/MD-06-2023-1095

European Bioplastics. (n.d.). Available online: https://www.european-bioplastics.org/

Exchange, T. (2022). Preferred fiber & materials market report 2022. Available at: https://textileexchange.org/app/uploads/2022/10/Textile-Exchange_PFMR_2022.pdf

Faccia, A., & Petratos, P. (2021). Blockchain, Enterprise Resource Planning (ERP) and Accounting Information Systems (AIS): Research on e-Procurement and System Integration. *Applied Sciences, 11*(15), 6792. DOI: 10.3390/app11156792

Fibre2Fashion (2011). Good scope for organised retailing in Indian handicrafts. 23 November Retrieved from www.fibre2fashion.com/news/textile-news/newsdetails.aspx?news_id=105452

Fidan, F. ¸. S., Aydo˘gan, E. K., & Uzal, N. (2021). An integrated life cycle assessment approach for denim fabric production using recycled cotton fibers and combined heat and power plant. *Journal of Cleaner Production*, 2021(287), 125439. DOI: 10.1016/j.jclepro.2020.125439

Ghosh, S. (2009). Gandhi's khadi: A history of contention and conciliation. *European Journal of Development Research*, 21(2), 322–324. DOI: 10.1057/ejdr.2009.1

Gnyawali, D. R., Fan, W. & Penner, J. (2010) Competitive Actions and Dynamics in the Digital Age: An Empirical Investigation of Social Networking Firms. Information Systems Research, 21(3), 594-613.

Gopalan, B. (2022, March). Value Co-creation-based Information Management in the Digital Economy. *Asia Pacific Journal of Information Systems*, 32(1), 1–31. Advance online publication. DOI: 10.14329/apjis.2022.32.1.1

Gray, P. H., Parise, S. & Iyer, B. (2011). Innovation impacts of using social bookmarking systems. MIS Quarterly, 35(3), 629-643.

Grover, V. & Kohli, R. (2012). Cocreating IT Value: New Capabilities and Metrics for Multifirm Environments. MIS Quarterly, 36(1), 225-232.

Gummesson, E., & Mele, C. (2010). Marketing as Value Co-Creation through Network Interaction and Resource Integration. *Journal of Business Market Management*, 4(4), 181–198. DOI: 10.1007/s12087-010-0044-2

Hazen, B. T., Russo, I., Confente, I., & Pellathy, D. (2021). Supply chain management for circular economy: Conceptual framework and research agenda. *International Journal of Logistics Management*, 32(2), 510–537. DOI: 10.1108/IJLM-12-2019-0332

Hill, I. R. (2021). Spotlight on UK artisan entrepreneurs' situated collaborations: Through the lens of entrepreneurial capitals and their conversion. *International Journal of Entrepreneurial Behaviour & Research*, 27(1), 99–121. DOI: 10.1108/IJEBR-11-2019-0642

Kabbaj, M., Hadi, K. E. Q. E., Elamrani, J., & Lemtaoui, M. (2018). A study of the social entrepreneurship ecosystem: The case of Morocco. *Journal of Developmental Entrepreneurship*, 21(4), 1650021. Advance online publication. DOI: 10.1142/S1084946716500217

Ketonen-Oksi, S., & Valkokari, K. (2019). Innovation Ecosystems as Structures for Value Co-Creation. *Technology Innovation Management Review*, 9(2), 25–35. DOI: 10.22215/timreview/1216

Kim, J. W., Choi, J., Qualls, W., & Han, K. (2008). It Takes a Marketplace Community to Raise Brand Commitment: The Role of Online Communities. *Journal of Marketing Management*, 24(3), 409–431. DOI: 10.1362/026725708X306167

Kirchherr, J., Yang, N.-H. N., Schulze-Spüntrup, F., Heerink, M. J., & Hartley, K. (2023). Conceptualizing the circular economy (revisited): An analysis of 221 definitions. *Resources, Conservation and Recycling*, 194, 107001. DOI: 10.1016/j.resconrec.2023.107001

Kohler, T., Fueller, J., Matzler, K., Stieger, D., & Füller, . (2011). Co-creation in virtual worlds: The design of the user experience. *Management Information Systems Quarterly*, 35(3), 773. DOI: 10.2307/23042808

Korhonen, J., Honkasalo, A., & Seppälä, J. (2018). Circular economy: The concept and its limitations. *Ecological Economics*, 143, 37–46. DOI: 10.1016/j.ecolecon.2017.06.041

Lechner, U., & Hummel, J. (2002). Business models and system architectures of virtual communities: From a sociological phenomenon to peer-to-peer architectures. *International Journal of Electronic Commerce*, 6(3), 41–53. DOI: 10.1080/10864415.2002.11044242

Mainardes, E. W., Teixeira, A., & Romano, P. C. S. (2017). Determinants of co-creation in banking services. *International Journal of Bank Marketing*, 35(2), 187–204. DOI: 10.1108/IJBM-10-2015-0165

Martínez-Martínez, A., Cegarra-Navarro, J.-G., Garcia-Perez, A., & De Valon, T. (2023). Active listening to customers: Eco-innovation through value co-creation in the textile industry. *Journal of Knowledge Management*, 27(7), 1810–1829. DOI: 10.1108/JKM-04-2022-0309

Matzler, K., Strobl, A., & Bailom, F. (2016). Leadership and the wisdom of crowds: How to tap into the collective intelligence of an organization. *Strategy and Leadership*, 44(1), 30–35. DOI: 10.1108/SL-06-2015-0049

McClelland, D. C. (1961). *The Achieving Society*. D. Van Nostrand Company. DOI: 10.1037/14359-000

McGowan, A. (2016). Khadi curtains and swadeshi bed covers: Textiles and the changing possibilities of home in western India, 1900-1960. *Modern Asian Studies*, 50(2), 518–563. DOI: 10.1017/S0026749X14000705

Messinger, P. R., Stroulia, E., Lyons, K., Bone, M., Niu, R. H., Smirnov, K., & Perelgut, S. (2009). Virtual Worlds - Past, Present, and Future: New Directions in Social Computing. *Decision Support Systems*, 47(3), 204–228. DOI: 10.1016/j.dss.2009.02.014

Montes, J. O., & Olleros, F. X. (2020). Microfactories and the new economies of scale and scope. *Journal of Manufacturing Technology Management*, 31(1), 72–90. DOI: 10.1108/JMTM-07-2018-0213

Moran, E., & Gossieaux, F. (2010). Marketing in a Hyper-Social World: The Tribalization of Business Study and Characteristics of Successful Online Communities. *Journal of Advertising Research*, 50(3), 232–239. DOI: 10.2501/S0021849910091397

Morris, D. R. (1991). Exergy analysis and cumulative exergy consumption of complex chemical processes: The industrial chlor-alkali processes. *Chemical Engineering Science*, 46(2), 459–465. DOI: 10.1016/0009-2509(91)80007-L

Nambisan, P., & Watt, J. H. (2011). Managing Customer Experiences in Online Product Communities. *Journal of Business Research*, 64(8), 889–895. DOI: 10.1016/j.jbusres.2010.09.006

O'Hern, M., & Rindfleisch, A. (2010). 'Customer co-creation: A typology and research agenda', *Review of Marketing Research. Emerald Group Publishing*, 6, 84–106.

Oh, L. & Teo, H., (2010). Consumer value co-creation in a hybrid commerce service-delivery system. International Journal of Electronic Commerce, 14(3), 35-62.

Parel, A., & Trivedi, L. (2009). Clothing Gandhi's nation: Homespun and modern India. *The Journal of Asian Studies*, 68(1), 329–331. DOI: 10.1017/S0021911809000552

Perera, G. A., & Ranaweera, A. (2023). Fashion localism: Evaluation and extensions of utility in Sri Lankan fashion brands. *Research Journal of Textile and Apparel*, 27(2), 264–280. DOI: 10.1108/RJTA-08-2021-0099

Pinto, L. (2023). Investigating the relationship between green supply chain purchasing practices and firms' performance. *Journal of Industrial Engineering and Management*, 16(1), 78–101. DOI: 10.3926/jiem.3686

Piribauer, B., Bartl, A., & Ipsmiller, W. (2021). Enzymatic textile recycling—Best practices and outlook. *Waste Management & Research*, 39(10), 1277–1290. DOI: 10.1177/0734242X211029167 PMID: 34238113

Rae, D., & Blenker, P. (2024). The role of collective intelligence and collective agency in enterprising communities. *Journal of Enterprising Communities: People and Places in the Global Economy*, 18(1), 7–28. DOI: 10.1108/JEC-09-2022-0141

Rai, A., Pavlou, P., Im, G. & Du, S. (2012). Interfirm IT capability profiles and communications for cocreating relational value: Evidence from the logistics industry. MIS Quarterly, 36(1), 233-262.

Ramaswamy, V., & Ozcan, K. (2016). Brand value co-creation in a digitalized world: An integrative framework and research implications. *International Journal of Research in Marketing*, 33(1), 93–106. DOI: 10.1016/j.ijresmar.2015.07.001

Rapp, A., Beitelspacher, L. S., Grewal, D., & Hughes, D. E. (2013). Understanding social media effects across seller, retailer, and consumer interactions. Journal of the Academy of Marketing Science, 41(5), 547-566. doi:http://dx.doi.org.proxy.uwasa.fi/10.1007/s11747-013-0326-9

Rathore, A. K., Ilavarasan, P. V., & Dwivedi, Y. K. (2016). Social media content and product co-creation: An emerging paradigm. *Journal of Enterprise Information Management*, 29(1), 7–18. DOI: 10.1108/JEIM-06-2015-0047

Romero, D., & Molina, A. (2011). Collaborative networked organizations and customer communities: Value co-creation and co-innovation in the networking era. *Production Planning and Control*, 22(5-6), 447–472. DOI: 10.1080/09537287.2010.536619

Sarker, S., Sahaym, A. & Bjørn-Andersen, N. (2012). Exploring value cocreation in relationships between an ERP vendor and its partners: A revelatory case study. MIS Quarterly, 36(1), 317-338.

Shah, N. (2018). The political economy of branding: Khadi, colonialism and Indian nationhood. *Journal of Historical Research in Marketing*, 10(3), 197–223. DOI: 10.1108/JHRM-06-2017-0035

Shen, Y., Huang, C., Chu, C., & Liao, H. (2010). Virtual community loyalty: An interpersonal-interaction perspective. *International Journal of Electronic Commerce*, 15(1), 49–74. DOI: 10.2753/JEC1086-4415150102

Short, , Moss, T. W., & Lumpkin, G. T. (2009). Research in social entrepreneurship: Past contributions and future opportunities. *Strategic Entrepreneurship Journal*, 3(2), 161–194. DOI: 10.1002/sej.69

Sigala, M. (2018). Implementing social customer relationship management. *International Journal of Contemporary Hospitality Management*, 30(7), 2698–2726. DOI: 10.1108/IJCHM-10-2015-0536

Singh, N., Moid, S., Rushdi, N. J., & Shankar, N. (2024). Finding a digital silver line during COVID-19 pandemic: A case of Madhubani Paints. *Emerald Emerging Markets Case Studies*, 14(1), 1–26. Advance online publication. DOI: 10.1108/EEMCS-07-2023-0246

Singh, P., & Chaudhary, K. (2023). Jharcraft: A gift of transformational leadership in an Indian state-owned enterprise. *International Journal of Public Leadership*, 19(4), 339–354. DOI: 10.1108/IJPL-01-2023-0003

Soundri, G. M., Kavitha, S., & Kumar, B. S. (2023). Dimensional, moisture, and thermal properties of bi-layered knitted fabric for sportswear application. *Research Journal of Textile and Apparel*, 27(4), 543–559. DOI: 10.1108/RJTA-05-2021-0074

Stam, E. (2014). The Dutch entrepreneurial ecosystem. DOI: 10.2139/ssrn.2473475

Summatavet, K., & Raudsaar, M. (2015). Cultural heritage and entrepreneurship – inspiration for novel venture creation. *Journal of Enterprising Communities: People and Places in the Global Economy*, 9(1), 31–44. DOI: 10.1108/JEC-03-2013-0010

Swain, S., & Patoju, S. K. S. (2022). Global Enterprises: contemporarisation of khadi products in India. *CASE Journal, 18*(6), 1–16. DOI: 10.1108/TCJ-12-2021-0214

Teixeira, S. J., & Ferreira, J. J. M. (2019). Entrepreneurial artisan products as regional tourism competitiveness. *International Journal of Entrepreneurial Behaviour & Research*, 25(4), 652–673. DOI: 10.1108/IJEBR-01-2018-0023

Tiwari, S. K., & Korneliussen, T. (2022). Entrepreneurial internationalisation of Nepalese artisanal firms: A dynamic capabilities perspective. *International Journal of Entrepreneurial Behaviour & Research*, 28(6), 1369–1390. DOI: 10.1108/IJEBR-09-2020-0635

Trivedi, L. N. (2003). Visually mapping the "nation": Swadeshi politics in nationalist India, 1920-1930. *The Journal of Asian Studies*, 62(1), 11–41. https://search.proquest.com/docview/230429907?accountid=177896. DOI: 10.2307/3096134

Verma, R., Teixeira, J., Patrıcio, L., Nunes, N. J., Nobrega, L., Fisk, R. P., & Constantine, L. (2012). Customer experience modeling: From customer experience to service design. *Journal of Service Management*, 23(3), 362–376. DOI: 10.1108/09564231211248453

Wall, G. (2010). On exergy and sustainable development in environmental engineering. *The Open Environmental Engineering Journal*, 3(1), 21–32. DOI: 10.2174/1874829501003010021

Yadav, U.S. & Tripathi, R. (2024). Impact of innovation, entrepreneurial orientation and entrepreneurial leadership on supply chain resilience in handicraft industry: moderating role of supply chain orientation. Benchmarking: An International Journal. DOI: 10.1108/BIJ-09-2023-0615

Yang, S., Song, Y., Chen, S., & Xia, X. (2017). Why are Customers Loyal in Sharing-Economy Services? A Relational Benefits Perspective. *Journal of Services Marketing*, 31(1), 48–62. https://www.proquest.com/scholarly-journals/why-are-customers-loyal-sharing-economy-services/docview/1862042626/se-2. DOI: 10.1108/JSM-01-2016-0042

Zomerdijk, L. G., & Voss, C. A. (2010). Service design for experience-centric services. *Journal of Service Research*, 13(1), 67–82. DOI: 10.1177/1094670509351960

KEY TERMS AND DEFINITIONS

Bar Code / RFID: A unique product code that enables a part or product type to be identified when read by a bar-code scanner.

Capacity: The maximum level of value-added activity that an operation, or process, or facility is capable of over a period of time.

Continuous Improvement: An approach to operations improvement that assumes many, relatively small, incremental, improvements in performance, stressing the momentum of improvement rather than the rate of improvement; also known as 'kaizen', often contrasted with breakthrough improvement.

Customization: The variation in product or service design to suit the specific needs of customers.

Division of Labour: An approach to job design that involves dividing a task down into relatively small parts, each of which is accomplished by a single person.

E-Commerce: Online commerce that sells products and services.

Eco-Labeling: A seal of approval for environmentally safe products.

Environmental Protection: Activities and decisions in operations management that minimize the negative impact of processes, products and services on the environment.

Goods: Tangible objects that can be created and sold at a later date.

Infrastructure: The physical support structures in a community, including roads, water and sewage systems, and utilities.

ISO 14000: An international standard that guides environmental management systems and covers initial planning, implementation and objective assessment.

Job Design: The way in which we structure the content and environment of individual staff members' jobs within the workplace and the interface with the technology or facilities that they use.

Khadi: Indian homespun cloth made with a spinning wheel called charka.

Chapter 10
Collective Intelligence for Sustainable Society:
A Study Through the Lens of Corporate Social Responsibility

Jipson Joseph
https://orcid.org/0009-0005-1795-5051
Christ University, India

Ananya Pandey
https://orcid.org/0000-0002-2419-6314
Christ University, India

ABSTRACT

Sustainability is a catchword of the present generation. The evolution of sustainability through the sustainable development model of Brundtland report and Sustainable Development Goals (SDGs) affirms that the present generation is not only focused on its developmental needs but also concerned about the survival needs of the future generations. This constructive and progressive vision emerged from the positive mentality of many people affirming that the existence of collective intelligence (CI) is advantageous to society. CI insists that open dialogue, mutual sharing, and collaborative efforts can make wonders in human existence. Human coexistence becomes more meaningful with CI. It has also shaped the idea of corporate social responsibility (CSR), which stands for the firms' responsibility towards society. CSR also tries to share a portion of the economic benefits to the marginalized sections of society. From this perspective, the chapter analyzes the role of CI-guided CSR for establishing a sustainable society.

DOI: 10.4018/979-8-3693-7272-2.ch010

INTRODUCTION

Decision-making is the most vital dimension and unique capacity of an individual. This ability depends on factors like education, experience, and social and cultural background. It evolves from the logical and systematic application of one's intelligence. Every person's intelligence is unique and it makes decisions differently from others by analyzing various factors. Collective intelligence (CI) is the sum-total of many individual intelligences. For example, if there is an individual business initiative then mostly the decisions are taken by that individual's intelligence and decision-making capacity; whereas if there are two or more persons, they make collective effort and thereby arrive at a more meaningful and effective decision by applying the intelligence of all of them. As an idea it originated in 1785 with the contribution of Marquis de Condorcet, but it became popular in the last decades of the 20th century. CI, if properly employed, will have more effective results compared to individual intelligence. The present society and its business activities are more complex necessitating collaborative and collective efforts.

Sustainability became a catchword of discussions and policy makings from the last quarter of the 20th century. The Brundtland Commission report of 1987 is to be credited for the wide acceptance of this term. Sustainability refers to people's choice to coexist for a long time on Earth. Coexistence requires CI and collaborative efforts. Coexistence does not merely mean the peaceful existence of the present generation but it also refers to the existence of the present generation without compromising the future generation's right of existence. Accordingly, there emerged the widespread understanding of sustainable development that stands for the collective and collaborative efforts of people to satisfy their needs without endangering the needs of future generation. Sustainability thus entails a process of bridging between the present and future generations. Such a process cannot be achieved without the precise application of CI. Corporate Social Responsibility (CSR) is assessed as an attempt to strengthen the sustainable development projects. It has given many advantages to society in view of sustainable development goals (SDGs). Sustainable society evolves from this enlarged perspective, which refers to a society in which the values of justice, equality, non-discrimination, equitable distributions of the benefits of economic growth, and respect towards the environment are practiced.

There were studies on the various aspects of CI like the understanding of CI from the life of insects (Solé, 2011; Drouin, 2019), an overview of CI (Leimeister, 2010), importance of CI for the better understanding of group priorities (Woolley et al., 2015), CI and its benefits (Mashingaidze, 2014), CI for climate resilience (Nik & Moazami, 2021), and the use of CI for changing the world (Mulgan, 2018). The connection between CSR and sustainable development is also made by various researchers ((McWilliams & Siegel, 2001; Patuelli et al., 2022; Wu & Jin, 2022).

This chapter therefore attempts to analyze the role of CI for establishing a sustainable society through the lens of CSR. The chapter, compared to the previous studies, seeks to make an interconnection between CI and CSR to explore their possibilities for a policy design in connection with sustainable future.

This chapter consists of four main parts. In the first part, the chapter tries to give a basic understanding of CI; in the second part, it focuses on the idea of sustainability and connects it with coexistence and CI; in the third part, the chapter advances CSR as an idea that stands for bridging the gaps so that the aspirations for sustainable society can be achieved; in the fourth section, the chapter explores the possibilities for a policy design that interconnects CI and CSR for establishing sustainable society.

COLLECTIVE INTELLIGENCE: CONCEPTUAL FRAMEWORK

Collective Intelligence, a unique characteristic of majority of animals, originates from the idea of group living (Krause et al., 2010). This concept emerged from the application of self-organization theory in collective animal behavior particularly with regard to the realization that their group living and thinking can solve cognitive problems that are beyond the capacity of individual animals (Bonabeau et al., 1999). An understanding of CI was present throughout human history in different forms. Aristotle argued that the intelligence of a group of people is stronger than that of a single individual. Cicero followed the same line. Teilhard de Chardin used the term "noosphere" to refer to the CI of whole humanity (Bhasin, 2023). Nicolas de Condorcet in the 18th century was the first researcher, who claimed that individuals can benefit from collective thinking and decision-making. But he prioritized the need of correct information (Krause et al., 2010). Galton used empirical data to explain the functioning of CI in humans (1907). But CI developed as a distinct research area in the second half of the 20th century (Woolley & Fuchs, 2011). It functions based on the supposition that although no one knows everything, everyone knows something of everything (Lévy & Bonomo, 1999). This specific term was first used in its modern understanding by Tim O'Reily in 1997 (Bhasin, 2023).

Researchers use variety of terms to explain CI like "collective cognition," "citizen science," "crowdsourcing," "participatory modelling," "swarm intelligence," "wisdom of crowds," and "knowledge co-production" (Gray et al., 2020). All these refer to the same phenomenon. Krause et al. (2010) use swarm intelligence (SI) to refer to all these terminologies, but in this chapter, the authors prefer collective intelligence (CI) to refer to all these terms as to emphasize the cooperative and collaborative efforts. Collective symbolizes the collective personality that can express itself with a *we* identity like a university, firm, political party, or government. It denotes to a group of individuals, who may not be even having the same attitude or perspective

(Leimeister, 2010). But *we-ness* is an important characteristic of CI. It is not quite easy to immediately transform into 'we perspective' from an 'individual perspective.' It requires codes, roles, and rules that govern individuals and define the identity and status of the group. However, the collective should not become so large as it becomes difficult to collaborate and coordinate (Mulgan, 2018). Performance capability is a unique group trait that can result in CI (Woolley, 2011). When the group becomes extremely larger it can adversely affect its performance quality and also its CI.

Defining Collective Intelligence

Individual and collective intelligences are different but intimately related (Watson & Levin, 2023). Multiple studies on individual's intelligence have taken place in psychology but not many attempts have been done to measure group intelligence (Woolley et al., 2010). Intelligence is always perceived as a specific category of an individual, not of a group. But Reidl et al. argue that an evaluation of group living establishes the existence of various factors of common intelligence (2021). Individual intelligence is the dependency of an individual on one's own reasoning or decision-making capacity, whereas CI originates from the ability of a group of individuals to collaborate, share, and employ their decision-making capacities for solving complex problems. In such a way CI outweighs individual intelligence (Gray et al., 2020). It argues that the problems that cannot be solved individually can be positively addressed by the group's strength (Krause et al., 2010). It also leads to convergence and interdependence of action against the divergent and independent perspectives of individuals (Woolley, 2011).

Just as there is lack of consensus among the names given to CI, there is also no consensus on its definition (Woolley et al., 2010; Krause et al., 2010; Skaržauskienè & Mačiulienè, 2015). CI can be defined as a system of functioning in which "two or more individuals independently, or at least partially independently, acquire information and these different packages of information are combined and processed through social interaction, which provides a solution to a cognitive problem in a way that cannot be implemented by isolated individuals" (Krause et al., 2010, p. 29). The definition underlines the essential characteristics of CI such as there should be at least two individuals, they should acquire information either independently or partially independently, the acquired information should be combined and processed through social interaction, and it should lead to the solution of a cognitive problem that isolated individuals cannot easily do. It means that mere staying together of individuals or the crowd in a market place cannot considered as examples of CI. Woolley et al. give a simpler definition to CI as "the general ability of the group to perform a wide variety of tasks" (2010, p. 687). It affirms that CI is a characteristic of the group and not of the individuals who are its parts. Individuals contribute to formulate CI but it belongs to the group. Accordingly, CI will be "more productive for coordinating the efforts of free individuals" (Lévy, 2005, p. 194). The characteristic features of CI are a group of individuals, motivations and incentives, collecting of inputs, and collaboration of ideas (Recker et al., 2013).

CI can offer variety of benefits to the society at large. An individual has a limitation to solve complex problems but when many individuals collectively think and collaborate with each other, it has the capacity to see the problem from different angles and give appropriate solutions (Gray et al., 2020). Individuals' efficiency is more effective than the individual's capacity in problem-solving (Page, 2007). This is because of the active and progressive use of their CI, which gives valuable insights to decision-makers and resource managers by actively interacting with many people who can solve the problems (Woolley et al., 2010). Teachers can use CI to improve crowd-teaching's functioning (Recker et al., 2013). Scientific communities use CI for research, inventions, and knowledge sharing through conferences, collaborative experiments, special issues of journals, and mutual sharing process (Woolley & Fuchs, 2011). CI technologies like swarm platforms and online surveys "can act as a middleman between resource users and managers by providing a venue for inclusive forms of decision making and improving methods of incorporating stakeholder inputs" (Gray et al., 2020, p. 469). This is also useful for improved production, election prediction, media sector interactions, and company management (Krause et al., 2010). Besides, it can empower humankind's creativity, efficiency, and decision-making capacity (Bhasin, 2023).

Collective Intelligence and Collaborative Efforts

CI is a measure to understand and evaluate the general effectiveness of a group in carrying out a multiple range of tasks (Woolley et al., 2015). Cognitive diversity and diversity of opinion among the group members empower the strength of CI (Kozhevnikov et al., 2014). In the contemporary scenario, education and research rely on CI and collaborative efforts. Compared to previous centuries, the present researchers focus more on collaborative works as they give better results. Even the research articles with many authors and international collaborators are more valued and prioritized. It affirms that group of people can produce better results (under certain conditions) rather than any individual of that group (Leimeister, 2010). Efficient and effective collaboration among individuals is a prerequisite of CI as diverse opinions can thus be converted into a decision. Participation, sharing, and collaboration are vital for achieving common goals (Skaržauskienė & Mačiulienė, 2015). The group's diversity is also essential for its effectiveness (Mann & Helbing, 2017) as CI "emerges from the synergy of individual creative efforts" (Flores et al., 2015, p. 852). Mutual interaction is prioritized over social interaction to achieve better results in CI (Woolley et al., 2015) as social interaction may lead to unnecessary external influence. But mutual interaction must be qualified by transparency and honesty for having more effectiveness in employing their CI (Bhasin, 2023). However, high social perceptiveness enhances the group's CI (Woolley et al., 2015). Social perceptiveness must lead to effective mutual interaction among the group members triggering their CI, which will help to solve multitude of problems and engage in a wide range of tasks.

Different Perceptions of Truth for Decision-Making

Collective Intelligence is not a mere collection of individual opinions and thinking. Individuals have different opinions about a particular subject and they can make judgments independent of each other without any external influence or bias that can result in different perceptions of truth (Surowiecki, 2004). There can be both convergence and divergence among the individuals and the process of bridging is employed to enable CI (Woolley & Fuchs, 2011). When put together by an intelligent coordinator, the different perceptions of truth become the CI, which can lead to a favorable decision (Straub et al., 2023). At the same time, there is every possibility for individuals to be biased or influenced by others and their ideologies (Leimeister, 2010). In such cases, their own unique intelligence that perceives truth will not emerge. Independent and unbiased perception of truth is the rationale for CI, which can lead to meaningful decision-making (UNDP, 2021). CI is a consensus decision-making far beyond the combined decision-making. In combined decision-making, the decisions are taken individually without a consensus but depends on other individuals' behavior patterns. Whereas, in consensus decision-making, individuals come to consensus through coordination, cooperation, deliberation, and collaboration (Mashingaidze, 2014).

Enhanced Capacity for Economic Growth

The traditional understanding of economic growth is clubbed with the evolution of GDP. This can happen even without a convincing development of the whole society. Economic progress must be envisioned as sustainable economic growth (García-Monleón et al., 2024). No societal growth is possible without the contribution of all protagonists. But its advantages are mainly concentrated into the hands of a few. Every individual in the society should become beneficiaries of economic growth. CI is being understood as an "enhanced capacity" that emerges from the working together of a group of individuals (UNDP, 2021, p. 5). Enhanced capacity helps to achieve more benefits. Since CI is more used in economic interaction, it can contribute to economic development. Using CI in various fields like research, innovation, production, manufacturing, energy consumption, and environmental protection can increase economic growth (Woolley, 2021). CI helps policy-makers, coordinators, or managers to easily interact with different fields in such a way to examine whether a particular thing is advantageous compared to others. Such a mechanism advances the possibility to opt for the best possible method that can lead to sustainable economic growth. CI also enhances the group's capacity to do various tasks, resulting in economic development (Woolley et al., 2010). Collaborative works of entrepreneurs or employers can leverage their CI and collective know-how, which will empower their economic growth as well.

Collective Intelligence and Sustainable Society

Intelligence is action-oriented. Human actions resulting from intelligence's capacities of analysis and reasoning lead to growth. Intelligence provides an internal framework and when it aligns with the external environment through its expressions, it gives sustainable results (Mulgan, 2018). Sustainable society is the ultimate objective of all individual actions, if rightly oriented. In the absence of sustainable society perspective, no individual can achieve true well-being. Sustainable society refers to a society "that has learned to live within the boundaries established by ecological limits. It can be maintained as a collective and ongoing entity because practices that imposed excessive burdens upon the environment have been reformed or abolished" (Meadowcroft, 2024). Sustainable society is thus the one which takes into account the environmental concerns in its social and economic development interests. The concept of sustainable society revolves around the principle of justice with its distributive and environmental elements.

CI approach can contribute positively to the demands of sustainable society as it can provide better strategies for both environmental protection and economic development (Gray et al., 2020). CI can speed up the achievement of SDGs. SDG 17 affirms the importance of partnerships or collective intelligence for achieving the society's goals for a sustainable future. Based on SDG 17, the UNDP conducted case studies of various programs in different States that advanced the attempts for a sustainable society. In Argentina, DIY hardware and citizen sensing were used to measure changes in air quality. The use of CI helped researchers effectively understand the reasons of air pollution (2021). A study conducted by Nik and Moazami in Stockholm says that "CI can help to gradually and effectively decrease the energy demand during extreme climate events" (2021, p. 13). In Ukraine, there was a practice of open burning of waste, especially in rural areas. The researchers gave awareness to the indigenous people, addressed their concerns, and after a series of mutual interactions and employing their CI, they found other methods of waste disposal. Serbia, one of the fastest shrinking populations in the world, faces massive external migration issues. The UNDP researchers together with the local support found out the reasons for this huge migration. UNDP, State government, NGOs, and citizens, using their CI, contributed to formulate appropriate policies against this unfavorable situation. In the same way, case studies were conducted in Mexico, Ecuador, Columbia, Vietnam, and the like to understand how CI can enhance the attempts to establish a sustainable society (UNDP, 2021). Besides, Beckett and O'Loughlin identify indigenous knowledge as CI and emphasizes its importance for achieving the SDGs (2024).

SUSTAINABILITY: THEORETICAL FOUNDATION FOR EGALITARIAN SOCIETY

Sustainability is an age-old term. But it received required attention in the second half of the 20th century. Sustainability is "the integration of environmental health, social equity, and economic vitality in order to create thriving, healthy, diverse, and resilient communities for this generation and generations to come" (UCLA, 2016). It bridges environment, equity, and economic growth. These were individual elements in the past, but sustainability balances them. Sustainability thus becomes the cornerstone for an egalitarian society. Egalitarianism demands that all people should be treated equally irrespective of gender, race, religion, ethnicity, and economic status as they have equal dignity and rights (UDHR, Arts. 1 & 2), equal recognition everywhere as a person before the law (UDHR, Art. 6), equal status before the law and equal protection of the law (UDHR, Art. 7), equal consideration for a fair hearing (UDHR, Art. 10), equality of opportunities (UDHR, Art. 21), and equality of conditions (UDHR, Arts. 25-27). Equality of opportunities also underscores the principle of equal access (Fleurbaey, 2001). Egalitarianism originated with the Christianity's perspective of creation of human beings as equals (Arneson, 2013). But it became more influential through the philosophies of John Locke (1690), Karl Marx (1875), John Rawls (1999; Leif, 2021), Amartya Sen (1992, 1997, 2009), and Marta Nussbaum (1992, 2000). The aspirations for an egalitarian society cannot be achieved without substantial economic growth that ensures basic standard of life to all people, principle of equity that echoes equality of living conditions and opportunities, and a healthy environment for the present and past generations. That is, egalitarian society will be unimaginable without the inclusion of justice. Justice demands equitable distribution of economic benefits and opportunities, positive and progressive concerns towards the needs of others, and an environmental justice perspective that respects and values the needs for a healthy environment of the present and future generations.

Evolution of Sustainability

Sustainability has received wide acceptance in the present global order. This word is often equated with a systematic and equitable global order. The term got its momentum in the second half of the 20th century but the idea was already prevalent in the ancient and medieval civilizations as well. Humans were always aware of the importance of economic growth, environmental protection, and equitable distribution. In the past, the idea of sustainability was not given much attention due to many reasons such as, small size of population, lack of industrial and other polluting sectors, and the society's specific mindset. It was practiced to a great extent, but not propagated. It was an integral part of the society, and so, there was no much effort required to implement it as the societies were basically agrarian and ecofriendly (Combs, 2024).

The shift from traditional agrarian practices took place with the Industrial Revolution. Ecofriendly practices were substituted with eco-utilizing practices that are primarily oriented towards profit. It made substantial alterations in the relationship between humans and the environment. It gave economic benefits to a few, but risked the lives of many people and other species. Accordingly, the environmental health was damaged. However, this consumptive economic model also raised questions on balancing progress and conservation (Combs, 2024). Various movements like conservation movement, environmental movement, 'no growth' philosophy, discipline of ecology, counter-technology movement, resource/environment concept, and global model approach shaped the concept of sustainability (Kidd, 1992). But yet, sustainability was very poorly defined and many people perceived it differently (Wilkinson, 2016).

Sustainability appeared as a major theme for the first time in the book *Blueprint for Survival* (Goldsmith et al., 1972). In the same year the International Union for the Conservation of Nature (IUCN) in its *Yearbook* used 'sustainable' in the context of environment. In 1974, the preparatory document of the planning committee for the Woodlands conferences used the term in connection with development (Kidd, 1992). In 1977, the first book with the word sustainability in its title was published, which demanded the need for an environmental policy in relation to economic development (Pirages, 1977). The word made its first appearance in the UN documents with the World Environment Report of 1978 (UNEP). The Worldwatch institute popularized the term in the 1980s. In the annual meeting of Indian Science Congress Association, T. N. Khoshoo reminded that sustainability has to be given specific importance in the planning process (Kidd, 1992). All these individual and organizational attempts achieved its finality with the publication of Brundtland report, *Our Common Future* (WCED, 1987). Sustainability is radical and closely associated with achieving justice, which is possible only through changes in the priorities and practices of human beings (Dower, 2004).

Sustainable Development: A Paradigm Shift

From the time of Brundtland report both sustainability and sustainable development are used interchangeably. But some authors claim that both are different as one is a means whereas the other is an end. Sustainability is an end-state wherein a dynamic equilibrium takes place between the needs of humankind and nature. It is considered a perfect balance between nature and humankind. It stands for the end result of the sustainable form of development. Sustainable development, on the other hand, is a process or a means to achieve sustainability (Basiago, 1995; Hector et al., 2014). However, a close analysis shows that the objective of sustainable development is predominantly anthropocentric and not to strive for any dynamic equilibrium. Its objective is to satisfy the present generation's needs without denying the future generation's availability of resources (Hector et al., 2014). But in practice, it has become eco-centric due to the influence of environmentalists and other international actors who highly advocate for the preservation of the ecosystem. In reality, sustainable development should be anthropo-eco-centric without neglecting one for the other or using one for the advantage of the other. Only then, sustainable development will be able to epitomize both environmental and distributive justice.

Sustainable form of development was first used in World Environment Report without a specific definition (UNEP, 1978). Sustainable development was also occasionally used by some individual researchers or organizations, but it became a well-defined concept only with the Brundtland report. The UN General Assembly in 1983 formulated an independent group to study the relationship between environment and development. G. H. Brundtland was the chairman of this committee (Kidd, 1992). It defined sustainable development as the ability of the present generation to meet its needs through development without compromising the ability of the future generations to meet their own needs, particularly their environmental needs (WCED, 1987). This concept thus clubbed the developmental aspirations of the present generation with the environmental needs of the future generations. It is an inter-generational concept that addresses the needs of both generations (Habib, 2013). It is also intra-generational as it focuses on economic development and environmental health of the present generation. In this perspective, sustainable development links the two diverse concepts of anthropocentrism and ecocentrism as it does not prioritize one over the other (Wilkinson, 2016).

Sustainable development encompasses three basic concepts: economic growth, environmental health, and social justice. These three are essential for a sustainable society (Elkington, 1997). They are interconnected. It is not a pyramidal but a triangular relationship. All these three aspects have equal importance. Economic growth is achievable mainly through development. Sustainable model of development implies that the benefits of development should be equally distributed to address various issues like poverty, unemployment, and inequality. It will ensure social justice. Sustainable developmental model also affirms that the developmental aspirations should not damage environmental health (Wilkinson, 2016). But sustainability is all the more related with the results of economic development. Economic development's impact on social and environmental dimensions is the major concern of sustainability. Sustainable development thus stands for an economic development that does not have an adversarial impact on environment and society. Accordingly, this model can be termed as totalitarian as it addresses the welfare of the whole ecosystem including the humans. Sustainable society in that sense refers to a society where the interests of people and the ecosystem are protected and respected.

Balancing Sustainable Development and Coexistence

Sustainable development paradigm is strengthened by an understanding of its 'four pillars' with the Rio Conference. These interconnected pillars are economic growth, protection of environment, social responsibility, and institutional reform (UNDFSD, 1993). However, this is often confined to the "Triple Stool" of sustainability encompassing ecology, economic growth, and equity (Sanford, 2017). Institutional reform was not sidelined as it is the underlining and interconnecting tool of the other three fundamental principles. Without significant institutional reform, no society can achieve a sustainable future consisting of economic growth, environmental protection, and equitable distribution. It also balances with the idea of coexistence. The principle of coexistence demands coexistence of humans and also their sustainable existence with other beings (Vogel et al., 2023). It necessitates the coexistence of industries and other sectors that are oriented towards sustainable development (López, 2010). Coexistence of economy, ecology, and equity are essential for a sustainable society (Parida et al., 2022). Coexistence and Sustainable development are mutually empowering and one cannot exist without the other (García-Monleón et al., 2024).

Bridging Coexistence and Collective Intelligence

As mentioned above, CI is the intelligence of a collective or a group. Mutual cooperation and coordination of individuals is a critical parameter of CI (Leonard & Levin, 2022). Living, thinking, or working together using the tools of mutual interaction and open dialogue enhances CI (Watson & Levin, 2023). It does not mean that the collective or group should live or work in a same space. It demands sharing of intelligence (Pooley, 2021), which can be done through real or virtual space. The group must have the same identity, orientation, or objective as it should guide the functioning of individual intelligence to solve a particular problem or carry out a significant task. For example, a group of researchers from different countries come together in the cyberspace and share their ideas and studies on CI among elephants and its inputs for humankind as we see in the research of Vogel et al. (2023). Coexistence is often emphasized in human-human interaction in the context of war and terrorism and human-wildlife interaction (Pooley, 2021). Coexistence has undoubtedly great value in such contexts. But it cannot be limited to such situations only. Coexistence demands people to exist meaningfully and peacefully with other creatures and the ecosystem for the well-being of the whole society. In that sense, it is creature-creature interaction for sustainable society. Besides, coexistence is also an essential factor for the growth of CI, which is advantageous to societal well-being.

Failures in the System: Threats for Sustainable Society

A small minority possesses majority of economic benefits and such an unequal distribution is one of the main concerns of sustainable society. Sustainable development is understood only in terms of economic growth without degrading the environment. Its social dimension is mostly neglected or given lesser importance. No serious reflection is undertaken on the aftereffects of unfair social structures of economic growth and environmental burdens (Sanford, 2017). Occasional studies were conducted without succeeding in redefining policies and reforming societal attitude. Sustainable development and coexistence have become a monopoly of the developed countries and rich people. Due to the failure of the distributive justice system, developing countries and poor people succumb to the monopoly of the richest few people. Many hazardous industries are situated in developing countries or in poor rural areas. Hazardous waste is dumped near the living areas of impoverished or vulnerable population (Sanford, 2017). Both sustainable development and coexistence become vain in the absence of sincere efforts to uplift the marginalized and vulnerable sections of the society. This endangers the aspirations for sustainable society.

Urbanization, undoubtedly, leads to economic growth. But unplanned urbanization, especially in the developing world, is an important area of concern. It increases ecological burden, economic disparity, and social inequalities among the people. As a result, the coexistence of people becomes a complex issue (Parida et al., 2022). Gender inequality and discrimination endangers peaceful coexistence and sustainable development paradigm. Without thoughtful efforts to tackle gender inequality, the demands for a sustainable society cannot be achieved (Stevens, 2010). CI should depend on the entire potential of the society without any discrimination, then only it will lead to sustainability (Parida et al., 2022). Fund allocation and distribution is also crucial for sustainable development. The overall development, progress, and prosperity should be the concern of each government (Frey, 2017). Inequitable distribution leads to injustice and inequality. This challenges the foundations of coexistence. This is also same with employment opportunities. Lack of income and opportunities cannot promote a sustainable future (Parida et al., 2022).

CORPORATE SOCIAL RESPONSIBILITY: BRIDGING THE GAPS

Disproportionate distribution and concentration of the economic benefits into the hands of a minority causes enormous gap in the society. Justice demands responsible social action for societal well-being. Corporates should give more emphasis on social responsibility as they cause various problems like environmental pollution, ecological imbalances, food insecurity, inefficient production, quality issues, gender discrimination, unstable employment situations, and unfair income distribution (Wu & Jin, 2022). Many think that the prime objective of CSR is to advance sustainable development programs. Hersh and Levin thus argue that they are "umbrella constructs" (1999, p. 200). But the language of CSR is more normative than the formal and rational style of sustainability (Strand et al., 2015). Though the language and style of CSR and sustainable development differ, they underline the desired attitude towards society. Social responsibility should become the prime and inevitable choice of corporates and enterprises to ensure sustainable development (Wu & Jin, 2022). Scandinavian countries and their industries perform well in their CSR as per the various data available (Strand et al., 2015). This model should be followed throughout the world for a substantial growth.

The 21st century economic growth can be equated with corporate culture. This trend started from the last quarter of the 20th century. The leading business personnel are either MNCs or TNCs. Even the small-scale business people work as subsidiary units of many of these corporates. Accordingly, there emerged the relevance of CSR, a concept which had its beginning in the 1950s (Mariani et al., 2021). The first official reference to CSR can be seen in the book *Social Responsibilities of the Businessman* (Bowen, 1953). Carroll specifically presented it as the businessmen's responsibility towards society (1978, 2008). Enlarging the scope of CSR Freeman argued that corporates and firms have responsibility not only to shareholders but also to all stakeholders (1984). There are manifold definitions of CSR. It is defined as "actions that further some social good, beyond the interests of the firm and that which is required by law" (McWilliams & Siegel, 2001, p. 117). The European Commission defines it as "the responsibility of enterprises for their impacts on society" (2011). CSR thus aims to ensure maximum benefits to maximum number of people by going far beyond the interests of the firm and the law and thereby establishing its impact on the society. It thus tries to bridge the gap between people, societies, and States. CSR has two different levels of demand. From the perspective of customers, that is, to avail quality, healthy, and ecofriendly products; and from the perspective of all stakeholders, that is, to undertake projects of sustainable development so that a portion of their economic benefits will be shared with the vulnerable sections of the society (McWilliams & Siegel, 2001). The second level of demand includes the firm's employees as well. In this section, we focus only on this second perspective/demand of CSR excluding the demands of the employees.

Unparalleled Gap between the Rich and the Poor: A Critical Analysis

Compared to previous generation, the present generation's economic development is clubbed with the growth of MNCs and TNCs. Individual initiatives, which mainly result from individual intelligence, are being shifted with collaborative and corporate efforts that employ CI (Figueroa &Vargas-Perez, 2018). Though corporates utilize CI for the progress of their business activities, their ownership lie in the hands of a very few persons. Accordingly, the fruits of economic growth are being concentrated into a small group of individuals. This leads to a huge gap between the rich and the poor. According to the World Inequality Report of 2022, the richest 1% owns 38% and the poorest 50% owns just 2% of global increment in wealth. Such extreme inequality leads to the cry of the majority that 'we belong to the 99%.' The example of the most populous country in the world, India, underlines this claim as it moved from British Raj to Billionaire Raj due to the over concentration of wealth in the hands of few people (Chancel & Piketty, 2019; Oxfam India, 2023). Increase in the poverty rate of the advanced economies also affirms that economic inequality is not a specific feature of the developing world (Dabla-Norris et al., 2015). Growing gap between the rich and the poor has become a global phenomenon.

The economic divide has far-reaching adversarial impacts on social welfare, economic growth, and overall development of the society (Majumdar et al., 2023). This results in social inequality and injustice. This also leads to an exclusion mentality (Francis, 2013) that excludes the concerns and needs of the marginalized from policy-making and its implementation. Both inequality of income and opportunities cause economic inequality that challenges societal well-being and individual growth (Stiglitz, 2012). Higher the inequality is, lower the sustainable economic growth (Dabla-Norris et al., 2015). Since economic benefits are the results of CI and collaborative efforts of many stakeholders, there should be an effective mechanism to share its benefits to all the deserving people. Distributive justice demands that there must be fair and equitable distribution. Fair sharing encompasses equitable distribution of basic resources, economic benefits, capabilities, opportunities, and also burdens (Habib, 2013).

CSR: Model for Bridging the Gaps

CSR is a self-regulation process for the private business people in such a way that they share at least some percentage of their annual turnover for some philanthropic activities (Carroll, 2008; Carroll & Shabana, 2010; Kasturi Rangan et al., 2015). Many countries do not draw a particular line but countries like India demand that they should share at least 2% of their net profits. This sharing can contribute to various projects that are oriented towards the welfare of society. Such initiatives can energize the aspirations for a sustainable society. CSR underlines the richest entrepreneurs' responsibility towards the poor and helps to realize an egalitarian society. People should have an equal chance to enjoy the basic essentials for a meaningful life, fulfil their potential, and participate in societal life (Coote, 2015). Only through policy designs like CSR the triangular relationship between economic, environmental, and social dimensions of sustainability can be achieved. CSR affirms that economically advanced entrepreneurs have an obligation to positively respond to the society's sustainable needs. This requires operational effectiveness, transformation of business model, and unified practice platform (Kasturi Rangan et al., 2015).

CSR attempts to uplift the society's downtrodden sections by using a portion of the economic benefits of the corporates or industrialists. It is a process of bridging. A nexus-building was needed otherwise the society would have been divided into two very extreme unequal units. There are arguments either in favor or against of the CSR of firms (Carroll & Shabana, 2010). This chapter does not enter into that debate. Since the firms function in a society using many of its resources, a share of their profit should be returned back to the society for its welfare. This is a matter of justice and accountability. This is to create value, balance, and accountability in the society (Schwartz & Carroll, 2008). CSR includes ethical and legal responsibilities of the firms. But more noticeably it underlines philanthropic responsibilities towards the society as it will improve the community's well-being (Kotler & Lee, 2005) and promote activities of human welfare (Carroll, 1991). The ultimate objective of CSR is thus to reduce inequality, which is prevalent in the society, in order to ensure a sustainable future for humankind. Most of these CSR initiatives originate from the application of CI of many stakeholders. CI leads to CSR, which results in establishing a sustainable society.

Harmonizing CSR and SDGs

Elkington argues that the SDGs, which epitomize the economic, environmental, and social dimensions of sustainable development, balance perfectly with the framework of CSR (1997). Both SDGs and CSR have the same objective, that is, the well-being of society. CSR's attempts to reduce poverty, hunger, unemployment, discrimination, inequality, and irresponsible consumption are closely linked to SDGs (Shayan et al., 2022). SDGs revolve around the 5Ps such as people, planet, peace, partnering, and prosperity (UN, 2015) and CSR also aims to focus on these 5Ps as its prime objective in the present times is to support the sustainable future endeavors of the UN's 2030 agenda. Since corporations have proper and efficient resources, manpower, and technology to pursue the targets of SDGs, the CSR model will be more effective in the efforts for a sustainable society (Shayan et al., 2022). The triple bottom line framework that upholds the balance between economic interests, environmental concerns, and social expectations (Elkington, 1997) will be sustainable only in a harmonious interaction between SDGs and CSR. Besides, they both are complementary as they target socioeconomic development and environmental protection (Shayan et al., 2022).

While SDGs are the goals set for humanity's sustainable future, CSR is one vital means for achieving those goals. CSR is a key to sustainable development (An & Yoon, 2021), whereas SDGs provide "a reputable, comprehensive, and practical framework for CSR" (Shayan et al., 2022, p. 10). To advance social responsibility, corporates should not limit their objective by creating a CSR fund, but they should also properly address how they will utilize this fund to realize the SDGs (Wu & Jin, 2022). Prioritization of SDGs targets on account of its necessity and urgency is essential in the utilization of CSR fund (Zagloel & Hasibuan, 2021). Corporations should invest more resources to confront the most urgent issues, mostly SDGs targets, of their immediate neighborhoods. Such efforts can be slowly extended to the whole society (Shayan et al., 2022).

CSR: A Critical Analysis

CSR is not a burden but a positive and progressive attempt to distribute the benefits of economic growth to the weaker sections of the society and to promote societal well-being. This echoes the Indian Vedic principle of *Vasudhaiva ku u - bakam* (*Maha Upani ad* 6:71-72), which implies that the whole earth is one family (Parecattil, 2020). The familial nature of the earth demands that the stronger should support the weaker sections of the society. Familial vision insists on unity in diversity. CSR attempts to expand the horizon of familial space in order to include all without any divisive mentality (Gupta, 2021). Accordingly, CSR should guarantee fair and sustainable distribution of its benefits to a maximum number of marginalized people (Wu & Jin, 2022). Nevertheless, how far this ideological setting is being practiced in real life is a complex point of discussion. Do the firms undertake philanthropic activities to promote a positive vision towards the sustainable growth of others or to greenwash their activities? Do their social responsibility activities come from their humanitarian perspective or from their duplicity to hide their harmful practices by creating a public image? CSR, if it does not evolve from a positive vision, will not be beneficial for the deserving people. Both management and administration teams should consider it as a means to enhance a culture of sustainable love and life.

CSR activities have helped in many ways to bridge the gap between the rich and the poor (Shetty & Potdar, 2023). A wise and effective CSR fund spending is essential for realizing sustainable development (McWilliams & Siegel, 2001). However, many companies lack coordination and logic that result in poor performance of CSR (Kasturi Rangan et al., 2015). Many MNCs and TNCs have their charitable organizations, like the Bill and Melinda Gates Foundation of Microsoft founder, Reliance Foundation of Reliance Group, Tata Foundation of Tata Group, and Adani Foundation of Adani Group. They undertake manifold philanthropic activities supporting millions of people to secure their lives. However, their main objective is to ensure a high reputation for their group. Some companies use CSR as a publicity tool rather than impacting people's life (Shetty & Potdar, 2023). Transparency and accountability about the utilization of CSR fund is essential for a real impact (Kumar, 2019). All the above-mentioned foundations have specific sectorial preferences like education, health, and women empowerment programs (Shetty & Potdar, 2023). These areas are vital for sustainable development. But if there is proper and systematic coordination among all these foundations and other firms in the allotment and spending of CSR funds, it can reach to truly deserving people.

Many companies do not spend their prescribed CSR fund (Gouda M et al., 2024). Proper mechanism should be established to check the actual spending of the CSR fund to ensure the firms' responsibility towards the society. The government should also give a priority list consisting of the sectors, areas, etc., to each firm so that the State can achieve a sustainable future through such collaborative efforts. The firms and their central offices are situated in certain areas depending on many factors and if the CSR allotment is based on the location of the head office, most of such funds would go to a particular area. In such a situation, allocating certain areas or sectors to the firms by a coordinating agency can provide a comprehensive vision of progress in view of sustainable society.

CSR and Collective Intelligence

CI, as already mentioned, is the intelligence of a group of individuals (Krause et al., 2010). CSR evolved from the self-regulation process of a firm that includes many shareholders (Carroll & Shabana, 2010). CSR embodies CI as it results from many stakeholders' active and progressive visionary approach. The beginning of CSR underlines that it originated not from any external pressure but from the progressive thinking of its management to secure human progress and societal well-being (Schwartz & Carroll, 2008). Though they had some biased interests, they undertook some positive steps that epitomized their social responsibility. CSR is a meaningful mechanism for energizing sustainable development. It also can contribute in many ways to advance various programs to realize SDGs (Shayan et al., 2022). All these activities and programs, from the initiation of CSR projects, allocation of funds, coordination, implementation, and monitoring to its completion, involve the collaborative efforts of many individuals. From these collaborations of individual intelligences evolve the intelligence of the collective (CI), which finally makes possible the CSR projects. CSR cannot function without the sustainable use of CI.

SUGGESTIONS FOR A POLICY DESIGN: A WAY FORWARD

From the Brundtland report onwards, sustainable development has been a policy matter for almost all nations (WCED, 1987). The 21st century initiatives of Millennium Development Goals (MDGs) and SDGs redefined this policy framework with more positivity. The 2030 agenda of a sustainable future, though it received a setback with the COVID-19 crisis, is a serious concern for all countries. The sole efforts of international organizations or national governments cannot achieve a sustainable future. It requires the collaborative efforts of various actors. International organizations like UN, WHO, WTO, and IMF, regional cooperations like EU, BRICS, and ASEAN, national governments, NGOs, MNCs and TNCs, and various civic societies actively engage in this 2030 project. Among the 17 SDGs, both 16 and 17 affirm the importance of strong institutions and partnerships for achieving other 15 SDGs. Such an emphasis on collaborative efforts underlines the significance of CI and CSR (Kasturi Rangan et al., 2015). Depending on individual intelligence or initiatives has limited access but CI can widen the initiatives and approach of people or corporations towards sustainability. Hence, specific attention should be given to the positive usage of CI in policy-making and implementation strategies.

Diversity of opinion is the foundational element of CI (Kozhevnikov et al., 2014). Both international organizations and State governments should accept and respect the diverse opinions of opposition leaders, corporates, NGOs, and laymen so that the policies and decision-makings can better empower the aspirations for a sustainable society (Surowiecki, 2004). No society can sustainably grow if there is no possibility for diverse thinking and open dialogue. Differences in individual intelligence should harmonize into CI through mutual interaction. Such kind of sharing and interaction should be encouraged in the society.

CSR is an efficient mechanism for realizing equitable distribution of economic benefits among the people (Wu & Jin, 2022). All the stakeholders of a firm should be able to reap the fruits of the firm's economic growth. Every society, in many ways, supports the progress of a firm. It thus necessitates responsible social actions from the part of the firm. Many countries through legal enactments made CSR a compulsory project. The governments need to prioritize projects and missions for the firms to establish a sustainable society. A proper coordinating and monitoring agency is also vital for effectively implementing CSR fund (McWilliams & Siegel, 2001).

CONCLUSION

Both globalization and open policy frameworks have reshaped the globe. The world has become so intimately interconnected, which no one could imagine in the first half of the 20th century. Communication, information, and transportation facilities have become so progressive as to enhance the claims of the traditional Vedic concept of *Vasudhaiva ku u bakam.* Based on the concept of globalization some people consider world as global village whereas some others add more inclusivity and call it, global family. The inclusiveness of *Vasudhaiva ku u bakam* is echoed in the interconnectedness of global family. Such an interconnectedness, either through virtual or real platforms, supports people's collective interests. The present society does not value individual interests but prioritizes collective interests. This shift is visible in the evolution of the concept of CI. Almost all the essential sectors uphold the importance of CI over individual intelligence. It is believed that since CI depends on the diverse thinking capacities of people, it can provide better results.

CI was the inspirational source behind the visionary approach towards sustainability. The concept of sustainable development evolved from many people's progressive and positive thinking. They argued that the economic needs, environmental concerns, and social expectations should balance for a sustainable future. This vision for a balanced society has been taken up by the UN and other international organizations, and it became more intense with the introduction of SDGs in 2015. Various agents are actively cooperating with each other in order to ensure a positive result with the 2030 agenda of a sustainable future. CSR, being a mechanism of positivity and an offshoot of CI, can augment the various projects with regard to SDGs.

CSR is not a publicity campaign, but an attempt to support the aspirations for an equitable society. Some firms might use it as a publicity tool without understanding its importance and value. The CI, which was behind the CSR designed it as a key for sustainable development. Accordingly, the MNCs, TNCs, and other firms should dedicate their CSR fund to empower the society and marginalized sections. This should not be viewed as a charitable contribution of the rich but as a progressive mechanism to promote the familial nature of the Earth.

REFERENCES

An, S. B., & Yoon, K. C. (2021). The Effects of Socially Responsible Activities on Management Performance of Internationally Diversified Firms: Evidence from KOSPI Market. *Journal of Asian Finance. Economics and Business*, 8, 251–265.

Arneson, R. (2013). Egalitarianism. *The Stanford Encyclopedia of Philosophy*. https://plato.stanford.edu/entries/egalitarianism/

Basiago, A. D. (1995). Methods of Defining Sustainability. *Sustainable Development (Bradford)*, 3(3), 110–119. DOI: 10.1002/sd.3460030302

Beckett, R. C., & O'Loughlin, A. (2024). The Unity of Indigenous Knowledge in the Pursuit of a UN Sustainable Development Goal. *Collective Intelligence*, 3(2), 26339137241241295. Advance online publication. DOI: 10.1177/26339137241241295

Bhasin, H. (2023). What is Collective Intelligence? Benefits and Limitations. *Marketing91*. https://www.marketing91.com/collective-intelligence/

Bonabeau, E., Dorigo, M., & Theraulaz, G. (1999). *Swarm Intelligence: From Natural to Artificial Systems*. Academic. DOI: 10.1093/oso/9780195131581.001.0001

Bowen, H. R. (1953). *Social Responsibilities of the Businessman*. University of Iowa Press.

Carroll, A. B. (1979). A Three-Dimensional Conceptual Model of Corporate Performance. *Academy of Management Review*, 4(4), 497–505. DOI: 10.2307/257850

Carroll, A. B. (1991). The Pyramid of Corporate Social Responsibility: Toward the Moral Management of Organizational Stakeholders. *Business Horizons*, 34(4), 39–48. DOI: 10.1016/0007-6813(91)90005-G

Carroll, A. B. (2008). A History of Corporate Social Responsibility: Concepts and Practices. In Crane, A., Matten, D., McWilliams, A., Moon, J., & Siegel, D. S. (Eds.), *The Oxford Handbook of Social Responsibility* (pp. 19–46). Academic. DOI: 10.1093/oxfordhb/9780199211593.003.0002

Carroll, A. B., & Shabana, K. (2010). The Business Case for Corporate Social Responsibility: A Review of Concepts, Research and Practice. *International Journal of Management Reviews*, 12(1), 85–105. DOI: 10.1111/j.1468-2370.2009.00275.x

Chancel, L., & Piketty, T. (2019). Indian Income Inequality, 1922-2015: From British Raj to Billionaire Raj? *Review of Income and Wealth*, 65(S1), S33–S62. DOI: 10.1111/roiw.12439

Combs, S. (2024). The Evolution of Sustainability: A Historical Perspective. *Emerald Ecovations*. https://emeraldecovations.com/2024/05/evolution-of-sustainability/#

Coote, A. (2015). People, Planet, Power: Toward a New Social Settlement. *International Journal of Social Quality*, 5(1), 8–34. DOI: 10.3167/IJSQ.2015.050102

Dabla-Norris, E., Kochhar, K., Suphaphiphat, N., Ricka, F., & Tsounta, E. (2015). *Causes and Consequences of Income Inequality: A Global Perspective*. IMF.

Dower, N. (2004). Global Economy, Justice and Sustainability. *Ethical Theory and Moral Practice*, 7(4), 399–415. DOI: 10.1007/s10677-004-2215-2

Drouin, J.-M. (2019). *A Philosophy of the Insect*. Columbia University Press. DOI: 10.7312/drou17578

Elkington, J. (1997). Cannibals with Forks: The Triple *The Bottom Line*.

Figueroa, J. L., & Vargas-Perez, C. (2018). Collective Intelligence: A New Model of Business Management in the Big-Data Ecosystem. *European Journal of Economics and Business Studies*, 10(1), 209–220. DOI: 10.26417/ejes.v10i1.p208-219

Fleurbaey, M. (2001). Egalitarian Opportunities. *Law and Philosophy*, 20(5), 499–530.

Flores, R. P., Negny, S., Belaud, J. P., & Lann, J.-M. (2015). Collective Intelligence to Solve Creative Problems in Conceptual Design Phase. *Procedia Engineering*, 131, 850–860. DOI: 10.1016/j.proeng.2015.12.394

Francis. (2013). *Evangelii Gaudium*. Libreria Editrice Vaticana.

Freeman, R. E. (1984). *Strategic Management: A Stakeholder Approach*. Pitman Publishing.

Frey, D. F. (2017). Economic Growth, Full Employment and Decent Work: The Means and Ends in SDGs 8. *International Journal of Human Rights*, 21(8), 1164–1184. DOI: 10.1080/13642987.2017.1348709

Galton, F. (1907). Vox populi. *Nature*, 75(1949), 450–451. DOI: 10.1038/075450a0

García-Monleón, F., González-Rodrigo, E., & Bordonado-Bermejo, M.-J. (2024). Coexistence of Sustainability and Growth in Different Economies. *Journal of Business Research*, 170, 114352. DOI: 10.1016/j.jbusres.2023.114352

Gauda, M. S., Parasuraman, S., & Khan, A. G. (2024). Opportunities and Challenges for Corporate Social Responsibility in India. *IOSR Journal for Humanities and Social Sciences*, 29(3), 36–45.

Gray, S., Aminpour, P., Reza, C., Scyphers, S., Grabowski, J., Murphy, R.Jr, Singer, A., Baltaxe, D., Jordan, R., Jetter, A., & Introne, J. (2020). Harnessing the Collective Intelligence of Stakeholders for Conservation. *Frontiers in Ecology and the Environment*, 18(8), 465–472. DOI: 10.1002/fee.2232

Gupta, A. (2021). Reimagining Multilateralism: The Ethos and Philosophy of *Vasudhaiva Ku u bakam. National Security*, 4(1), 20–24.

Habib, A. (2013). Sharing the Earth: Sustainability and the Currency of Inter-Generational Environmental Justice. *Environmental Values*, 22(6), 751–764. DOI: 10.3197/096327113X13781997646575

Hector, D. C., Christensen, C. B., & Petrie, J. (2014). Sustainability and Sustainable Development: Philosophical Distinctions and Practical Implications. *Environmental Values*, 23(1), 7–28. DOI: 10.3197/096327114X13851122268963

Kasturi Rangan, V., Chase, L., & Karim, S. (2015). The Truth about CSR. *Harvard Business Review*, 93(1/2), 40–49.

Kidd, C. V. (1992). The Evolution of Sustainability. *Journal of Agricultural & Environmental Ethics*, 5(1), 1–26. DOI: 10.1007/BF01965413

Kotler, P., & Lee, N. (2005). *Corporate Social Responsibility: Doing the Most Good for Your Company and Your Cause*. Wiley.

Kozhevnikov, M., Evans, C., & Kosslyn, S. M. (2014). Cognitive Style as Environmentally Sensitive Individual Differences in Cognition: A Modern Synthesis and Applications in Education, Business, and Management. *Psychological Science in the Public Interest*, 15(1), 3–33. DOI: 10.1177/1529100614525555 PMID: 26171827

Krause, J., Ruxton, G. D., & Krause, S. (2010). Swarm Intelligence in Animals and Humans. *Trends in Ecology & Evolution*, 25(1), 28–34. DOI: 10.1016/j.tree.2009.06.016 PMID: 19735961

Kumar, N. (2019). Corporate Social Responsibility: An Analysis of Impact and Challenges in India. *International Journal of Social Sciences. Management and Entrepreneurship*, 3(2), 53–63.

Leif, W. (2021). John Rawls. *The Stanford Encyclopedia of Philosophy*. https://plato.stanford.edu/entries/rawls/

Leimeister, J. M. (2010). Collective Intelligence. *Business & Information Systems Engineering*, 4(4), 245–248. DOI: 10.1007/s12599-010-0114-8

Leonard, N. E., & Levin, S. A. (2022). Collective Intelligence as a Public Good. *Collective Intelligence*, 1(1), 1–18. DOI: 10.1177/26339137221083293

Lévy, P. (2005). Collective Intelligence, a Civilization: Towards a Method of Positive Interpretation. *International Journal of Politics Culture and Society*, 18(3/4), 189–198.

Locke, J. (1690). *Second Treatise of Government*. Hackett.

López, R. (2010). Sustainable Economic Development: On the Coexistence of Resource-Dependent and Resource-Impacting Industries. *Environment and Development Economics*, 15(6), 687–705. DOI: 10.1017/S1355770X10000331

Majumdar, S., Roy, S., Bose, A., & Chowdhury, I. R. (2023). Multiscale GIS based-model to Assess Urban Social Vulnerability and Associated Risk: Evidence from 146 Urban Centers of Eastern India. *Sustainable Cities and Society*, 96, 104692. DOI: 10.1016/j.scs.2023.104692

Mann, R. P., & Helbing, D. (2017). Optimal Incentives for Collective Intelligence. *Proceedings of the National Academy of Sciences of the United States of America*, 114(20), 5077–5082. DOI: 10.1073/pnas.1618722114 PMID: 28461491

Marx, K. (1875). Critique of the Gotha Program. In R. C. Tucker (Ed.), *The Marx-Engels Reader* (pp. 525-541). W. W. Norton (1978).

Mashingaidze, S. (2014). Benefits of Collective Intelligence: Swarm Intelligent Foraging. *Journal of Governance and Regulation*, 3(4), 193–201. DOI: 10.22495/jgr_v3_i4_c2_p2

McWilliams, A., & Siegel, D. (2001). Corporate Social Responsibility: A Theory of the Firm Perspective. *Academy of Management Review*, 26(1), 117–127. DOI: 10.2307/259398

Meadowcroft, J. (2024). Sustainability. *Britannica*. https://www.britannica.com/science/sustainability#ref1225913

Mulgan, G. (2018). *Big Mind: How Collective Intelligence can Change our World*. Princeton University Press. DOI: 10.1515/9781400888511

Nik, V. M., & Moazami, A. (2021). Using Collective Intelligence to Enhance Demand Flexibility and Climate Resilience in Urban Areas. *Applied Energy*, 281, 1–17. DOI: 10.1016/j.apenergy.2020.116106

Nussbaum, M. (1992). Human Functioning and Social Justice: In Defense of Aristotelian Essentialism. *Political Theory*, 20(2), 202–246. DOI: 10.1177/0090591792020002002

Nussbaum, M. (2000). Aristotle, Politics, and Human Capabilities: A Response to Antony, Arneson, Charlesworth, and Mulgan. *Ethics*, 111(1), 102–140. DOI: 10.1086/233421

Oxfam India. (2023). *Survival of the Richest: The India Story*. Oxfam India.

Page, S. E. (2007). Making the Difference: Applying a Logic of Diversity. *The Academy of Management Perspectives*, 21(4), 6–20. DOI: 10.5465/amp.2007.27895335

Parecattil, J. (2020). *Darśanavī : A Theology of Inclusive Home in Saint Chavara*. Dharmaram Publications.

Patuelli, A., Carungu, J., & Lattanzi, N. (2022). Drivers and Nuances of Sustainable Development Goals: Transcending Corporate Social Responsibility in Family Firms. *Journal of Cleaner Production*, 373, 133723. DOI: 10.1016/j.jclepro.2022.133723

Pirages, D. (1977). *The Sustainable Society: Implications for Limited Growth*. Praeger.

Pooley, S. (2021). Coexistence for Whom? *Frontiers in Conservation Science*, 2, 1–7. DOI: 10.3389/fcosc.2021.726991

Rawls, J. (1999). *A Theory of Justice* (Rev. Ed.). Harward University Press. DOI: 10.4159/9780674042582

Recker, M. M., Yuan, M., & Ye, L. (2013). CrowdTeaching: Supporting Teacher Collective Intelligence Communities. *Educational Technology*, 53(6), 18–23.

Reidl, C., Kim, Y. J., Gupta, P., Malone, T. W., & Woolley, A. W. (2021). Quantifying Collective Intelligence in Huma Groups. *Proceedings of the National Academy of Sciences of the United States of America*, 118(21), 1–5.

Sanford, A. W. (2017). *Living Sustainably: What International Communities can teach us about Democracy, Simplicity, and Nonviolence*. University Press of Kentucky.

Sen, A. (1992). *Inequality Reexamined*. Harvard University Press.

Sen, A. (1997). *On Economic Inequality*. Clarendon Press.

Sen, A. (2009). *The Idea of Justice*. Harvard University Press.

Shayan, N. F., Mohabbati-Kalejahi, N., Alavi, S., & Zahed, M. A. (2022). Sustainable Development Goals (SDGs) as a Framework for Corporate Social Responsibility (CSR). *Sustainability (Basel)*, 14(3), 1222. DOI: 10.3390/su14031222

Shetty, S., & Potdar, P. (2023). A Study of Corporate CSR Spending of Companies Operating in Maharashtra. *The Online Journal of Distance Education and e-Learning : TOJDEL*, 11(1), 469–482.

Skaržauskienė, A., & Mačiulienė, M. (2015). The Potential of Collective Intelligence in Online Community Projects. *Journal of Information Warfare*, 14(3), 66–74.

Solé, R. V. (2011). *Phase Transitions*. Princeton University Press.

Stevens, C. (2010). Are Women the Key to Sustainable Development? *Sustainable Development Insights*, 3(11), 1–8.

Stiglitz, J. (2012). *The Price of Inequality: How Today's Divided Society Endangers Our Future*. W. W. Norton.

Strand, R., Freeman, R. E., & Hockerts, K. (2015). Corporate Social Responsibility and Sustainability in Scandinavia: An Overview. *Journal of Business Ethics*, 127(1), 1–15. DOI: 10.1007/s10551-014-2224-6

Surowiecki, J. (2004). *The Wisdom of Crowds: Why the Many are Smarter than the Few and How Collective Wisdom shapes Business, Economies, Societies, and Nations*. Doubleday.

UCLA. (2016). The Charter for the Sustainability Committee. *UCLA Sustainability*. https://www.sustain.ucla.edu/wp-content/uploads/UCLA-Sustainability-Charter.pdf

UN. (2015). *Transforming Our World: The 2030 Agenda for Sustainable Development*. UN.

UNDP (United Nations Development Program). (2021). *Collective Intelligence for Sustainable Development: 13 Stories from the UNDP Accelerator Labs*. UNDP.

Vogel, S. M., Vasudev, D., Ogutu, J. O., Taek, P., Berti, E., Goswami, V. R., Kaelo, M., Buitenwerf, R., Munk, M., Li, W., Wall, J., Chala, D., Amoke, I., Odingo, A., & Svenning, J.-C. (2023). Identifying Sustainable Coexistence Potential by Integrating Willingness-to-coexist with Habitat Sustainability Assessments. *Biological Conservation*, 279, 1–12. DOI: 10.1016/j.biocon.2023.109935

Watson, R., & Levin, M. (2023). The Collective Intelligence of Evolution and Development. *Collective Intelligence*, 2(2). Advance online publication. DOI: 10.1177/26339137231168355

WCED (World Commission on Environment and Development). (1987). *Our Common Future*. WCED.

Wilkinson, S. (2016). Understanding Sustainability and the Australian Property Professions. *The Journal of Sustainable Real Estate*, 8(1), 95–119. DOI: 10.1080/10835547.2016.12091888

Woolley, A. W. (2011). Responses to Adversarial Situations and Collective Intelligence. *Journal of Organizational Behavior*, 32(7), 978–983. DOI: 10.1002/job.753

Woolley, A. W. (2021). Assessing Collective Intelligence in Human Groups. In OECD, *AI and the Future of Skills, Volume 1: Capabilities and Assessments* (pp. 117-133). OECD.

Woolley, A. W., Aggarwal, I., & Malone, T. W. (2015). Collective Intelligence and Group Performance. *Current Directions in Psychological Science*, 24(6), 420–424. DOI: 10.1177/0963721415599543

Woolley, A. W., Chabris, C. F., Pentland, A., Hashmi, N., & Malone, T. W. (2010). Evidence for a Collective Intelligence Factor in the Performance of Human Groups. *Science*, 330(6004), 686–688. DOI: 10.1126/science.1193147 PMID: 20929725

Woolley, A. W., & Fuchs, E. (2011). Collective Intelligence in the Organization of Science. *Organization Science*, 22(5), 1359–1367. DOI: 10.1287/orsc.1110.0648

Wu, L., & Jin, S. (2022). Corporate Social Responsibility and Sustainability: From a Corporate Governance Perspective. *Sustainability (Basel)*, 14(22), 15457. DOI: 10.3390/su142215457

Chapter 11

Organizing in Democratic Organizational Forms and Constitution of Collective Intelligence

Magali Pérez Camacho
https://orcid.org/0000-0002-5947-6666
Universidad Autónoma Metropolitana, Mexico

ABSTRACT

This chapter explores how democratic organizational forms enhance collective intelligence, which is a group's ability to collaborate, reason, and solve problems. It highlights how such organizations promote participation, decentralization, and diversity, creating environments where information flows freely and diverse perspectives are valued. Mechanisms like shared sensemaking and self-organization support this. Theories from Karl Weick and Barbara Czarniawska are used to explain these processes, with case studies like the Political Task Committees in Gentofte and "Sager der Samler" in Aarhus illustrating the effectiveness of decentralized approaches. The chapter concludes that democratic organizations are well-suited for developing collective intelligence and calls for more research on optimizing organizational structures.

INTRODUCTION

Collective intelligence has been a consistent phenomenon throughout history. In contemporary times, this form of intelligence has notably manifested in organizational phenomena involving groups of individuals and technologies, exemplified by

DOI: 10.4018/979-8-3693-7272-2.ch011

entities such as Wikipedia, social networks, and open-source software. Like many others, the concept of collective intelligence has undergone various interpretations. It can be perceived as the ability to make decisions, perform collective tasks in unison, reason, plan, solve problems, learn from experience, or effectively adapt to an environment, among other definitions (Malone & Bernstein, 2015).

In this study, our focus is on the organizational sphere. Specifically, we talk about democratic forms of organization (Kerr, 2004; Harrison & Freeman 2004; Yazdani, 2010; Adobor,2020) and the phenomena of organizing. The aim is to elucidate how organizing enables the construction of collective intelligence within democratic organizational forms. This choice is driven by the intrinsic characteristics of democratic organizations that promote the development of collective intelligence (Christakis & Bausch, 2006; Rough, 2008; Landemore, 2013; Boucher, Hallin & Paulson, 2023). Furthermore, the phenomenon of organizing involves a process of sense-making that is collectively shared and thus becomes a mechanism that facilitates the construction of collective intelligence.

The Democratic organizational forms are characterized by fostering the full participation of all members, thereby encouraging collective learning, cooperation, coordination, and decision-making—essential elements for cultivating collective intelligence. This work aims to elucidate how organizing, understood as how an organization structures itself, facilitates the emergence and strengthening of collective intelligence. A documentary review of cases providing evidence of this phenomenon will be conducted to achieve this.

The phenomenon of collective intelligence has sparked interest across multiple fields of study, including computer science, cognitive science, network sciences, and social sciences. The exploration of collective intelligence as a research topic is not recent, as descriptions of the phenomenon date back to the 19th century. Examples can be found in various disciplinary fields, such as medicine, where Robert Graves (in Malone & Bernstein, 2015) used the term to denote the rapid advancement of medical knowledge, and in political science, where John Pumroy employed it to describe the sovereignty of the people in governance, their will against the State (Malone & Bernstein, 2015).

Salminen (2012) proposes a three-level approach to studying collective intelligence. The micro-level focuses on the factors enabling human beings, recognizing that collective intelligence combines psychological, cognitive, and behavioral elements. Various studies assume that human behavior is predictable at this level because "our unconscious ability to read and display social signals allows smooth coordination within the network" (Salminen, 2012, p.2).

The macro-level concentrates on the resulting products of the system, suggesting that collective intelligence can lead to a "wisdom of crowds" where, under certain conditions, large groups of people can achieve better results than an individual within the group. The third level, termed the emergence level by Salminen (2012), is situated in an intermediate position, exploring how collective intelligence emerges towards the macro level through interactions among individuals, revealing self-organization phenomena.

Similarly, Ha and Tang (2022) propose understanding collective intelligence as a field of study that "[analyzes] a group intelligence that emerges from the interactions of many individuals. Thus, it sparks interest in self-organization, emergent behavior, swarm and cellular automata optimization, complex systems modeling, and deep learning" (Ha & Tang, 2022, p.3). These authors also recognize collective intelligence as

> *"a form of distributed intelligence that constantly improves and coordinates to achieve better results than any individual in the group through mutual recognition and individual enrichment. [Thus] collective intelligence promotes outcomes through diversity, independence, and decentralization" (Ha & Tang, 2022, p.3).*

Another approach to the concept of collective intelligence is reflected in Ammiar's (2022) proposal, which posits that it is a mode of work and collaboration in which the energy of each individual is directed toward a collective goal, thus implying a high degree of co-responsibility. According to this author, every group in which collective intelligence develops assumes three logical levels: the content, referring to the elements or objectives the group carries out; the process, which involves how tasks are accomplished; and the sense, which addresses why and for what purpose the group mobilizes its energy and performs its tasks.

Given that collective intelligence is an interdisciplinary field of study and recognizing the significance of this phenomenon, it is essential to analyze it through a framework that incorporates factors such as self-organization, diversity, independence, and decentralization. In this regard, situating the study of collective intelligence within Organization Studies is pertinent. This field of study, dedicated to examining the elements that constitute organizations and organized phenomena, analyzes organizations both as entities and as social processes through which these entities evolve (Clegg & Hardy, 1996). By doing so, Organizational Studies naturally addresses the phenomenon of collective intelligence as it manifests in groups such as organizations and other organized systems. Moreover, collective intelligence itself can influence the structure and dynamics of these organizations and phenomena.

To consider the study of collective intelligence as pertinent within the field of Organizational Studies leads to emphasizing the relevance of organizations in society. Contemporary civilization relies on organizations, which facilitate the coordination of life. "Our society is an organizational society" (Etzioni, 1997, p.1), and "organization ultimately imposes socialization" (Presthus, 1979, p.4), from which collective intelligence derives.

The organization, under its notion of entity in organizational studies, can be defined according to Montaño (2001) from different perspectives. The author suggests that an organization can be defined as follows:

> *"Conventional and idealized, as an orderly, harmonious, monolithic, functional, transparent, homogeneous space, with well-defined boundaries. Alternatively, it can be understood as a multidimensional space, where different logics of action - technical, economic, political, emotional, cultural, etc. - intersect, involving multiple actors with their own interests, making conflict and power basic ingredients of its functioning; built on diverse structures and representing multiple projects, hardly dissociable from the rest of the social constructions that make up everyday life" (Montaño, 2001, p. 108-109).*

Under this definition, it can be argued that collective intelligence can be a product of the organization. In an organization, multiple actors with a diversity of interests are involved, creating both a sense of order and a certain degree of disorder that facilitates human agency to achieve collective creations such as wisdom of crowds. However, since collective intelligence can be understood as a social construction, it can also be associated with the organization, as the latter is constructed by diverse social structures.

This chapter's argument posits that the contribution of Organization Studies lies in understanding how organizing enables the construction of collective intelligence in organizations and organized phenomena.

The organizing process, facilitating the construction of collective intelligence, is based on creating a complex network of democratic collaborations. In other words, it manifests primarily when democratic forms of organization emerge. These forms of organization are characterized by fostering the full participation of all members, thereby promoting the decentralization of information and decision-making, the free expression of its members, the encouragement of diversity in experiences and knowledge, and self-organization. These constitute fundamental mechanisms for the development of collective intelligence.

In this context, this paper examines how organizing, conceived as how an organization evolves, supports the emergence and strengthening of collective intelligence. The chapter is divided into five sections. The first section addresses two main theoretical proposals that explain the organizing. In the second section, various explanations of the mechanisms leading to the formation of collective intelligence are presented. The third section offers a reflection on how organizing facilitates the construction of collective intelligence by reproducing some of the mechanisms that constitute collective intelligence and proposes that sensemaking is one of these mechanisms. The fourth section presents empirical cases of the organizing process in democratic forms of organization and the formation of collective intelligence within them. Finally, the fifth section provides concluding reflections.

THEORETICAL PROPOSITIONS ON THE ORGANIZING

Organizing as an organizational phenomenon was first acknowledged by Karl Weick (1979) in his book *The Social Psychology of Organizing* (Clegg & Hardy, 1996). This work marked a critical turn against Organizational Theory at that time, emphasizing the need to focus on organizing rather than viewing the organization as a distinct entity (Clegg & Hardy, 1996). Weick argued that for an organization to be what it is, it requires the convergence of procedures, interpretations, behaviors, and enigmas.

Weick's (1979) concept of organizing is also recognized as one of the early proposals shaping the theoretical approach to organizational processes, with a particular interest in the ongoing process of "becoming." It acknowledges that entities are constructed and experienced (Langley & Tsoukas, 2017).

According to Weick (1979), individuals seek to organize to make sense of the ambiguity surrounding them. It involves "bringing all interdependent actions together, where reflective sequences generate reasonable outcomes" (Weick, 1979, p.3).

Weick (1979, p.42) posits that organizations deal with multiple, heterogeneous flows moving at variable speeds, representing materials, people, money, time, solutions, problems, and choices. Describing this elusive and complex activity, Weick (1979, p.43) employs the metaphor of a pseudopod inspired by Von Foerster, visualizing the movement of this animal through capillarity. This movement captures static aspects, represented by nouns (animal, place, pseudopod, capillary), and temporal aspects, conveyed by verbs and verb forms (moving, extending, pulling).

Weick (1979, p.45) initially suggests that organizing could be viewed as "a set of formulas for connecting episodes of social interactions in an orderly manner. These episodes would be called interlaced cycles and constitute the ingredients organized into recipes." These recipes involve the processes of execution, selection, and retention.

The execution, selection, and retention processes are portrayed through a model of natural selection. This model begins with an ecological change, expressed when differences within the flows, although multiple and heterogeneous, are detected and draw attention, providing an opportunity to clarify ambiguity or generate meaning. This ecological change creates a conducive environment for execution and sensemaking.

Execution in this model resembles variation in natural selection and leads actors to take one of two actions: first, actors facing an ecological change take measures to isolate and pay more attention to the changes, and second, they independently initiate changes that ultimately define their future actions (Weick, 1979).

Selection involves imposing various structures on execution to reduce ambiguity. These structures often take the form of causal maps, acting as molds that reveal configurations that make sense or not. This process involves organizing select interpretation schemes, which, when proven useful, are retained (Weick, 1979).

Retention, as part of this organizing process, involves storing the products derived from successful sensemaking. It represents a coherent version of what was once ambiguous (Weick, 1979).

Weick (1995) introduces a crucial element to this model: sensemaking, which is emerging in organizing. For Weick (1995), meaning arises from the interaction of "frames" and "cues." Weick (1995) proposes that embedded clues exist in explanatory frames created in the past and signals in the present about experiences. By combining these elements, individuals generate meanings.

Thus, for Weick, organizations result from structuring events that fit into an ever-changing and non-stop structure through connecting and making sense of the feedback process (Czarniawska, 2006).

Sensemaking is, therefore, a process through which organizational situations are structured, narrated, and characterized, using words and even gestures. This structuring becomes a form of learning when actors cognitively recognize regularities within an experience. These regularities, even when captured as broad conceptual frameworks, can guide perceptions, inferences, and behaviors (Holt & Cornelissen, 2014). Holt and Cornelissen (2014) argue that cognition seeks stability, and experience is interpreted through signals that are framed within conceptual structures. These structures allow an individual's experience to align with that of others in a collective and historical manner.

Sensemaking is not a solitary endeavor; it emerges as a collective exercise, grounded in the messages, conversations, and words co-constructed by groups, known as shared meanings. Sensemaking becomes a collective process as it is deeply embedded within the institutional contexts of agents (Coburn, 2001). From an institutionalist perspective, one of the pillars explaining how environments shape action patterns within an organizational field is the cognitive pillar, through which meanings, while having subjective elements, ultimately manifest through collective interaction (Scott, 1998).

The interrelation of institutions in shaping sensemaking supports the collective nature of this process, as institutions provide the necessary contexts. Actors operating under different institutional logics will construct varied meanings and be inclined toward distinct courses of action (Pham et al., 2021). Weber and Glynn (2006) propose that multiple institutional processes underpin this, such as activation, editing, and triggering. Institutions activate sensemaking by presenting available measures to generate a course of action. Similarly, institutions edit sensemaking by providing social evaluations that press actors to act. They also trigger sensemaking by directing attention to specific issues, demanding the reconciliation of contradictions and ambiguities.

Public attention to events can also initiate a process of environmental sensemaking, where actors generate meaning not only regarding the event itself but also the broader organizational field in which it unfolds, selectively focusing on certain aspects (Nigam & Ocasio, 2010). Authors like Nigam and Ocasio (2010) argue that this collective sensemaking even leads to the emergence of institutional logics, whether through a theorization process that facilitates the formation of abstract models of understanding within the collective or through representation that constructs localized and context-specific reasoning to explain the novelty.

Following Weick's proposal, Barbara Czarniawska's work can be identified, building upon the notion of social construction to inquire into the construction of organizations and their realization. Czarniawska (2014) starts with the idea that actors, through their actions, continuously construct the organization. It aligns with Weick's critique of various organizational theoretical approaches that have concentrated on thinking and, consequently, studying the organization as an entity. According to Czarniawska (2014), organizational theoretical models should analyze verbs, as verbs give meaning to the organizational phenomenon since verbs are actions.

The starting point in this proposal is actions, as organizing involves connecting various collective actions into a network under an institutionalized pattern at a specific moment and place (Lindberg & Czarniawska, 2006, p.293). Viewing the connection of collective actions as a network allows understanding that organizing goes beyond the physical boundaries of a specific organization, moving away from the idea of a static organization.

What happens is that networks of collective action gradually create, according to institutionalized patterns, a "formal organization," meaning a network of action generates boundaries around it that shape a "formal organization" (Lindberg & Czarniawska, 2006, p.293).

The theoretical foundations of the "network theory of action" by Czarniawska (2014) correspond to new sociological institutionalism and the sociology of translation. New institutionalism starts from the premise that each place and time is influenced by an institutional order, determining how to organize, as certain connections between actions are legitimized by aligning with these orders. An example of this is actions legitimized in Research Centers, where reading, writing, publishing, and teaching are carried out, and it is on these actions that actors, identities such as being an editor or a professor, are constituted. This process stabilizes patterns that ultimately result in a normative explanation, an institution (Czarniawska, 2014).

As for the sociology of translation, it explains how these networks are built and maintained in everyday life in the network theory of action proposal. Czarniawska and Sevón (1996) state that organizational life involves a history of ideas that become actions, emerge, and institutionalize. They begin "the story in a local time/space, where an idea is objectified in a specific place and time, and then it continues through different moments and places towards a global time/space" (Czarniawska & Joerges, 1996, p. 39). As ideas objectified in one place travel to a new location, they translate into action and institutionalize when becoming a booming trend.

The idea of translation, borrowed by Czarniawska and Sevón (1996) from Latour, suggests moving away from the concept of diffusion to that of translation, as it has more extraordinary richness in meaning by promoting movement, transfer, interpretation, transformation, change, even renewal. Thus, the formation of a stabilized network of action does not become static because, in each action, there will always be a translation that represents the hinge between the structured and the transformative.

In summary, Weick's (1979) concept of "organizing" redefines our understanding of organizations, emphasizing dynamic processes over static structures. Rather than viewing an organization as a fixed entity, Weick sees it as a continuous flow of activities and interactions aimed at making sense of an ambiguous world. He presents organizing as a process akin to natural selection, involving stages of execution, selection, and retention. Execution allows individuals to recognize and respond to environmental changes; selection creates interpretive frameworks to reduce ambiguity; and retention consolidates these understandings, preserving them for future reference. Central to this is "sensemaking," where individuals construct meaning by combining past frameworks with present cues. This collective sensemaking process fosters shared interpretations, grounded in institutional contexts, and allows for coordinated action within organizations.

Building on Weick's foundations, Barbara Czarniawska (2014) expands this notion by introducing the "network theory of action," where organizing is seen as an ongoing construction of interconnected actions within institutional patterns. Czarniawska suggests that organizations are shaped by actions in context, forming networks that extend beyond physical spaces and adapt across various settings. Her concept of "translation," adapted from Latour, posits that as ideas move across locations, they transform rather than merely diffuse, adding layers of interpretation and adaptation. Thus, organizations are not static structures but evolving networks that both stabilize and adapt, influenced by collective meanings and institutional logics. Together, Weick and Czarniawska's insights invite a view of organizations as fluid, contextually bound systems, where meaning and order emerge through a continuous interplay of action and sensemaking.

ON THE FORMATION OF COLLECTIVE INTELLIGENCE

It is necessary to elucidate the mechanisms through which such formation is promoted. As previously noted, the study of collective intelligence originates from various disciplines, each offering insights into the definition of mechanisms that foster the formation of collective intelligence. This section will showcase some studies from diverse fields where these mechanisms are evident.

For instance, Heylighen's work (2013) highlights that the requirements for collective intelligence and its mechanisms include diversity in knowledge and experiences among group members, independence of group members in expressing their opinions, decentralization enabling the collection and processing of information from members, and aggregation, an effective mechanism for synthesizing diverse opinions into a singular collective response, such as voting.

Heylighen (2013) also underscores the importance of having a shared language within the community, indicating communicative alignment as the foundation for sequential interactions. Communicative alignment involves not only sharing the same language but also managing intonation, rhythm, lexicon, contextual reference, and grammatical structure. This dynamic communication facilitates self-organization, reducing frictions in information interpretation and enabling the production of simple and efficient references, ultimately accelerating information flow (Heylighen, 2013).

Additionally, Heylighen (2013) emphasizes the mechanism of self-organization, understanding it as a spontaneous coordination of actions performed by different agents. This organization is based on local trial and error, variation, and selection, where agents adapt to each other by finding a coordinated pattern that spreads through positive feedback processes.

Some of the mechanisms highlighted by Heylighen (2013) are also described by Richard Foss (2016) within the field of behavioral sciences. Foss conducted a study on a colony of honeybees, observing that decentralization facilitates the information process for decision-making regarding selecting a nest site. Foss (2016) uses a cybernetic model to identify characteristics necessary for intelligent decision-making in groups of individuals, emphasizing the decentralization of power. In the case of bees, Foss notes that although the queen has pheromonal influence in enclosed spaces, it is less influential in the field, and there is no hierarchical group or performed information networks influencing decisions within the bee collective.

> *"The swarm's decisions are made by scouts who accumulate the necessary evidence about sites to place a nest. The center of decision-making is determined by the flow of information, not by any pre-existing command structure" (Foss, 2016, p. 747).*

Bees' decentralization allows them to trigger massive information production in local spaces and improve their respective processing. It enables enhanced decision-making capacity and a more robust response to changes (Foss, 2016).

The implications for human groups and the phenomenon of collective intelligence are that these groups should consist of individuals with diverse opinions who actively listen to each other. It fosters participatory decision-making, leveraging collective wisdom and promoting collective intelligence. It also facilitates equitable access to information, providing a more comprehensive understanding of the presented context.

Kurvers, Wolf, Naguib, and Krause (2015) are researchers in the field of biology who recognize self-organization as one of the mechanisms generating collective intelligence. Specifically, they conducted simulation experiments on predator detection using human groups. They found that individuals adjust their response time during collective decision-making based on their personal information. If individuals possess accurate information, collective decision-making becomes faster, highlighting the importance of individuals having precise information in promoting collective intelligence.

Regarding the mechanism of aggregation, Ganser and Keuschnigg (2018) argue that while taking the average of individual judgments can derive a reliable strategy, social influence should also be considered. Social influence narrows the variation in individual opinions. In a simulation study on voting contexts, Ganser and Keuschnigg (2018) argue that social influence contributes to information aggregation, strengthening collective judgment.

They suggest that the disadvantages of voting compared to other aggregation tools diminish when social influence is incorporated. The fact that agents initially review their judgments allows them to converge on the opinions of others, emphasizing the importance of exchanging viewpoints and opinions for better opinion aggregation through tools such as voting.

One mechanism that has been studied in enhancing collective intelligence are "nudges," understood as subtle prompts or incentives. According to Gupta et al. (2024), digital nudges have the potential to facilitate skill utilization, task strategy formulation, and collective effort in temporary online teams, which in turn enhances collaborative processes and increases collective intelligence. The concept of digital nudges is grounded in behavioral economics, which posits that changes in choice architecture can subtly guide behavior without limiting available options, thereby making specific outcomes more likely.

In their study, Gupta et al. (2024) analyzed the impact of digital nudges on 168 temporary online teams, employing the POGS platform—a web-based tool designed to facilitate synchronous collaboration. Teams were engaged in a structured Test of Collective Intelligence (TCI), a task battery aimed at measuring the team's ability to collaborate effectively across a variety of scenarios. The study implemented four types of nudges: two automated "facilitator" bots and two interactive digital tools.

The first bot, referred to as the Skill Facilitator, prompted team members to identify their individual skills relevant to the task at the outset, thereby enhancing awareness of team resources. The second bot, the Strategy Facilitator, encouraged discussions on task coordination to help align member contributions more effectively. In addition to these bots, two tools provided ongoing guidance: one tool, a To-Do List feature, highlighted pending tasks to ensure structured task progression, while the other tool displayed real-time feedback on each member's level of engagement and effort. This feedback display aimed to counteract "social loafing" by making each member's contribution visible to the team, thus encouraging equal participation.

The findings of Gupta et al. (2024) underscore the potential of well-designed digital nudges to improve essential collaborative processes within teams, even when team members are strangers and lack established norms. However, the study also highlights complexities, as certain nudges, while generally beneficial, occasionally led to unintended effects. This suggests that for digital nudges to be effective, they must be carefully calibrated to the team context, with consideration of how individuals interpret and respond to different forms of feedback within a collaborative digital environment.

In the work by He et al. (2019), three paradigms are proposed in the field of computational collective intelligence, each defined by the underlying mechanisms of interaction and feedback that shape its formation. The first paradigm is isolation, in which individuals act independently, and collective intelligence emerges through the aggregation of individual judgments without interaction or feedback among them. Here, statistical methods play a central role in synthesizing individual knowledge into a collective set of estimates.

The second paradigm is collaboration, where both direct and indirect interactions among participants are allowed. In this context, factors such as social influence and diversity become key drivers of collective intelligence, as a variety of perspectives and skills within the group enhances problem-solving effectiveness and enriches outcomes (He et al, 2019).

Finally, the third paradigm identified by He et al. (2019) is feedback. In this case, alongside interaction, a continuous feedback process is introduced, allowing individuals to adjust their behaviors based on observed group outcomes. This feedback mechanism encourages adaptive behaviors, promoting self-organization and optimization in dynamic environments, thus enhancing the collective system's ability to tackle complex problems.

Up to this point, various mechanisms and factors have been identified across fields as key promoters of collective intelligence. In the field of education, Rowe, Hattie, and Munro (2024) make a notable contribution by arguing that the development of collective intelligence is not governed by a single factor but rather by at least two major dimensions: crystallized and fluid intelligences. Crystallized intelligence involves knowledge and skills previously acquired, while fluid intelligence refers to the ability to solve new problems and adapt quickly. Additionally, motivation, cohesion, and even personality traits also play an essential role in shaping collective intelligence.

In conclusion, the formation of collective intelligence emerges as a multifaceted phenomenon that requires a blend of diverse mechanisms across various disciplines. Key to its development are factors such as diversity in knowledge, independence of thought, decentralization, aggregation, and effective communication, as underscored by Heylighen (2013) and exemplified in studies by Foss (2016) and Kurvers et al. (2015). Each of these elements fosters an environment where collective judgment can be synthesized effectively, allowing for enhanced decision-making and a robust response to change.

Furthermore, digital "nudges," as studied by Gupta et al. (2024), reveal the power of subtle prompts in guiding collaborative efforts and counteracting issues like social loafing in temporary online teams. By facilitating skill awareness and structured task progression, these nudges enhance team functionality, though they require careful calibration to avoid unintended effects.

Computational approaches to collective intelligence, outlined by He et al. (2019), illustrate three paradigms—isolation, collaboration, and feedback—that promote different facets of collective behavior. Each paradigm shows that feedback and social influence are essential to optimizing group responses in dynamic settings.

Finally, the educational perspective offered by Rowe, Hattie, and Munro (2024) highlights the role of both crystallized and fluid intelligence in collective endeavors, along with motivational and personality factors. Together, these insights underscore that collective intelligence is not merely an aggregation of individual knowledge but a dynamic interplay of diverse mechanisms that collectively enhance the problem-solving capabilities of groups.

ORGANIZING AND THE FORMATION OF COLLECTIVE INTELLIGENCE

Up to this point, we have explored the mechanisms enabling collective intelligence formation, as described across various disciplinary fields. However, when considering organizational studies, how does the organizing process facilitate the construction of collective intelligence? Examining theoretical proposals on the organizing process reveals several mechanisms identified in other disciplines as constitutive of collective intelligence and uncovers new mechanisms contributing to collective intelligence.

Within the organizing process, a fundamental element is coordination, which seeks to harmonize actions to become interdependent (Weick, 1979). Coordination involves organizing agreements based on consensus validation or a high-level common sense.

Agreements and, consequently, coordination of actions are reached as participants' common sense and interpersonal experiences allow specific decision alternatives to be perceived as objective (Weick, 1979). Thus, since agreements are part of collective decision-making, sensemaking, according to Weick's proposal (1979), not only forms the basis of the organizing process but also contributes to forming collective intelligence, becoming a mechanism.

As highlighted in the first section, sensemaking not only facilitates the formation of meaning for actors but also, as sense is generated within actors, contributes to organizing the flow of activities in organizations or forms of organization. Actors identify signs of disturbance in multiple and heterogeneous or routine activities (Weick et al., 2005; Brown, Colville & Pye, 2015; Maitlis, Christianson, 2014).

These signs of disturbance in activities are detected, selected, and subsequently interpreted, labeled, and categorized – in other words, the sense is generated, and decisions are made about them. In the case of collective intelligence, sensemaking within the organizing process becomes a mechanism because it facilitates the formation of meaning and processing of large information flows.

However, both sensemaking and collective intelligence depend on a central component: communication. Communication is the conduit through which sensemaking takes place and can be preserved. In the case of collective intelligence, as mentioned in the second section, communicative alignment becomes necessary by reducing friction in information interpretation.

Communication is essential in sensemaking, and several theoretical approaches identify it as a constitutive element of the organizing process (Cooren et al., 2011). According to McPhee and Zaug (2009), communication shapes the organizing process and the organization itself through four distinct communicative flows. This work considers these flows critical points to achieve communicative alignment and collective intelligence.

These flows are membership negotiation, self-structuring, coordination activity, and institutional positioning. According to McPhee and Zaug (2009, p.33), these four flows generate a social structure involving an interactive communication episode that invariably includes reproduction and sometimes resistance to the organization's rules and resources. They are synthetically presented in the Table 1.

Table 1. Communication flows in the constitution of organizing (CCO).

Flow	Description
Membership Negotiation	Membership is required for actors to join an organization or a form of organization. Prospecting members involves a communicative process that spans recruitment, evaluation, and categorization. Through this dialectical flow, the members and the organization decide to establish a relationship.
Self-structuring	To coordinate work within an organization, sustained reflection on organizational operations is necessary, involving a flow of communication. Self-structuring necessitates a collective communicative exercise, which involves disseminating the organizational structure, arrangements, and norms. This type of reflective communication constitutes the organization for itself.
Coordination activity	While self-structuring achieves work organization, it is widely acknowledged that such structural directions may still need to be fully understood. These necessitate coordinated adjustments, which require communication to foster cooperative efforts for an organization to establish itself.
Institutional positioning	Another type of communication flow links organization members to the external environment. Here, one crucial exercise is positioning identity.

Source: This source is a personal elaboration base on McPhee, R., & Zaug, P. (2009). The communicative constitution of organizations. In L. Putnam, A. M. Nicotera (Eds.), *Building theories of organization: the constitutive role of communication* (21-48). Routledge.

In the case of collective intelligence, negotiating membership entails a crucial aspect of communication alignment. It serves as the communicative starting point through which identity is defined. Actors' performance establishes a communicative flow between actors and the organization, thus forming the basis for mutual understanding. Self-structuring is relevant to achieving communication alignment as it establishes behavior patterns reinforced in coordination activities.

Recognizing self-organization as a critical mechanism in collective intelligence emphasizes the idea of coordination through trial and error, forming a coordinated pattern (Heylighe, 2013). In the context of the organizing process, Weick's proposal (1979) acknowledges that, in response to environmental changes, experimental adjustments are made to adapt what was previously familiar, reducing ambiguity. This adjustment may result in a coordinated pattern that is useful and retained for later feedback. From Czarniawska's perspective (2014), activities can be interpreted as a trial-and-error exercise that, when stabilized, institutionalizes into a practice.

Concerning decentralization and aggregation, these representative mechanisms of collective intelligence may emerge or strengthen depending on the type of organizational form emerging in organizing. If the configuration of the organizational form adopts democratic characteristics, the emergence and strengthening of these mechanisms in organizing are plausible. The features of a democratic organizational form will favor decentralization in information production and decision-making, essential elements for the development of collective intelligence. Additionally, they will provide the means to facilitate actor expression when making decisions, going beyond the simple act of casting a vote.

In summary, organizing fosters the formation of collective intelligence by structuring communication, coordination, and sensemaking within an organization. Weick (1979) emphasizes that collective intelligence is achieved through sensemaking, where actors interpret and respond to disturbances, facilitating meaning-making and decision-making processes. Communication, as McPhee and Zaug (2009) propose, further enables collective alignment through membership negotiation, self-structuring, coordination, and institutional positioning. Meanwhile, Czarniawska (2014) adds that coordinated patterns emerge through trial and error, often within democratic organizational forms, enhancing decentralization and enabling collective intelligence to evolve as a stable, adaptive network of actions.

In the following section, we will explore more clearly what democratic organizational forms mean and empirically illustrate how organizing gives rise to the formation of collective intelligence in these organizational forms, drawing on documented cases.

ORGANIZING IN DEMOCRATIC ORGANIZATIONAL FORMS AND THE EMERGENCE OF COLLECTIVE INTELLIGENCE: CASE ANALYSIS

When addressing the term "organizational form," the classical reference invariably encounters the Weberian proposal on the ideal type of bureaucracy, defining such organizational form structurally as a means for an organization to achieve rationality and efficiency through rules defining hierarchies and levels of authority (Mouzelis, 1975). However, for this work, Romanelli's definition (Romanelli, 1991, pp. 81-82) of the organizational form will be considered, referring to "those characteristics of an organization that identify it as a distinct entity and simultaneously classify it as a member of a group of similar organizations."

In the case of democratic organizational forms, it is necessary to consider that their organizational characteristics are grounded in an understanding of the term democracy, recognizing various conceptions thereof. Specifically, Kerr (2004, p.83) states that "participatory democracy implies that citizens influence decisions that affect them through their direct participation." He adds that it also "involves the equitable distribution of participation rights, ensuring that each person, regardless of their social, economic, or political position, has a vote" (Kerr, 2004, p.84).

On the other hand, Dahl (2015) proposes five principles characterizing democracy: a) Effective participation, where members have equal opportunities to express their views to other members; b) Equity in voting, ensuring that each member has the opportunity to vote, and each vote counts as equal for every member; c) Relevant understanding, ensuring that each member has equitable opportunities to understand policies and their consequences; d) Agenda control, granting members the authority to decide which matters will be included in the agenda; e) Inclusion of all adults, promoting the participation of any gender and minority.

From the above, it can be stated that the organizational characteristics of democratic organizational forms will promote these democratic principles and conceptions. Standard features of these forms of organization include flat, flexible, and even informal structures, allowing free deliberation among members.

Coupling can be loose, and the form of governance is characterized by a pursuit of democracy, evident in figures such as assemblies and councils, where representation is ensured through electoral processes. Authority rests with the collective, implying that decision-making usually occurs through consensus and collective voting. Learning is socialized and externalized. Hence, access to information is open and guaranteed. A high level of involvement is encouraged through active and assured participation of all organization members. Regarding control mechanisms, accountability is directed towards the collective, and the need for gender equity is recognized to ensure the full participation of all members.

The next step is to present some empirical cases illustrating how the organizing process, integrated into these forms of organization, facilitates, and fosters the formation of collective intelligence. Having addressed the recognition of democratic organizational forms to ensure comprehensive coverage of both elements—the democratic organizational forms and organizing leading to the configuration of collective intelligence—this work will rely on the text by Boucher, Hallin, and Paulson (2023) titled "The Routledge Handbook of Collective Intelligence for Democracy and Governance." This text provides empirical cases involving both aspects.

The first case pertains to the text by Sørensen and Torfing (2023), who explain that in 2015, the City Council of Gentofte, Denmark, embarked on a transformative shift in policymaking by implementing Political Task Committees (PTCs) to foster collective political intelligence. Driven by growing dissatisfaction with traditional decision-making processes—which largely excluded citizen input and led to isolated policy development within City Hall—the Council sought a more inclusive approach. The new model aimed to integrate diverse perspectives by creating ad hoc committees composed of politicians from different parties and citizens from various backgrounds. This shift was part of a broader trend recognizing the potential of collective intelligence, where group collaboration generates insights that exceed individual capabilities.

Gentofte's model of collective political intelligence hinges on interactive political leadership, emphasizing the importance of dialogue among stakeholders. Unlike conventional governance models that focus on internal city administration, Gentofte's PTCs bring politicians and citizens together, engaging them in extended discussions to identify, negotiate, and implement policy solutions. The chapter defines collective political intelligence as the ability to understand divergent perspectives, balance competing interests, and address potential compromises involved in decision-making (Sørensen and Torfing, 2023). By fostering deep connections between politicians and citizens, Gentofte's PTCs not only improved the quality of policy decisions but also enhanced the perceived legitimacy of the government (Sørensen and Torfing, 2023).

The model demonstrated its effectiveness through practical examples, such as involving young people in policy formulation for a local skate center. When initial top-down plans were met with skepticism from young citizens, the PTC engaged these stakeholders directly, resulting in a more suitable and popular design. Over six years, Gentofte's Council established over 42 PTCs addressing a range of issues, from youth policy and environmental sustainability to health services and cultural initiatives (Sørensen and Torfing, 2023)..

Gentofte's innovative approach serves as a model for other municipalities seeking to enhance democratic engagement and policy effectiveness. This experiment underscores the value of collective political intelligence in fostering an inclusive and responsive government that balances expert input with real-world insights from citizens. Through this model, Gentofte illustrates that structured citizen engagement can be a cornerstone of effective democratic governance.

The second case, authored by Natrop (2023), explores the work of Sager der Samler, a Danish platform that empowers citizen-led initiatives to tackle social issues through collective action. Sager der Samler facilitates the transformation of personal initiatives into collective movements, promoting the concept of "everyday activism"—a form of civic engagement that transcends traditional volunteering by centering on social change grounded in individual experience and daily life.

One prominent example is *Social Sundhed* (Social Health), founded by Kristina Louise Bliksted. This initiative arose from Bliksted's concern about inequalities in the Danish healthcare system, especially for vulnerable citizens, such as those facing language barriers, mental health issues, or homelessness. With support from *Sager der Samler*, *Social Sundhed* mobilizes health students to accompany individuals to medical appointments, acting as "bridges" between patients and the medical system. Over time, *Social Sundhed* has expanded nationally, showcasing how an individual idea can scale up through community support and shared resources (Natrop, 2023).

Sager der Samler operates on key principles: starting from one's own experience, working alongside others as equals, and taking action without waiting for external permission or funding. This approach allows citizens like Bliksted to access a support network that enhances their confidence, encourages mutual learning, and facilitates collaboration with formal institutions. Additionally, the platform creates a supportive environment where members share resources and are empowered to lead change within their communities (Natrop, 2023).

The organization also emphasizes the power of narrative to inspire and legitimize civic activism. By retelling success stories across various media, *Sager der Samler* reinforces the role of citizens as co-creators of society, redefining civic engagement beyond passive roles. This perspective fosters a culture in which citizens are the authors of social change, transforming systems from their experiences and community networks (Natrop, 2023).

To facilitate the analysis of these cases, they will be presented in tables below, outlining the organizational characteristics of the form of organization within the case, organizing using any of the theoretical proposals by Weick, Czarniawska, or the CCO perspective, and the mechanisms of collective intelligence present.

Table 2. Organizing in the formation of intelligence in the political task committees of Gentofte, Denmark

Author	Sørensen & Torfing
Case	Political Task Committees in Gentofte, Denmark
Context	In 2015, the municipality of Gentofte, Denmark, changed the process of public decision-making by establishing Political Task Committees. It was enacted that all new public policies in the municipality would be developed through these committees with citizen participation. The City Council started by establishing eight committees, and by 2021, there were already more than 42
Organizational characteristics	They bring together politicians from different parties and citizens with diverse backgrounds to develop and negotiate policy proposals. Decision-making Committees have the facilities to gather information from various sources of expertise. The principle for appointing Committee participants is to maximize the group's diversity. Committees are free to organize their work processes. There are facilitators in the consensus-building processes. Their structure is flat, with each Committee having a president and vice-president. Open discussions are conducted. Citizen participation is voluntary and selected based on competency profiles. Those not selected can participate in subcommittees, workshops, innovation camps, and public hearings.

continued on following page

Table 2. Continued

Author	Sørensen & Torfing
Organizing	The process of forming Committees begins with a call for proposals to promote a change in some aspect of the municipality. Each Committee, through gathering information from different sources and open discussions on these topics, develops proposals that are eventually formalized. Throughout this process, there has been a learning curve in understanding how Committees function best, to the point of establishing a culture of facilitation among municipal public administrators who support this process.
Mechanisms of collective intelligence	Organizing that unfolds in the Committees has played a crucial role in strengthening political dialogue to address complex issues. In this context, various mechanisms contributing to the formation of collective intelligence can be identified. Firstly, promoting diversity in the Committees facilitates the presence of a wide range of knowledge and experiences, thereby enriching the perspective on the addressed issues. Additionally, decentralization in collecting and processing information is essential for obtaining necessary data and developing practical solutions. Similarly, a degree of independence allows participants to express their opinions openly and transparently. Finally, the presence of facilitators contributes to effective communicative alignment, ensuring a proper flow of information among Committee members.

Source: This source is a personal elaboration base on Sørensen, E., & Torfing, J. (2023). How Collective Political Intelligence produced better policy. Political Task Committees in Gentofte, Denmark. In S. Boucher, C. A. Hallin, L. Paulson. *The Routledge Handbook of Collective Intelligence for Democracy and Governance* (181- 189). Routledge.

Table 3. Organizing in forming Sager der Samler Intelligence or causes that gather in Aarhus, Denmark.

Author	Natrop
Case	Non-profit organization Sager der Samler or Causes that Gather
Context	After Kristina Louise Bliksted's citizen proposal to improve healthcare services, Sager der Samler emerged. This organization promotes citizen initiatives in more than seven cities and has become a mechanism for improving the national healthcare system.
Organizational characteristics	The organization's structure is networked. It has a strong culture of mutual support among its members. Work is carried out through volunteering. The principles that govern Sager der Samler are: 1) Start in the situation of your own life where you have knowledge and legitimacy; 2) Stay at eye level and work with people (not for them) to grow your platform and impact. 3) Use your freedom and start where you do not need to ask for permission or money. It is organized as a platform that facilitates the exchange of resources to support citizen initiatives. The platform's role is to scale individual initiatives into public solutions. Socialized learning is achieved through regular interactions to exchange knowledge and skills. The goal is to create meaning from things to promote engagement. The organization serves as an intermediary between citizens and government organizations..

continued on following page

Table 3. Continued

Author	Natrop
Organizing	The process begins with attracting citizens through narratives; upon joining the organization, the citizen assumes the identity of an 'everyday activist' imbued with agency. By organizing as an analogous platform, members provide mutual support, generate elements of mutual exchange, and use informal meetings to build relationships among members and with the outside. For instance, lunches and coffees are proposed as a basis for developing connections between citizens and public officials to facilitate the development of initiatives. The organization intends to create narratives that connect citizens on the platform and promote their agency.
Mechanisms of collective intelligence	The organizing process carried out in Sager der Samler begins with the narrative used to incorporate its members. The networked platform structure, regulated through face-to-face or eye-level communication, facilitates resources and coordinates members to generate solutions to public issues. A clear example is the Vaskeriet (The Laundry) initiative, founded by Pia Stabell and Katrine Knudsen. Vaskeriet aims to be a practice field for people with developmental disabilities, seeking to help them develop courage, skills, and dreams to adapt to the work and community environment. To carry out this initiative, Vaskeriet borrowed two washing machines from the community laundry at Søvangen. In this collaborative space, while picking up or delivering laundry, people can enjoy a coffee and address community issues for mutual assistance. It implies an ease in developing self-organization, communication alignment, and decentralization in decision-making and community problem-solving.

Source: This source is a personal elaboration base on Natorp, P. (2023). Scaling personal initiatives into collective action. In S. Boucher, C. A. Hallin, L. Paulson. *The Routledge Handbook of Collective Intelligence for Democracy and Governance* (369- 374). Routledge.

The presented cases make evident how the organizing process promotes various mechanisms, giving rise to collective intelligence, and this is achieved more effectively when the organizational characteristics of a democratic form of organization are built into the organizing process. These democratic forms of organization, as observed, can be found in various sectors such as government and civil society.

For instance, considering the Political Task Committees of Gentofte, Denmark, the organizing process can be understood through Karl Wieck's model. The Committees' organization begins with the idea of instigating a change. Once established, a process of execution takes place by implementing measures rooted in democratic principles and the successful outcomes of previous Committees, addressing collective problem-solving. Aspects such as promoting diversity in the Committees, decentralization practices in information recovery and processing, and decision-making autonomy, acting as mechanisms of collective intelligence, would not be achievable without this framework.

In the case of the Sager der Samler or Causes Gathering in Aarhus, Denmark, the organizing process is linked to CCO and Czarniawska's theoretical proposals. The essential element is the communication flow among organization members, structuring a network that attracts resources. These narrative invites members to participate, forming a structure connecting individuals with objectives, purposes, and resources to address a specific social issue.

This process leads to the recognition and institutionalization of proposals, as seen in the case of Vaskeriet. Additionally, from a set of collective actions structured in a network, institutionalized patterns are formed, giving rise to formal organizations with their own identity, like Vaskeriet. The democratic principles and organizational characteristics, when structured as a network, facilitate mechanisms of collective intelligence.

We explore how organizing processes foster collective intelligence within democratic organizational forms, drawing on theoretical frameworks from organizational studies. The foundation of collective intelligence in organizations lies in coordinating actions, facilitating sensemaking, and maintaining open communication flows. Weick (1979) emphasizes that coordination and consensus-building are vital, as they harmonize individual actions into collective efforts, thus forming a shared understanding or "common sense" that enables decision-making. Sensemaking, or the ability to interpret and respond to organizational signals, becomes essential for processing complex information flows and aligning individual contributions toward collective goals.

Communication is integral to collective intelligence, structuring the interactions necessary for sensemaking. McPhee and Zaug's (2009) communicative constitution of organizing (CCO) highlights four key flows—membership negotiation, self-structuring, coordination activities, and institutional positioning—that establish organizational coherence and facilitate alignment among members. Each flow supports collective intelligence by creating mutual understanding, reinforcing organizational norms, and facilitating coordination, while Czarniawska's (2014) concept of self-organization underscores how these processes enable adaptation through trial and error.

The cases of Gentofte's Political Task Committees and the Sager der Samler organization illustrate collective intelligence in action within democratic structures. Gentofte's model, fostering citizen engagement in decision-making, demonstrates that diverse perspectives and decentralized information processing can yield innovative, community-driven solutions. Sager der Samler's "everyday activism" approach transforms individual initiatives into collective action, leveraging narratives and networked resources to scale local solutions into national movements. Both cases underscore the importance of democratic principles, such as inclusivity, open participation, and community-based decision-making, which support decentralized coordination and information aggregation essential for collective intelligence.

In sum, these democratic organizing processes demonstrate that collective intelligence thrives through structured communication, adaptive sensemaking, and democratic engagement, allowing organizations to respond effectively to complex societal challenges.

CONCLUSION

This study sheds light on the organizational dimensions of collective intelligence by examining the processes and mechanisms that facilitate its emergence, particularly within democratic organizational forms. Understanding collective intelligence from the perspective of organizational studies emphasizes the centrality of organizing processes—those actions that shape an organization beyond its static, structural boundaries. By focusing on how democratic forms of organizing can nurture collective intelligence, this research identifies several fundamental mechanisms: sensemaking, communicative alignment, coordination, and decentralization. These mechanisms, embedded in the organizational structure, enable groups to act intelligently and cohesively in complex environments, adapting to changes, processing information, and making collective decisions that are not only efficient but also inclusive and participatory.

One of the most significant contributions of this study is its examination of sensemaking as a key mechanism that underpins both organizing and collective intelligence. Sensemaking, as introduced by Weick (1979), provides a framework for individuals within an organization to interpret and respond to ambiguity, enabling the development of shared understandings that facilitate coordinated action. In this context, sensemaking serves not only as a means of organizing but also as a foundational process through which collective intelligence emerges. By allowing individuals to interpret and respond to disturbances collectively, sensemaking fosters an adaptive, resilient form of intelligence that strengthens an organization's ability to process information and navigate complex situations.

Furthermore, communicative alignment is emphasized as a core requirement for collective intelligence. Through structured and purposeful communication, alignment reduces interpretative friction, ensuring that members can share information seamlessly and develop common ground for decision-making. This alignment is crucial in democratic organizations, where the open exchange of perspectives and the integration of diverse viewpoints are essential for robust collective intelligence. Communicative alignment thus serves as a linchpin for fostering a shared understanding that enables effective, responsive action. It highlights that intelligence in groups is not merely the sum of individual contributions, but rather the result of cohesive, structured communication that brings together disparate perspectives into a unified collective response.

The study also incorporates the perspective of Communicative Constitution of Organizations (CCO) theory, specifically McPhee and Zaug's (2009) communicative flows—membership negotiation, self-structuring, activity coordination, and institutional positioning. These flows offer a communicative framework for understanding how organizing processes can facilitate collective intelligence. By fostering an inclusive environment where members can actively negotiate their roles and engage in self-structuring and coordinated activities, democratic organizations provide an environment conducive to collective sensemaking and intelligence. This inclusive engagement, rooted in the communicative structure, enables individuals to align on shared goals, organize effectively, and address challenges through collective action. The integration of CCO's communicative flows thus underlines that collective intelligence is inherently a communicative process, continuously shaped and reshaped through interactions among organizational members.

Decentralization emerges as another critical component, particularly within democratic organizational forms, where the distribution of decision-making authority is essential for fostering autonomy and engagement. By decentralizing decision-making processes, organizations not only empower individuals to contribute their insights but also create a system where diverse perspectives can be incorporated into the decision-making process. Decentralization supports the principles of democratic engagement and, as such, provides a fertile ground for collective intelligence to flourish. This feature is particularly relevant to complex and dynamic environments, where adaptive responses are crucial. Decentralized structures enable organizations to act swiftly and effectively, drawing on the collective wisdom of all members to make informed and balanced decisions.

The case studies analyzed in this work, including the Political Task Committees in Gentofte and the citizen-led initiatives of Sager der Samler in Denmark, provide empirical evidence of how democratic organizational structures can foster collective intelligence. In Gentofte, the task committees demonstrate how diversity, decentralization, and facilitation can enrich the policymaking process, making it more responsive and representative. By encouraging open discussion among citizens and politicians with varied backgrounds, these committees not only enhance the decision-making process but also create a model of governance grounded in the principles of collective intelligence. Similarly, Sager der Samler illustrates how a networked organizational structure, grounded in narrative and mutual support, can facilitate citizen-driven initiatives that address pressing social issues. This networked approach enables the organization to harness the knowledge, skills, and resources of diverse actors, scaling individual contributions into broader social solutions. Both cases underscore that collective intelligence thrives in environments that promote open participation, decentralization, and a culture of mutual learning and support.

This study's findings have important implications for the broader field of organizational studies and beyond. The mechanisms of collective intelligence identified in democratic organizational contexts are applicable across a wide array of domains, including policy development, team management, and social innovation. Decentralization, sensemaking, communicative alignment, and flexible organizational structures are principles that can inform how various organizations—whether in education, technology, or urban development—structure themselves to support effective, collective problem-solving. Organizations that incorporate these mechanisms are better positioned to foster a dynamic form of intelligence that is responsive to complex and evolving challenges.

The study also highlights the need for methodological advancements in investigating the relationship between organizing processes and collective intelligence mechanisms. By focusing on the interaction between organizational form and the processes that enable collective intelligence, this research opens up avenues for further empirical exploration. Future studies could benefit from developing simulation models or conducting in-depth case studies that examine how specific organizing processes foster collective intelligence. These methodological approaches would allow researchers to gain a deeper understanding of the conditions under which collective intelligence emerges and the factors that sustain it over time.

In conclusion, collective intelligence is a dynamic, emergent property of democratic organizing, shaped by mechanisms that encourage participation, foster communication, and allow for decentralized decision-making. The findings of this study demonstrate that collective intelligence within organizations is not merely the aggregation of individual knowledge but the result of continuous interactions, shared sensemaking, and structured communication. This collective process enables organizations to act cohesively, adaptively, and intelligently in the face of complexity.

The implications of these findings extend beyond organizational studies, suggesting that democratic organizational forms have the potential to shape collective intelligence in ways that benefit society at large. By promoting inclusivity, decentralization, and alignment, democratic organizations can become models of intelligent collective action, responding to social challenges with agility and insight. This work invites further investigation into the dynamics of collective intelligence, encouraging organizational studies to integrate new theoretical perspectives that acknowledge the power of collective action in addressing contemporary challenges.

REFERENCES

Adobor, H. (2020). Open strategy: Role of organizational democracy. *Journal of Strategy and Management*, 13(2), 310–331. DOI: 10.1108/JSMA-07-2019-0125

Ammiar, B. (2022). *Intelligence Collective. Stimuler le collectif. Créer ensemble a distance Surmonter les situations difficiles*. Éditions Eyrolles.

Boucher, S., Hallin, C. A., & Paulson, L. (2023). *The Routledge Handbook of Collective Intelligence for Democracy and Governance*. Routledge. DOI: 10.4324/9781003215929

Brown, A., Colville, I., & Pye, A. (2015). Making sense of sensemaking in organization studies. *Organization Studies*, 36(2), 265–277. DOI: 10.1177/0170840614559259

Christakis, A., & Bausch, K. (2006). *How people harness their collective wisdom and power to construct the future in co-laboratories of democracy*. Information Age Publishing.

Clegg, S. R., & Hardy, C. (1996). Introduction. Organizations, Organization and Organizing. In *Handbook of Organization Studies* (pp. 1-28). Sage.

Coburn, C. (2001). Collective Sensemaking about Reading: How Teachers Mediate Reading Policy in their Professional Communities. *Educational Evaluation and Policy Analysis*, 23(2), 145–170. DOI: 10.3102/01623737023002145

Cooren, F., Kuhn, T., Cornelissen, J., & Clark, T. (2011). Communication, Organizing and Organization: An Overview and Introduction to the Special Issue. *Organization Studies*, 32(9), 1149–1170. DOI: 10.1177/0170840611410836

Czarniawska, B. (2006). A Golden Braid: Allport, Goffman, Weick. *Organization Studies*, 27(11), 1661–1674. DOI: 10.1177/0170840606068344

Czarniawska, B. (2014). *A Theory of Organizing*. Edward Elgar Publishing Limited.

Czarniawska, B., & Joerges, B. (1996). Travels of Ideas. In Czarniawska, B., & Sevón, G. (Eds.), *Translating organizational change* (pp. 13–48). Walter de Gruyter & Co. DOI: 10.1515/9783110879735.13

Czarniawska, B., & Sevón, G. (1996). *Translating organizational change*. Walter de Gruyter & Co. DOI: 10.1515/9783110879735

Dahl, R. (2015). *On Democracy*. Yale University Press.

Etzioni, A. (1997). *Organizaciones modernas*. Editorial Limusa.

Foss, R. (2016). Major Mechanism Contributing to Swarm Intelligence. *Systems Research and Behavioral Science*, 34(6), 746–758. DOI: 10.1002/sres.2416

Ganser, C., & Keuschnigg, M. (2018). Social influence strengthens crowd wisdom under voting. *Advances in Complex Systems*, 21(6-7). DOI: 10.1142/S0219525918500133

Gupta, P., Kim, Y. J., Glikson, E., & Williams Woolley, A. (2024). Using Digital Nudges To Enhance Collective Intelligence In Online Collaboration: Insights From Unexpected Outcomes. *Management Information Systems Quarterly*, 48(1), 393–408. DOI: 10.25300/MISQ/2023/16752

Ha, D., & Tang, Y. (2022). Collective intelligence for deep learning: A survey of recent developments. *Collective Intelligence*, 1(1). Advance online publication. DOI: 10.1177/26339137221114874

Harrison, J. S., & Freeman, R. E. (2004). Special Topic: Democracy in and Around Organizations. *The Academy of Management Perspectives*, 18(3), 49–53. DOI: 10.5465/ame.2004.14776168

He, F., Pan, Y., Lin, Q., Miao, X., & Chen, Z. (2019). Collective intelligence: A taxonomy and survey. *IEEE Access : Practical Innovations, Open Solutions*, 7, 170213–170225. DOI: 10.1109/ACCESS.2019.2955677

Heylighen, F. (2013). Self-organization in Communicating Groups: the emergence of coordination, shared references and collective intelligence. In Massip-Bonet, A., & Bastardas-Boada, A. (Eds.), *Complexity perspectives on language, communication, and society* (pp. 117–149). Springer. DOI: 10.1007/978-3-642-32817-6_10

Holt, R., & Cornelissen, J. (2013). Sensemaking revisited. *Management Learning*, 45(5), 525–539. DOI: 10.1177/1350507613486422

Kerr, J. L. (2004). The limits of organizational democracy. *The Academy of Management Perspectives*, 18(3), 81–95. DOI: 10.5465/ame.2004.14776172

Kurvers, R. H. J. M., Wolf, M., Naguib, M., & Krause, J. (2015). Self-organized flexible leadership promotes collective intelligence in human groups. *Royal Society Open Science*, 2(12), 150222. Advance online publication. DOI: 10.1098/rsos.150222 PMID: 27019718

Landemore, H. (2013). *Democratic reason: politics, collective intelligence, and the rule of the many*. Princeton University Press.

Langley, A., & Tsoukas, H. (2017). Introduction. In *The SAGE Handbook of Process Organization Studies* (pp. 1–25). SAGE Publications.

Lindberg, K., & Czarniawska, B. (2006). Knotting the action net, or organizing between organizations. *Scandinavian Journal of Management*, 22(4), 292–306. DOI: 10.1016/j.scaman.2006.09.001

Maitlis, S., & Christianson, M. (2014). Sensemaking in organizations: Taking stock and moving forward. *The Academy of Management Annals*, 8(1), 57–125. DOI: 10.5465/19416520.2014.873177

Malone, T., & Bernstein, M. (2015). Introduction. In Malone, T., & Bernstein, M. (Eds.), *Handbook of Collective Intelligence* (pp. 1–15). The MIT Press.

McPhee, R., & Zaug, P. (2009). The communicative constitution of organizations. In Putnam, L., & Nicotera, A. M. (Eds.), *Building theories of organization: the constitutive role of communication* (pp. 21–48). Routledge.

Montaño, L. (2001). Los nuevos desafíos de la docencia. Hacia la construcción-siempre inacabada- de la Universidad. In *Universidad, organización y sociedad: arreglos y controversias* (p. 105-132). Miguel Ángel Porrúa.

Natorp, P. (2023). Scaling personal initiatives into collective action. In Boucher, S., Hallin, C. A., & Paulson, L. (Eds.), *The Routledge Handbook of Collective Intelligence for Democracy and Governance* (pp. 369–374). Routledge. DOI: 10.4324/9781003215929-34

Nigam, A., & Ocasio, W. (2010). Event attention, environmental sensemaking, and change in institutional logics: An inductive analysis of the effects of public attention to Clinton's health care reform initiative. *Organization Science*, 21(4), 823–841. DOI: 10.1287/orsc.1090.0490

Pham, C. H., Nguyen, T. V., Bach, T. N., Le, C. Q., & Nguyen, H. V. (2022). Collective sensemaking within institutions: Control of the COVID-19 epidemic in Vietnam. *Public Administration and Development*, 1–13. DOI: 10.1002/pad.1996 PMID: 36248011

Presthus, R. (1979). *The Organizational Society* (Revised Edition). St. Martin's Press Inc. DOI: 10.1007/978-1-349-16095-2

Romanelli, E. (1991). The Evolution of New Organizational Forms. *Annual Review of Sociology*, 17(1), 79–103. DOI: 10.1146/annurev.so.17.080191.000455

Rough, J. (2008). The circle organization: Structuring for collective wisdom. In *Collective Intelligence: Creating a Prosperous World at Peace* (pp. 75-82). Earth Intelligence Network (EIN).

Rowe, L. I., Hattie, J., & Munro, J. (2024). High-performing teams: Is collective intelligence the answer? *PLoS One*, 19(8), e0307945. Advance online publication. DOI: 10.1371/journal.pone.0307945 PMID: 39133757

Salminen, J. (2012). Collective intelligence in humans: A literature review. *arXiv*. https://doi.org//arXiv.1204.3401DOI: 10.48550

Scott, R. (1998). *Institutions and organizations*. Sage Publications.

Sørensen, E., & Torfing, J. (2023). How Collective Political Intelligence produced better policy. Political Task Committees in Gentofte, Denmark. In Boucher, S., Hallin, C. A., & Paulson, L. (Eds.), *The Routledge Handbook of Collective Intelligence for Democracy and Governance* (pp. 181–189). Routledge. DOI: 10.4324/9781003215929-13

Weber, K., & Glynn, M. A. (2006). Making sense with institutions: Context, thought and action in Karl Weick's theory. *Organization Studies*, 27(11), 1639–1660. DOI: 10.1177/0170840606068343

Weick, K. (1979). *The social psychology of organizing*. McGraw-Hill.

Weick, K. (1995). *Sensemaking in organizations*. SAGE Publications.

Yazdani, N. (2010). Organizational democracy and organization structure link: Role of strategic leadership & environmental uncertainly. *Business Review (Federal Reserve Bank of Philadelphia)*, 5(2), 51–74. DOI: 10.54784/1990-6587.1244

Compilation of References

Abaid, E. A., Cordera, A., & Pasco, A. (2021). Resiliencia organizacional en una microempresa: Estudio preliminar. *RILCO: Revista de Investigación Latinoamericana en Competitividad Organizacional*, (12), 52–59.

Accenture. (2023). A new era of generative AI for everyone. Accenture. https://www.accenture.com/content/dam/accenture/final/accenture-com/document/Accenture-A-New-Era-of-Generative-AI-for-Everyone.pdf

Adams, J., & DeFleur, M. (2005). The Acceptability of a Doctoral Degree Earned Online as Credential for Obtaining a Faculty Position. *The American Journal of Distance Education*, 19(2), 71-85.

Adekola, J., & Clelland, D. (2020). Two sides of the same coin: Business resilience and community resilience. *Journal of Contingencies and Crisis Management*, 28(1), 50–60. DOI: 10.1111/1468-5973.12275

Adler, P. S., & Borys, B. (1996). Two types of bureaucracy: Enabling and coercive. *Administrative Science Quarterly*, 41(1), 61–89. DOI: 10.2307/2393986

Adner, R. (2017). Ecosystem as structure: An actionable construct for strategy. *Journal of Management*, 43(1), 39–58. DOI: 10.1177/0149206316678451

Adner, R., & Kapoor, R. (2010). Value creation in innovation ecosystems: How the structure of technological interdependence affects firm performance in new technology generations. *Strategic Management Journal*, 31(3), 306–333. DOI: 10.1002/smj.821

Adobor, H. (2020). Open strategy: Role of organizational democracy. *Journal of Strategy and Management*, 13(2), 310–331. DOI: 10.1108/JSMA-07-2019-0125

Aggarwal, R., Singh, H., & Krishna, V. (2023). Doodlage: Contributing to circular economy in fashion. *CASE Journal*, 20(3), 747–756. DOI: 10.1108/TCJ-05-2023-0117

Ahmad, A., Javaid, N., Guizani, M., Alrajeh, N., & Khan, Z. A. (2016). An accurate and fast converging short-term load forecasting model for industrial applications in a smart grid. *IEEE Transactions on Industrial Informatics*, 13(5), 2587–2596. DOI: 10.1109/TII.2016.2638322

Alaerjan, A., Jabeur, R., Ben Chikha, H., Karray, M., & Ksantini, M. (2024). Improvement of Smart Grid Stability Based on Artificial Intelligence with Fusion Methods. *Symmetry*, 2024(16), 459. DOI: 10.3390/sym16040459

Alañón, A. & Arauzo, J. (2011). On the Geographical Scope of Location Decisions: Empirical Evidence from Spanish Municipalities. *The Empirical Economics Letters*, 10(2).

Albright, S., & Winston, W. (2003). *Business Analytics: Data Analysis and Decision Making* (6th ed.). Cengage Learning.

Al-Emran, M. (2023). Beyond technology acceptance: Development and evaluation of technology-environmental, economic, and social sustainability theory. *Technology in Society*, 75, 102383. DOI: 10.1016/j.techsoc.2023.102383

AlKuwaiti, R. H., El-Sayed, W. T., Farag, H. E. Z., Al-Durra, A., & El-Saadany, E. F. (2024). Power system resilience against climatic faults: An optimized self-healing approach using conservative voltage reduction. *International Journal of Electrical Power & Energy Systems*, 155, 109519. DOI: 10.1016/j.ijepes.2023.109519

Alles, M. (2002*). Dirección Estratégica de Recursos Humanos*. Gestión por competencias: El Direccionario. Editorial Garnica, 1-86.

Almond, K., & Iszoro, E. (2023). Virtual Reality as a New Means of Communication: A Case Study Analysis of Fashion Brand, Accidental Cutting. *Fashion, Style & Popular Culture*, 10(3).

Aly, H. H. (2020). A proposed intelligent short-term load forecasting hybrid models of ANN, WNN and KF based on clustering techniques for smart grid. *Electric Power Systems Research*, 182, 106191. DOI: 10.1016/j.epsr.2019.106191

Ambrosio, M. (2017). Ciclo adaptativo y cambio rural: El enfoque territorial en la gestión de la resiliencia rural. *Revista de Fomento Social*, 72(3-4), 665–682. DOI: 10.32418/rfs.2017.287-288.1470

Ammiar, B. (2022). *Intelligence Collective. Stimuler le collectif. Créer ensemble a distance Surmonter les situations difficiles*. Éditions Eyrolles.

Anaya, A., & Boticario, J. (2009, April). Clustering learners according to their collaboration. In *2009 13th International Conference on Computer Supported Cooperative Work in Design* (pp. 540-545). IEEE. DOI: 10.1109/CSCWD.2009.4968115

Ancona, D. G., Goodman, P. S., Lawrence, B. S., & Tushman, M. L. (2001). Time: A new research lens. *Academy of Management Review*, 26(4), 645–663. DOI: 10.2307/3560246

Anderson, P. (1999). Complexity Theory and Organization Science. *Organization Science*, 10(3), 216–232. DOI: 10.1287/orsc.10.3.216

An, S. B., & Yoon, K. C. (2021). The Effects of Socially Responsible Activities on Management Performance of Internationally Diversified Firms: Evidence from KOSPI Market. *Journal of Asian Finance. Economics and Business*, 8, 251–265.

Ansorena, Á. (1996). *15 pasos para la selección de personal con éxito: Método e instrumentos* (41). *Grupo Planeta.*

An, W., & Alarcón, S. (2020). How Can Rural Tourism Be Sustainable? A Systematic Review. *Sustainability (Basel)*, 12(18), 7758. DOI: 10.3390/su12187758

Arafat, M. Y., Hossain, M. J., & Alam, M. M. (2024). Machine learning scopes on microgrid predictive maintenance: Potential frameworks, challenges, and prospects. *Renewable & Sustainable Energy Reviews*, 190, 114088. DOI: 10.1016/j.rser.2023.114088

Aristoteles Nicomachean Ethics, b. (n.d.). Nicomachean Ethics. Retrieved march 15th, 2023, from http://classics.mit.edu/Aristotle/nicomachaen.2.ii.html

Arneson, R. (2013). Egalitarianism. *The Stanford Encyclopedia of Philosophy*. https://plato.stanford.edu/entries/egalitarianism/

Athanasopoulou, A., de Reuver, M., Nikou, S., & Bouwman, H. (2019). What technology enabled services impact business models in the automotive industry? An exploratory study. *Futures*, 109, 73–83. DOI: 10.1016/j.futures.2019.04.001

Atmanspacher, H. (2023). Why Physics Does Not Inform the Human Condition, But Its Boundaries Do. *Foundations of Science*. Advance online publication. DOI: 10.1007/s10699-023-09915-y

Atmanspacher, H., & Rickles, D. (2022). *Dual-Aspect Monism and the Deep Structure of Meaning*. Routledge., DOI: 10.4324/9781003270584

Attri, R., & Bairagi, R. (2022). Guthali – challenges in marketing Indian handicrafts and handloom. *Emerald Emerging Markets Case Studies*, 12(1), 1–23. DOI: 10.1108/EEMCS-09-2021-0298

Austin, J. E., & Seitanidi, M. M. (2012). Collaborative value creation: A review of partnering between nonprofits and businesses. Part I: Value creation spectrum and collaboration stages. *Nonprofit and Voluntary Sector Quarterly*, 41(5), 726–758. DOI: 10.1177/0899764012450777

Autio, E., & Thomas, L. D. W. (2014). Innovation ecosystems: Implications for innovation management. In Dodgson, M., Gann, D. M., & Phillips, N. (Eds.), *The Oxford Handbook of Innovation Management* (pp. 204–228). Oxford University Press.

Azizi, A. A., Shamim, A. G., & Mosayebian, M. E. (2023). Robust island-mode operation of power distribution network using game theory for resilience enhancement, Sustainable Energy. *Grids and Networks*, 33, 100978.

Aziz, T., Waseem, M., Liu, S., Ma, Y., Lin, Z., & Memon, Q.-U.-D. (2023). A self-healing restoration of power grid based on two-stage adaptive decision-making strategy to enhance grid resilience. *International Journal of Electrical Power & Energy Systems*, 154, 109435. DOI: 10.1016/j.ijepes.2023.109435

Bachmann, R. (2003). Trust and power as means of coordinating the internal relations of the organization: A conceptual framework. In *The trust process in organizations: Empirical studies of the determinants and the process of trust development* (pp. 58-74). DOI: 10.4337/9781843767350.00010

Baert, J. M., De Laender, F., Sabbe, K., & Janssen, C. R. (2016). Biodiversity increases functional and compositional resistance, but decreases resilience in phytoplankton communities. *Ecology*, 97(12), 3433–3440. DOI: 10.1002/ecy.1601 PMID: 27912020

Bailey, N., & Kurland, N. (1999). The advantages and challenges of working here, there, anywhere, and anytime. *Organizational Dynamics*, 28(2), 53–68. DOI: 10.1016/S0090-2616(00)80016-9

Bakti, L., Lew, A., & Kim, Y. (2017). A Resilient Approach to Collaborative Coral Reef Conservation on Gili Trawangan, Indonesia. In Lew, A., & Cheer, J. (Eds.), *Understanding Tourism Resilience: Adapting to Environmental Change*. Routledge. DOI: 10.4324/9781315463971-12

Ballie, J., & Woods, M. (2018). Circular by Design: A Model for Engaging Fashion/Textile SMEs with Strategies for Designed Reuse. In *Unmaking Waste in Production and Consumption: Towards the Circular Economy*. Emerald Publishing Limited. DOI: 10.1108/978-1-78714-619-820181010

Bandeiras, F., Gomes, Á., Gomes, M., & Coelho, P. (2023). Exploring Energy Trading Markets in Smart Grid and Microgrid Systems and Their Implications for Sustainability in Smart Cities. *Energies*, 16(2), 801. DOI: 10.3390/en16020801

Bankins, S., & Formosa, P. (2023, February). The Ethical Implications of Artificial Intelligence (AI) For Meaningful Work. *Journal of Business Ethics*, 185(4), 725–740. Advance online publication. DOI: 10.1007/s10551-023-05339-7

Barker, J. (1993, September). Tightening the Iron Cage: Concertive Control in Self-Managing Teams. *Administrative Science Quarterly*, 38(3), 408–437. DOI: 10.2307/2393374

Barroso, A. P., Machado, V. H., & Machado, V. C. (2011). Supply chain resilience using the mapping approach. *Supply Chain Management*, 161–184.

Basiago, A. D. (1995). Methods of Defining Sustainability. *Sustainable Development (Bradford)*, 3(3), 110–119. DOI: 10.1002/sd.3460030302

Bassanino, M., Fernando, T., & Wu, K. (2014). Can virtual workspaces enhance team communication and collaboration in design review meetings? *Architectural Engineering and Design Management*, 10(3-4), 200–217. DOI: 10.1080/17452007.2013.775102

Bastakis, C., Buhalis, D., & Butler, R. (2004). The Perception of Small and Medium-Sized Tourism Accommodation Providers on the Impacts of the Tour Operator's Power in Easter Mediterranean. *Tourism Management*, 25(2), 151–170. DOI: 10.1016/S0261-5177(03)00098-0

Batta, A., Bandameeda, G., & Parayitam, S. (2023). Human Resource Management Practices, Job Satisfaction and Performance: Evidence from Transportation Sector in India. *Asia-Pacific Journal of Management Research and Innovation*, 19(1), 47–62. DOI: 10.1177/2319510X231166800

Baum, J. A. C., Li, S. X., & Usher, J. M. (2000). Making the next move: How experiential and vicarious learning shape the locations of chains' acquisitions. *Administrative Science Quarterly*, 45(4), 766–801. DOI: 10.2307/2667019

Bavdaž, M., Bounfour, A., Martin, J., Nonnis, A., Perani, G., & Redek, T. (2023). Measuring investment in intangible assets. *Advances in Business Statistics, Methods and Data Collection*, 79-103.

Beall, A. (2020). Why clothes are so hard to recycle. BBC Future. Available at: www.bbc.com/future/article/20200710-why-clothes-are-so-hard-to-recycle

Beck, D. E., & Cowan, C. (2007/2014). *Spiral Dynamics: Leadership, Werte undWandel* (5th ed.). Inspire.

Beckett, R. C., & O'Loughlin, A. (2024). The Unity of Indigenous Knowledge in the Pursuit of a UN Sustainable Development Goal. *Collective Intelligence*, 3(2), 26339137241241295. Advance online publication. DOI: 10.1177/26339137241241295

Behrangrad, M. (2015). A review of demand side management business models in the electricity market. *Renewable & Sustainable Energy Reviews*, 47, 270–283. DOI: 10.1016/j.rser.2015.03.033

Beni, G., & Wang, J. (1989). Swarm Intelligence in Cellular Robotic Systems. *NATO Advanced Workshop on Robots and Biological Systems*, 703–712.

Benkler, Y. (2006). *The wealth of networks: How social production transforms markets and freedom*. Yale University Press.

Benner, M. J., & Tushman, M. L. (2003). Exploitation, exploration, and process management: The productivity dilemma revisited. *Academy of Management Review*, 28(2), 238–256. DOI: 10.2307/30040711

Bennett, J., & Strange, N. (Eds.). (2014). *Media independence: Working with freedom or working for free?* Routledge. DOI: 10.4324/9781315776392

Berman, S. J. (2012). Digital transformation: Opportunities to create new business models. *Strategy and Leadership*, 40(2), 16–24. DOI: 10.1108/10878571211209314

Bernauer, J. (1999). Emerging standards: Empowerment with purpose. *Kappa Delta Pi Record*, 35(2), 68–74. DOI: 10.1080/00228958.1999.10518419

Bhamra, R., Dani, S., & Burnard, K. (2011). Resilience: The concept, a literature review, and future directions. *International Journal of Production Research*, 49(18), 5375–5393. DOI: 10.1080/00207543.2011.563826

Bhasin, H. (2023). What is Collective Intelligence? Benefits and Limitations. *Marketing91*. https://www.marketing91.com/collective-intelligence/

Bhattacharya, S., & Roy, P. (2017). Organisational climate and team effectiveness – A study on small scale industries. ASBM Journal of Management, 10(2), 17-24. Retrieved from https://search.proquest.com/docview/1963102034?accountid=177896

Black, E. (2012). IBM and the Holocaust: The Strategic Alliance Between Nazi Germany and America's Most Powerful Corporation-Expanded Edition.

Boden, M. A. (2016). *AI*. Oxford University Press.

Boder, A. (2006). Collective intelligence: A keystone in knowledge management. *Journal of Knowledge Management*, 10(1), 81–93. DOI: 10.1108/13673270610650120

Bogers, M., Chesbrough, H., & Moedas, C. (2018). Open innovation: Research, practices, and policies. *California Management Review*, 60(2), 5–16. DOI: 10.1177/0008125617745086

Bøllingtoft, A. (2019). The role of government in fostering collaborative ecosystems: Lessons from practice. *The Journal of Business Strategy*, 40(2), 22–30.

Bonabeau, E., Dorigo, M., & Theraulaz, G. (1999). *Swarm Intelligence: From Natural to Artificial Systems*. Academic. DOI: 10.1093/oso/9780195131581.001.0001

Borderías, C., & Martini, M. (2020). En las fronteras de la precariedad. Trabajo feme-nino y estrategias de subsistencia (XVIII-XXI). *Historia y Sociedad (Rio Piedras, San Juan, P.R.)*, (96), 63–78.

Borin, L. C., Hollweg, G. V., Osório, C. R. D., Carnielutti, F. M., Oliveira, R. C. L. F., & Montagner, V. F. (2024). Automated test-driven design for robust optimized current control of GTIs operating under normal and abnormal grid conditions. *Control Engineering Practice*, 143, 105790. DOI: 10.1016/j.conengprac.2023.105790

Boromisza-Habashi, D. (2015). *Speaking hatefully: Culture, communication, and political action in Hungary*. Penn State University Press.

Boucher, S., Hallin, C. A., & Paulson, L. (2023). *The Routledge Handbook of Collective Intelligence for Democracy and Governance*. Routledge. DOI: 10.4324/9781003215929

Bouncken, R. B., Clauss, T., & Fredrich, V. (2016). Product innovation through coopetition in alliances: Singular or plural governance? *Industrial Marketing Management*, 53, 77–90. DOI: 10.1016/j.indmarman.2015.11.011

Bourdieu, P. (1990). The Logic of Practice (R. Nice, Trans.). Stanford University. DOI: 10.1515/9781503621749

Bourdieu, P. (1986). The forms of capital. In Richardson, J. (Ed.), *Handbook of Theory and Research for the Sociology of Education, Greenwood, New York* (pp. 241–258).

Bourdieu, P., & Passero, J. (1996). *La reproducción*. Fontamara.

Bowen, H. R. (1953). *Social Responsibilities of the Businessman*. University of Iowa Press.

Bresciani, S., Ferraris, A., & Bresciani, S. (2020). Artificial intelligence in collaborative ecosystems: Implications for business model innovation. *Journal of Business Research*, 114, 30–39.

Brooks, R. (1991). Intelligence without representation. *Artificial Intelligence*, 47(1-3), 139–159. DOI: 10.1016/0004-3702(91)90053-M

Brown, A., Colville, I., & Pye, A. (2015). Making sense of sensemaking in organization studies. *Organization Studies*, 36(2), 265–277. DOI: 10.1177/0170840614559259

Brown, M., Silberman, J., & Spiegel, F. (2012). A contemporary evaluation of the acrasids (Acrasidae, Heterolobosea, Excavata). *European Journal of Protistology*, 48(2), 103–123. DOI: 10.1016/j.ejop.2011.10.001 PMID: 22154141

Brynjolfsson, E., & Mac Afee, A. (2023). *The Impact of Generative AI on Workforce Productivity*. https://www.youtube.com/watch?v=4i1a-ApM00M

Brynjolfsson, E. (2022). The Turing Trap: The promise and peril of human-like artificial intelligence. *Daedalus*, 151(2), 272–287. DOI: 10.1162/daed_a_01915

Brynjolfsson, E., & McElheran, K. (2016). The rapid evolution of digital businesses: Digital transformation and data-driven decision making. *MIT Sloan Management Review*, 57(3), 1–7.

Buckley, P. J., & Casson, M. (2010). *The Multinational Enterprise Revisited*. Palgrave MacMillan. DOI: 10.1057/9780230250468

Bui, H., Jones, T., Weaver, D., & Le, A. (2020). The adaptive resilience of living cultural heritage in a tourism destination. *Journal of Sustainable Tourism*, 28(7), 1022–1040. DOI: 10.1080/09669582.2020.1717503

Burnard, K., & Bhamra, R. (2011). Organisational resilience: Development of a conceptual framework for organisational responses. *International Journal of Production Research*, 49(18), 5581–5599. DOI: 10.1080/00207543.2011.563827

Buzzao, G., & Rizzi, F. (2023). The role of dynamic capabilities for resilience in pursuing business continuity: An empirical study. *Total Quality Management & Business Excellence*, 34(11-12), 1–33. DOI: 10.1080/14783363.2023.2174427

Cabanelas, P., Parkhurst, G., Thomopoulos, N., & Lampón, J. F. (2023). A dynamic capability evaluation of emerging business models for new mobility. *Research in Transportation Business & Management*, 47, 100964. DOI: 10.1016/j.rtbm.2023.100964

Campbell-Kelly, M., Aspray, W. F., Yost, J. R., Tinn, H., & Díaz, G. C. (2023). *Computer: A history of the information machine*. Taylor & Francis. DOI: 10.4324/9781003263272

Cánovas, P. (2014). Innovación tecnológica y crecimiento en la Unión Europea. *Revista Universitaria Europea, 20*.

Carmichael, T., & Hadžikadić, M. (2019). The fundamentals of complex adaptive systems. In *Complex Adaptive Systems*. Springer. DOI: 10.1007/978-3-030-20309-2_1

Carrasquillo, M. (2023, November 15). Infrastructure Apartheid to Liberatory Infrastructures. *Shareable*.

Carroll, A. B. (1979). A Three-Dimensional Conceptual Model of Corporate Performance. *Academy of Management Review*, 4(4), 497–505. DOI: 10.2307/257850

Carroll, A. B. (1991). The Pyramid of Corporate Social Responsibility: Toward the Moral Management of Organizational Stakeholders. *Business Horizons*, 34(4), 39–48. DOI: 10.1016/0007-6813(91)90005-G

Carroll, A. B. (2008). A History of Corporate Social Responsibility: Concepts and Practices. In Crane, A., Matten, D., McWilliams, A., Moon, J., & Siegel, D. S. (Eds.), *The Oxford Handbook of Social Responsibility* (pp. 19–46). Academic. DOI: 10.1093/oxfordhb/9780199211593.003.0002

Carroll, A. B., & Shabana, K. (2010). The Business Case for Corporate Social Responsibility: A Review of Concepts, Research and Practice. *International Journal of Management Reviews*, 12(1), 85–105. DOI: 10.1111/j.1468-2370.2009.00275.x

Carvalho, H., Azevedo, S. G., & Cruz-Machado, V. (2012). Agile and resilient approaches to supply chain management: Influence on performance and competitiveness. *Logistics Research*, 4(1-2), 49–62. DOI: 10.1007/s12159-012-0064-2

Castro, F. (2019). *Filosofía tuitera y estética columnista*. Micromegas.

Cervantes, F. (2023). *Del algoritmo a la inteligencia colectiva. Un experimento con el potencial de ayudar a la mejora continua de los programas públicos*. PNUD.

Chancel, L., & Piketty, T. (2019). Indian Income Inequality, 1922-2015: From British Raj to Billionaire Raj? *Review of Income and Wealth*, 65(S1), S33–S62. DOI: 10.1111/roiw.12439

Chang, H.-W., Chang, T., Ling, Y. H., & Yang, Y.-L. (2023). Dynamical linkages between the Brent oil price and stock markets in BRICS using quantile connectedness approach. *Finance Research Letters*, 54, 103748. DOI: 10.1016/j.frl.2023.103748

Chan, K. W., & Li, S. Y. (2010). Understanding consumer-to-consumer interactions in virtual communities: The salience of reciprocity. *Journal of Business Research*, 63(9/10), 1033–1040. DOI: 10.1016/j.jbusres.2008.08.009

Charles, I. I., & Uford, I. C. (2023). Comparative analysis and evaluation of business and financial performance of Amazon. Com: A three-year period critical review of exceptional success. European Journal of Business. *Economics and Accountancy*, 11(2), 69–92.

Chen, J., & Zhang, J. (2023). Crude oil price shocks, volatility spillovers, and global systemic financial risk transmission mechanisms: Evidence from the stock and foreign exchange markets. *Resources Policy*, 85, 103875. DOI: 10.1016/j.resourpol.2023.103875

Chesbrough, H., & Appleyard, M. M. (2007). Open innovation and strategy. *California Management Review*, 50(1), 57–76. DOI: 10.2307/41166416

Cheung, C. M. K., & Lee, M. K. O. (2010). A theoretical model of intentional social action in online social networks. *Decision Support Systems*, 49(1), 24–30. DOI: 10.1016/j.dss.2009.12.006

Chikersal, P., Tomprou, M., Yi, J., Williams, A., & Dabbish, L. (2017). Deep Structures of Collaboration: Physiological Correlates of Collective Intelligence and Group Satisfaction. *CSCW '17: Proceedings of the 2017 ACM Conference on Computer Supported Cooperative Work and Social Computing*. DOI: 10.1145/2998181.2998250

Choi, J. N., Sung, S. Y., & Kim, M. U. (2010). How Do Groups React to Unexpected Threats? Crisis Management in Organizational Teams. *Social Behavior and Personality*, 38(6), 805–828. DOI: 10.2224/sbp.2010.38.6.805

Christakis, A., & Bausch, K. (2006). *How people harness their collective wisdom and power to construct the future in co-laboratories of democracy*. Information Age Publishing.

Chroust, G., & Aumayr, G. (2017). Resilience 2.0: Computer-aided disaster management. *Journal of Systems Science and Systems Engineering*, 26(3), 321–335. DOI: 10.1007/s11518-017-5335-7

Chun, Y. H., Choi, S., & Song, M. (2018). Analyzing the Link Between Job Satisfaction and Performance in Educational Institutions. *International Journal of Public Administration*. Advance online publication. DOI: 10.1080/01900692.2018.1498101

CIA. (1944). Simple Sabotage Field Manual. In *Strategic Services* (p. 20). Office of Strategic Services.

Čirjevskis, A. (2023). Measuring dynamic capabilities-based synergies using real options in M&A deals: Amazon's acquisition of Whole Foods. *International Journal of Applied Management Science*, 15(1), 73–85. DOI: 10.1504/IJAMS.2023.128296

Clegg, S. R., & Hardy, C. (1996). Introduction. Organizations, Organization and Organizing. In *Handbook of Organization Studies* (pp. 1-28). Sage.

Coburn, C. (2001). Collective Sensemaking about Reading: How Teachers Mediate Reading Policy in their Professional Communities. *Educational Evaluation and Policy Analysis*, 23(2), 145–170. DOI: 10.3102/01623737023002145

Cohen, W., & Levinthal, D. (1990). Absorptive Capacity: A New Perspective on learning and innovation. *Administrative Science Quarterly*, 35(1), 128–152. DOI: 10.2307/2393553

Colbert, B. A. (2004). The complex resource-based view: Implications for theory and practice of strategic human resource management. *Academy of Management Review*, 29(3), 341–358. DOI: 10.2307/20159047

Colella, V., Klopfer, E., & Resnick, M. (2001). *Adventures in modeling: Exploring complex, dynamic systems with StarLogo*. Teachers College Press.

Collective | Search Online Etymology Dictionary. (n.d.). Retrieved November 12, 2023, from Link https://www.etymonline.com/search?q=collective

Colliander, J., & Dahlén, M. (2011). Following the Fashionable Friend: The Power of Social Media - Weighing the Publicity Effectiveness of Blogs Versus Online Magazines. *Journal of Advertising Research*, 51(1), 313–320. DOI: 10.2501/JAR-51-1-313-320

Combs, S. (2024). The Evolution of Sustainability: A Historical Perspective. *Emerald Ecovations*. https://emeraldecovations.com/2024/05/evolution-of-sustainability/#

Contractor, F. J., Kumar, V., Kundu, S. K., & Pedersen, T. (2010). Revisiting the role of culture in MNC performance: The case of management practices. *Journal of International Business Studies*, 41(5), 852–875.

Contreras, F., & González, T. (2021). Business Resilience and Social Inclusion: A Critical Reflection on Internal Marketing. *Mercados y negocios*, 22(43), 77-96.

Conz, E., & Magnani, G. (2020). A dynamic perspective on the resilience of firms: A systematic literature review and a framework for future research. *European Management Journal*, 38(3), 400–412. DOI: 10.1016/j.emj.2019.12.004

Cook, A., Faulconbridge, J., & Muzio, D. (2012). *Legal Elite: Recruitment Through Cultural Capital and the 'London's Reproduction of Social Exclusivity in City Professional Service Field.*

Cooper, B., Wang, J., Bartram, T., & Cooke, F. L. (2019). Well-being-oriented human resource management practices and employee performance in the Chinese banking sector: The role of social climate and resilience. *Human Resource Management*, 58(1), 85–97. DOI: 10.1002/hrm.21934

Cooren, F., Kuhn, T., Cornelissen, J., & Clark, T. (2011). Communication, Organizing and Organization: An Overview and Introduction to the Special Issue. *Organization Studies*, 32(9), 1149–1170. DOI: 10.1177/0170840611410836

Coote, A. (2015). People, Planet, Power: Toward a New Social Settlement. *International Journal of Social Quality*, 5(1), 8–34. DOI: 10.3167/IJSQ.2015.050102

Costa, C., & Buhalis, D. (2006). *Tourism Business Frontiers: Consumers, Products and Industry*. Elsevier.

Covey, F. (2023). *The 7 Habits of Highly Effective People*. FranklinCovey.

Coy, D., Malekpour, S., Saeri, A. K., & Dargaville, R. (2021). Rethinking community empowerment in the energy transformation: A critical review of the definitions, drivers and outcomes. *Energy Research & Social Science*, 72, 101871. DOI: 10.1016/j.erss.2020.101871

Czarniawska, B. (2014). *A Theory of Organizing*. Edward Elgar Publishing Limited.

Czarniawska, B. (2006). A Golden Braid: Allport, Goffman, Weick. *Organization Studies*, 27(11), 1661–1674. DOI: 10.1177/0170840606068344

Czarniawska, B., & Joerges, B. (1996). Travels of Ideas. In Czarniawska, B., & Sevón, G. (Eds.), *Translating organizational change* (pp. 13–48). Walter de Gruyter & Co. DOI: 10.1515/9783110879735.13

Dabbous, A., & Barakat, K. A. (2023). The road towards environmental sustainability: Investigating the role of information and communication technologies and green technology innovations. *Journal of Cleaner Production*, 432, 139826. DOI: 10.1016/j.jclepro.2023.139826

Dabla-Norris, E., Kochhar, K., Suphaphiphat, N., Ricka, F., & Tsounta, E. (2015). *Causes and Consequences of Income Inequality: A Global Perspective*. IMF.

Dahlberg, R. (2015). Resilience and complexity: Conjoining the discourses of two contested concepts. *Culture Unbound*, 7(3), 541–557. DOI: 10.3384/cu.2000.1525.1572541

Dahles, H., & Susilowati, T. P. (2015). Business resilience in times of growth and crisis. *Annals of Tourism Research*, 51, 34–50. DOI: 10.1016/j.annals.2015.01.002

Dahl, R. (2015). *On Democracy*. Yale University Press.

Dassouli, S., Bodolica, V., Satt, H., & M'hamdi, M. (2024). Adaptation strategy, international experience and export performance of Moroccan handicraft firms: The mediating role of partnerships. *International Journal of Emerging Markets*, 19(2), 412–434. DOI: 10.1108/IJOEM-01-2021-0127

Davenport, T. H., & Harris, J. G. (2007). *Competing on analytics: The new science of winning*. Harvard Business Review Press.

Davies, A., & Brady, T. (2016). Explicating the Dynamics of Project. *International Journal of Project Management*, 34(2), 314–327. DOI: 10.1016/j.ijproman.2015.04.006

Dayo-Olupona, O., Genc, B., Celik, T., & Bada, S. (2023). Adoptable approaches to predictive maintenance in mining industry: An overview. *Resources Policy*, 86, 104291. DOI: 10.1016/j.resourpol.2023.104291

de Bono, E. (1995). *De Bono's Thinking Course*. BBC Books.

de Koster, R., Roy, D., Yun, F. L., & Kumar, S. (2021). Special Issue of Production and Operations Management Journal "Managing Autonomous and IoT-driven Intralogistics Operations". *Production and Operations Management*, 30(1), 293–294. DOI: 10.1111/poms.13372

de la Rosa-Navarro, M., & Carmona-Lavado, A. (2010). Cómo afecta la relación del empleado con el líder a su compromiso con la organización. *Universia Business Review*, (26), 112–132.

de Oliveira Neto, G. C., Teixeira, M. M., Souza, G. L. V., Arns, V. D., Tucci, H. N. P., & Amorim, M. (2022). Assessment of the Eco-Efficiency of the Circular Economy in the Recovery of Cellulose from the Shredding of Textile Waste. Polymers, 14(7), 1317. DOI: 10.3390/polym14071317

De Santis, E., Rizzi, A., Sadeghian, A., & Mascioli, F. M. F. (2015). A learning intelligent system for fault detection in Smart Grid by a One-Class Classification approach. Proceedings of the International Joint Conference on Neural Networks, 2015-September, Article 7280756. DOI: 10.1109/IJCNN.2015.7280756

de Valck, K., van Bruggen, G. H., & Wierenga, B. (2009). Virtual communities: A marketing perspective. *Decision Support Systems*, 47(3), 185–203. DOI: 10.1016/j.dss.2009.02.008

de Vreede, G., Antunes, P., Vassileva, J., Gerosa, M., & Wu, K. (2016). Collaboration technology in teams and organizations: Introduction to the special issue. *Information Systems Frontiers*, 18(1), 1–6. DOI: 10.1007/s10796-016-9632-3

Defourny, J., & Nyssens, M. (2010). Conceptions of social enterprises and social entrepreneurship in Europe and the United States: Convergences and divergences. *Journal of Social Entrepreneurship*, 1(1), 32–53. DOI: 10.1080/19420670903442053

Demir, K., & Cicibaş, H. (2019). The Next Industrial Revolution: Industry 5.0 and Discussions on Industry 4.0. *4th International Management Information Systems Conference "Industry 4.0,"* February, 247–260.

Denckla, C., Cicchetti, D., Kubzansky, L., Seedat, S., Teicher, M., Williams, D., & Koenen, K. (2020). Psychological resilience: An update on definitions, a critical appraisal, and research recommendations. *European Journal of Psychotraumatology*, 11(1), 1822064. DOI: 10.1080/20008198.2020.1822064 PMID: 33244362

Deng, H., Wang, J., Shao, Y., Zhou, Y., Cao, Y., Zhang, X., & Li, W. (2023). Optimization of configurations and scheduling of shared hybrid electric-hydrogen energy storages supporting to multi-microgrid system. *Journal of Energy Storage*, 74, 109420. DOI: 10.1016/j.est.2023.109420

Dennis, C., Bourlakis, M., Alamanos, E., Papagiannidis, S., & Brakus, J. (2017). 'Value Co-Creation Through Multiple Shopping Channels: The Interconnections with Social Exclusion and Well-Being', International Journal of Electronic Commerce, 21(4), 517-547.

Derrida, J. (2005). At This Very Moment in This Work Here I Am. *Emmanuel Levinas: Levinas, phenomenology and his critics, 1*, 174.

Deryugina, T., Moore, F., & Tol, R. (2021). Environmental Applications of the Coase Theorem. *Environmental Science & Policy*, 120, 81–88. DOI: 10.1016/j.envsci.2021.03.001

Descartes, R. (1897). Meditationes de prima philosophia. In Adam, C., & Tannery, P. (Eds.), *Oevres de Descartes*. Cerf. DOI: 10.5962/bhl.title.39750

Dhanaraj, C., & Parkhe, A. (2006). Orchestrating innovation networks. *Academy of Management Review*, 31(3), 659–669. DOI: 10.5465/amr.2006.21318923

Díaz de Rada, V., & Portilla, I. (2015). Encuestas telefónicas: Estrategias para mejorar la colaboración. *Perspectiva Empresarial*, 2(1), 97–115. DOI: 10.16967/rpe.v2n1a7

Dictionary.com Affect. (2023, March 15th). Retrieved from affect: https://www.dictionary.com/browse/affect

Dioni, J. (2021). *La España de las piscinas*. Arpa.

Doak, D. F., Bigger, D., Harding, E. K., Marvier, M. A., O'malley, R. E., & Thomson, D. (1998). The statistical inevitability of stability-diversity relationships in community ecology. *American Naturalist*, 151(3), 264–276. DOI: 10.1086/286117 PMID: 18811357

Dower, N. (2004). Global Economy, Justice and Sustainability. *Ethical Theory and Moral Practice*, 7(4), 399–415. DOI: 10.1007/s10677-004-2215-2

Drouin, J.-M. (2019). *A Philosophy of the Insect*. Columbia University Press. DOI: 10.7312/drou17578

Drucker, P. (1999). Knowledge-Worker Productivity. *California Management Review*, 41(2), 79–94. DOI: 10.2307/41165987

Drucker, P. (2017). *The Age of Discontinuity. Guidelines to our Changing Society*. Heinemann. DOI: 10.4324/9781315130873

Duchek, S. (2020). Organizational resilience: a capability-based conceptualization. *Business research*, 13(1), 215-246.

Duncan, R. (1976). The ambidextrous organization: Designing dual structures for innovation. In Killman, R. H., Pondy, L. R., & Sleven, D. (Eds.), *The management of organization*. North Holland.

Durkheim, É. (1995). *The Elementary Forms of Religious Life*.

Duro, J., Perez, A., & Fernandez, M. (2022). Territorial tourism resilience in the COVID-19 summer. *Annals of Tourism Research Empirical Insights*, 3(1), 100039. DOI: 10.1016/j.annale.2022.100039

Dwyer, L., & Kim, C. (2003). Destination Competitiveness: Determinants and Indicators. *Current Issues in Tourism*, 6(5), 369–414. DOI: 10.1080/13683500308667962

Dyer, J. H., & Singh, H. (1998). The relational view: Cooperative strategy and sources of inter-organizational competitive advantage. *Academy of Management Review*, 23(4), 660–679. DOI: 10.2307/259056

Dziubaniuk, O., Ivanova-Gongne, M., Kaipainen, J., & Nyholm, M. (2024), Exploring the heuristics behind the transition to a circular economy in the textile industry. Management Decision. DOI: 10.1108/MD-06-2023-1095

EC. (2016). *Open Innovation, Open Science, Open to the World - a Vision for Europe*. European Commission.

EC: Directorate-General for Research and Innovation. (2023). *Harnessing the power of collaboration for nature-based solutions – New ideas and insights for local decision-makers*, Publications Office of the European Union.

Edgington, U. (2017). *Emotional Labour and Lesson Observation: A Study of England's Further Education*. Springer. DOI: 10.1007/978-981-10-2991-2

Edmondson, A. (2023, March 24). Den richtigen Ton setzen. *Manager-magazin*. Link: https://www.manager-magazin.de/harvard/fuehrung/leadership-professorin-amy-edmondson-ueber-zusammenarbeit-a-00000000-0002-0001-0000-000174106563

Edmondson, A. C., Kramer, R. M., & Cook, K. S. (2004). Psychological safety, trust, and learning in organizations: A group-level lens. *Trust and distrust in organizations: Dilemmas and approaches*, 12(2004), 239-272.

Edwards, S. (2020). How to encourage collaboration and break down silos in remote teams? *Strategic HR Review*, 19(4), 157–158. DOI: 10.1108/SHR-05-2020-0043

Einwiller, S., Ruppel, C., & Stranzl, J. (2021). Achieving employee support during the COVID-19 pandemic–the role of relational and informational crisis communication in Austrian organizations. *Journal of Communication Management (London)*, 25(3), 233–255. DOI: 10.1108/JCOM-10-2020-0107

Elkington, J. (1997). Cannibals with Forks: The Triple *The Bottom Line*.

Elkington, J. (1998). *Cannibals With Forks. The Triple Bottom Line of 21st Century Business*. Capstone Publishing Limited. DOI: 10.1002/tqem.3310080106

Elkington, J. (2018). *The triple bottom line: Does it all add up?* Routledge.

Eloundou, T., Manning, S., Mishkin, P., & Rock, D. (2023). GPTs are GPTs: An Early Look at the Labor Market Impact Potential of Large Language Models. *arXiv*. https://doi.org/https://doi.org/10.48550/arXiv.2303.10130

Encinas, M. (2022). *La innovación disruptiva como recurso para la transformación de modelos de negocios en medios de comunicación*. Complutense University of Madrid.

Engert, A. (2020). *Collective intelligence: Crowd Wisdom versus Herding Collective Intelligence* (44).

Etzioni, A. (1997). *Organizaciones modernas*. Editorial Limusa.

European Bioplastics. (n.d.). Available online: https://www.european-bioplastics.org/

Exchange, T. (2022). Preferred fiber & materials market report 2022. Available at: https://textileexchange.org/app/uploads/2022/10/Textile-Exchange_PFMR_2022.pdf

Extremadura. (2022). *Estructura de actuación: ecosistema 2030*. Extremadura 2030. Link: https://extremadura2030.com/ecosistema-extremadura-2030/

Eylon, D., & Au, K. (1999). Exploring empowerment cross-cultural differences along the power distance dimension. *International Journal of Intercultural Relations*, 23(3), 373–385. DOI: 10.1016/S0147-1767(99)00002-4

Faccia, A., & Petratos, P. (2021). Blockchain, Enterprise Resource Planning (ERP) and Accounting Information Systems (AIS): Research on e-Procurement and System Integration. *Applied Sciences, 11*(15), 6792. DOI: 10.3390/app11156792

Falandays, J., Kaaronen, R., Moser, C., Rorot, W., Tan, J., Varma, V., Williams, T., & Youngblood, M. (2023). All intelligence is collective intelligence. *Journal of Multiscale Neuroscience*. https://doi.org/DOI: 10.56280/1564736810

Faquir, D., Chouliaras, N., Sofia, V., Olga, K., & Maglaras, L. (2021). Cybersecurity in smart grids, challenges and solutions. *AIMS Electronics and Electrical Engineering*, 5(1), 24–37.

Fetterman, D. (2001). Foundations of empowerment evaluation. *Sage (Atlanta, Ga.)*.

Fibre2Fashion (2011). Good scope for organised retailing in Indian handicrafts. 23 November Retrieved from www.fibre2fashion.com/news/textile-news/newsdetails .aspx?news_id=105452

Fidan, F. ¸. S., Aydo˘gan, E. K., & Uzal, N. (2021). An integrated life cycle assessment approach for denim fabric production using recycled cotton fibers and combined heat and power plant. *Journal of Cleaner Production*, 2021(287), 125439. DOI: 10.1016/j.jclepro.2020.125439

Figueroa, H. (2014). *Estrategias de Atracción y Retención de Talento Humano en la Industria Minera Colombiana*. Económicas CUC, 61-77.

Figueroa, J. L., & Vargas-Perez, C. (2018). Collective Intelligence: A New Model of Business Management in the Big-Data Ecosystem. *European Journal of Economics and Business Studies*, 10(1), 209–220. DOI: 10.26417/ejes.v10i1.p208-219

Firlej, K., Firlej, C., & Luty, L. (2023). Economic growth and decent work as a goal of sustainable development in the European Union in the pre-pandemic and pandemic period. *International Entrepreneurship Review*, 9(1), 61–76. DOI: 10.15678/IER.2023.0901.05

Fischer, F. (2012). Participatory Governance: From Theory to Practice. In *The Oxford Handbook of Governance*. Oxford University Press.

Fisher, M. (2009). *Capitalist Realism: Is There no Alternative?* Zero Books.

Fleurbaey, M. (2001). Egalitarian Opportunities. *Law and Philosophy*, 20(5), 499–530.

Flex. (2023). Our mask-making journey | Flex. Link: https://flex.com/resources/our-mask-making-journey-three-dimensions-of-success

Flores, R. P., Negny, S., Belaud, J. P., & Lann, J.-M. (2015). Collective Intelligence to Solve Creative Problems in Conceptual Design Phase. *Procedia Engineering*, 131, 850–860. DOI: 10.1016/j.proeng.2015.12.394

Flórez, J., Rubio, G., & Rapallo, C. (2020). Corporate social responsibility and crowdfunding: The experience of the colectual platform in empowering economic and sustainable projects. *Sustainability (Basel)*, 12(13), 5251. Advance online publication. DOI: 10.3390/su12135251

Foss, R. (2016). Major Mechanism Contributing to Swarm Intelligence. *Systems Research and Behavioral Science*, 34(6), 746–758. DOI: 10.1002/sres.2416

Foster, & Keys, C. (1997). The person/environment dynamics of employee empowerment: An organizational culture analysis. *American Journal of Community Psychology,* 25(3), 345-369.

Foster, P., Salem, D., Chibnall, S., Legler, R., & Yapchai, C. (1998). Empirical support for the critical assumptions of empowerment theory. *American Journal of Community Psychology*, 26(4), 507–536. DOI: 10.1023/A:1022188805083

Francis. (2013). *Evangelii Gaudium*. Libreria Editrice Vaticana.

Franck, G. (2012). Modern Science: A Case of Collective Intelligence? On the Role of Thought Economy and Gratifying Attention in Knowledge Production. *Angewandte Chemie International Edition*, 51(29), 7088–7092. Advance online publication. DOI: 10.1002/anie.201201013 PMID: 22707208

Frankl, V. (2006). *Man's Search for Meaning*. Beacon Press.

Frederiksen, M. (2023). *Mette Frederiksen lässt Rede teilweise von KI schreiben, DER SPIEGEL*. Spiegel Online.

Freeman, R. E. (1984). *Strategic Management: A Stakeholder Approach*. Pitman Publishing.

Frey, D. F. (2017). Economic Growth, Full Employment and Decent Work: The Means and Ends in SDGs 8. *International Journal of Human Rights*, 21(8), 1164–1184. DOI: 10.1080/13642987.2017.1348709

Future of Life. (2023). *Pause Giant AI Experiments: An Open Letter*. Future of Life.

Gainsworth, S. (2021). *Airbnb Ciudad Mercancía. Historias de resistencia a la gentrificación digital.* Marmol Izquierdo Editores.

Galderisi, A., & Limongi, G. (2024). A methodological path to foster inner peripheries' sustainable and resilient futures: A research experience from Southern Italy. *Futures*, 156, 103320. DOI: 10.1016/j.futures.2024.103320

Galesic, M., Barkoczi, D., Berdahl, A., Biro, D., Carbone, G., Giannoccaro, I., Goldstone, R. L., Gonzalez, C., Kandler, A., Kao, A. B., Kendal, R., Kline, M., Lee, E., Massari, G. F., Mesoudi, A., Olsson, H., Pescetelli, N., Sloman, S. J., Smaldino, P. E., & Stein, D. L. (2023). Beyond collective intelligence: Collective adaptation. *Journal of the Royal Society, Interface*, 20(200), 20220736. DOI: 10.1098/rsif.2022.0736 PMID: 36946092

Galton, F. (1907). Vox populi. *Nature*, 75(1949), 450–451. DOI: 10.1038/075450a0

Ganser, C., & Keuschnigg, M. (2018). Social influence strengthens crowd wisdom under voting. *Advances in Complex Systems*, 21(6-7). DOI: 10.1142/S0219525918500133

Garayalde, M., González, S., & Mascareñas, J. (2019). *"Project Finance" y desarrollo económico. Estudio de un caso*. REVESCO. DOI: 10.5209/reve.64302

Garcês, S., Pocinho, M., Jesus, S., & Rieber, M. (2018). Positive psychology and tourism: A systematic literature review. *Tourism & Management Studies*, 14(3), 41–51. DOI: 10.18089/tms.2018.14304

García, J., Fernández, J., & Mascareñas, J. (2024). Cómo financiar un futuro sostenible: un estudio descriptivo del mercado de bonos verdes europeo. *Revista Universitaria Europea,* 41.

García, M. (2019). Del riesgo a la resiliencia. Hacia el diseño y gestión adaptativo del paisaje. *Estudios del Hábitat*, 17(1), 1–15.

García-Monleón, F., González-Rodrigo, E., & Bordonado-Bermejo, M.-J. (2024). Coexistence of Sustainability and Growth in Different Economies. *Journal of Business Research*, 170, 114352. DOI: 10.1016/j.jbusres.2023.114352

Garrosa, E., & Carmona, I. (2011). Salud laboral y bienestar: Incorporación de modelos positivos a la comprensión y prevención de los riesgos psicosociales del trabajo. *Medicina y Seguridad del Trabajo*, 57, 224–238. DOI: 10.4321/S0465-546X2011000500014

Gauda, M. S., Parasuraman, S., & Khan, A. G. (2024). Opportunities and Challenges for Corporate Social Responsibility in India. *IOSR Journal for Humanities and Social Sciences*, 29(3), 36–45.

Gawer, A., & Cusumano, M. A. (2014). Industry platforms and ecosystem innovation. *Journal of Product Innovation Management*, 31(3), 417–433. DOI: 10.1111/jpim.12105

GE. (2016). *Ecomagination: Strategy and impact report*. General Electric.

Genest, J., & Legg, D. (2003). *Premier-ranked tourist destinations: development of a framework for analysis and its self-guided workbook*. Ontario. Link: http://www.tourism.gov.on.ca/english/research/pdf/self-guidedworkbook.pdf

Gheorghe, A., Masera, M., & Katina, P. (2014). *Infranomics. Sustainability, Engineering Design and Governance*. Springer. DOI: 10.1007/978-3-319-02493-6

Ghosh, S. (2009). Gandhi's khadi: A history of contention and conciliation. *European Journal of Development Research*, 21(2), 322–324. DOI: 10.1057/ejdr.2009.1

Gibson, C. B., & Birkinshaw, J. (2004). The antecedents, consequences, and mediating role of organizational ambidexterity. *Academy of Management Journal*, 47(2), 209–226. DOI: 10.2307/20159573

Gilan, D. (2021). *Resilienz – die Kunst der Widerstandskraft*. Verlag Herder GmbH.

Gnyawali, D. R., Fan, W. & Penner, J. (2010) Competitive Actions and Dynamics in the Digital Age: An Empirical Investigation of Social Networking Firms. Information Systems Research, 21(3), 594-613.

Gnyawali, D. R., & Park, B. J. (2011). Co-opetition between giants: Collaboration with competitors for technological innovation. *Research Policy*, 40(5), 650–663. DOI: 10.1016/j.respol.2011.01.009

Gong, Wong, Peng, Khamdamov, Albasher, Hoa, & Nhan. (2023). Exploring an interdisciplinary approach to sustainable economic development in resource-rich regions: An investigation of resource productivity, technological innovation, and ecosystem resilience, 87, 104294.

González, T., & Córdova, K. (2020). Capacidad dinámica y recursos para la resiliencia en empresas artesanales de cerámica en Jalisco, México. Cuadernos Latinoamericanos de Administración, 16(30).

González-Alvarado, T. E., Kubus, R., & Sánchez-Gutiérrez, J. (2021). Business Resilience and Complex Adaptive Systems. Business Resilience & Adaptive System, 7.

González, T., & Martin, V. (2016). *Emprendimiento e innovación para el desarrollo local*. México UNAM FCA.

Gopalan, B. (2022, March). Value Co-creation-based Information Management in the Digital Economy. *Asia Pacific Journal of Information Systems*, 32(1), 1–31. Advance online publication. DOI: 10.14329/apjis.2022.32.1.1

GPTW. (2019). Que es el trust index: Diagnóstico de la experiencia del empleado. *Great place to work*. http://greatpacetowork.es/que-es-trust-index/

Grassé, P. (1959). La reconstruction du nid et les coordinations interindividuelles chez Bellicositermes natalensis et Cubitermes sp. La théorie de la stigmergie: Essai d'interprétation du comportement des termites constructeurs. *Insectes Sociaux*, 6(1), 41–83. DOI: 10.1007/BF02223791

Gray, P. H., Parise, S. & Iyer, B. (2011). Innovation impacts of using social bookmarking systems. MIS Quarterly, 35(3), 629-643.

Gray, S., Aminpour, P., Reza, C., Scyphers, S., Grabowski, J., Murphy, R.Jr, Singer, A., Baltaxe, D., Jordan, R., Jetter, A., & Introne, J. (2020). Harnessing the Collective Intelligence of Stakeholders for Conservation. *Frontiers in Ecology and the Environment*, 18(8), 465–472. DOI: 10.1002/fee.2232

Gross, C. (2008). *Complex and Adaptive Dynamical Systems: A Primer*. Springer-Verlag. DOI: 10.1007/978-3-540-71874-1

Grover, V. & Kohli, R. (2012). Cocreating IT Value: New Capabilities and Metrics for Multifirm Environments. MIS Quarterly, 36(1), 225-232.

Gulati, R. (2007). *Managing network resources: Alliances, affiliations, and other relational assets*. Oxford University Press. DOI: 10.1093/oso/9780199299355.001.0001

Gulati, R., Puranam, P., & Tushman, M. (2012). Meta-organization design: Rethinking design in inter-organizational and community contexts. *Strategic Management Journal*, 33(6), 571–586. DOI: 10.1002/smj.1975

Gulati, R., Wohlgezogen, F., & Zhelyazkov, P. (2012). The two facets of collaboration are cooperation and coordination in strategic alliances. *The Academy of Management Annals*, 6(1), 531–583. DOI: 10.5465/19416520.2012.691646

Gummesson, E., & Mele, C. (2010). Marketing as Value Co-Creation through Network Interaction and Resource Integration. *Journal of Business Market Management*, 4(4), 181–198. DOI: 10.1007/s12087-010-0044-2

Gunderson, L., & Holding, C. (2002). *Panarchy: Understanding Transformations in Human and Natural Systems*. Island Press.

Gunduz, M. Z., & Das, R. (2020). Cyber-security on smart grid: Threats and potential solutions. *Computer Networks*, 169, 107094. DOI: 10.1016/j.comnet.2019.107094

Guo & Stan. (2017). Implications of accelerated self-healing as a key design knob for cross-layer resilience. Integration, the VLSI Journal, 56, 167-180.

Gupta, A. (2021). Reimagining Multilateralism: The Ethos and Philosophy of *Vasudhaiva Ku u bakam. National Security*, 4(1), 20–24.

Gupta, A. K., Smith, K. G., & Shalley, C. E. (2006). The interplay between exploration and exploitation. *Academy of Management Journal*, 4(4), 693–706. DOI: 10.5465/amj.2006.22083026

Gupta, P., Kim, Y. J., Glikson, E., & Williams Woolley, A. (2024). Using Digital Nudges To Enhance Collective Intelligence In Online Collaboration: Insights From Unexpected Outcomes. *Management Information Systems Quarterly*, 48(1), 393–408. DOI: 10.25300/MISQ/2023/16752

Güttel, W. H., & Konlechner, S. W. (2023). *Strategic Change: Exploration, Exploitation & Ambidexterityi*. Successful in Turbulent Times.

Habbak, H., Mahmoud, M., Metwally, K., Fouda, M. M., & Ibrahem, M. I. (2023). Load forecasting techniques and their applications in smart grids. *Energies*, 16(3), 1480. DOI: 10.3390/en16031480

Habib, A. (2013). Sharing the Earth: Sustainability and the Currency of Inter-Generational Environmental Justice. *Environmental Values*, 22(6), 751–764. DOI: 10.3197/096327113X13781997646575

Ha, D., & Tang, Y. (2022). Collective intelligence for deep learning: A survey of recent developments. *Collective Intelligence*, 1(1). Advance online publication. DOI: 10.1177/26339137221114874

Hafeez, G., Alimgeer, K. S., & Khan, I. (2020). Electric load forecasting based on deep learning and optimized by heuristic algorithm in smart grid. *Applied Energy*, 269, 114915. DOI: 10.1016/j.apenergy.2020.114915

Hafeez, G., Khan, I., Jan, S., Shah, I. A., Khan, F. A., & Derhab, A. (2021). A novel hybrid load forecasting framework with intelligent feature engineering and optimization algorithm in smart grid. *Applied Energy*, 299, 117178. DOI: 10.1016/j.apenergy.2021.117178

Hamid, S., Azhar, M., & Sujood, . (2023). Behavioral intention to order food and beverage items using e-commerce during COVID-19: An integration of theory of planned behavior (TPB) with trust. *British Food Journal*, 125(1), 112–131. DOI: 10.1108/BFJ-03-2021-0338

Handy, C. (1995). *Gods of management: The changing work of organizations*. Oxford University Press.

Han, X., Li, J., & Zhang, Z. (2023). Dynamic game optimization control for shared energy storage in multiple application scenarios considering energy storage economy. *Applied Energy*, 350, 121801. DOI: 10.1016/j.apenergy.2023.121801

Hao, J., Yuan, J., Wu, D., Xu, W., & Li, J. (2023). A dynamic ensemble approach for multi-step price prediction: Empirical evidence from crude oil and shipping market. *Expert Systems with Applications*, 234, 121117. DOI: 10.1016/j.eswa.2023.121117

Harari, Y. N. (2023). AI and the future of humanity. *Frontiers Forum*.

Harrison, J. S., & Freeman, R. E. (2004). Special Topic: Democracy in and Around Organizations. *The Academy of Management Perspectives*, 18(3), 49–53. DOI: 10.5465/ame.2004.14776168

Hartman, S. (2018). Resilient tourism destinations? Governance implications of bringing theories of resilience and adaptive capacity to tourism practice. In Innerhofer, Fontanari, & Pechlaner (Eds.). *Destination resilience – Challenges and opportunities for destination management and governance* (pp. 66–75). Abingdon: Routledge. DOI: 10.4324/9780203701904-5

Hartman, S. (2020). Adaptative tourism areas in times of change. *Annals of Tourism Research*, 87, 102987. Advance online publication. DOI: 10.1016/j.annals.2020.102987 PMID: 32836568

Hasanien, H. M., Alsaleh, I., Tostado-V'eliz, M., Alassaf, A., Alateeq, A., & Jurado, F. (2023). Optimal parameters estimation of lithium-ion battery in smart grid applications based on gazelle optimization algorithm. *Energy*, 285, 129509. DOI: 10.1016/j.energy.2023.129509

Hazen, B. T., Russo, I., Confente, I., & Pellathy, D. (2021). Supply chain management for circular economy: Conceptual framework and research agenda. *International Journal of Logistics Management*, 32(2), 510–537. DOI: 10.1108/IJLM-12-2019-0332

Hector, D. C., Christensen, C. B., & Petrie, J. (2014). Sustainability and Sustainable Development: Philosophical Distinctions and Practical Implications. *Environmental Values*, 23(1), 7–28. DOI: 10.3197/096327114X13851122268963

He, F., Pan, Y., Lin, Q., Miao, X., & Chen, Z. (2019). Collective intelligence: A taxonomy and survey. *IEEE Access : Practical Innovations, Open Solutions*, 7, 170213–170225. DOI: 10.1109/ACCESS.2019.2955677

Heidegger. (1993). *Sein und Zeit*. Tübingen: Max Niemeyer Verlag.

Heider, F., Jahic, A., Plenz, M., & Schulz, D. (2022). Extended residential power management interface for flexibility communication and uncertainty reduction for flexibility system operators. *Energies*, 15(4), 1257. Advance online publication. DOI: 10.3390/en15041257

Helfat, C. (1997). Know-How and Asset Complementarity and Dynamic Capability Accumulation: Thee Case Of R&D. *Strategic Management Journal*, 18(5), 339–360. DOI: 10.1002/(SICI)1097-0266(199705)18:5<339::AID-SMJ883>3.0.CO;2-7

Heylighen, F. (2002). The Global Superorganism: An Evolutionary-cybernetic Model of the Emerging Network Society. *Journal of Social and Evolutionary Systems*, 1–37.

Heylighen, F. (2013). Self-organization in Communicating Groups: the emergence of coordination, shared references and collective intelligence. In Massip-Bonet, A., & Bastardas-Boada, A. (Eds.), *Complexity perspectives on language, communication, and society* (pp. 117–149). Springer. DOI: 10.1007/978-3-642-32817-6_10

Heylighen, F. (2016). Stigmergy as a universal coordination mechanism I: Definition and components. *Cognitive Systems Research*, 38, 4–13. DOI: 10.1016/j.cogsys.2015.12.002

He, Z. L., & Wong, P. K. (2004). Exploration vs. exploitation: An empirical test of the ambidexterity hypothesis. *Organization Science*, 15(4), 481–494. DOI: 10.1287/orsc.1040.0078

Hidayat, K., & Idrus, M. (2023). The effect of relationship marketing towards switching barrier, customer satisfaction, and customer trust on bank customers. *Journal of Innovation and Entrepreneurship*, 12(1), 29. DOI: 10.1186/s13731-023-00270-7 PMID: 37193581

Hill, I. R. (2021). Spotlight on UK artisan entrepreneurs' situated collaborations: Through the lens of entrepreneurial capitals and their conversion. *International Journal of Entrepreneurial Behaviour & Research*, 27(1), 99–121. DOI: 10.1108/IJEBR-11-2019-0642

Hoffmann, M. W., Wildermuth, S., Gitzel, R., Boyaci, A., Gebhardt, J., Kaul, H., Amihai, I., Forg, B., Suriyah, M., Leibfried, T., Stich, V., Hicking, J., Bremer, M., Kaminski, L., Beverungen, D., zur Heiden, P., & Tornede, T. (2020). Integration of novel sensors and machine learning for predictive maintenance in medium voltage switchgear to enable the energy and mobility revolutions. *Sensors (Basel)*, 20(7), 2099. DOI: 10.3390/s20072099 PMID: 32276442

Holbeche, L. (2019). Designing sustainably agile and resilient organizations. *Systems Research and Behavioral Science*, 36(5), 668–677. DOI: 10.1002/sres.2624

Holling, C. (1996). *Engineering Resilience versus Ecological Resilience*. Engineering Within Ecological Constraints, National Academy of Engineering, National Academy Press.

Holling, C., Gunderson, L., & Peterson, G. (2002). Sustainability and Panarchies. In *Panarchy: understanding transformations in human and natural systems*. Island Press.

Holling, C. (1973). Resilience and Stability of Ecological Systems. *Annual Review of Ecology and Systematics*, 4(1), 1–23. DOI: 10.1146/annurev.es.04.110173.000245

Holt, R., & Cornelissen, J. (2013). Sensemaking revisited. *Management Learning*, 45(5), 525–539. DOI: 10.1177/1350507613486422

Hong, Y., Zhou, Y., Li, Q., Xu, W., & Zheng, X. (2020). A deep learning method for short-term residential load forecasting in smart grid. *IEEE Access : Practical Innovations, Open Solutions*, 8, 55785–55797. DOI: 10.1109/ACCESS.2020.2981817

Hulland, J., & Houston, M. (2020). Why Systematic Review Papers and Meta-Analyses Matter: An Introduction to the Special Issue on Generalizations in Marketing. *Journal of the Academy of Marketing Science*, 48(3), 351–359. DOI: 10.1007/s11747-020-00721-7

Humbert, G., & Sciacovelli, A. (2024). Design of effective heat transfer structures for performance maximization of a closed thermochemical energy storage reactor through topology optimization. *Applied Thermal Engineering*, 239, 122146. DOI: 10.1016/j.applthermaleng.2023.122146

Hurtado, J., Salvati, D., Semola, R., Bosio, M., & Lomonaco, V. (2023). Continual learning for predictive maintenance: Overview and challenges. *Intelligent Systems with Applications*, 19, 200251. DOI: 10.1016/j.iswa.2023.200251

Huxham, C., & Vangen, S. (2013). *Managing to collaborate: The theory and practice of collaborative advantage*. Routledge. DOI: 10.4324/9780203010167

Hu, Y., Lang, C., Corbet, S., Hou, Y. G., & Oxley, L. (2023). Exploring the dynamic behaviour of commodity market tail risk connectedness during the negative WTI pricing event. *Energy Economics*, 125, 106829. DOI: 10.1016/j.eneco.2023.106829

Iansiti, M., & Levien, R. (2004). Strategy as ecology. *Harvard Business Review*, 82(3), 68–78. PMID: 15029791

Ibrahim, B., Rabelo, L., Gutierrez-Franco, E., & Clavijo-Buritica, N. (2022). Machine learning for short-term load forecasting in smart grids. *Energies*, 15(21), 8079. DOI: 10.3390/en15218079

Ibrahim, N., Said, A., Abas, N., & Shahreki, J. (2020). Relationship between well-being perspectives, employee engagement and intrinsic outcomes: A literature review. *Journal of Critical Reviews*, 7(12), 69–74.

Intelligence | Etymology, origin and meaning of intelligence by etymonline. (n.d.). Retrieved November 12, 2023, from https://www.etymonline.com/word/intelligence

Interregnum | Search Online Etymology Dictionary. (n.d.). Retrieved September 28, 2024, from https://www.etymonline.com/search?q=interregnum

Iqbal, S., Sarfraz, M., Ayyub, M., Tariq, M., Chakrabortty, R. K., Ryan, M. J., & Alamri, B. (2021). A comprehensive review on residential demand side management strategies in smart grid environment. *Sustainability (Basel)*, 13(13), 7170. DOI: 10.3390/su13137170

Jacobides, M. G., Cennamo, C., & Gawer, A. (2018). Towards a theory of ecosystems. *Strategic Management Journal*, 39(9), 2255–2276. DOI: 10.1002/smj.2904

Jänke, L., Korte, M., & Stern, E. (2022). *The Answer to Almost Everything: Are we getting stupider?* (42). Retrieved from https://www.arte.tv/en/videos/104841-001-A/42-the-answer-to-almost-everything/

Jha, R. K.Rahul Kumar Jha. (2023). Cybersecurity and Confidentiality in Smart Grid for Enhancing Sustainability and Reliability. *Recent Research Reviews Journal*, 2(2), 215–241. DOI: 10.36548/rrrj.2023.2.001

Jiang, Y., Ritchie, B. W., & Verreynne, M. L. (2019). Building tourism organizational resilience to crises and disasters: A dynamic capabilities view. *International Journal of Tourism Research*, 21(6), 882–900. DOI: 10.1002/jtr.2312

Jiménez, P., & Aquino, F. (2012). Propuesta de un modelo de competitividad de destinos turísticos. *Estudios y Perspectivas en Turismo*, 21(4), 977–995.

Johnson, N. L., Rasmussen, S., Joslyn, C., Rocha, L., & Smith, S. (1998). Symbiotic Intelligence: Self-Organizing Knowledge on Distributed Networks Driven by Human Interaction (1998-05–039).

Jo, J., & Park, J. (2020). Demand-side management with shared energy storage system in smart grid. *IEEE Transactions on Smart Grid*, 11(5), 4466–4476. DOI: 10.1109/TSG.2020.2980318

Jose, S., Nguyen, K. T. P., Medjaher, K., Zemouri, R., Lévesque, M., & Tahan, A. (2023). Fault detection and diagnostics in the context of sparse multimodal data and expert knowledge assistance: Application to hydrogenerators. *Computers in Industry*, 151, 103983. DOI: 10.1016/j.compind.2023.103983

Jung, J., & Gómez-Bengoechea, G. (2022). A literature review on firm digitalization: drivers and impacts. *Estudios sobre la Economía Española.*

Jurt, J. (2010). Die Habitus-Theorie von Pierre Bourdieu. *Zeitschrift für Literaturund Theatersoziologie*, 3, 5–17.

Jüttner, U., & Maklan, S. (2011). Supply chain resilience in the global financial crisis: An empirical study. *Supply Chain Management*, 16(4), 246–259. DOI: 10.1108/13598541111139062

Kabbaj, M., Hadi, K. E. Q. E., Elamrani, J., & Lemtaoui, M. (2018). A study of the social entrepreneurship ecosystem: The case of Morocco. *Journal of Developmental Entrepreneurship*, 21(4), 1650021. Advance online publication. DOI: 10.1142/S1084946716500217

Kabeyi, M. J. B., & Olanrewaju, O. A. (2022). The use of smart grids in the energy transition. Proceedings - 30th Southern African Universities Power Engineering Conference, SAUPEC 2022. DOI: 10.1109/SAUPEC55179.2022.9730635

Kamargianni, M., Li, W., Matyas, M., & Schäfer, A. (2016). A critical review of new mobility services for urban transport. *Transportation Research Procedia*, 14, 3294–3303. DOI: 10.1016/j.trpro.2016.05.277

Kaplan, R. S., & Norton, D. P. (1996). *The balanced scorecard: Translating strategy into action.* Harvard Business School Press.

Karduri, R. K. (2018). Integrating Renewable Energy into Existing Power Systems: Challenges and Opportunities. International Journal of Advanced Research in Management Architecture Technology & Engineering.

Karduri, R. K. R., & Ananth, C. (2023). Sustainable Urban Energy: Integrating Smart Grids into Smart Cities. International Journal of Advanced Research In Basic Engineering Sciences and Technology, 10.

Karman, A. (2020). Flexibility, coping capacity and resilience of organizations: Between synergy and support. *Journal of Organizational Change Management*, 33(5), 883–907. DOI: 10.1108/JOCM-10-2019-0305

Kasturi Rangan, V., Chase, L., & Karim, S. (2015). The Truth about CSR. *Harvard Business Review*, 93(1/2), 40–49.

Kerr, J. L. (2004). The limits of organizational democracy. *The Academy of Management Perspectives*, 18(3), 81–95. DOI: 10.5465/ame.2004.14776172

Ketonen-Oksi, S., & Valkokari, K. (2019). Innovation Ecosystems as Structures for Value Co-Creation. *Technology Innovation Management Review*, 9(2), 25–35. DOI: 10.22215/timreview/1216

Khan, A. R., Mahmood, A., Safdar, A., Khan, Z. A., & Khan, N. A. (2016). Load forecasting, dynamic pricing and DSM in smart grid: A review. *Renewable & Sustainable Energy Reviews*, 54, 1311–1322. DOI: 10.1016/j.rser.2015.10.117

Khan, H. W., Usman, M., Hafeez, G., Albogamy, F. R., Khan, I., Shafiq, Z., & Alkhammash, H. I. (2021). Intelligent optimization framework for efficient demand-side management in renewable energy integrated smart grid. *IEEE Access : Practical Innovations, Open Solutions*, 9, 124235–124252. DOI: 10.1109/ACCESS.2021.3109136

Khan, S. A. R., Zhang, Y., Kumar, A., Zavadskas, E., & Streimikiene, D. (2020). Measuring the impact of renewable energy, public health expenditure, logistics, and environmental performance on sustainable economic growth. *Sustainable Development (Bradford)*, 28(4), 833–843. DOI: 10.1002/sd.2034

Kidd, C. V. (1992). The Evolution of Sustainability. *Journal of Agricultural & Environmental Ethics*, 5(1), 1–26. DOI: 10.1007/BF01965413

Kimberly, J., & Bouchikhi, H. (1995). The dynamics of organizational development and change: How the past shapes the present and constrains the future. *Organization Science*, 6(1), 9–18. DOI: 10.1287/orsc.6.1.9

Kim, J. W., Choi, J., Qualls, W., & Han, K. (2008). It Takes a Marketplace Community to Raise Brand Commitment: The Role of Online Communities. *Journal of Marketing Management*, 24(3), 409–431. DOI: 10.1362/026725708X306167

Kim, W., & Braun, J. E. (2020). Development, implementation, and evaluation of a fault detection and diagnostics system based on integrated virtual sensors and fault impact models. *Energy and Building*, 226, 110368. DOI: 10.1016/j.enbuild.2020.110368

Kim, Y. (2020). Managing supply chain disruptions with resilience strategies: A review and future research directions. *Journal of Business Logistics*, 41(2), 123–137.

Kirchherr, J., Yang, N.-H. N., Schulze-Spüntrup, F., Heerink, M. J., & Hartley, K. (2023). Conceptualizing the circular economy (revisited): An analysis of 221 definitions. *Resources, Conservation and Recycling*, 194, 107001. DOI: 10.1016/j.resconrec.2023.107001

Kohler, T., Fueller, J., Matzler, K., Stieger, D., & Füller, . (2011). Co-creation in virtual worlds: The design of the user experience. *Management Information Systems Quarterly*, 35(3), 773. DOI: 10.2307/23042808

Kolla, J. (2017). *How Artificial Intelligence benefits companies and ups their game*. MINT.

Konlechner, S., Güttel, W., & Keller, A. (2023). Ambidexterity for continuous change: Forms, operating conditions & organizational learning. In Güttel, W. (Ed.), *Successful in turbulent times. Leadership, change management and ambidexterity* (pp. 302–328). Nomos.

Konstantinou, C., & Mohanty, S. P. (2020). Cybersecurity for the smart grid. *Computer*, 53(5), 10–12. DOI: 10.1109/MC.2020.2975901

Korhonen, J., Honkasalo, A., & Seppälä, J. (2018). Circular economy: The concept and its limitations. *Ecological Economics*, 143, 37–46. DOI: 10.1016/j.ecolecon.2017.06.041

Kotler, P., & Lee, N. (2005). *Corporate Social Responsibility: Doing the Most Good for Your Company and Your Cause*. Wiley.

Kozhevnikov, M., Evans, C., & Kosslyn, S. M. (2014). Cognitive Style as Environmentally Sensitive Individual Differences in Cognition: A Modern Synthesis and Applications in Education, Business, and Management. *Psychological Science in the Public Interest*, 15(1), 3–33. DOI: 10.1177/1529100614525555 PMID: 26171827

Krause, J., Ruxton, G. D., & Krause, S. (2010). Swarm Intelligence in Animals and Humans. *Trends in Ecology & Evolution*, 25(1), 28–34. DOI: 10.1016/j.tree.2009.06.016 PMID: 19735961

Kubus, R. (2020). *Innovation Ecosystems in the European Union*. UNED.

Kuhn, T. (2017). *The structure of scientific revolutions*. The University of Chicago Press.

Kuldas, S., & Foody, M. (2022). Neither resiliency-trait nor resilience-state: Transactional Resiliency/e. *Youth & Society*, 54(8), 1352–1376. DOI: 10.1177/0044118X211029309

Kumar, N. (2019). Corporate Social Responsibility: An Analysis of Impact and Challenges in India. *International Journal of Social Sciences. Management and Entrepreneurship*, 3(2), 53–63.

Kumar, P. (2023). Gig Workers in Chhattisgarh: Emerging Opportunities in the New Economy. *Central Asian Journal of Innovations on Tourism Management and Finance*, 4(6), 140–148.

Kurtzberg, T. (2014). *Virtual teams: Mastering communication and collaboration in the digital age*. Bloomsbury Publishing USA. DOI: 10.5040/9798216032564

Kurvers, R. H. J. M., Wolf, M., Naguib, M., & Krause, J. (2015). Self-organized flexible leadership promotes collective intelligence in human groups. *Royal Society Open Science*, 2(12), 150222. Advance online publication. DOI: 10.1098/rsos.150222 PMID: 27019718

Lampón, J. F. (2020). The impact of uncertainty on production relocation: Implications from a regional perspective. *Papers in Regional Science*, 99(3), 427–446. DOI: 10.1111/pirs.12493

Lampón, J. F. (2023). Efficiency in design and production to achieve sustainable development challenges in the automobile industry: Modular electric vehicle platforms. *Sustainable Development (Bradford)*, 31(1), 26–38. DOI: 10.1002/sd.2370

Lampón, J. F., Cabanelas, P., & Delgado-Guzmán, J. A. (2018). Keys in the evolution of Mexico within the global value chain in the automobile components industry: The case of Bajio. *El Trimestre Economico*, 85(3), 483–514.

Lampón, J. F., Lago-Peñas, S., & Cabanelas, P. (2016). Can the periphery achieve core? The Case of the automobile components industry in Spain. *Papers in Regional Science*, 95(3), 595–612. DOI: 10.1111/pirs.12146

Lampón, J. F., Lago-Peñas, S., & González-Benito, J. (2015). International relocation and production geography in the European automobile components sector: The case of Spain. *International Journal of Production Research*, 53(5), 1409–1424. DOI: 10.1080/00207543.2014.942757

Lampón, J. F., & Muñoz-Dueñas, P. (2023). Are sustainable mobility firms reshaping the traditional relationships in the automotive industry value chain? *Journal of Cleaner Production*, 413, 137522. DOI: 10.1016/j.jclepro.2023.137522

Lampón, J. F., Pérez-Moure, H., Carballo-Cruz, F., & Velando-Rodríguez, M. E. (2024). New mobility technologies and regional status in the automotive industry value chain: The case of Spain and Portugal. *Technology in Society*, 78, 102624. DOI: 10.1016/j.techsoc.2024.102624

Lampón, J. F., Rodríguez-De La Fuente, M., & Fraiz-Brea, J. A. (2022). The dilemma of domestic suppliers on the periphery of the automotive industry global value chain. *Kybernetes*, 51(12), 3637–3655. DOI: 10.1108/K-01-2021-0073

Landemore, H. (2013). *Democratic reason: politics, collective intelligence, and the rule of the many*. Princeton University Press.

Landemore, H., & Elster, J. (Eds.). (2012). *Collective Wisdom: Principles and Mechanisms*. Cambridge University Press. DOI: 10.1017/CBO9780511846427

Langley, A., & Tsoukas, H. (2017). Introduction. In *The SAGE Handbook of Process Organization Studies* (pp. 1–25). SAGE Publications.

Lazarsfeld, P. (1994). The controversy over detailed interviews. *Public Opinion Quarterly*, 38–60.

Leander, A. (2009). *Habitus and Field. Department of Intercultural Communication and Management*. Copenhagen Business School. DOI: 10.1093/acrefore/9780190846626.013.51

Lechner, U., & Hummel, J. (2002). Business models and system architectures of virtual communities: From a sociological phenomenon to peer-to-peer architectures. *International Journal of Electronic Commerce*, 6(3), 41–53. DOI: 10.1080/10864415.2002.11044242

Lee, M. Y., & Edmondson, A. C. (2017). Self-managing organizations: Exploring the limits of less-hierarchical organizing. *Research in Organizational Behavior*, 37, 35–58. DOI: 10.1016/j.riob.2017.10.002

Lee, Y., & Kim, J. (2021). Cultivating employee creativity through strategic internal communication: The role of leadership, symmetry, and feedback seeking behaviors. *Public Relations Review*, 47(1), 101998. DOI: 10.1016/j.pubrev.2020.101998

Leif, W. (2021). John Rawls. *The Stanford Encyclopedia of Philosophy*. https://plato.stanford.edu/entries/rawls/

Leimeister, J. M. (2010). Collective intelligence. *Business & Information Systems Engineering*, 2(4), 245–248. DOI: 10.1007/s12599-010-0114-8

Leminen, S., Rajahonka, M., Wendelin, R., Westerlund, M., & Nyström, A. (2022). Autonomous vehicle solutions and their digital servitization business models. *Technological Forecasting and Social Change*, 185, 122070. DOI: 10.1016/j.techfore.2022.122070

Leonard, N. E., & Levin, S. A. (2022). Collective Intelligence as a Public Good. *Collective Intelligence*, 1(1), 1–18. DOI: 10.1177/26339137221083293

Levit, G. (2000). The Biosphere and Noosphere theories of V. I. Vernadsky and P. Teilhard de Chardin: A Methodological Essay. *Archives Internationales d'Histoire des Sciences*, 50(144), 160–176.

Lévy, P. (1997). *Collective Intelligence*. Perseus Books.

Levy, P. (1997). *Collective intelligence: Mankind's emerging world in cyberspace*. Plenum Press.

Levy, P. (1997). Vers L'intelligence Collective. *Sciences Humaines*, 59, 31.

Lévy, P. (2005). Collective Intelligence, a Civilization: Towards a Method of Positive Interpretation. *International Journal of Politics Culture and Society*, 18(3/4), 189–198.

Lewis, M. W. (2000). Exploring paradox: Toward a more comprehensive guide. *Academy of Management Review*, 25(4), 760–777. DOI: 10.2307/259204

Licklider, J. (1960). *Man-Computer Symbiosis. IRE Transactions on Human Factors in Electronics*, 4–11.

Li, J. Y., Sun, R., Tao, W., & Lee, Y. (2021). Employee coping with organizational change in the face of a pandemic: The role of transparent internal communication. *Public Relations Review*, 47(1), 101984. DOI: 10.1016/j.pubrev.2020.101984 PMID: 36568504

Li, J., Deng, D., Zhao, J., Cai, D., Hu, W., Zhang, M., & Huang, Q. (2020). A novel hybrid short-term load forecasting method of smart grid using MLR and LSTM neural network. *IEEE Transactions on Industrial Informatics*, 17(4), 2443–2452. DOI: 10.1109/TII.2020.3000184

Lindberg, K., & Czarniawska, B. (2006). Knotting the action net, or organizing between organizations. *Scandinavian Journal of Management*, 22(4), 292–306. DOI: 10.1016/j.scaman.2006.09.001

Lings, I. (2004). Internal market orientation: Construct and consequences. *Journal of Business Research*, 57(4), 405–413. DOI: 10.1016/S0148-2963(02)00274-6

Lin, J., Liu, S., & Wang, G. (2023). Stability analysis and control parameter optimization of multi-VSG parallel grid-connected system. *Electric Power Systems Research*, 221, 109478. DOI: 10.1016/j.epsr.2023.109478

Lin, M., Xie, M., & Li, Z. (2023). Organizational error tolerance and change-oriented organizational citizenship behavior: Mediating role of psychological empowerment and moderating role of public service motivation. *Psychology Research and Behavior Management*, 16, 4133–4153. DOI: 10.2147/PRBM.S431373 PMID: 37850190

Liu, T., & Yu, Z. (2022). The Relationship between Open Technological Innovation, Intellectual Property Rights Capabilities, Network Strategy, and AI Technology under the Internet of Things. *Operations Management Research : Advancing Practice Through Research*, 15(3–4), 793–808. DOI: 10.1007/s12063-021-00242-8

Locke, J. (1690). *Second Treatise of Government*. Hackett.

Locke, J., Hume, D., & Rousseau, J. (1960). *Social Contract, Essays by Locke, Hume and Rousseau*. Oxford University Press.

López, R. (2010). Sustainable Economic Development: On the Coexistence of Resource-Dependent and Resource-Impacting Industries. *Environment and Development Economics*, 15(6), 687–705. DOI: 10.1017/S1355770X10000331

Lovelock, J. (1979). *Gaia: A New look at Life on Earth*. Oxford University Press.

Lucia, S. (2016). Análisis de componentes y definición del concepto resiliencia: una revisión narrativa. Investig. psicol.

Lusch, R. F., & Nambisan, S. (2015). Service innovation: A service-dominant logic perspective. *Management Information Systems Quarterly*, 39(1), 155–175. DOI: 10.25300/MISQ/2015/39.1.07

Lu, X., & Zhou, K. (2024). A distributionally robust optimization approach for optimal load dispatch of energy hub considering multiple energy storage units and demand response programs. *Journal of Energy Storage*, 78, 110085. DOI: 10.1016/j.est.2023.110085

Lu, Y., Zhang, M., Yang, M., & Wang, Y. (2023). Sustainable human resource management practices, employee resilience, and employee outcomes: Toward common good values. *Human Resource Management*, 62(3), 331–353. DOI: 10.1002/hrm.22153

Madhok, A., & Keyhani, M. (2012). Acquisitions as a strategy for globalization: A review and theoretical integration. *Journal of International Business Studies*, 43(3), 234–259.

Madni, A. M., & Jackson, S. (2009). Towards a conceptual framework for resilience engineering. *IEEE Systems Journal*, 3(2), 181–191. DOI: 10.1109/JSYST.2009.2017397

Ma, F., Xue, T., & Huang, S. (2020). On the Conceptual Framework of Tourism Complex Research from the Perspective of the Theory of Complex Adaptive System. *Tourism Management and Technology Economy*, 3, 1–15.

Mahela, O. P., Khosravy, M., & Gupta, N. (2022). Comprehensive Overview of Multi-agent Systems for Controlling Smart Grids. *CSEE Journal of Power and Energy Systems*, 8(1), 115–131. DOI: 10.17775/CSEEJPES.2020.03390

Mahmood, Z. (2020). *Connected vehicles in the Internet of Things*. Springer. DOI: 10.1007/978-3-030-36167-9

Mahmoud, M. A., Md Nasir, N. R., Gurunathan, M., Raj, P., & Mostafa, S. A. (2021). The current state of the art in research on predictive maintenance in smart grid distribution network: Fault's types, causes, and prediction methods—A systematic review. *Energies*, 14(16), 5078. DOI: 10.3390/en14165078

Mainardes, E. W., Teixeira, A., & Romano, P. C. S. (2017). Determinants of co-creation in banking services. *International Journal of Bank Marketing*, 35(2), 187–204. DOI: 10.1108/IJBM-10-2015-0165

Maitlis, S., & Christianson, M. (2014). Sensemaking in organizations: Taking stock and moving forward. *The Academy of Management Annals*, 8(1), 57–125. DOI: 10.5465/19416520.2014.873177

Majumdar, S., Roy, S., Bose, A., & Chowdhury, I. R. (2023). Multiscale GIS based-model to Assess Urban Social Vulnerability and Associated Risk: Evidence from 146 Urban Centers of Eastern India. *Sustainable Cities and Society*, 96, 104692. DOI: 10.1016/j.scs.2023.104692

Makrooni, G. (2020). From Challenge to Empowerment. *Journal of Ethnic and Cultural Studies*, 7(3), 112–128. DOI: 10.29333/ejecs/522

Malone, T., & Bernstein, M. (2015). Introduction. In Malone, T., & Bernstein, M. (Eds.), *Handbook of Collective Intelligence* (pp. 1–15). The MIT Press.

Mannix, E., Neale, M., & Northcraft, G. (1995). Equity, equality, or need? The effects of organizational culture on the allocation of benefits and burdens. *Organizational Behavior and Human Decision Processes*, 63(3), 276–286. DOI: 10.1006/obhd.1995.1079

Mann, R. P., & Helbing, D. (2017). Optimal Incentives for Collective Intelligence. *Proceedings of the National Academy of Sciences of the United States of America*, 114(20), 5077–5082. DOI: 10.1073/pnas.1618722114 PMID: 28461491

Manservigi, L., Bahlawan, H., Losi, E., Morini, M., Spina, P. R., & Venturini, M. (2022). A diagnostic approach for fault detection and identification in district heating networks. *Energy*, 251, 123988. DOI: 10.1016/j.energy.2022.123988

March, J. G. (1991). Exploration and Exploitation in Organizational Learning. *Organization Science*, 2(1), 71–87. DOI: 10.1287/orsc.2.1.71

Marlin, S. (2024). A comprehensive comparative study on intelligence based optimization algorithms used for maximum power tracking in grid-PV systems. *Sustainable Computing : Informatics and Systems*, 41, 100946. DOI: 10.1016/j.suscom.2023.100946

Martínez-Martínez, A., Cegarra-Navarro, J.-G., Garcia-Perez, A., & De Valon, T. (2023). Active listening to customers: Eco-innovation through value co-creation in the textile industry. *Journal of Knowledge Management*, 27(7), 1810–1829. DOI: 10.1108/JKM-04-2022-0309

Martin, F. (1995). *Comunicación en Empresas e Instituciones: de la Consultora a la Dirección de Comunicación*. Universidad de Salamanca.

Martín, M., & González, T. (2016). *Negocios internacionales y estrategias empresariales para la sustentabilidad*. UNAM.

Marx, K. (1875). Critique of the Gotha Program. In R. C. Tucker (Ed.), *The Marx-Engels Reader* (pp. 525-541). W. W. Norton (1978).

Mashingaidze, S. (2014). Benefits of Collective Intelligence: Swarm Intelligent Foraging. *Journal of Governance and Regulation*, 3(4), 193–201. DOI: 10.22495/jgr_v3_i4_c2_p2

Mastropietro, C., & Vervaeke, J. (2023). What is a Meaning Crisis? *The Side View*

Matzler, K., Strobl, A., & Bailom, F. (2016). Leadership and the wisdom of crowds: How to tap into the collective intelligence of an organization. *Strategy and Leadership*, 44(1), 30–35. DOI: 10.1108/SL-06-2015-0049

Mazaro, R., & Varzin, G. (2008). Modelos de Competitividad para Destinos Turísticos en el Marco de la Sostenibilidad. *Revista de Administração contemporánea*, 12, 789-809.

Mazzucato, M., Schaake, M., Krier, S., & Entsminger, J. (2022). Governing artificial intelligence in the public interest. UCL Institute for Innovation and Public Purpose, *Working Paper Series* (IIPP WP 2022-12). https://www.ucl.ac.uk/bartlett/public-purpose/wp2022-12

McClelland, D. C. (1961). *The Achieving Society*. D. Van Nostrand Company. DOI: 10.1037/14359-000

McGowan, A. (2016). Khadi curtains and swadeshi bed covers: Textiles and the changing possibilities of home in western India, 1900-1960. *Modern Asian Studies*, 50(2), 518–563. DOI: 10.1017/S0026749X14000705

McPhee, R., & Zaug, P. (2009). The communicative constitution of organizations. In Putnam, L., & Nicotera, A. M. (Eds.), *Building theories of organization: the constitutive role of communication* (pp. 21–48). Routledge.

McWilliams, A., & Siegel, D. (2001). Corporate Social Responsibility: A Theory of the Firm Perspective. *Academy of Management Review*, 26(1), 117–127. DOI: 10.2307/259398

Meadowcroft, J. (2024). Sustainability. *Britannica*. https://www.britannica.com/science/sustainability#ref1225913

Medina, E., Mazaira, A., & Alén, E. (2022). Innovation in the broadcasters' business model: A bibliometric and review approach. *European Research on Management and Business Economics*, 28(3), 100202. DOI: 10.1016/j.iedeen.2022.100202

Mei, S., Tan, Q., Liu, Y., Trivedi, A., & Srinivasan, D. (2023). Optimal bidding strategy for virtual power plant participating in combined electricity and ancillary services market considering dynamic demand response price and integrated consumption satisfaction. *Energy*, 284, 128592. DOI: 10.1016/j.energy.2023.128592

Messinger, P. R., Stroulia, E., Lyons, K., Bone, M., Niu, R. H., Smirnov, K., & Perelgut, S. (2009). Virtual Worlds - Past, Present, and Future: New Directions in Social Computing. *Decision Support Systems*, 47(3), 204–228. DOI: 10.1016/j.dss.2009.02.014

Miles, R., Snow, C., Meyer, A., & Coleman, H.Jr. (1978). Organizational Strategy, Structure, and Process. *Academy of Management Review*, 3(3), 546–562. https://www.jstor.org/stable/257544. DOI: 10.5465/amr.1978.4305755 PMID: 10238389

Ming, W., Xie, Z., Ma, J., Du, J., Zhang, G., Cao, C., & Zhang, Y. (2021). Critical review on sustainable techniques in electrical discharge machining. *Journal of Manufacturing Processes*, 72, 375–399. DOI: 10.1016/j.jmapro.2021.10.035

Mintzberg, H. (1983). *Power in and around organizations*. Prentice Hall.

Mohammad, N., & Mishra, Y. (2019). Demand-side management and demand response for smart grid. Smart grids and their communication systems, 197-231.

Mohammadi, F. (2021). Emerging challenges in smart grid cybersecurity enhancement: A review. *Energies*, 14(5), 1380. DOI: 10.3390/en14051380

Mokhtar, I., Abdullah, N., Ismael, D., Othman, B., & Ali, R. (2019). The Development of training participation conceptual framework among academic staff: A qualitative study based on training officers perception at Malaysian public universities. *International Journal of Psychosocial Rehabilitation*, 23(3), 544–572. DOI: 10.37200/IJPR/V23I3/PR190346

Mokhtari, S., & Yen, K. K. (2024). False data injection attack detection, isolation, and identification in industrial control systems based on machine learning: Application in load frequency control. *Electronics (Basel)*, 13(16), 3239. Advance online publication. DOI: 10.3390/electronics13163239

Monett, D., Lewis, C. W., Thórisson, K. R., Bach, J., Baldassarre, G., Granato, G., & Shevlin, H. (2020). Introduction to the JAGI special issue 'On defining artificial intelligence'–commentaries and author's response. *Journal of Artificial General Intelligence*, 11(2), 1–100. DOI: 10.2478/jagi-2020-0003

Montaño, L. (2001). Los nuevos desafíos de la docencia. Hacia la construcción-siempre inacabada- de la Universidad. In *Universidad, organización y sociedad: arreglos y controversias* (p. 105-132). Miguel Ángel Porrúa.

Montes, J. O., & Olleros, F. X. (2020). Microfactories and the new economies of scale and scope. *Journal of Manufacturing Technology Management*, 31(1), 72–90. DOI: 10.1108/JMTM-07-2018-0213

Moore, J. F. (1996). *The death of competition: Leadership and strategy in the age of business ecosystems*. Harper Business.

Moore, J. F. (2006). Business ecosystems and the view from the firm. *Antitrust Bulletin*, 51(1), 31–75. DOI: 10.1177/0003603X0605100103

Morando, M., Zehnter, M., & Platania, S. (2023). Reverse Sexism and Its Impact on Job Satisfaction and Career Planning: Italian Validation of the "Belief in Sexism Shift Scale". *Social Sciences (Basel, Switzerland)*, 12(6), 357. DOI: 10.3390/socsci12060357

Moran, E., & Gossieaux, F. (2010). Marketing in a Hyper-Social World: The Tribalization of Business Study and Characteristics of Successful Online Communities. *Journal of Advertising Research*, 50(3), 232–239. DOI: 10.2501/S0021849910091397

Moreira, C., Ferreira, R., & Santos, T. (2021). Smart Tourism and Local Heritage: Phygital Experiences and the Development of Geotourism Routes. In Oliveira, L., Amaro, A., & Melro, A. (Eds.), *Handbook of Research on Cultural Heritage and Its Impact on Territory Innovation and Development* (pp. 206–232). IGI Global. DOI: 10.4018/978-1-7998-6701-2.ch012

Morel, L., Dupont, L., & Boudarel, M.-R. (2018). Innovation spaces: new places for collective intelligence? In U. D (Ed.), *Collective Innovation Processes*. John Wiley & Sons. DOI: 10.1002/9781119557883.ch5

Morgan, M. (2023). *Model Narratives*. ICI Berlin. Retrieved from https://www.ici-berlin.org/events/mary-s-morgan/DOI: 10.25620/e230530

Moriano, J., Topa, G., Valero, E., & Lévy, J. (2009). Identificación organizacional y conducta "intraemprendedora". *Anales de Psicología/Annals of Psychology, 25*(2), 277-287.

Moriano, J., Molero, F., Topa, G., & Lévy Mangin, J. (2014). The influence of transformational leadership and organizational identification on intrapreneurship. *The International Entrepreneurship and Management Journal*, 10(1), 103–119. DOI: 10.1007/s11365-011-0196-x

Morozov, E. (2013). *To Save Everything, Click Here. The Folly of Technological Solutionism*. PublicAffairs.

Morris, D. R. (1991). Exergy analysis and cumulative exergy consumption of complex chemical processes: The industrial chlor-alkali processes. *Chemical Engineering Science*, 46(2), 459–465. DOI: 10.1016/0009-2509(91)80007-L

Mukherjee, D., Nuruzzaman, N., Gaur, A., & Singh, D. (2023). Pro-market reforms and the outsourcing tradeoffs: Evidence from the transition economies. *International Business Review*, 32(4), 102105. DOI: 10.1016/j.ibusrev.2023.102105

Mulgan, G. (2018a). Artificial intelligence and collective intelligence: The emergence of a new field. *AI & Society*, 33(4), 631–632. DOI: 10.1007/s00146-018-0861-5

Mulgan, G. (2018b). *Big Mind. How Collective Intelligence Can Change Our World.* Princeton University Press. DOI: 10.1515/9781400888511

Müller, S., Kirst, A., Bergmann, H., & Bird, B. (2023). Entrepreneurs' actions and venture success: A structured literature review and suggestions for future research. *Small Business Economics*, 60(1), 199–226. DOI: 10.1007/s11187-022-00644-3

Murino, T., Romano, E., & Santillo, L. C. (2011, December). Supply chain performance sustainability through resilience function. In *Proceedings of the 2011 Winter Simulation Conference (WSC)* (pp. 1600-1611). IEEE. DOI: 10.1109/WSC.2011.6147877

Nambisan, P., & Watt, J. H. (2011). Managing Customer Experiences in Online Product Communities. *Journal of Business Research*, 64(8), 889–895. DOI: 10.1016/j.jbusres.2010.09.006

Nambisan, S. (2018). Digital innovation and dynamic capabilities: How digital transformation shapes firms' dynamic capabilities. *Information Systems Research*, 29(2), 461–475.

Nasir, T., Bukhari, S. S. H., Raza, S., Munir, H. M., Abrar, M., Muqeet, H. A. U., Bhatti, K. L., Ro, J.-S., & Masroor, R. (2021). Recent challenges and methodologies in smart grid demand side management: State-of-the-art literature review. *Mathematical Problems in Engineering*, 2021, 1–16. DOI: 10.1155/2021/5821301

Nguyen, T. N., Liu, B. H., Nguyen, N. P., & Chou, J. T. (2020, June). Cyber security of smart grid: attacks and defenses. In ICC 2020-2020 IEEE International Conference on Communications (ICC) (pp. 1-6). IEEE. DOI: 10.1109/ICC40277.2020.9148850

Nie, S., & Fan, B. (2023). The Dynamics of Collaborative Emergency Capability: A Qualitative Comparative Analysis Based on Contingency Plans. *Natural Hazards Review*, 24(2), 05023002. DOI: 10.1061/NHREFO.NHENG-1645

Nigam, A., & Ocasio, W. (2010). Event attention, environmental sensemaking, and change in institutional logics: An inductive analysis of the effects of public attention to Clinton's health care reform initiative. *Organization Science*, 21(4), 823–841. DOI: 10.1287/orsc.1090.0490

Nik, V. M., & Moazami, A. (2021). Using Collective Intelligence to Enhance Demand Flexibility and Climate Resilience in Urban Areas. *Applied Energy*, 281, 1–17. DOI: 10.1016/j.apenergy.2020.116106

Nilsson, N. J. (2005). Human-Level Artificial Intelligence? Be Serious! *AI Magazine*. Advance online publication. DOI: 10.1609/aimag.v26i4.1850

Nishat, F. M., Chakraborty, R., Oh, H.-J., Yoo, D.-Y., Mohapoo, R., & Yeon, J. H. (2023). Design and performance evaluation of an electrically heated concrete panel for sustainable winter maintenance. *Developments in the Built Environment*, 16, 100259. DOI: 10.1016/j.dibe.2023.100259

Nkhata, A., Breen, C., & Freimund, W. (2008). Resilient social relationships and collaboration in the management of social–ecological systems. *Ecology and Society*, 13(1), art2. DOI: 10.5751/ES-02164-130102

Nussbaum, M. (1992). Human Functioning and Social Justice: In Defense of Aristotelian Essentialism. *Political Theory*, 20(2), 202–246. DOI: 10.1177/0090591792020002002

Nussbaum, M. (2000). Aristotle, Politics, and Human Capabilities: A Response to Antony, Arneson, Charlesworth, and Mulgan. *Ethics*, 111(1), 102–140. DOI: 10.1086/233421

O'Hern, M., & Rindfleisch, A. (2010). 'Customer co-creation: A typology and research agenda', *Review of Marketing Research. Emerald Group Publishing*, 6, 84–106.

Oad, A., Ahmad, H. G., Talpur, M. S. H., Zhao, C., & Pervez, A. (2023). Green smart grid predictive analysis to integrate sustainable energy of emerging V2G in smart city technologies. *Optik (Stuttgart)*, 272, 170146. DOI: 10.1016/j.ijleo.2022.170146

Ogali, O. I. O., & Orodu, O. D. (2022). Fault characterization and flow barrier detection using capacitance-resistance model and diagnostic plots. *Journal of Petroleum Science Engineering*, 209, 109817. DOI: 10.1016/j.petrol.2021.109817

Oh, L. & Teo, H., (2010). Consumer value co-creation in a hybrid commerce service-delivery system. International Journal of Electronic Commerce, 14(3), 35-62.

Omitaomu, O. A., & Niu, H. (2021). Artificial intelligence techniques in smart grid: A survey. *Smart Cities*, 4(2), 548–568. DOI: 10.3390/smartcities4020029

Onu, P., Mbohwa, C., & Pradhan, A. (2023). Advancements, challenges, and recommendations for resilient and decarbonized future smart grids. International Conference on Electrical, Computer and Energy Technologies, ICECET 2023. . 2023.10389344DOI: 10.1109/ICECET58911.2023.10389344

Osterwalder, A., & Pigneur, Y. (2010). *Business model generation: a handbook for visionaries, game changers, and challengers*. Wiley.

Oxfam India. (2023). *Survival of the Richest: The India Story*. Oxfam India.

Oxford-Review. (2023, March 21). *Collective Intelligence*. Oxford.

Page, S. E. (2007). Making the Difference: Applying a Logic of Diversity. *The Academy of Management Perspectives*, 21(4), 6–20. DOI: 10.5465/amp.2007.27895335

Pal, C., & Shankar, R. (2023). A hierarchical performance evaluation approach for the sustainability of smart grid. *International Journal of Energy Sector Management*, 17(3), 569–594. DOI: 10.1108/IJESM-02-2022-0011

Parecattil, J. (2020). *Darśanavī : A Theology of Inclusive Home in Saint Chavara*. Dharmaram Publications.

Parel, A., & Trivedi, L. (2009). Clothing Gandhi's nation: Homespun and modern India. *The Journal of Asian Studies*, 68(1), 329–331. DOI: 10.1017/S0021911809000552

Parker, L. D. (2023). Third sector crisis management and resilience: Reflections and directions. *Financial Accountability & Management*.

Patel, K. R. (2023). Enhancing Global Supply Chain Resilience: Effective Strategies for Mitigating Disruptions in an Interconnected World. *BULLET: Jurnal Multidisiplin Ilmu*, 2(1), 257–264.

Patuelli, A., Carungu, J., & Lattanzi, N. (2022). Drivers and Nuances of Sustainable Development Goals: Transcending Corporate Social Responsibility in Family Firms. *Journal of Cleaner Production*, 373, 133723. DOI: 10.1016/j.jclepro.2022.133723

Peerdom. (2019). Discovering the dark side of self-organization: 7 common challenges. Peerdom. Link: https://peerdom.medium.com/discovering-the-dark-side-of-self-organisation-7-common-challenges-272fafe98927

Pelacho, M., Rodríguez, H., Broncano, F., Kubus, R., García, F., Gavete, B., & Lafuente, A. (2021). Science as a commons: Improving the governance of knowledge through citizen science. In *The Science of Citizen Science* (pp. 57–78). Springer International Publishing. DOI: 10.1007/978-3-030-58278-4_4

Pendall, R., Foster, A., & Cowell, M. (2009). Resilience and regions: Building understanding of the metaphor. *Cambridge Journal of Regions, Economy and Society*, 3(1), 71–84. DOI: 10.1093/cjres/rsp028

Peng, B., Galley, M., He, P., Cheng, H., Xie, Y., Hu, Y., . . . Gao, J. (2023). Check your facts and try again: Improving large language models with external knowledge and automated feedback. arXiv preprint arXiv:2302.12813. https://doi.org//arXiv.2302.12813DOI: 10.48550

Perera, G. A., & Ranaweera, A. (2023). Fashion localism: Evaluation and extensions of utility in Sri Lankan fashion brands. *Research Journal of Textile and Apparel*, 27(2), 264–280. DOI: 10.1108/RJTA-08-2021-0099

Pérez, M. (2009) La relación entre la tecnología de la información, las prácticas de gestión de la calidad y el Desarrollo de las capacidades dinámicas: una aproximación empírica. Tesis Doctoral, Universidad de Granada, España.

Pérez-Moure, H., Lampón, J. F., & Cabanelas, P. (2023a). Mobility business models toward a digital tomorrow: Challenges for automotive manufacturers. *Futures*, 103309. Advance online publication. DOI: 10.1016/j.futures.2023.103309

Pérez-Moure, H., Lampón, J. F., Velando-Rodríguez, M. E., & Rodríguez-Comesaña, L. (2023b). Revolutionizing the road: How sustainable, autonomous, and connected vehicles are changing digital mobility business models. *European Research on Management and Business Economics*, 29(3), 100230. Advance online publication. DOI: 10.1016/j.iedeen.2023.100230

Peterson, J. (2017a). *Personality*. Toronto University.

Peterson, J. (2017b). *Maps of meaning*. Toronto University.

Peterson, J. B. (2013). Three forms of meaning and the management of complexity. In Markman, K. D., Proulx, T., & Lindberg, M. J. (Eds.), *The psychology of meaning* (pp. 17–48). American Psychological Association., DOI: 10.1037/14040-002

Pettit, T. J., Croxton, K. L., & Fiksel, J. (2013). Ensuring supply chain resilience: Development and implementation of an assessment tool. *Journal of Business Logistics*, 34(1), 46–76. DOI: 10.1111/jbl.12009

Pham, C. H., Nguyen, T. V., Bach, T. N., Le, C. Q., & Nguyen, H. V. (2022). Collective sensemaking within institutions: Control of the COVID-19 epidemic in Vietnam. *Public Administration and Development*, 1–13. DOI: 10.1002/pad.1996 PMID: 36248011

Pham, Q., Nguyen, D., Mirjalili, S., Hoang, D., Nguyen, D., Pathirana, P., & Hwang, W. (2021). Swarm intelligence for next-generation networks: Recent advances and applications. *Journal of Network and Computer Applications*, 191, 103141. DOI: 10.1016/j.jnca.2021.103141

Pinto, L. (2023). Investigating the relationship between green supply chain purchasing practices and firms' performance. *Journal of Industrial Engineering and Management*, 16(1), 78–101. DOI: 10.3926/jiem.3686

Pirages, D. (1977). *The Sustainable Society: Implications for Limited Growth*. Praeger.

Piribauer, B., Bartl, A., & Ipsmiller, W. (2021). Enzymatic textile recycling—Best practices and outlook. *Waste Management & Research*, 39(10), 1277–1290. DOI: 10.1177/0734242X211029167 PMID: 34238113

Połok, B., & Bilski, P. (2021). Intelligent diagnostic system for the rachet mechanism faults detection using acoustic analysis. *Measurement*, 183, 109637. DOI: 10.1016/j.measurement.2021.109637

Ponomarov, S. Y., & Holcomb, M. C. (2009). Understanding the concept of supply chain resilience. *International Journal of Logistics Management*, 20(1), 124–143. DOI: 10.1108/09574090910954873

Pooley, S. (2021). Coexistence for Whom? *Frontiers in Conservation Science*, 2, 1–7. DOI: 10.3389/fcosc.2021.726991

Poseck, B. V., Baquero, B. C., & Jiménez, M. L. V. (2006). La experiencia traumática desde la psicología positiva: resiliencia y crecimiento postraumático. Papeles del Psicólogo, 27(1), 40-49.

Powell, W. W., & Grodal, S. (2005). Networks of innovators. In Fagerberg, J., Mowery, D. C., & Nelson, R. R. (Eds.), *The Oxford Handbook of Innovation* (pp. 56–85). Oxford University Press.

Poyyamozhi, N., Senthil Kumar, S., & Ashok Kumar, R. (2024). An investigation into enhancing energy storage capacity of solar ponds integrated with nanoparticles through PCM coupling and RSM optimization. *Renewable Energy*, 221, 119733. DOI: 10.1016/j.renene.2023.119733

Pradono, N., Sulistyo, H., & Zulfa, M. (2024). Waqi'iyah networking power based on cross-function integration on marketing performance. *Quality - Access to Success*, 25(198).

Presthus, R. (1979). *The Organizational Society* (Revised Edition). St. Martin's Press Inc. DOI: 10.1007/978-1-349-16095-2

Prieto, J. (2015). *Gestión Estratégica Organizacional*. ECOE Ediciones, 1-8.

Provan, K. G., & Kenis, P. (2008). Modes of network governance: Structure, management, and effectiveness. *Journal of Public Administration: Research and Theory*, 18(2), 229–252. DOI: 10.1093/jopart/mum015

Puerta, M. E., Pindado, J., González, T. (2023). The resilience of corporate tourism: bleisure, digitalization, and sustainability. *Mercados y Negocios*, (48).

Purkarthofer, E., & Mäntysalo, R. (2022). Enhancing Knowledge, Skills, and Identity Development Through Collaborative Student-Led Learning: Experiences With the Gradual Empowerment of Students in a Planning Studio Course. *Journal of Planning Education and Research*.

Puttamadappa, C., & Parameshachari, B. D. (2019). Demand side management of small scale loads in a smart grid using glow-worm swarm optimization technique. *Microprocessors and Microsystems*, 71, 102886. DOI: 10.1016/j.micpro.2019.102886

Qaisar, F., & Muhamad, N. (2021). Internal marketing: A review and future research agenda. *Asia Pacific Business Review*, 27(2), 267–300. DOI: 10.1080/13602381.2021.1858590

Qiao, D., Yuan, W., & Li, H. (2024). Regulation and resilience: Panarchy analysis in forest socio-ecosystem of Northeast National Forest Region, China. *Journal of Environmental Management*, 353, 120295. DOI: 10.1016/j.jenvman.2024.120295 PMID: 38330839

Qing, L., Abbas, J., Najam, H., Ma, X., & Dagestani, A. A. (2024). Investment in renewable energy and green financing and their role in achieving carbon-neutrality and economic sustainability: Insights from Asian region. *Renewable Energy*, 221, 119830. DOI: 10.1016/j.renene.2023.119830

Quang, D. V., Milani, D., & Abu Zahra, M. (2023). A review of potential routes to zero and negative emission technologies via the integration of renewable energies with CO2 capture processes. *International Journal of Greenhouse Gas Control*, 124, 103862. DOI: 10.1016/j.ijggc.2023.103862

Quayson, M., Bai, C., Sun, L., & Sarkis, J. (2023). Building blockchain-driven dynamic capabilities for developing circular supply chain: Rethinking the role of sensing, seizing, and reconfiguring. *Business Strategy and the Environment*, 32(7), 4821–4840. DOI: 10.1002/bse.3395

Rae, D., & Blenker, P. (2024). The role of collective intelligence and collective agency in enterprising communities. *Journal of Enterprising Communities: People and Places in the Global Economy*, 18(1), 7–28. DOI: 10.1108/JEC-09-2022-0141

Rahbari, H. R., Mando, M., & Arabkoohsar, A. (2024). Real-time modeling and optimization of molten salt storage with supercritical steam cycle for sustainable power generation and grid support. *Process Safety and Environmental Protection*, 182, 866–879. DOI: 10.1016/j.psep.2023.12.024

Rai, A., Pavlou, P., Im, G. & Du, S. (2012). Interfirm IT capability profiles and communications for cocreating relational value: Evidence from the logistics industry. MIS Quarterly, 36(1), 233-262.

Raisch, S., & Birkinshaw, J. (2008). Organizational ambidexterity: Antecedents, outcomes, and moderators. *Journal of Management*, 34(3), 375–409. DOI: 10.1177/0149206308316058

Ramaswamy, V., & Ozcan, K. (2016). Brand value co-creation in a digitalized world: An integrative framework and research implications. *International Journal of Research in Marketing*, 33(1), 93–106. DOI: 10.1016/j.ijresmar.2015.07.001

Ramezani, J., & Camarinha-Matos, L. (2020). Approaches for Resilience and Antifragility in Collaborative Business Ecosystems. *Technological Forecasting and Social Change*, 151, 119846. Advance online publication. DOI: 10.1016/j.techfore.2019.119846

Ramprasad, C., Gwenzi, W., Chaukura, N., Izyan Wan Azelee, N., Upamali Rajapaksha, A., Naushad, M., & Rangabhashiyam, S. (2022). Strategies and options for the sustainable recovery of rare earth elements from electrical and electronic waste. *Chemical Engineering Journal*, 442, 135992. DOI: 10.1016/j.cej.2022.135992

Rapp, A., Beitelspacher, L. S., Grewal, D., & Hughes, D. E. (2013). Understanding social media effects across seller, retailer, and consumer interactions. Journal of the Academy of Marketing Science, 41(5), 547-566. doi:http://dx.doi.org.proxy.uwasa.fi/10.1007/s11747-013-0326-9

Raskin, P. (2006). *World Lines. Pathways, Pivots, and the Global Future*. Tellus Institute.

Rathore, A. K., Ilavarasan, P. V., & Dwivedi, Y. K. (2016). Social media content and product co-creation: An emerging paradigm. *Journal of Enterprise Information Management*, 29(1), 7–18. DOI: 10.1108/JEIM-06-2015-0047

Rawls, J. (1999). *A Theory of Justice* (Rev. Ed.). Harward University Press. DOI: 10.4159/9780674042582

Raworth, K. (2018). *Doughnut Economics: Seven Ways to Think Like a 21st-Century Economist*. Random House International.

Recker, M. M., Yuan, M., & Ye, L. (2013). CrowdTeaching: Supporting Teacher Collective Intelligence Communities. *Educational Technology*, 53(6), 18–23.

Rehan, M., Raza, M. A., & Abro, A. G. (2023). A sustainable use of biomass for electrical energy harvesting using distributed generation systems. *Energy*, 278, 128036. DOI: 10.1016/j.energy.2023.128036

Reidl, C., Kim, Y. J., Gupta, P., Malone, T. W., & Woolley, A. W. (2021). Quantifying Collective Intelligence in Huma Groups. *Proceedings of the National Academy of Sciences of the United States of America*, 118(21), 1–5.

Ren, H., Gao, D., Ma, Z., Zhang, S., & Sun, Y. (2024). Data-driven surrogate optimization for deploying heterogeneous multi-energy storage to improve demand response performance at building cluster level. *Applied Energy*, 356, 122312. DOI: 10.1016/j.apenergy.2023.122312

Renugadevi, N., Saravanan, S., & Sudha, C. N. (2023). IoT based smart energy grid for sustainable cites. *Materials Today: Proceedings*, 81, 98–104. DOI: 10.1016/j.matpr.2021.02.270

Reyes, R. (2009). Diccionario _ UCM. Retrieved from Habitus. De: https://webs.ucm. es/info/eurotheo/diccionario/H/habitus. htm

Rhaiem, K., & Halilem, N. (2023). The worst is not to fail, but to fail to learn from failure: A multi-method empirical validation of learning from innovation failure. *Technological Forecasting and Social Change*, 190, 122427. DOI: 10.1016/j.techfore.2023.122427

Rheingold, H. (2002). *Smart Mobs: The Next Social Revolution*. Perseus Books.

Richardson, J. (1986). 'The Forms of Capital. In Richardson (Ed.), *Handbook of Theory and Research for the Sociology of Education* (pp. 241-58). New York, Greenwood.

Ridley, M. (2020). *How innovation works: And why it flourishes in freedom*. Harper.

Ring, P. S., & Van de Ven, A. H. (1994). Developmental processes of cooperative interorganizational relationships. *Academy of Management Review*, 19(1), 90–118. DOI: 10.2307/258836

Ritchie, J., & Crouch, G. (2003). *The competitive destination*. CAB International Publishing.

Rodríguez, R., & Ricárdez, J. (2020). Aproximación a la gestión ambiental proactiva como capacidad dinámica en el sector turístico hotelero mexicano. Elementos determinantes para su desarrollo. *El Periplo Sustentable*, (38), 194–218. DOI: 10.36677/elperiplo.v0i38.7029

Romanelli, E. (1991). The Evolution of New Organizational Forms. *Annual Review of Sociology*, 17(1), 79–103. DOI: 10.1146/annurev.so.17.080191.000455

Romero, D., & Molina, A. (2011). Collaborative networked organizations and customer communities: Value co-creation and co-innovation in the networking era. *Production Planning and Control*, 22(5-6), 447–472. DOI: 10.1080/09537287.2010.536619

Rong, K., Hu, G., Lin, Y., Shi, Y., & Guo, L. (2015). Understanding business ecosystem using a 6C framework in Internet-of-Things-based sectors. *International Journal of Production Economics*, 159, 41–55. DOI: 10.1016/j.ijpe.2014.09.003

Rønne, A. (2012). Smart grids and intelligent energy systems: A European perspective. In *Energy Networks and the Law*. Innovative Solutions in Changing Markets. DOI: 10.1093/acprof:oso/9780199645039.003.0008

Rose, A. (2017). *Defining and measuring economic resilience from a societal, environmental and security perspective*. Springer Singapore., DOI: 10.1007/978-981-10-1533-5

Rough, J. (2008). The circle organization: Structuring for collective wisdom. In *Collective Intelligence: Creating a Prosperous World at Peace* (pp. 75-82). Earth Intelligence Network (EIN).

Rowe, L. I., Hattie, J., & Munro, J. (2024). High-performing teams: Is collective intelligence the answer? *PLoS One*, 19(8), e0307945. Advance online publication. DOI: 10.1371/journal.pone.0307945 PMID: 39133757

Russell, S. (2023). What AI Expert Prof Stuart J Russell: Said On Artificial Intelligence. Youtube. https://www.youtube.com/watch?v=Bzre5fWr6Ec

Russo, D., & Ciancarini, P. (2017). Towards antifragile software architectures. *Procedia Computer Science*, 109, 929–934. DOI: 10.1016/j.procs.2017.05.426

Saad, M. H., Hagelaar, G., Van Der Velde, G., & Omta, S. W. F. (2021). Conceptualization of SMEs' business resilience: A systematic literature review. *Cogent Business & Management*, 8(1), 1938347. DOI: 10.1080/23311975.2021.1938347

Sanahuja, J., & Rodríguez Díaz, J. (2023). The European Union and Latin America in the Interregnum: Limits and Challenges of a Needed Partnership. *Development Corporation Review*, 6(3).

Sánchez, M. (2016). Cultura y Comunicación Organizacional. In *Comunicación institucional y cambio social. Claves para la comprensión de los factores relacionales de la comunicación estratégica y el nuevo ecosistema comunicacional* (pp. 15-38).

Sanford, A. W. (2017). *Living Sustainably: What International Communities can teach us about Democracy, Simplicity, and Nonviolence*. University Press of Kentucky.

Sardesai, S., & Klingebiel, K. (2023). Maintaining viability by rapid supply chain adaptation using a process capability index. *Omega*, 115, 102778. DOI: 10.1016/j.omega.2022.102778

Sargeant, A., & Asif, S. (2000). Modelling internal communications in the financial services sector. *European Journal of Marketing*, 34(3/4), 299–317. DOI: 10.1108/03090560010311867

Sarker, S., Sahaym, A. & Bjørn-Andersen, N. (2012). Exploring value cocreation in relationships between an ERP vendor and its partners: A revelatory case study. MIS Quarterly, 36(1), 317-338.

Sarker, E., Halder, P., Seyedmahmoudian, M., Jamei, E., Horan, B., Mekhilef, S., & Stojcevski, A. (2021). Progress on the demand side management in smart grid and optimization approaches. *International Journal of Energy Research*, 45(1), 36–64. DOI: 10.1002/er.5631

Satish & Kishore. (2023). AI and ML for Intelligent Battery Management in the Age of Energy Efficiency. International Journal for Recent Developments in Science & Technology, 134-140.

Saul, J. (2022). *Collective trauma, collective healing: Promoting community resilience in the aftermath of disaster*. Routledge.

Schaltegger, S., Christ, K. L., Wenzig, J., & Burritt, R. L. (2022). Corporate sustainability management accounting and multi-level links for sustainability–A systematic review. *International Journal of Management Reviews*, 24(4), 480–500. DOI: 10.1111/ijmr.12288

Scheffler, I. (1967). *Science and Subjectivity*. The Bobbs-Merrill Company.

Schein, E. H. (2010). *Organizational culture and leadership* (4th ed.). Jossey-Bass.

Schnell, T. (2010). Existential Indifference: Another Quality of Meaning in Life. *Journal of Humanistic Psychology*, 50(3), 351–373. DOI: 10.1177/0022167809360259

Schoenmaker, D., & Schramade, W. (2019). *Principles of Sustainable Finance*. Oxford University Press.

Schönborn, G., Berlin, C., Pinzone, M., Hanisch, C., Georgoulias, K., & Lanz, M. (2019). Why social sustainability counts: The impact of corporate social sustainability culture on financial success. *Sustainable Production and Consumption*, 17, 1–10. DOI: 10.1016/j.spc.2018.08.008

Scott, R. (1998). *Institutions and organizations*. Sage Publications.

Sedarati, P., Santos, S., & Pintassilgo, P. (2018). System Dynamics in Tourism Planning and Development. *Tourism Planning & Development*, 1–25. DOI: 10.1080/21568316.2018.1436586

Sen, A. (1992). *Inequality Reexamined*. Harvard University Press.

Sen, A. (1997). *On Economic Inequality*. Clarendon Press.

Sen, A. (2009). *The Idea of Justice*. Harvard University Press.

Shah, C., & González, R. (2011). Evaluating the synergic effect of collaboration in information seeking. In *Proceedings of the 34th international ACM SIGIR conference on Research and Development in Information Retrieval* (pp. 913-922). DOI: 10.1145/2009916.2010038

Shah, N. (2018). The political economy of branding: Khadi, colonialism and Indian nationhood. *Journal of Historical Research in Marketing*, 10(3), 197–223. DOI: 10.1108/JHRM-06-2017-0035

Shayan, N. F., Mohabbati-Kalejahi, N., Alavi, S., & Zahed, M. A. (2022). Sustainable Development Goals (SDGs) as a Framework for Corporate Social Responsibility (CSR). *Sustainability (Basel)*, 14(3), 1222. DOI: 10.3390/su14031222

Sheng, X., Kim, W. J., Gupta, R., & Ji, Q. (2023). The impacts of oil price volatility on financial stress: Is the COVID-19 period different? *International Review of Economics & Finance*, 85, 520–532. DOI: 10.1016/j.iref.2023.02.006

Shen, Y., Huang, C., Chu, C., & Liao, H. (2010). Virtual community loyalty: An interpersonal-interaction perspective. *International Journal of Electronic Commerce*, 15(1), 49–74. DOI: 10.2753/JEC1086-4415150102

Shepherd, D., & Williams, T. (2023). Different response paths to organizational resilience. *Small Business Economics*, 61(1), 23–58. DOI: 10.1007/s11187-022-00689-4 PMID: 38625189

Shetty, S., & Potdar, P. (2023). A Study of Corporate CSR Spending of Companies Operating in Maharashtra. *The Online Journal of Distance Education and e-Learning : TOJDEL*, 11(1), 469–482.

Shittua, E., Tibrewala, A., Kalla, S., & Wang, X. (2021). Meta-analysis of the strategies for self-healing and resilience in power systems. *Advances in Applied Energy*, 4, 100036. DOI: 10.1016/j.adapen.2021.100036

Short, , Moss, T. W., & Lumpkin, G. T. (2009). Research in social entrepreneurship: Past contributions and future opportunities. *Strategic Entrepreneurship Journal*, 3(2), 161–194. DOI: 10.1002/sej.69

Shutterstock. (2023). Imágenes libres de regalías. Link: https://www.shutterstock .com/es/search/2023

Siemens. (2020). *MindSphere: The Industrial IoT as a service solution*. Siemens AG.

Sigala, M. (2018). Implementing social customer relationship management. *International Journal of Contemporary Hospitality Management*, 30(7), 2698–2726. DOI: 10.1108/IJCHM-10-2015-0536

Singh, N., Moid, S., Rushdi, N. J., & Shankar, N. (2024). Finding a digital silver line during COVID-19 pandemic: A case of Madhubani Paints. *Emerald Emerging Markets Case Studies*, 14(1), 1–26. Advance online publication. DOI: 10.1108/EEMCS-07-2023-0246

Singh, P., & Chaudhary, K. (2023). Jharcraft: A gift of transformational leadership in an Indian state-owned enterprise. *International Journal of Public Leadership*, 19(4), 339–354. DOI: 10.1108/IJPL-01-2023-0003

Singh, V., Mathur, J., & Bhatia, A. (2022). A comprehensive review: Fault detection, diagnostics, prognostics, and fault modeling in HVAC systems. *International Journal of Refrigeration*, 144, 283–295. DOI: 10.1016/j.ijrefrig.2022.08.017

Sisto, V. (2009). Cambios en el trabajo, identidad e inclusión social en Chile: Desafíos para la investigación. [Talca]. *Universum (Talca)*, 24(2), 192–216. DOI: 10.4067/S0718-23762009000200011

Skaržauskienė, A., & Mačiulienė, M. (2015). The Potential of Collective Intelligence in Online Community Projects. *Journal of Information Warfare*, 14(3), 66–74.

Smite, D., Moe, N., Hildrum, J., Gonzalez, J., & Mendez, D. (2023). Work-from-home is here to stay: Call for flexibility in post-pandemic work policies. *Journal of Systems and Software*, 195, 111552. DOI: 10.1016/j.jss.2022.111552 PMID: 36320721

Solé, R. V. (2011). *Phase Transitions*. Princeton University Press.

Soni, U., Jain, V., & Kumar, S. (2014). Measuring supply chain resilience using a deterministic modeling approach. *Computers & Industrial Engineering*, 74, 11–25. DOI: 10.1016/j.cie.2014.04.019

Soundri, G. M., Kavitha, S., & Kumar, B. S. (2023). Dimensional, moisture, and thermal properties of bi-layered knitted fabric for sportswear application. *Research Journal of Textile and Apparel*, 27(4), 543–559. DOI: 10.1108/RJTA-05-2021-0074

Speer, P. (2000). Intrapersonal and interactional empowerment: Implications for theory. *Journal of Community Psychology*, 28(1), 51–61. DOI: 10.1002/(SICI)1520-6629(200001)28:1<51::AID-JCOP6>3.0.CO;2-6

Spencer, B., & Guillen, F. (1899). *The Native Tribes of Central Australia.* The Macmillan. DOI: 10.2307/2842887

Stam, E. (2014). The Dutch entrepreneurial ecosystem. DOI: 10.2139/ssrn.2473475

Steggemann, M. (2023, May- August). Collective Intelligence synergizing into Collective Resilience. *Mercados y Negocios,* 65-82. DOI: 10.32870/myn.vi48.7686

Steggemann, M. (2015). *Complementarity between universalism and particularism in the filial of the German transnational located in Mexico.* Universidad La Salle. DOI: 10.13140/rg.2.1.3687.8564

Stevens, C. (2010). Are Women the Key to Sustainable Development? *Sustainable Development Insights*, 3(11), 1–8.

Stewart, K., & Perren, R. (2023). Under the spell of your smartphone: How dependence evokes a halo of trust in advertising. *Journal of Promotion Management*, 29(1), 106–124. DOI: 10.1080/10496491.2022.2108188

Stiegler, B. (2010). *What Makes Life Worth Living: On Pharmacology.* Polity Press.

Stiglitz, J. (2012). *The Price of Inequality: How Today's Divided Society Endangers Our Future.* W. W. Norton.

Strand, R., Freeman, R. E., & Hockerts, K. (2015). Corporate Social Responsibility and Sustainability in Scandinavia: An Overview. *Journal of Business Ethics*, 127(1), 1–15. DOI: 10.1007/s10551-014-2224-6

Stufflebeam, D. (1994). Empowerment evaluation, objectivist evaluation, and evaluation standards: Where the future of evaluation should not go and where it needs to go. *Evaluation Practice*, 15(3), 321–338. DOI: 10.1177/109821409401500313

Sturgeon, T. J., Van Biesebroeck, J., & Gereffi, G. (2008). Value chains, networks and clusters: Reframing the global automotive industry. *Journal of Economic Geography*, 8(3), 297–321. DOI: 10.1093/jeg/lbn007

Subhan, M., Irfan, M., Pan, X., Ahmad, G., Naeem, M. H., & Zamir, M. N. (2024). Unveiling the dynamic impact of energy generation on economic sustainability in Canada: A roadmap towards sustainable development. *Journal of Cleaner Production*, 434, 139783. DOI: 10.1016/j.jclepro.2023.139783

Sugden, R. (1989). Spontaneous Order. *The Journal of Economic Perspectives*, 3(4), 85–97. DOI: 10.1257/jep.3.4.85

Summatavet, K., & Raudsaar, M. (2015). Cultural heritage and entrepreneurship – inspiration for novel venture creation. *Journal of Enterprising Communities: People and Places in the Global Economy*, 9(1), 31–44. DOI: 10.1108/JEC-03-2013-0010

Supriharyanti, E., & Sukoco, B. M. (2023). Organizational change capability: A systematic review and future research directions. *Management Research Review*, 46(1), 46–81. DOI: 10.1108/MRR-01-2021-0039

Surowiecki, J. (2004). *The wisdom of crowds*. Anchor Books.

Surowiecki, J. (2004). *The Wisdom of Crowds: Why the Many are Smarter than the Few and How Collective Wisdom shapes Business, Economies, Societies, and Nations*. Doubleday.

Sutaguna, I., Achmad, G., Risdwiyanto, A., & Yusuf, M. (2023). Marketing Strategy For Increasing Sales Of Cooking Oil Shoes In Barokah Trading Business. *International Journal of Economics and Management Research*, 2(1), 132–152. DOI: 10.55606/ijemr.v2i1.73

Swain, S., & Patoju, S. K. S. (2022). Global Enterprises: contemporarisation of khadi products in India. *CASE Journal, 18*(6), 1–16. DOI: 10.1108/TCJ-12-2021-0214

Swart, K., Bond, T., & Chugh, R. (2022). Challenges and critical success factors of digital communication, collaboration and knowledge sharing in project management virtual teams: A review. *International Journal of Information Systems and Project Management*, 10(4), 84–103. DOI: 10.12821/ijispm100404

Syed, M. M., Lemma, T. A., Vandrangi, S. K., & Ofei, T. N. (2020). Recent developments in model-based fault detection and diagnostics of gas pipelines under transient conditions. *Journal of Natural Gas Science and Engineering*, 83, 103550. DOI: 10.1016/j.jngse.2020.103550

Taheri, S., Ahmadi, A., Mohammadi-Ivatloo, B., & Asadi, S. (2021). Fault detection diagnostic for HVAC systems via deep learning algorithms. *Energy and Building*, 250, 111275. DOI: 10.1016/j.enbuild.2021.111275

Tang, C. S. (2006). Robust strategies for mitigating supply chain disruptions. *International Journal of Logistics*, 9(1), 33–45. DOI: 10.1080/13675560500405584

Tapscott, D., & Tapscott, A. (2016). *Blockchain revolution: How the technology behind Bitcoin is changing money, business, and the world*. Penguin.

Tapsott, D., & Williams, A. (2008). *Wikinomics: How Mass Collaboration Changes Everything*. Penguin.

Tardivo, G., Scilla, A., & Viassone, M. (2014). A New Frontier in the Satisfaction of the Cultural Tourist: The QR Code. In Aiello, L. (Ed.), *Handbook of Research on Management of Cultural Products: E-Relationship Marketing and Accessibility Perspectives* (pp. 348–366). IGI Global. DOI: 10.4018/978-1-4666-5007-7.ch017

Tarun Kataray, B. (2023). Integration of smart grid with renewable energy sources: Opportunities and challenges – A comprehensive review. *Sustainable Energy Technologies and Assessments*, 58, 103363. DOI: 10.1016/j.seta.2023.103363

Tashtoush, B., Wa'ed, A., Al Ghadi, M., Al-Omari, J., & Morosuk, T. (2023). Renewable energy integration in water desalination: State-of-the-art review and comparative analysis. *Applied Energy*, 352, 121950. DOI: 10.1016/j.apenergy.2023.121950

Teece, D. (2007). Explicating dynamic capabilities: The nature and micro foundations of (sustainable) enterprise performance. *Strategic Management Journal*, 28(13), 1319–1350. DOI: 10.1002/smj.640

Teece, D. J. (2018). Profiting from innovation in the digital economy: Enabling technologies, standards, and licensing models in the wireless world. *Research Policy*, 47(8), 1367–1387. DOI: 10.1016/j.respol.2017.01.015

Teece, D. J., & Al-Aali, A. (2012). Knowledge assets, capabilities, and the theory of the firm. Handbook of organizational learning and knowledge management, 505-534.

Teece, D. J., Pisano, G., & Shuen, A. (1997). Dynamic capabilities and strategic management. *Strategic Management Journal*, 18(7), 509–533. DOI: 10.1002/(SICI)1097-0266(199708)18:7<509::AID-SMJ882>3.0.CO;2-Z

Teixeira, S. J., & Ferreira, J. J. M. (2019). Entrepreneurial artisan products as regional tourism competitiveness. *International Journal of Entrepreneurial Behaviour & Research*, 25(4), 652–673. DOI: 10.1108/IJEBR-01-2018-0023

Thórrison, K. R. (2020). Discretionarily Constrained Adaptation under Insufficient Knowledge & Resources. *Journal of Artificial Intelligence*, 11(2), 7–12.

Tiwari, S. K., & Korneliussen, T. (2022). Entrepreneurial internationalisation of Nepalese artisanal firms: A dynamic capabilities perspective. *International Journal of Entrepreneurial Behaviour & Research*, 28(6), 1369–1390. DOI: 10.1108/IJEBR-09-2020-0635

Toledo, G., Valdés, J., & Pollero, A. (1998). *Empresas turísticas en ambiente globalizado: marketing y competitividad. Estudio de casos de clústeres turísticos.* FEA/USP.

Trinh, V. L., & Chung, C. K. (2023). Renewable energy for SDG-7 and sustainable electrical production, integration, industrial application, and globalization. *Cleaner Engineering and Technology*, 15, 100657. DOI: 10.1016/j.clet.2023.100657

Trivedi, L. N. (2003). Visually mapping the "nation": Swadeshi politics in nationalist India, 1920-1930. *The Journal of Asian Studies*, 62(1), 11–41. https://search.proquest.com/docview/230429907?accountid=177896. DOI: 10.2307/3096134

Tufail, S., Parvez, I., Batool, S., & Sarwat, A. (2021). A survey on cybersecurity challenges, detection, and mitigation techniques for the smart grid. *Energies*, 14(18), 5894. DOI: 10.3390/en14185894

Tushamn, M. L., Smith, W. K., & Wood, R. C. (2010). *Organizational designs and innovation streams*. Industrial and Corporate Change. DOI: 10.1093/icc/dtq040

Tushman, M. L., & O'Reilly, C. A.III. (1996). Ambidextrous organizations: Managing evolutionary and revolutionary change. *California Management Review*, 38(4), 8–30. DOI: 10.2307/41165852

UCLA. (2016). The Charter for the Sustainability Committee. *UCLA Sustainability*. https://www.sustain.ucla.edu/wp-content/uploads/UCLA-Sustainability-Charter.pdf

UN. (2015). *Transforming Our World: The 2030 Agenda for Sustainable Development*. UN.

Uña, R. (2023). *La humanidad como ente político soberano: Una aproximación al cosmopolitismo jurídico-político*. Dykinson.

UNCTAD. (2021). El comercio electrónico mundial crece hasta los 26,7 billones de dólares, impulsado por la COVID-19. United Nations. https://news.un.org/es/story/2021/05/1491592

UNDP (United Nations Development Program). (2021). *Collective Intelligence for Sustainable Development: 13 Stories from the UNDP Accelerator Labs*. UNDP.

UNWTO. (2021). *The Importance of SMEs in the Tourism Industry*. UNWTO. Link https://www.unwto.org/es/node/12378

Ustun, T. S., & Hussain, S. S. (2019, November). A review of cybersecurity issues in smartgrid communication networks. In *2019 International Conference on Power Electronics, Control and Automation (ICPECA)* (pp. 1-6). IEEE. DOI: 10.1109/ICPECA47973.2019.8975629

Valentinov, V., Van Assche, K., & Hermans, F. (2023). Toward a digital transformation of the theory of the firm: Emergence as framework for organizational sustainability. Canadian Journal of Administrative Sciences/Revue Canadienne des Sciences de l'Administration, 40(3), 270-282.

van der Straaten, K., Narula, R., & Giuliani, E. (2023). The multinational enterprise, development, and the inequality of opportunities: A research agenda. *Journal of International Business Studies*, 54(9), 1623–1640. DOI: 10.1057/s41267-023-00625-y

Vanhaverbeke, W., & Chesbrough, H. W. (2014). A classification of open innovation and open business models. In H. Chesbrough, W. Vanhaverbeke, & J. West (Eds.), *New Frontiers in Open Innovation* (pp. 50-68). Oxford University Press. DOI: 10.1093/acprof:oso/9780199682461.003.0003

Vecchiola, C., Anjomshoa, H., Bernstein, Y., Dumitrescu, I., Garnavi, R., von Känel, J., & Wightwick, G. (2013). Engineering resilient information systems for emergency management. *IBM Journal of Research and Development*, 57(5), 2–1. DOI: 10.1147/JRD.2013.2259432

Verčič, A. (2021). The impact of employee engagement, organisational support and employer branding on internal communication satisfaction. *Public Relations Review*, 47(1), 102009. DOI: 10.1016/j.pubrev.2021.102009

Verma, R., Teixeira, J., Patrıcio, L., Nunes, N. J., Nobrega, L., Fisk, R. P., & Constantine, L. (2012). Customer experience modeling: From customer experience to service design. *Journal of Service Management*, 23(3), 362–376. DOI: 10.1108/09564231211248453

Vernadsky, V. (1998). *The Biosphere*. Springer Science+Business Media.

Verweij, F., Hoose, N., Kuiken, M., Pommer, J., & Savenije, W. (2010). *Cooperative Vehicle- Infrastructure Systems. Deployment Roadmap*. Report D.DEPN.8.1. ERTICO – ITS Europe.

Vieira, T. (2023). The unbearable precarity of pursuing freedom: A critical overview of the Spanish Sí soy autónomo movement. *Sociological Research Online*, 28(1), 244–260. DOI: 10.1177/13607804211040090

Vina, A., & Liu, J. (2023). Effects of global shocks on the evolution of an interconnected world. *Ambio*, 52(1), 95–106. DOI: 10.1007/s13280-022-01778-0 PMID: 35997989

Vlados, C., & Chatzinikolaou, D. (2024). The emergence of the new globalization: The approach of the evolutionary structural triptych. *Journal of Global Responsibility*. Advance online publication. DOI: 10.1108/JGR-04-2023-0063

Vogel, S. M., Vasudev, D., Ogutu, J. O., Taek, P., Berti, E., Goswami, V. R., Kaelo, M., Buitenwerf, R., Munk, M., Li, W., Wall, J., Chala, D., Amoke, I., Odingo, A., & Svenning, J.-C. (2023). Identifying Sustainable Coexistence Potential by Integrating Willingness-to-coexist with Habitat Sustainability Assessments. *Biological Conservation*, 279, 1–12. DOI: 10.1016/j.biocon.2023.109935

Vollero, A., Sardanelli, D., & Siano, A. (2023). Exploring the role of the Amazon effect on customer expectations: An analysis of user-generated content in consumer electronics retailing. *Journal of Consumer Behaviour*, 22(5), 1062–1073. DOI: 10.1002/cb.1969

Voskamp, de Luca, C., Polo, M., Hulsman, H., & Brolsma, R. (2021). Nature-based solutions tools for planning urban climate adaptation: State of the art. *Sustainability*, 13(11).

Vu, K., Hanafizadeh, P., & Bohlin, E. (2020). ICT as a driver of economic growth: A survey of the literature and directions for future research. *Telecommunication Policy*, 44(2).

Vylobkova, V., & Heintz, S. (2023). A meeting of positive behaviors: The relations of three aspects of flexibility with character strengths. *Frontiers in Psychology*, 13, 1078764. DOI: 10.3389/fpsyg.2022.1078764 PMID: 36817377

Wall, G. (2010). On exergy and sustainable development in environmental engineering. *The Open Environmental Engineering Journal*, 3(1), 21–32. DOI: 10.2174/1874829501003010021

Wang, P. (2023). *A General Theory of Intelligence*. A developing eBook. Link: https://cis.temple.edu/~pwang/GTI-book/index.html

Wang, P. (2019). On Defining Artificial Intelligence. *Journal of Artificial General Intelligence*, 10(2), 1–37. DOI: 10.2478/jagi-2019-0002

Wang, S., & Sun, C. (2023). Blockchain empowered dynamic spectrum sharing: Standards, state of research and road ahead. *IEEE Communications Standards Magazine*, 7(3), 72–80. DOI: 10.1109/MCOMSTD.0010.2200026

Wang, T., Yang, Z., Han, F., Yu, J., Ma, X., & Han, J. (2024). Assessment of tourism socio-ecological system resilience in arid areas: A case study of Xinjiang, China. *Ecological Indicators*, 159, 111748. DOI: 10.1016/j.ecolind.2024.111748

Wang, W., Kang, K., Sun, G., & Xiao, L. (2023). Configuration optimization of energy storage and economic improvement for household photovoltaic system considering multiple scenarios. *Journal of Energy Storage*, 67, 107631. DOI: 10.1016/j.est.2023.107631

Wang, X., Wang, X., Shi, Y., Wu, D., Ma, L., & Huang, M. (2023). Core-selecting auction-based mechanisms for service function chain provisioning and pricing in NFV markets. *Computer Networks*, 222, 109557. DOI: 10.1016/j.comnet.2023.109557

Watson, R., & Levin, M. (2023). The collective intelligence of evolution and development. *Collective Intelligence*, 2(2). DOI: 10.1177/26339137231168355

WCED (World Commission on Environment and Development). (1987). *Our Common Future*. WCED.

Weber, K., & Glynn, M. A. (2006). Making sense with institutions: Context, thought and action in Karl Weick's theory. *Organization Studies*, 27(11), 1639–1660. DOI: 10.1177/0170840606068343

Webster, F. (2006). *Theories of the Information Society*. Routledge. Taylor & Francis.

Weick, K. (1979). *The social psychology of organizing*. McGraw-Hill.

Weick, K. (1995). *Sensemaking in organizations*. SAGE Publications.

Wells, H. (1938). *World Brain*. Double Day, Doran & Co.

Wen, L., Zhou, K., Feng, W., & Yang, S. (2022). Demand side management in smart grid: A dynamic-price-based demand response model. *IEEE Transactions on Engineering Management*.

Westerman, G., Bonnet, D., & McAfee, A. (2014). *Leading digital: Turning technology into business transformation*. Harvard Business Review Press.

Whelan, E., & Fink, L. (2020). Collaborative business ecosystems: The dynamics of collective intelligence. *Journal of Business Research*, 116, 1–12.

Who Cares Wins. (2004). *Connecting Financial Markets to a Changing World*. UN Global Compact.

Wilkinson, M., Dumontier, M., Aalbersberg, J., Appleton, G., Axton, M., Baak, A., Blomberg, N., Boiten, J.-W., da Silva Santos, L. B., Bourne, P. E., Bouwman, J., Brookes, A. J., Clark, T., Crosas, M., Dillo, I., Dumon, O., Edmunds, S., Evelo, C. T., Finkers, R., & Mons, B. (2016). Comment: The FAIR Guiding Principles for Scientific Data Management and Stewardship. *Scientific Data*, 3(1), 1–9. DOI: 10.1038/sdata.2016.18 PMID: 26978244

Wilkinson, S. (2016). Understanding Sustainability and the Australian Property Professions. *The Journal of Sustainable Real Estate*, 8(1), 95–119. DOI: 10.1080/10835547.2016.12091888

Williamson, P. J., & De Meyer, A. (2012). Ecosystem advantage: How to successfully harness the power of partners. *California Management Review*, 55(1), 24–46. DOI: 10.1525/cmr.2012.55.1.24

Williams, W., Chabris, C., Pentland, A., Hashimi, N., & Malone, T. (2010). Evidence for a Collective Intelligence Factor in the Performance of Human Groups. *Science*, 330(6004), 683–686. PMID: 21030660

Wilson, R., Herziger, A., & Hamilton, M. (2020). From incremental to transformative adaptation in individual responses to climate-exacerbated hazards. *Nature Climate Change. Nature*, 10(3), 200–208.

Wood, S., Luers, A., Garard, J., Gambhir, A., Chaudhari, K., Ivanova, M., & Cronin, C. (2021). Collective foresight and intelligence for sustainability. *Global Sustainability*, 4.

Woolley, A. W. (2021). Assessing Collective Intelligence in Human Groups. In OECD, *AI and the Future of Skills, Volume 1: Capabilities and Assessments* (pp. 117-133). OECD.

Woolley, A. W. (2011). Responses to Adversarial Situations and Collective Intelligence. *Journal of Organizational Behavior*, 32(7), 978–983. DOI: 10.1002/job.753

Woolley, A. W., & Fuchs, E. (2011). Collective Intelligence in the Organization of Science. *Organization Science*, 22(5), 1359–1367. DOI: 10.1287/orsc.1110.0648

Woolley, A., Aggarwal, I., & Malone, T. (2015). Collective Intelligence and Group Performance. *Current Directions in Psychological Science*, 24(6), 420–424. DOI: 10.1177/0963721415599543

World Economic Forum. (2018). *The future of jobs report 2018*. Geneva, Switzerland: WEF.

World Economic Forum. (2023a). *Strategic Intelligence* Geneva, Switzerland: WEF.

World Economic Forum. (2023b). *The future of job reports*. Geneva, Switzerland: WEF.

Wu, L., & Jin, S. (2022). Corporate Social Responsibility and Sustainability: From a Corporate Governance Perspective. *Sustainability (Basel)*, 14(22), 15457. DOI: 10.3390/su142215457

Yadav, U.S. & Tripathi, R. (2024). Impact of innovation, entrepreneurial orientation and entrepreneurial leadership on supply chain resilience in handicraft industry: moderating role of supply chain orientation. Benchmarking: An International Journal. DOI: 10.1108/BIJ-09-2023-0615

Yang, S., Song, Y., Chen, S., & Xia, X. (2017). Why are Customers Loyal in Sharing-Economy Services? A Relational Benefits Perspective. *Journal of Services Marketing*, 31(1), 48–62. https://www.proquest.com/scholarly-journals/why-are-customers-loyal-sharing-economy-services/docview/1862042626/se-2. DOI: 10.1108/JSM-01-2016-0042

Yang, Z., Yin, M., Xu, J., & Lin, W. (2019). Spatial evolution model of tourist destinations based on complex adaptive system theory: A case study of Southern Anhui, China. *Journal of Geographical Sciences*, 29(8), 1411–1434. DOI: 10.1007/s11442-019-1669-z

Yan, W., Shi, Y., Ji, Z., Sui, Y., Tian, Z., Wang, W., & Cao, Q. (2023). Intelligent predictive maintenance of hydraulic systems based on virtual knowledge graph. *Engineering Applications of Artificial Intelligence*, 126, 106798. DOI: 10.1016/j.engappai.2023.106798

Yazdani, N. (2010). Organizational democracy and organization structure link: Role of strategic leadership & environmental uncertainly. *Business Review (Federal Reserve Bank of Philadelphia)*, 5(2), 51–74. DOI: 10.54784/1990-6587.1244

Yeung, A., & Ulrich, D. (2020). *Reinventando la organización: Cómo crear mayor valor en mercados en constante evolución*. Editorial Almuzara.

Yi, H., Cho, Y., & Amenuvor, F. (2023). Internal marketing and salespeople's out-of-role behaviour: The mediating role of job satisfaction. *European Research on Management and Business Economics*, 29(2), 100216. DOI: 10.1016/j.iedeen.2023.100216

Yi, K. (2003). Can vertical specialization explain the growth of world trade? *Journal of Political Economy*, 111(1), 52–102. DOI: 10.1086/344805

Yin, X., Zhao, Z., & Yang, W. (2023). Ensemble prediction aided multi-objective co-design optimizations of grid-connected integrated renewables for green hydrogen production. *Journal of Cleaner Production*, 425, 138585. DOI: 10.1016/j.jclepro.2023.138585

You, W., Sarpong, D., & O'Regan, N. (2022). Global value chains in a digitalized era. *Strategic Change*, 31(1), 5–8. DOI: 10.1002/jsc.2476

Zeng, M., Xie, X., & Tam, C. M. (2010). Relationship between cooperation networks and innovation performance of SMEs. *Technovation*, 30(3), 181–194. DOI: 10.1016/j.technovation.2009.08.003

Zeren, G., Tan, J., Zhang, Q., & Qiuying, B. (2023). Rebuilding rural community cooperative institutions and their role in herder adaptation to climate change. *Climate Policy*, 23(4), 522–537. DOI: 10.1080/14693062.2023.2184763

Zhakupov, A., Yessilov, A., Yelemessov, A., & Ismailova, N. (2023). The Impact of the Pandemic on the Economic Development about Small and Medium Sized Businesses. *Theoretical and Practical Research in Economic Fields*, 14(1), 146–163. DOI: 10.14505/tpref.v14.1(27).12

Zhang, F. (2021). Evaluating public organization performance under extreme weather events: Does organizational adaptive capacity matter? *Journal of Environmental Management*, 296, 113388. DOI: 10.1016/j.jenvman.2021.113388 PMID: 34328864

Zhang, J., & Gong, X. (2023). From clicks to change: The role of Internet use in fostering environmental sustainability awareness. *Journal of Environmental Management*, 348, 119275. DOI: 10.1016/j.jenvman.2023.119275 PMID: 37827071

Zhang, L., Leach, M., Bae, Y., Cui, B., Bhattacharya, S., Lee, S., Im, P., Adetola, V., Vrabie, D., & Kuruganti, T. (2021). Sensor impact evaluation and verification for fault detection and diagnostics in building energy systems: A review. *Advances in Applied Energy*, 3, 100055. DOI: 10.1016/j.adapen.2021.100055

Zhang, M., Hu, E., & Lin, Y. (2023). The impact of flexibility-oriented HRM systems on innovative behaviour in China: A moderated mediation model of dualistic passion and inclusive leadership. *Asia Pacific Business Review*, 29(1), 114–135. DOI: 10.1080/13602381.2022.2076446

Zhang, Z., Cheng, X., Xing, Z., & Wang, Z. (2024). Energy management strategy optimization for hybrid energy storage system of tram based on competitive particle swarm algorithms. *Journal of Energy Storage*, 75, 109698. DOI: 10.1016/j.est.2023.109698

Zheng, X., Wang, R., Hoekstra, A. Y., Krol, M. S., Zhang, Y., Guo, K., & Wang, C. (2021). Consideration of culture is vital if we are to achieve the Sustainable Development Goals. *One Earth*, 4(2), 307–319. DOI: 10.1016/j.oneear.2021.01.012

Zhong, D., Xia, Z., Zhu, Y., & Duan, J. (2023). Overview of predictive maintenance based on digital twin technology. *Heliyon*, 9(4), e14534. DOI: 10.1016/j.heliyon.2023.e14534 PMID: 37025897

Zhuang, P., Zamir, T., & Liang, H. (2020). Blockchain for cybersecurity in smart grid: A comprehensive survey. *IEEE Transactions on Industrial Informatics*, 17(1), 3–19. DOI: 10.1109/TII.2020.2998479

Zhu, L., & Zhou, Z. (2016). Blockchain technology and trust relationships in business: A literature review. *Journal of Business and Technology*, 9(2), 155–168.

Zolli, A., & Haely, A. M. (2012). Introduction. United Kingdom. In Resilience: Why Things Bounce Back (pp. 12-132). Free Press.

Zolli, A., & Healy, A. (2012). *Resilience: Why things bounce back. Hachette UK.* Free Press.

Zolli, A., & Healy, A. (2012). *Resilience: Why Things Bounce Back.* Headline Publishing Group.

Zomerdijk, L. G., & Voss, C. A. (2010). Service design for experience-centric services. *Journal of Service Research*, 13(1), 67–82. DOI: 10.1177/1094670509351960

About the Contributors

Tania Elena González Alvarado is Full Research Professor C T.C. in Marketing and International Business at the University of Guadalajara (Mexico). She has at least three decades of experience, during which she has conducted research activities, directed theses and/or taught at the following universities: Universidad Nacional Autónoma de México, Universidad La Salle, Escuela Bancaria y Comercial and Universidad Complutense de Madrid. Her current research interests are collective intelligence, resilience, the future of work, internal marketing, social value and artificial intelligence. She is the author of more than thirty articles, has co-authored three books and coordinated twelve collective works.

Pablo Cabanelas Lorenzo is an Associate Professor of Marketing at the University of Vigo (Spain). He also belongs to the UNAM (México) faculty in the post-graduate studies, and cooperate with different European and Latin-American universities. His current research interests are value creation, industrial marketing, and relationship marketing. He has participated and directed several research projects with different European, National and Regional institutions and companies. His research has been published in several books and journals such as Industrial Marketing Management, Regional Studies, Journal of Business Research, Journal of Business & Industrial Marketing, International Marketing Review, and Journal of Business Research, among others. He acts as associate editor in the Journal of Business and Industrial Marketing and European Research on Management and Business Economics, and guest editor in Reviews of Managerial Science.

* * *

Karima Belmabrouk received her engineering degree in 1998 and her magister degree in 2006 and her PhD degree in 2017 from the University of Science and Technology of Oran, USTO-MB. Since December 2006, she is an assiocate professor and researcher in the computer science department of the USTO-MB. Her research interests are based on agent-based modeling and simulation, Web services composition, ontology and semantic Web as well as planning in artificial intelligence. Currently, she is working on cybersecurity and supply chain optimization.

Abhijit Pramod Chandratreya is currently working as Deputy Director in the Department of Post Graduate Research Centre at SCES's Indira Institute of Management, Pune for the past 16 years. He joined IIMP after working in various Industries for 17 years. He graduated in Production Engineering from Birla Vishwakarma Mahavidyalaya (Sardar Patel University), Anand, Gujarat, India. He secured a Master of Business Administration in Human Resource Development from IGNOU. He has been awarded a Ph.D. in the field of Marketing Management from Savitribai Phule Pune University, India. He has presented several papers in National and International Journals, conferences, and Symposiums and has published 15 research papers both in referred and SCOPUS / ABDC-listed Journals. He has published three patents. He is a certified trainer of CSCP, CPTP, CLDM, MTF, and CID certified by MiddleEarth HR. His main areas of interest include Marketing, HRM, SCM, Statistics, Business Analytics, and Research Methodologies. ORCID ID; https://orcid.org/0000-0001-9403-2094 ; SCOPUS ID: 58695471800 Google Scholar ID: jJN5ZcQAAAAJ.

Latifa Dekhici is an associate professor in computer sciences and vice dean of external relationship in mathematics and computer science faculty in the university of sciences and technology of Oran; and a researcher in LDREI, Smart Grid Development laboratory in the Higher School of Electrical Engineering and Energetic of Oran. Her research interests include power dispatch, power system design, healthcare scheduling and green optimization as well as optimization methods especially metaheuristic. DEKHICI has been a member of Inside Project (Inclusion of Students With impairments in Distance Education) in 2023 and a Responsible of Digitalisation Strategy Office in her university. She is currently a member of DIGITAQ project of digitalization of quality in higher education. As a trainer, she participated in many sustainability; digitalization; accessibility activities.

Balaji Gopalan is an Assistant Professor with the Department of Decision Sciences at the Faculty of Management Studies, CMS Business School in Bangalore, India, (Jain-Deemed-to-be University). His area of specialization is Production and Operations Management, Logistics and Supply Chain Management and Value Co-creation. He has more than 20 years of experience that includes working in academics, research and consulting and has worked at institutes and companies in Finland, USA and India. He holds a Doctor of Science in Industrial Management from the University of Vaasa, Finland. He has completed his M.Sc in Information Studies from Florida State University (USA). He has a M.E. in Manufacturing Systems from BITS-Pilani (Rajasthan, India) and a B.E. in Industrial and Production Engineering from SJCE, University of Mysore (India). He has also published his research in Scopus and ABDC indexed journals. For Details - 0000-0002-1082-5597 Scopus Author ID: 57638534500

Khaled Guerraiche, born in Oran, Algeria, received his engineering diploma in Electrical Engineering from the Institute of Electrical Engineering at the University of Science and Technology of Oran (USTOMB) in 2004, his Master's degree in Electrical Engineering in 2008, and his Ph.D. from the University of Science and Technology of Oran (USTO) in 2016. He is currently an Associate Professor at the Higher School of Electrical and Energetic Engineering in Oran, Algeria. His research interests include the design, reconfiguration, planning, and economics of electrical energy systems, as well as optimization theory and its applications in smart grids.

Jipson Joseph has a PhD in Ethics from DVK Bangalore. Currently, he is a Research Scholar in the School of Law at Christ University, Bangalore. His research interests are in the fields of ethics, gender studies, constitutional law, human rights, human security, collective intelligence, environmental justice, developmental policies and global poverty.

Renata Kubus is a professor in sustainable finance at the Complutense University with ANECA accreditation. PhD extraordinary prize by UNED. Research and practice in Collective Intelligence, Sustainability, Innovation Ecosystems & Finance. Expert evaluator for Horizon Europe (ERA). Founder and Leader of Network for Collective Intelligence Development (CID-N). InnovaCEF 2019 prize for scientific entrepreneurship. International Congress and Convention Association (ICCA) Poland national prize for degree thesis. More than 15 years of international professional experience in banking and risk sector.

Jesús F. Lampón, Industrial Engineer and PhD in Business Administration, is professor of Business Organization at the University of Vigo. He has been a lead researcher in more than fifty research projects with different institutions and firms. His research has been published in more than 40 journals such as the International Journal of Production Research, Journal of Business Research, Production Planning & Control, Papers in Regional Science, Regional Studies or Journal of Manufacturing Technology Management. He was Manager of the Programme to Promote Business Research and Innovation in the Economy and Industry Council of the Galicia Government (Spain). He is Editor of the European Research on Management and Business Economics and SAGE Open, and member of the Editorial Board of

Kybernetes, International Journal of Automotive Technology and Management, and Regional Science Policy & Practice.

Inés Martín de Santos has a PhD in Economics from the Complutense University of Madrid on 29 May 2012, at the age of 26, qualification outstanding cum laude. She is a member of the research group 970926 Humanities, Science and Health of the Complutense University of Madrid. Main responsible for the UCM teaching innovation project 'Open scientific training as a teaching complement to higher education in Economics and Business Studies'. Innova 2024-2025 call for proposals. Permanent member of the Agustín Millares University Institute of Information Management of the Carlos III University of Madrid. Member of the commission of the Vice-Deanship of International Relations. Erasmus Coordinator for students of the Faculty of Economics and Business Studies (UCM) from April 2019 to September 2020. Coordinator of the Master in Business Finance of the Faculty of Economics and Business Administration of the UCM from July 2020 to March 2023, ranked in 2021 as the fifth best Spanish Master in Finance and in fourth place in 2022. She has been Assistant Professor in the Department of Financial Management and Accounting at the Complutense University of Madrid since February 2019 and interim Associate Professor since March 2022. Currently, since January 2023, she is Associate Professor. Winner of the Juan de Goyeneche research prize, in its tenth edition, awarded annually by the Asociación del Patrimonio Histórico de Nuevo Baztán. Madrid, 2023.

Pilar Morales Valdez is a Subject Professor at the University of Guadalajara with a PhD in Managerial Sciences and a Master's degree in Marketing. Her research focuses on small and medium enterprises (SMEs) competitiveness, tourism resilience, and businesses as adaptive complex systems, as she specializes in examining SMEs and their role in rural tourism resilience, as well as the adaptation of businesses within complex systems. Her work as a professor bridges theory and practice, guiding undergraduate students in hands-on research projects that support SMEs through market strategies and advertising.

José Cabanelas Omil, PhD in Economics and Business Administration, is a professor at the University of Vigo. The main lines of research are Emerging Competitiveness, Organization Theory and Organizational Development, Regional Competitiveness and Development, Regenerative Governance and Disruption and New Genesis. He has written more than 50 books on competitive dynamics, cooperation, business management in open and complex environments and competitive evolution of regional and sectoral production systems and competitive intelligence on unique companies such as high-growth companies -gazelle-, high-performance companies -economic performance-, high productivity and high added value. He has also written articles on network governance, creating, transferring, and assimilating knowledge into networks, configurations of control and power in networks.

Ananya Pandey is a Research Scholar in School of Law at Christ University, Bangalore. She has her research interests in the field of Constitutional Law, Human Rights, Intellectual Property Law and Jurisprudence.

Magali Pérez Camacho is a distinguished academic with a rich background in administration and organizational studies. She holds a Bachelor's degree in Administration from the Universidad Nacional Autónoma de México (UNAM), along with a specialization in the History of Economic Thought from the same institution. Her commitment to deepening her expertise in the field led her to pursue both a Master's and a Ph.D. in Organizational Studies at the Metropolitan Autonomous University (UAM), cementing her position as a leading scholar in her domain. Currently a full-time professor in the Department of Administration at UAM's Azcapotzalco campus, Dr. Pérez is also a recognized member of the National System of Researchers under the National Council for Humanities, Science and Technology (CONAHCYT), a testament to her contributions to research and scholarship. Dr. Pérez's academic leadership is evident in her role as Chair of the Editorial Committee for *Gestión y Estrategia*, a prominent journal within the field of organizational studies, published by UAM Azcapotzalco. Additionally, she serves as the editor of the book series *Graduate Studies Documents in Organizational Studies*, affiliated with the Mexican Network of Researchers in Organizational Studies (REMINEO). Her involvement in these initiatives highlights her dedication to fostering and disseminating high-quality research within her field. As a member of notable academic networks, including REMINEO and the International Network of Researchers in Social Sciences and Humanities (Huika Mexihco), Dr. Pérez actively engages with interdisciplinary and international communities, reflecting her commitment to collaborative knowledge production and the advancement of organizational studies on a global scale. Her research spans critical topics such as the organizational perspective on international cooperation for development, intentional communities and ecovillages, and small and family-owned businesses. The theoretical frameworks that shape her work include organizational theory, process organization studies, institutionalism within organizations, and meta-organizations, underscoring her depth of expertise and analytical rigor. Dr. Pérez's research trajectory includes impactful collaborations with universities on projects addressing SME cooperation, international development cooperation, and public policy. Her sustained engagement with these themes has resulted in numerous publications, including articles and book chapters, through which she continues to contribute valuable insights to the field of organizational studies.

Hugo Pérez Moure graduate cum laude Doctor in Economic Analysis and Business Strategy from the University of Vigo, with two master's degrees: one in East Asian Studies from the Autonomous University of Madrid and another in International Trade from the University of Vigo. Despite his young age, he has collaborated on numerous European projects across a wide range of business-related fields, such as entrepreneurship and mobility. He also has several publications in high-impact JCR and Scopus journals, including Technology in Society, European Research on Management and Business Economics, Futures, Industrial Marketing Management, and Suma de Negocios y Dirección y Organización. Additionally, he is part of various international research networks, such as AEDEM, RIICO, and GERPISA. Through these networks and his participation in conferences, some of his research has received awards, including the ESIC Award for Knowledge Transfer to Business and Society.

José Sánchez Gutiérrez is a distinguished academic and professional leader in management and business competitiveness. He holds a PhD in Sciences, specializing in Administrative Sciences, from the National Polytechnic Institute in Mexico. He has furthered his education through executive programs at prestigious international institutions, such as Harvard Business School, in the advanced course for higher education leaders. Additionally, he holds a Master's in Administration with specializations in Organizational and Human Development, Marketing, and Finance from the ITESM, Mexico. His research and academic work have been widely recognized. He has published over 44 books and more than 100 articles in high-impact scientific journals. He's commitment to academic excellence, business development, and innovation inspires future leaders and entrepreneurs, cementing his position as a pillar in forming a new generation of executives committed to global competitiveness.

Michael Steggemann has extensive experience in project management and business administration, having worked internationally with companies from Germany, the United States, Canada, and Mexico. His career has provided him with deep understanding of cross-cultural business dynamics and strategic project leadership. He began his professional journey with an apprenticeship as a dairy technician, then graduated in Food & Dairy Engineering from the University of Applied Sciences in Hannover, Germany, in 1980. He later completed Master's degrees in Administration, Finance, and Marketing at the Escuela Bancaria y Comercial in Mexico City (2007–2012) and obtained his Ph.D. in Business

Administration from Universidad La Salle, Mexico City, in 2016. His current research interests include collective intelligence, resilience, coordination, cooperation, and collaboration when using artificial intelligence.

Index

E

G

I

K

L

M

N

O

P

R

S

T

V

www.ingramcontent.com/pod-product-compliance
Lightning Source LLC
LaVergne TN
LVHW080340011026
849161LV00009B/2132

* 9 7 9 8 3 6 9 3 7 2 7 2 2 *